The Impact of Globalization on the United States

Volume 1

Culture and Society

Edited by

MICHELLE BERTHO

Praeger Perspectives

Westport, Connecticut
London

Library of Congress Cataloging-in-Publication Data

The impact of globalization on the United States.
    v. cm. — (Praeger perspectives)
    Includes bibliographical references and index.
    Contents: v. 1. Culture and society / edited by Michelle Bertho —
    v. 2. Law and governance / edited by Beverly Crawford —
    v. 3. Business and economics / edited by Beverly Crawford
    and Edward A. Fogarty.
    ISBN 978-0-275-99181-4 (set : alk. paper) —
    ISBN 978-0-275-99182-1 (v. 1 : alk. paper) —
    ISBN 978-0-275-99183-8 (v. 2 : alk. paper) —
    ISBN 978-0-275-99184-5 (v. 3 : alk. paper)
    1. Globalization—United States. 2. United States—
Social conditions—21st century. 3. United States—
Economic conditions—21st century. I. Bertho, Michelle, 1956–
    HN90.G56I56 2008
    303.48'273009051—dc22   2008022075

British Library Cataloguing in Publication Data is available.

Library of Congress Catalog Card Number: 2008022075
ISBN: 978-0-275-99181-4 (set)
        978-0-275-99182-1 (vol. 1)
        978-0-275-99183-8 (vol. 2)
        978-0-275-99184-5 (vol. 3)

First published in 2008

Praeger Publishers, 88 Post Road West, Westport, CT 06881
An imprint of Greenwood Publishing Group, Inc.
www.praeger.com

Printed in the United States of America

The paper used in this book complies with the
Permanent Paper Standard issued by the National
Information Standards Organization (Z39.48-1984).
10 9 8 7 6 5 4 3 2 1

Contents

Preface

Over the past decade, bookshelves have begun to overflow with volumes describing the nature, origins, and impact of globalization. Largely and surprisingly absent from this literature, however, has been extensive discussion of the impact globalization has on the United States itself. We have launched this project to explore the nature and extent of that impact. This book series offers the first in-depth, systematic effort at assessing the United States not as a globalizing force but as a nation being transformed by globalization. Indeed, it is rarely even acknowledged that while the United States may be providing a crucial impetus to globalization, the process of globalization, once set in motion, has become a force unto itself. Thus globalization has its own logic and demands that are having a profound impact on the U.S. economy, on American society and culture, and on its legal and political system in ways that are often unanticipated.

We invited our contributors to explore how globalization is coming home. While the companion volumes to this one address globalization's effect on American government and law and its businesses and economy, the theme of this volume is the impact of globalization on U.S. society and culture. In the following essays, the authors attempt to connect the fundamental themes of social science with the complex forces that deform and transform American culture and society. They analyze social changes, the fears associated with these changes, and civil society's creativity, resilience, and adaptation.

It has been my privilege, as series coeditor, to participate in this process. In the course of this project, my coeditors—Beverly Crawford and Ed Fogarty—and I have constantly crossed borders between disciplines, from sociology to political science, from law to economics. I thank them for the great respect and trust they consistently expressed. My thanks also go to the authors. They made this volume possible. It was a pleasure to work with each of them; to a person, they brought their expertise and passion to their work, ensuring that this book represents a valuable contribution to the larger conversation about globalization.

This three-volume set has been a complex undertaking and would not have been possible without the support of many organizations and individuals. For financial support, I would like to thank the Ford Foundation, the Fisher Center for Real Estate and Urban Economics at the UC Berkeley Haas Business School, UC Berkeley's Townsend Center for the Humanities, Institute of Governmental Studies, the Institute of European Studies, and the Program on Globalization, Religion, and Politics. I would also like to express my gratitude to Sara Heitler Bamberger, Jessica Owen, Yana Feldman, Noga Wizansky, Charlene Nicholas, and Gia White-Forbes for their assistance with three meetings that brought the authors of these volumes together for discussion of early drafts of their chapters. I could not have completed a project of this magnitude without them. And I would like to express our heartfelt thanks to Ed Fogarty, who provided useful comments and criticism of the individual chapters and expert editorial assistance for all three volumes. Finally, I wish to thank Praeger Publishers and the excellent editorial advice and encouragement that we received from Hilary Claggett, Shana Jones, and Robert Hutchinson.

Michelle Bertho

Abbreviations

AAP	American Academy of Pediatrics
AAU	Amateur Athletic Union
AFL	American Football League
BAW/TAF	Border Art Workshop/Taller de Arte Fronterizo
BGL	Black Gay Language
ETA	Basque Homeland and Freedom (separatist organization)
EZLN	Ejército Zapatista de Liberación Nacional
FBI	Federal Bureau of Investigation
FEMA	Federal Emergency Management Agency
GME	Gay Men's English
LDC	less-developed country
LOTE	languages other than mainstream English
LPR	legal permanent resident
MDC	most-developed country
MLB	Major League Baseball
MOAD	Museum of the African Diaspora
NAFTA	North American Free Trade Agreement
NBA	National Basketball Association
NCAA	National Collegiate Athletic Association
NFL	National Football League
NGO	nongovernmental organization
OECD	Organization for Economic Cooperation and Development
PITB	Proyecto Internacional de Tierra-Boya

PLD	Partido de la Liberación Dominicana (Dominican Republic)
PRD	Partido Revolucionario Democrático (Dominican Republic)
TIDES	The Institute for Diversity and Ethics in Sport, University of Central Florida
TNC	transnational corporation
UNESCO	United Nations Educational, Scientific, and Cultural Organization
YCT	Yeshivat Chovevei Torah

Globalization's Impact on American Culture and Society: An Overview

Michelle Bertho

Rien ne se fera plus que le monde entier ne s'en mêle. [Nothing will be done anymore without the whole world meddling in it.]

—Paul Valery, *Critique de notre civilisation*

Is globalization "eating the hand that feeds it"? For decades, respected economists and advocates of engagement with the world economy have insisted that the United States gains from globalization. Now, they are not sure and the "coalition of doubters"[1] is growing. There is no doubt that American jobs are moving to the developing world—to call centers in Gurgaon, to research labs in Beijing, to auto plants in Bratislava. A new breed of multinational companies is arising from emerging economies to compete with the American giants. They are called Tata, Cemex, TCL, or RMC, and they are from India, Mexico, China, or Brazil. The accelerating pace of globalization profoundly affects life in poor and rich countries alike, transforming not only Bangalore but also Detroit, a once-thriving city that in less than twenty years has suffered economic evisceration at the hand of globalization.

Globalization was principally a topic of intellectual discourse until it moved into the public arena with the violent demonstrations against the World Trade Organization (WTO) in December 1999 in Seattle, and then again in 2001 in Genoa. "Globalization" is now a word on everyone's lips. In spite of the large amount of literature about it, the definition of the word itself is confusing. It appeared in the American vocabulary in the mid-1980s, and by the early 1990s had become part of news reporters' basic rhetoric. In this volume, *globalization* is understood to be the technology- and communications-driven integration of economic, political, and cultural systems across the globe.

Some studies point out that trade and capital markets are no more globalized today than they were at the end of the nineteenth century.[2] Nevertheless, there are more concerns about globalization now than ever before. The pace of the process is accelerating; the impact of new information technologies on market integration, efficiency, and industrial organization is enormous; the movement of people across borders, estimated at 200 million in 2006 (though most such figures, even those used by governments, are at best educated guesses), is increasing. The dizzying rhythm of change in the world of globalization is unprecedented and can be frightening. Globalization has unleashed powerful new forces under which elements of American culture and society—as well as American law and business[3]—are constantly in motion, perpetually in a creative, defensive, or even aggressive mode driven by concern of obsolescence or death.

People are quick to perceive the word *globalization* as another expression of the reach of American imperialism and the spread of capitalism. However, globalization is a two-way street, and no country, not even the United States, is immune to its effects. A flood of literature has explored the hegemonic role of the United States in determining the nature, scope, and speed of globalization and the consequences for the lives and livelihood of people all over the world. Very few scholars, however, have explored how American culture and society themselves have been transformed by the phenomenon. It is to that quest that this volume is directed.

Globalization is for some a force for economic growth, prosperity, and democratic freedom. Many fashionable and well-spoken apostles of globalization[4]—those John Clark refers to as the "ecstasy school"[5]—make compelling arguments, describing globalization as the most powerful force for economic and social good in the world. Some even have called globalization "the end of history," "the triumph of the laissez-faire." They argue that not only has the world become smaller, but it is also richer as a result of globalization, allowing us to live in a world of unprecedented opulence and comfort.

There have been remarkable changes far beyond the economic arena. In the twentieth century, democratic and participatory governance emerged as the preeminent model of political organization.[6] Concepts of human rights and political liberty are now part of the prevailing discourse in dominant media and international organizations. On average, people live much longer than ever before. Science has opened up new possibilities and capabilities, and the world literacy rate is rising. We are all more tightly linked together, not only in the field of trade and finance but also in the realm of communication and ideas.

Customs, art, religions, and social and cultural movements all follow the exchange of money or goods across national borders, speeding up the process of intercultural integration. In the same way that the silk trade brought Buddhism to the East, that Arab traders contributed to the propagation of Islam in Southeast Asia, and that Christian merchants and artisans transported their faith to Central Asia, Eastern Europe, and the Americas, today globalization and its modern traders are sending shock-waves through our cultures, our societies, and our systems of values. Something new is being born. The proponents of globalization see it as a global reality, a highly organized system encompassing the world's entire population. They think it is a natural phenomenon of modern evolution that has no center; it is developing from anywhere and everywhere and can expand infinitely.

Globalization has its detractors,[7] however, whom Clark called the "agony school."[8] This school is not limited to the usual disparagers of capitalist enterprise; even the gurus of economics are starting to doubt. Joseph E. Stiglitz argued that globalization not only leaves behind many of the world's poor and endangers the environment but also actually under-mines the stability of the global economy.[9] Alan Blinder, a former deputy chairman of the U.S. Federal Reserve who is "a free-trader down to his toes and always has been,"[10] is branded a heretic by many of his fellow econ-omists because he is questioning outsourcing and offshoring, both of which are phenomena germane to the broader process of free-market-oriented globalization. The dislocation of service jobs from rich countries such as the United States to poor ones such as India may affect tens of millions of American workers over the coming decade.[11] Paul A. Samuelson, winner of the Nobel Prize in economics, is also challenging the assumptions about free trade. The low-wage, high-innovation economies of China and India, he says, may present a historically unique challenge to U.S. economic competitiveness and prosperity—one that we are only beginning to come to grips with.

Beyond the ivory tower—in the real world—Americans are increasingly aware of globalization's dark side, and their leaders are struggling to respond. Democrats and Republicans alike search for adequate policy responses to enormous trade deficits and waves of outsourcing. Mike Huckabee, a pop-ulist candidate for the 2008 Republican nomination, speaks for many across the political spectrum when he claims, "There is no free trade with-out fair trade." New York senator Hillary Clinton, a more mainstream presidential candidate, also distanced herself from the idea of free trade, telling the *Financial Times* in December 2007 that she no longer believes that the old theory holds the only truth. In a speech in New Hampshire on December 19, 2007, her rival for the Democratic presidential nomina-tion, Illinois senator Barack Obama, said the fact that global trade makes products cheaper is no longer a valid argument if it costs people their jobs. The 2008 presidential campaign has found one of its issues: the other side of globalization.

Some critics go further and argue that the whole ideology of competi-tiveness divides workers, both domestically and internationally, and facilitates acquiescence to the redistribution of income from wages to profits.[12] These opponents assert that within a short two decades globalization has contrib-uted to reversing some of the working class's hard-won gains: minimum wages, security of employment, decent work, and social security. From this perspective, globalization drives unemployment, dislocates communities, depresses wages of unskilled workers, and exacerbates income inequalities both across and within countries. In addition, it is associated with the destruction of cultural identities—creating "victims of the accelerating encroachment of a homogenized, westernized, consumer culture"[13]—and environmental problems. A 2005 report by the Institute for Environment and Human Security in Bonn suggested that rising sea levels and extreme weather, among other things, could uproot 150 million people by 2050.

In sum, globalization is a process of immeasurable complexity, creating pressures for change viewed by some as opportunities and by others as threats. The transnational flows of capital, goods, services, people, ideas, and so forth tend to privilege actors that are themselves transnational—notably, multinational corporations—and to challenge actors that are territorially bound, especially states. Even the United States, so closely associated with much of the material and ideational content of globalization, is not immune.

This volume addresses the debate by studying the impact of globalization on culture and society in the United States. It presents distinctive and varied contributions that fall into three general groupings, each of which relates to a particular arena of globalization's social articulation, and each of which is inextricably bound up with the two others. The unifying theme of the first group, the fragmentation of society and the question of identity, leads to the theme of the second group, fear rooted in racial and xenophobic emotions and potential conflicts. Complementing those is the third theme, civil society's creativity, resilience, and adaptability. These three themes of social change run through and across the chapters, with some addressing two of them simultaneously.

This volume first tackles the fragmentation and transformation of American society as a result of global integration processes. Several of our contributors, including Ronnie Lipschutz, Andrew Barlow, James Cohen, Howard Winant, and Tyler Stovall, share the concern that American society is becoming less cohesive. They seek to make sense of the simultaneous processes of integration and fragmentation among nation-states, in American society, and even in the "self," as Winant puts it in his chapter, recalling W. E. B. Du Bois's articulation of "double consciousness."

Related to this question of fragmentation is that of fear, and whether and how globalization contributes to a climate of fear in the United States. While the authors work in different contexts and address different fears, several converge on those of xenophobia or racism. Lipschutz and Paul Cantor examine the fear of conflict along class, racial, or religious lines. Diana Crane and Susanne Janssen explore the fear of cultural homogeneity as a result of the cultural "hegemony" of those in the American "creative industry." And Barlow addresses a culture of fear in the political arena, maintained by politicians who prefer to inflame xenophobic emotions rather than to attempt to explain immigration's potential benefits.

Finally, this volume celebrates the remarkable creativity, imagination, and adaptability of both immigrants and American citizens. Cohen, Tirza True Latimer, William Leap, Tim Wendel, and Sara Heitler Bamberger demonstrate how a constantly evolving civil society attains empowerment and agency and innovates in governance as new circumstances arise. They laud the extraordinary resourcefulness of a multicultural American society, exploring how new communities help destroy the duality of "us versus them" or "in versus out," creating new spaces that transcend political, racial, and language boundaries. Bamberger and Wendel recognize the challenge and importance of maintaining religious practices or the spirit of sport as significant contributors to community unity and cohesiveness.

FRAGMENTATION AND TRANSFORMATION OF AMERICAN SOCIETY

Globalization's contribution to the fragmentation of society is a present concern that marks a sharp break from past American cultural critiques. In the 1950s and early 1960s, U.S. society was criticized for its conformity and homogeneity. Observers such as David Riesman (*The Lonely Crowd*, 1950), William H. Whyte (*The Organization Man*, 1956), C. Wright Mills (*The Power Elite*, 1956), and George William Domhoff (*Who Rules America?* 1960) decried what they perceived as the leveling and muffling effect of bureaucracy and mass society. But in recent years, these concerns about an overly oppressive community have been swept away and replaced by what is in some ways an opposite focus on the pronounced differences— and indifferences—in a society riven by race, ethnicity, immigration, class, and identity divisions.[14]

Globalization and fragmentation both involve questions of the geographical aspects of social interaction and the dissemination of cultural symbols and practices. Nevertheless, these processes pull in opposite directions. While globalization implies integration, fragmentation suggests disintegration. Globalization means interdependence, multilateralism, and openness, and fragmentation is associated with autarchy, unilateralism, and protectionism. And while globalization implies (American) universalism and hegemony, fragmentation tends toward national particularism and separatism.

These opposing processes are not simply international, but occur at multiple levels—in states, in communities, and in individuals. They threaten the cohesion of the group or of the state or prevent the individual from being fully integrated. In chapter 1 of this volume, Ronnie Lipschutz claims that history displays a recurrent tension between these integrative and disintegrative pressures. He discerns perennial struggles for hegemony in the United States, waged in religious terms: the "Great Awakenings," or populist revivals of religious fervor and institutions that have occurred in response to the dislocation, and "churn" associated with periodic industrial revolutions that threatened the social order. Andrew Barlow echoes Lipschutz with respect to the destabilization of American society—and the middle-class social order in particular—in the face of growing socioeconomic inequality and the erosion of governmental support.

James Cohen, for his part, underlines the inadequacy of U.S. immigration policy relative to the real nature of immigration. He focuses on the emergence of transnational communities whose identity is not primarily based on attachment to a specific geographic place or a specific country. These communities of migrants represent a powerful challenge to traditional ideas of nation-state, provoking rising nationalist suspicions and fears of losing the pure Anglo-Protestant identity "that made the United States great."

The fragmentation of society and the issue of identity, and in particular racial identity, are also at the center of both Howard Winant's and Tyler Stovall's chapters. Winant, in chapter 4, offers a provocative analysis of race, explaining that the internal conflict associated with having a dual identity applies not only to black Americans but to all Americans. All aspects of our lives are shaped in crucial ways by race; one cannot escape racial identity in the United States. Immigration's contribution to the increasing presence of multiple races stirs the anguish related to our own identity: Who are we as individuals and as a nation? Who are we in relation to one another? In chapter 3, Stovall addresses the lack of social cohesion by focusing on the unsettled relationship between African American and Diaspora communities, along with the increasing diversity of the black community. Within this context, *Time* columnist Joe Klein's question regarding senator and presidential candidate Barack Obama—"Is he African and American or African American?"—seems particularly pertinent.

Globalization's Churn

Ronnie Lipschutz skillfully unwinds the complex relationships among globalization, culture, and conflict. He argues that capitalism eats away at the foundations of social structures and hierarchies through the churn that it generates.[15] Lipschutz writes that churn weakens the "normal" or "commonsense" ideologies and relations that naturalize and justify particular institutionalized forms of domination, social organization, and hegemony. When both beliefs and practices begin to dissolve, the legitimacy of a social order comes under question and challenge, leading to cultural conflicts. The conflicts experienced today are manifestations of modernity and globalization, but they follow particular patterns observed in the past, when the cultural hegemony of the dominant elite was challenged and society was fractured by economic changes.

Lipschutz's chapter focuses on the "culture wars" for social and political hegemony that have been waged for at least the last thirty-five years. As noted, these culture wars recall past Great Awakenings associated with periods of great economic and social dislocation. He suggests, however, that since September 11, 2001, the American culture wars might be spreading to other parts of the world. Many powerful countries have experienced similar conflicts between religious and secular groups, often resulting in class and social struggles. These conflicts have often been resolved through expansionism or war, approaches readily discernable in current U.S. foreign policy.

A Polarized Society

For Thomas Friedman, globalization has created a new, "flat" global reality in which people everywhere potentially share new cosmopolitan connections and a global culture, thanks to the World Wide Web, computers, and microminiaturization.[16] However, Andrew Barlow in chapter 5 argues that this image is misleading: the world is not so much flat as it is polarized, with people retreating from larger frames of reference and gravitating toward coherent but isolating nationalism, ethnic group identification, and religious fundamentalism. According to Barlow, financial and economic integration has weakened the role of states and is seriously threatening national welfare systems, particularly in the United States. Key dynamics of globalization—notably, the emergence of a more global division of labor and the increased leverage for transnational corporations over workers and the state—have fractured American society. This is reflected more than ever in the reorganization of American cities. Furthermore, Barlow echoes Winant and Stovall when he argues that social instability and inequality fuel feelings of nationalism and racism, threatening a downward spiral of further social fragmentation.

From Barlow's perspective, we are facing an ironic truth about market globalization: rather than creating more cosmopolitanism and global connections among people, globalization is creating conditions in which people, feeling threatened, retreat from one another. In its current form, globalization does not take into account the richness of human diversity. It ignores the harshness of exploitation and social inequality and contributes to social and ecological tragedies. American society is exposed to deep and various faults threatening its cohesion and its stability.

For Friedman, technological progress fuels prosperity, economic forces shape society, and politics and culture are only secondary phenomena. But for Barlow, the world is uneven, and globalization intensifies the movement of its tectonic plates along social, racial, and gender fault lines.

The Need for a Broader Concept of Citizenship

James Cohen underlines with great eloquence the inadequacy of American immigration policies relative to the everyday life of immigrants. He demonstrates that policy makers have failed to appreciate the implications of the emergence of transnational networks of migrants. Existing policy is incapable of taking into account the real logic of human mobility in the current era of globalization. In the special case of the United States and Mexico, U.S. immigration policy does not recognize the importance of transnational migrants—despite the fact that communities transcending and traversing borders challenge basic notions of the nation-state and citizenship.

Yet Cohen is less interested in preserving outdated notions of nation and citizenship than in broadening them. Global or world citizenship may be unworkable, but it is possible to envision new "transnational forms of political authority that favor migrants"—including freedom of movement and respect for migrants' basic social rights, whatever side of the border they happen to be on at any given moment.[17] This idea remains well outside the mainstream of political debate within the United States, where the criteria of sovereignty remain unquestioned and national borders maintain great symbolic significance. Nevertheless, the rudiments of something resembling transnational law already exist, based largely in the Universal Declaration of Human Rights in 1948 and its subsequent covenants relating to economic, social, and cultural rights.

Society is fragmented in such a way that, as Lipschutz writes, "it will be difficult to put the pieces together" the way it was before. Perhaps a conceptualization of a larger meaning of citizenship is required to enable the emergence of a new cohesive society.

America's Multiracial Society and the Question of Identity

Howard Winant and Tyler Stovall engage brilliantly with the issue of race in twenty-first-century America and its multiracial society. Every day we consciously or unconsciously perform the most basic act of racialization—for example, using race labels to describe people—and uphold a certain racial organization in where we live or work, what we eat or wear or watch, the language we speak, and the idioms we use. What does it mean in modern America to be black, yellow, brown, or even white? Winant explains that we cannot escape the racial labels which U.S. society assigns to each of us, and at the same time, we cannot identify with their designations: we ourselves are fissured to an unprecedented extent by the conflicts and contradictions of the political struggles of the past decades. Stovall concurs, and takes racial identity further when he comments on contemporary philosophies of the African Diaspora. The new diasporic theory asserts the absence of certainties of fixed boundaries and settled definitions of race and culture, and challenges nationalist essentialism. For Stovall, black identity remains in flux as racial and national identifications sometimes diverge.

Both agree that the color blindness of the twenty-first century, a result of the "victory" of the twentieth century's civil rights movement, is one of the contradictions U.S. society faces today. In the 1900s, African Americans struggled to exercise their democratic rights as full-fledged American citizens; today, U.S. citizens and immigrants of various racial identities face a similar dilemma as they manage the disparate and contradictory meanings of race. Indeed, the dilemma W. E. B. Du Bois called "double consciousness" has ceased to be largely a "black thing" and has extended to Chinese, Latinos, and Native Americans. Its disruptive effect now touches all racial identities. Today we are all beset by double consciousness. Representing both African immigration and mixed race identity, Barack Obama highlights the significance of black diversity in America and demonstrates some of the political implications of that diversity.

GLOBALIZATION AND FEARS

The advance of globalization has coincided with the arrival of a variety of new threats, both natural and human-made, to Americans' security. The income gap between the rich and poor grows steadily; racial barriers contribute to the fragmentation of a multicultural-multiracial society; national borders' prophylactic powers erode; and cultural boundaries break down. Meanwhile, we are busy building physical fences between countries when environmental problems have cross-border effects—effects that will only be exacerbated by global warming and the resulting migration. These threats to Americans' well-being have not only fed the Great Awakenings discussed by Ronnie Lipschutz and the politics of fear identified by Andrew Barlow, but have even begun to call into question Americans' commitment to economic and political openness.

While many politicians and scholars, convinced of the benefits of international economic integration, are still quick to link free markets with prosperity and peace, many remain unconvinced that global markets can deliver the goods. Phenomena such as a persistent U.S. trade deficit with China, the downturn in housing markets, and the acceleration of companies' outsourcing activities do not reassure. According to a *Wall Street Journal*/NBC poll from late December 2007, there has been a decisive shift in Americans' attitudes about globalization, as many no longer see the link between free trade and "the wealth of nations."[18] Whereas this link once served as the bedrock principle of U.S. international economic leadership, Americans increasingly share anxieties about globalization voiced by people all over the world, writes Paul Cantor.

If culture is "a society's conglomeration of its language, spiritual practices, social norms, and values, transmitted from one generation to another; if it is tacit and esoteric; and if it is precious and fragile,"[19] the acceleration of "global culturization"—the diffusion of cultural values and ideas across national borders—is a risk for many. The consequence of technological progress such as the telephone, television, worldwide media, and the Internet has sped up the process, and we are experiencing the emergence of a more homogenous global culture consisting of Hollywood blockbusters, American television series, and American bestsellers. Diana Crane and Susanne Janssen argue, however, that in the United States itself, there is a significant resistance to the influence of foreign culture despite the growing number of immigrants and the broad availability of foreign cultural goods. This might be explained by an unsettled form of protectionism from the powerful media industry; it may also reflect a resistance to foreign cultural influences on the part of a population accustomed to cultural goods reflecting a high level of cultural proximity.

Recurrent Fears

During periods of cultural distortion and grave personal stress, when we lose faith in the legitimacy of our norms, the viability of our institutions, and the authority of our leaders in church and state, the masses return to traditional religious practices, religious movements of "purification."[20] There are times when we experience waves of xenophobia and social and political conflicts. These periodic social crises are also associated with peaks in imperialist expansion, the pursuit of "Manifest Destiny," or other utopian projects.[21] Expansion is not, however, merely driven by faith; it is also a means of resolving tensions of class and society that arise during such periods.

Ronnie Lipschutz observes that every fifty to seventy-five years, beginning in the mid-eighteenth century, the United States has gone through periods of great national fear that have led to national religious revivals, with consequent impacts on culture, economics, politics, and foreign policy. The transition from a material-based economy in the 1970s to an information-based economy and the latest cycle of capitalist globalization are the background of the "Fourth Awakening" and the social crisis we are experiencing today, writes Lipschutz. The global reorganization of production facilitated by electronic networks and new regulations in the global political economy impact families' structures and households, communities and consumption patterns, individual identity and freedom. They affect entire societies and cultures. The sundering of long-held authority relations and the melting away of political and social hierarchies engender fears, doubts, xenophobia, and racism, fostering the growth of evangelical churches and strong reactions against social liberalism of any variety.

A Politics of Fear

Why, after 9/11, did the U.S. government choose a political strategy based on fear to deal with terrorism, while other nations, including European nations that had also recently experienced terrorist attacks, chose instead strategies based on international cooperation? The Global Peace Campaign group, founded by Yumi Kikuchi, wrote to President George W. Bush just after the 9/11 attacks, urging him to seize the historic opportunity to prove that the United States was more than just an economic and military power to be feared. It was an opportunity to show the world that the United States was also a civilized country that could be trusted to follow the law, guided by wisdom and compassion. Instead, our government connected the horrible tragedy with urgency for military action and curtailing civil liberties. The Bush administration asserted that "September 11th changed everything."

In its 2007 International Report, Amnesty International writes that "powerful governments and armed groups are deliberately fomenting fear to erode human rights and to create an increasingly polarized and dangerous world."[22] If terrorists' goal is to generate a level of fear far beyond their real capacity to destroy, can we wonder why governments respond in kind, rather than by reassuring citizens? Despite the entreaties of pacifists and civil society groups, our "democratically elected politicians" are ignoring the dangers of cultivating a politics of fear. The U.S. government initiated a strategy of fear of "inevitable" attacks and of powerful, dangerous international networks aimed at destroying our free world. The media complicity in that strategy guaranteed its effectiveness: any terrorist attack anywhere in the world provides evidence that the strategy is perfectly grounded.

Why is the United States prisoner of this vicious rhetoric and of this political strategy? Andrew Barlow invokes Lipschutz's culture wars in his answer: the dynamics of globalization have undermined welfare systems in most developed countries, especially in the United States. Our governments—local, state, and national—have adopted policies aimed not at taming social conflicts and leveling inequalities but at fostering and maximizing the private accumulation of wealth.[23] Further, like Winant and Stovall, Barlow observes that the long history of racialization of American society provides a strong impetus to racialize this politics of fear. In addition to fostering intergroup conflicts, such racialization also provides politicians aligned with corporate interests a powerful weapon for undermining welfare state policies and programs.

Expression of Fear in Popular Culture

Ironically, a market economy has permitted a consolidation of media power that in turn is capitalizing on Americans' fears of globalization. Media outlets have distanced themselves from what many see as their primary role, objectively reporting news; they are profit-oriented and conduct themselves accordingly—they produce what *sells*, and one thing that sells is fear of globalization and its consequences.

In chapter 6, Paul Cantor argues that globalization's unsettling effects have been mirrored in many recent American television programs. Whereas American popular culture, especially from the late 1960s to the 1980s, has often reflected a sense of confidence and triumph, since the 1990s many television programs have expressed fears that sinister forces somewhere out there in the world are about to conquer America. These fears often take the form of nightmarish images of alien invasions and alien-human hybrids. Cantor gives special attention to the popular Fox science-fiction series *The X-Files* (1993–2002), which demonstrated a surprisingly sophisticated understanding of globalization, one that resonated with viewers' contemporary fears. It presented globalization as a process that affects all nations, including the United States—which created the system but became prisoner of its own creation, no longer in control of its own destiny. Whether via immigration or transnational conspiracy, something non-American, even un-American, is taking over the United States by masquerading as American.

Cantor also describes post-9/11 shows that have echoed the political paranoia of *The X-Files*, dealing with government conspiracies and cover-ups, imprisonment and interrogation, and chronicling the erosion of civil liberties in the United States. Throughout most of these series, however, there is a hero claiming, "Just because someone is different, it does not make him a monster." Cantor's interpretation is that while Americans may be anxious and even frightened about globalization, they are not incapable of detecting the silver lining.

Cultural Protectionism

Any traveler can witness the impact of globalization on public life and belief systems in just about every corner of the world. Yet the free flow of information and culture, leading to shared values, a common language, and harmonious international relations remains a utopian dream. Instead, the fear of globalization is a constant presence in cultural debates, and some literature even refers to a "culture world-system." Some argue that a homogenized world culture threatens local cultures. Others believe we are witnessing an increasing hybridization of cultures, and that global communication furthers social justice. For Nederveen Pieterse, for example, globalization is an open-ended process of interconnection of cultural influences, Eastern as well as Western. The growing awareness of cultural differences and the awareness of globalization itself are interdependent. There are both cultural differences and a striving for recognition on the global scale. This striving for recognition implies a claim to equal rights and equal treatment—in other words, a common universe of difference.[24] Although some equate globalization with "cultural imperialism" or even "Americanization," is it possible that local cultures are more robust and adaptive than such rhetoric would have us believe? Might American culture not also be subject to influences from the outside world?

Though the globalization of culture is often depicted as a one-way projection of American "content" from Hollywood and Madison Avenue, globalization and technological change have made it easier for cultural goods to flow in the other direction. As Diana Crane and Susanne Janssen demonstrate, however, there is a significant resistance to the influence of foreign culture in the United States, despite the easy access to it. This resistance is something of a puzzle: if the diversity of a multicultural society could be a comparative advantage and a source of continuing creativity and innovation, a hegemonic culture that alienates or destroys the "different" might be a source of impoverishment and, in the long run, sterility.

Crane and Janssen analyze UNESCO data to attempt to measure and explain this resistance. As they suggest, this resistance might reflect an unsettled form of protectionism from the powerful media industry. Driven to maximize market shares and profits, American media position themselves in opposition to Mahatma Gandhi's saying: "I want the cultures of all the lands to be blown about my house as freely as possible. But I refuse to be blown off my feet by any." This isolation may also reflect a resistance to foreign cultural influences on the part of a U.S. population that has been cultivated to prefer its own cultural goods. The result is that American culture remains relatively isolated from global influences.

GLOBALIZATION AS A SOURCE OF CREATIVITY AND INNOVATION IN CIVIL SOCIETY

In the twenty-first century, migration and globalization are so intertwined as to be integral to each other; as suggested by the *Economist*, "It is impossible to separate globalization of trade and capital from the global movement of people."[25] Millions of people around the world today do not live in the country of their citizenship; perhaps as many have multiple citizenships and live in more than one country; and many others are prohibited from gaining citizenship in their countries of residence. Considering the obstacles people crossing borders encounter and the rigidity and complexity of the systems they have to deal with, migrants worldwide seem to be coping remarkably well.

Porous borders and multiple identities undermine the territorial basis of cultural belonging, and consequently the basis of the nation-state.[26] Migrants are challenging the meaning of citizenship as a set of rights and responsibilities bestowed by the state. Yet they are also contributing to the growing, vibrant U.S. and transnational civil society among nongovernmental organizations (NGOs), trade unions, foundations, and many other grassroots organizations mentioned in the following chapters—including transmigrant networks, religious groups, sports organizations and communities, gay groups, and artists on the borderline.

James Cohen describes how emergent transnational networks of migrants are reinventing new strategies of living across borders. Tirza True Latimer argues that the border is not necessarily perceived as a constraint by artists, but rather can become a zone of creativity and sometimes connectedness, a place of intracultural vitality. When people cross borders, languages also become caught up in the dynamics of globalization; William Leap demonstrates that a striking feature of globalization includes new and unexpected forms of language pluralism, as well as more intense forms of linguistic backlash—a plethora of creativity. Creativity also comes to play in our relationship to sports, one of the most nationalistic of all cultural expressions, suggests Tim Wendel. Experienced often as the first rung of the social ladder for African Americans and as an element of stability and focus for youth, competition from a growing number of players from outside the United States might affect the cohesion of a community and the "dream" of its children. Meanwhile, as Sara Heitler Bamberger argues, religious practices and communities are by no means immune from the dynamics of globalization in which capitalism and consumerism have achieved the status of "golden calf." Willingly or not, religious communities are changing, resulting in either crystallization or a metamorphosis of their various faiths.

Despite globalization's challenges to citizenship and identity and to relationships of authority and legitimacy between government and citizens, civil society is creating new spaces both within and among countries for governance and agency.[27] Today, citizenship is claimed and rights are obtained through the agency and actions of the people themselves. Since at least the early 1990s, citizens' groups have grown tremendously in their capacity, scope, and influence. The "global associational revolution"[28] is enabled by the same technological and network-oriented dynamics as capitalism's globalization, yet promotes alternative values such as democracy, equality, freedom, participation, sustainability, human diversity, and solidarity.

Historically, much of the work of civil society organizations occurred at a micro level; today they have grown, and their credibility has increased tremendously. Some governments now integrate the expertise and local knowledge of civil society groups in their policy making. High-profile civil society groups have developed notoriety, and their endorsements or criticisms of business practices or political decisions carry significant weight with the public. They have become an important force with which the private and public sector must reckon. Above all, civil society groups generally enjoy a high level of public trust and fashion the cradle for new political forces. Robert D. Putnam gives us hope when he argues that civil society builds social capital, trust, and shared values, which are then transferred into the political sphere, helping hold society together. They facilitate an understanding of the interconnectedness of society and the interests within it.[29] There remains, however, a gap: in reality, the situations of poor and marginalized citizens preclude them from participating in civil society.

The Migrants' Will

The United States was built not only on the labor but also on the creativity and adaptability of immigrants. Millions from all over the world have made the United States their country, contributing to its diversity and economic strength. Immigrants and their children have moved far beyond the menial work domains with which they are traditionally associated, becoming a large section of the middle class. Such upward mobility can be explained by the fact that migrants need skills, determination, and a willingness to take risks; they need to adapt and evolve beyond the space known to them. In order to survive, they must reinvent their ways of relating to other groups and cultivate their own creativity. This move on their part already marks them as special people.

James Cohen investigates the complex patterns of cultural continuities and changes experienced by Mexicans and Mexican Americans living between Mexico and the United States. In chapter 2, he outlines the context of the current political struggle over Mexican immigration, describing the U.S.-Mexico border as a contested territory shaped by border crossings and fence building. Once they have successfully dealt with the fence, be it legally or illegally, immigrants face yet another set of barriers: mastering the English language, coping with the mores of American life without losing their identity or faith, and finding adequate employment, to name just a few. They frequently recast their individual ethnic identity, their concept of citizenship, and their national loyalty, often inventing a hybrid form of Mexican American culture reflecting their life between two worlds.

Remittances, a centuries-old component of migration, represent the human face of financial globalization. The flows of human and financial capital have profound implications for the economies, cultures, and societies of both the sending and the receiving countries. Latin America received about $68 billion in remittances in 2006, which many experts believe now exceeds the combined total of all foreign direct investment and overseas development assistance to the region; Mexico alone received $24.2 billion.[30]

Modern technology enables an unprecedented degree of ongoing involvement "back home," on the other side of the border. Immigrants form support associations for their home communities, contributing financially to infrastructure development and other improvements in their towns of origin. These associations, in turn, form networks of influence that can and do address larger political issues. Home country governments—local, regional, and national—often support these networks and associations by, for example, providing immigrants with legal defense or health care or providing the undocumented with identification to facilitate their integration into the host country.

Cohen cites Jonathan Fox, who wrote that Mexicans are creating new ways of becoming Americans, with membership organizations playing crucial roles.[31] He notes that while most migrant organizations began as hometown associations, many have now developed programs for families in the new communities in the United States. In his view, these transnational migrants are coming more and more to assume a new sort of civic binationality, having simultaneous membership in both Mexican and U.S. society. In this sense, immigrants show a great capacity to adapt to "multiple social settings" and display extraordinary "cross-cultural competences." Cohen concludes that in a mobile world of culturally open societies, such capacities should be seen as highly desirable, since individuals possessing such flexibility can perform as productive, civic-minded citizens, regardless of where they are.

On the Borderland

Gloria Anzaldua—Chicana, lesbian, feminist writer, scholar, and activist—writes of the geographical area where the United States and Mexico meet: "La frontera: the frontier, the edges, the limits, the boundaries, the borders, the cultures, the languages, the foods; but more than that, the unity and disunity: *es lo mismo y no lo es* (it's the same and it isn't)."[32] She explores the space of encounter, of integration and separation, of belonging and alienation, of inclusion and exclusion; she examines the duality of in and out, and of overlapping identities. Anzaldua describes living on the edge and trying to fit in and contemplates the "geographical, psychological, linguistic, and sexual borders where disenfranchised people reside."[33]

In this volume, Tirza True Latimer depicts the stand of Anzaldua and the borderland artists against popular media representations of borders as zones of perpetual conflict. They see the space between the United States and Mexico as a zone of creativity and connectedness; for them, the borderland is a model of intracultural vitality. Latimer sees the dynamism, idiosyncrasy, and creativity of the border arising from its physical demarcations, its particular space of transition, and the emotional life of the people who live in its sometimes surreal reality. These distinctive characteristics make it an infinite source of creativity.

In recent years, border zones have drawn the focus of politicians, free-trade apostles, human rights advocates, journalists, and many others. Artists have likewise turned their attention to the borderland. Latimer writes that, for these artists, work is not so much about the production of aesthetic objects as it is an important mode of raising social awareness and advocating social justice. They consider themselves to be peacemakers and troublemakers, intellectuals and educators, instigators of social change. The mixed-race community living and thriving on the borderland is reinventing the border, which is perceived both as the physical barrier between two countries and as the ideological line of scrimmage between corporate values and the interests of local populations.

Latimer describes the commitment that border artists have demonstrated to the public domain, especially to the creation of new forms and forums of what might be described as both public art and public education. She draws on Anzaldua's work, which weaves English, Spanish, and even Nahuatl into a new language of cultural emancipation, and she examines the Border Art Workshop/Taller de Arte Fronterizo (BAW/TAF), whose members confronted the meaning of deterritorialization and border politics through their work and lives. Latimer recalls Howard Winant's argument when she notes BAW/TAF's awareness of ambiguous and contradictory racial signifiers at play—describing a BAW/TAF production that dramatizes the extent to which ethnic stereotyping infiltrates American culture—in Hollywood productions, and even in "high culture" institutions such as museums. It exists in the American presentation of political and natural sciences, thus shaping our understanding of the world and our interaction with it. She also introduces the controversial exhibition organized by Chris Gilbert at the Berkeley Art Museum, "Now-Time Venezuela: Media along the Path of the Bolivarian Process." This exhibition, perceived by some to be too politically charged, ended in Gilbert's resignation. Latimer succeeds brilliantly in demonstrating that the border, instead of being a "defensive barricade," can be "a shared corridor where the terms of identity, community, and culture are incessantly negotiated, but never resolved."

Creativity and Language Purity

Languages around the world are changing faster than ever before. Over the past two or three decades, English has come to occupy the dominant position among world languages, and its global spread is closely tied to the forces of globalization and transcultural flows. While English has become the lingua franca of the global network, the fear of linguistic imperialism has frequently followed in the wake of economic and political imperialism.[34]

In the United States, however, the number of "languages other than mainstream English," which William Leap abbreviates to LOTE in his chapter, have increased significantly due to immigration and the fact that fluency in English does not spread evenly within these immigrant communities. Although English has never been officially declared the "national language," many wish that English would attain such a designation, and differences in English usage disturb some first-language U.S. English speakers.

In chapter 9, Leap explores the phenomenon through the linguistic practices of "Gay Men's English" in the United States, examining the influence of LOTE on it. Gay Men's English (GME) is a language constructed of linguistic codes and cultural practices that appear in conversations, storytelling, and other forms of communication among gay men. This coded language offers protection from public disclosure even as it allows for displays of gay identity. The creativity of this community, Leap notes, is demonstrated by the effectiveness of its language: highly political content and the centrality of gay identity are clearly communicated within the community, while being unintelligible to outsiders. Even though GME is predominantly a language of white, urban, affluent, gay men, it enjoys (as English more generally) a worldwide circulation for naming and discussing sexual experience when local languages and indigenous sexual cultures offer no framework for such discussion.

These sexualized linguistic codes used by gay men have evolved along with gay culture in the larger political and economic history of the United States. Over the last forty years, gay culture has moved from an oppositional stance to "a place at the table"; from a language of "the closet," reflecting a discrete lifestyle, to gay liberation; and now to a more conservative position. From the 1980s onward, GME became a white-centered, English-based, gay lexical purism, concerned with fitting into the mainstream. Gay men now find alternative ways to express their "gayness."

GME is at home in the United States, but globalization and immigration have introduced LOTEs, and speakers of LOTEs, into the GME speakers' space. Homosexual immigrants develop new ways of speaking about sexual experiences, drawing from the linguistic practices of their communities of origin as well as from patterns of speech in the context of their new U.S. resettlement. Through personal relationships, informal conversations in gay bars, restaurants, and other casual encounters with immigrants of different racial or ethnic backgrounds, speakers of Gay Men's English develop some level of second-language familiarity. Leap's research indicates that speakers of GME are simultaneously learning to speak a same-sex-oriented LOTE and resisting incorporating LOTE words and phrases into GME usage. The author concludes that the search for GME purity is an expression within the gay community of a broader inclination of American cultural and political nationalism, responding to the increasing pressures of globalization at home.

Hoop Dreams Gone

The World Baseball Classic was inaugurated in Tokyo on March 3, 2006. The competitiveness of the games, the national diversity of the spectators and players, and the high media ratings conclusively demonstrated that there is a rapidly growing global market for baseball. The results of individual games confirmed that globalization has also entered the realm of sports: who could have imagined that teams from Mexico and Canada would beat the United States at its own national pastime? The event also provided insight into the multiple identities of players such as Alex

Rodriguez, a Dominican raised in the United States who wrestled publicly with the decision of whether to play for his native or adopted country. (He chose to play for the United States.)

In chapter 10, Tim Wendel calls our attention to how globalization's effect on sports has altered the socioeconomic landscape in America. He sheds light on a harsh new reality for U.S.-born athletes, especially African Americans, who have often used sports to climb up from the bottom of the social ladder and to help promote social cohesion. He writes: "From the Bronx to Watts, the promise of a professional basketball career has long held many neighborhoods together. Even though the dream becomes reality for only a tiny percentage of those who play as kids, it provides a structure and discipline that other parts of our society often covet." The opening of professional sports to minorities offered direct or indirect opportunity for social mobility, a gateway to a better life; the increase in competition from sports globalization diminishes that opportunity for young Americans.

The globalization of American sports takes many forms. Athletes come from abroad to play for U.S. teams; American teams gain fans in foreign locations, among both expatriates and foreign sports enthusiasts; and sports that originated and are traditionally played in one country have spread throughout the world. Baseball originated in the United States, but is now very popular throughout Latin America and the Caribbean, with such countries as Cuba and the Dominican Republic providing many players to the (U.S.) major leagues. Several great basketball players drafted by the (U.S.) National Basketball Association are from Serbia and Russia. In 2002, Yao Ming became the first number-one draft pick in the United States coming from a foreign basketball league. The Institute for Diversity and Ethics in Sports at the University of Central Florida claims that the percentage of players from outside the United States continues to grow in most popular sports, such as baseball, basketball, football, and soccer.

Wendel notes that the consequences for the African American community—its youth and its cohesion—are already noticeable. He believes there are many ways to be a hero, and that today the academic track holds more promise for scholarship opportunities than the sports track. Wendel emphasizes the need for mentors and role models and calls on the creativity of sport communities to keep the youth dreaming another dream.

Between the "Golden Calf" and Fundamentalism

Religions, for the most part, have been profoundly affected by globalization and have been active consumers of the tools of modernity. Information technology has been used for almost two decades as an efficient means of proselytizing. Growing wealth has produced mega-churches and businesses of religion large in scale and ambition. The most prolific producer of Christian missionaries on a per-capita basis is now South Korea. The biggest Bible-publishing houses are located there and in Brazil. The

American Bible Society has published more than fifty million Bibles in officially atheist China. Muslims are going global as well: funded by Saudi wealth, thirty million Korans a year are distributed through a vast network of mosques, Islamic societies, embassies, and websites such as www.freekoran.com.[35]

Global networks and information technology are proving to be useful tools for religious groups trying to keep their followers together or to expand their influence. Several television channels and radio stations are "Godcasting" on all continents. The techniques and expertise of modern businesses are being applied to organized religions, and Christians reveal themselves to be quite proficient. Christian publishing houses are big businesses, and the religious section can be an important income for secular publishing houses. Bringing material concerns and practices into the Holy Kingdom is not universally welcomed, and some people of faith see conflict between capitalist free-market economy values and traditional, religion-based value systems.

In chapter 11, Sara Heitler Bamberger examines the complex relationship between globalization and religious fundamentalism. As globalization creates an increasingly interdependent, networked, and homogenized world, it also produces social, economic, and cultural dislocation. Bamberger focuses on how this dislocation is taking place in the political, economic, and social arenas, exposing millions of people to the vulnerability of clashing worldviews and at the same time bolstering religious identity and affiliation. She examines how globalization contributes to the dispersion of a subtle but distinct set of materialistic values characteristic of the free-market economy, values which have found a captive market in the United States.

Across the Abrahamic faiths of Christianity, Judaism, and Islam, Bamberger identifies three groups: those concerned with preserving and transmitting tradition, who resist modernity by creating enclavist communities; those who open their doors cautiously, appreciating the economic and social benefits of globalization but suspicious about the values it brings; and those who embrace globalization as a means of growth and prosperity. These three groups share the same concern about the erosion of religion and their role in society, but it is those who condemn globalization and adopt fundamentalist positions that develop organizations with the most clearly defined membership, the sharpest boundaries, the most authoritarian leadership, and strictest behavioral requirements. Often, members of this latter group define themselves in contrast to the pervasive secularism and materialism of American society, though they rarely employ the militant, adversarial techniques that typify fundamentalists in countries where the religious establishment, secular state, and civil society are seen as enemies of each other. In the United States, the climate is not conducive to militant religious activism. This relative moderation is a result of the United States' democratic political structure, freedom of religious practice, separation between church and state, relative affluence, economic stability, and enfranchisement of religious individuals.

CONCLUSION

Social theorists and contributors to this volume agree that globalization is fundamentally changing the nature of social interactions. Open for discussion is what has changed and how it has changed. Clearly, there are critically important economic changes favoring the emergence of transnational economic and political organizations enabled by a seamless web of information technology, with the Internet, mobile phones, and satellite networks shrinking space and time. Our contributors emphasize that the manifestations of globalization in both political and cultural processes are equally important; its constructive and salutary manifestations are fundamental to our future. The data available on trade capital and immigration flows testify that the benefits of globalization are not evenly distributed, with those excluded from its rewards becoming growing sources of resistance.

Contemporary globalization arose in the context of a postwar world economy structured by the overwhelming power of the United States. Since the end of the Cold War and the collapse of the Soviet Union, America has reigned supreme as the sole economic, cultural, and military giant. At a superficial level, one might believe that the United States has become Herbert Marcuse's "one-dimensional society,"[36] yet globalization's dispersing and diversifying dynamics appear to operate within the United States as well. The contributors to this volume have adroitly analyzed globalization in the American context, identifying a range of effects on American culture and society.

The challenges U.S. society faces are numerous, powerful, and often troubling. Some contributors argue that capitalism and the free trade doctrine preached since World War II have shaped an unjust American social structure, and "globalization coming home" is eroding the remaining pillars of social order and cohesion. The income gap between rich and poor in this country continues to widen. One-fifth of Americans today earn more than half of all wages and salaries, and 10 percent of the population owns 70 percent of all assets.[37] The American middle class is suddenly confronted with real wage decline and economic insecurity. Of the 300 million people living in the United States today, about 47 million have no health insurance. It is fair to ask whether these circumstances are consistent with core U.S. liberal democratic values, "that each person is created equal, that opportunity should be universal, that access to opportunity should be equal, and that a free and democratic society is one that treats each person with equal concern and respect."[38]

Fragmentation exists not only along class and wealth lines but also along color lines; race continues to be a significant factor dividing American society. Howard Winant, Tyler Stovall, Andrew Barlow, and Ronnie Lipschutz agree that race has been, and is still, at the center of American experience. They argue that race remains crucial both for contemporary politics and for conceptualizing identity and culture. The supposed color blindness of the century is tainted with contradictions because racial dualism, the whole apparatus of structural racism, has survived alongside new racial reforms. W. E. B. Du Bois's double consciousness is no longer only a black reality; it is all of ours. All racial and ethnic identities are now beset by uncertainty and anxiety.

Increasing immigration sharpens these tensions, and the volume of movement across borders is unlikely to abate. Lant Pritchett, a World Bank economist, explains why the global pressure for labor movement across national borders is intensifying:

> Big gaps in wages between rich and poor countries and the slow population growth of many developed countries ... will soon lead to a shrinking work-force unless more immigration is allowed. Cheap communications make a difference as well, because it is less psychically costly to move when one can stay in touch.[39]

These transmigrants are developing new networks, above or across borders, that challenge the concept of citizenship in civil, political, and social terms. James Cohen writes that in the United States, where the concept of national sovereignty remains mostly unquestioned and where national borders maintain a great symbolic significance, such networks foster fear, xenophobia, and racism, disrupt identities, and promote a desire for cultural sovereignty. Andrew Barlow, Tyler Stovall, William Leap, Paul Cantor, Diana Crane, and Susanne Janssen all confirm this argument in their own way.

Newton's third law states that for every action, there is an equal and opposite reaction. Does this same law apply to social science? If globalization has awakened forces in the United States that attempt to reaffirm America's global dominion, then the forces of civil society have found parallel modes of expression. We are witnessing a growing number of popular movements rising up in opposition to capitalist principles. Drawing inspiration from political, racial, and gender-based liberation movements, civil society groups focus on civil rights—the rights of women, immigrants, and gays and general human rights—as well as the environment and peace, all of which they perceive to be threatened in some way by globalization.

American civil society organizations are playing important roles in local, regional, and global politics, roles facilitated by the development of new information and communication technologies. In April 2006, there was an unprecedented number of street demonstrations in 102 cities across the country in response to proposed immigration restrictions. These demonstrations highlighted the power of networked actors using modern technologies, with Internet community sites containing personal blogs playing significant roles in "getting the word out" about the content of the policies and these demonstrations. Spanish-language radio stations and Internet sites targeted specific audiences. MySpace emerged as a particularly significant channel for engaging English-speaking Latino youth.

An early manifestation of the civil society movement as we know it today came at the Rio de Janeiro Earth Summit in 1992, when large groups of people became aware of the possibility of creating truly modern democratic societies that honor life, respect differences, and promote equality and development in a sustainable manner. Social justice organizations challenge the legitimacy of unfair systems, hegemonic powers, and institutions, inventing a new reality through individual and collective actions. Each one of them contributes a share to an emerging mosaic in which each tessera is indispensable, yet not enough to complete the beautiful and multicolored final image of our country and of the world. Also required are a more inclusive society and the creation of a complex web of alliances committed to creating a just, sustainable, and compassionate world. In such a system, globalization—the technology- and communications-driven integration of economic, political, and cultural systems across the globe— would be the cement that holds the tesserae of colors, races, religions, ethnicities, and genders together, forming a harmonious whole, a diverse, balanced, and sustainable world.

NOTES

1. Gabor Steingart, "The End of Globalization?" *Speigel*, December 11, 2007, translated from the German by Christopher Sultan.

2. See, among others, Kevin H. O'Rourke and Jeffrey G. Williamson, *Globalization and History* (Cambridge, MA: MIT Press, 1999); Harold James, *The End of Globalization: Lessons from the Great Depression* (Cambridge, MA: Harvard University Press, 2001); Sanjeev Mahajan, *Globalization and Social Change* (New Delhi: Lotus Press, 2006).

3. For globalization's impact on U.S. legal and economic institutions, see the two companion volumes to this book: Beverly Crawford, ed., *The Impact of Globalization on the United States: Law and Politics* (Westport, CT: Praeger, 2008); and Beverly Crawford and Edward A. Fogarty, eds., *The Impact of Globalization on the United States: Business and Economics* (Westport, CT: Praeger, 2008).

4. See, among others, Thomas L. Friedman, *The Lexus and the Olive Tree* (New York: Anchor Books, 2000); Francis Fukumaya, *The End of History and the Last Man* (New York: Free Press, 1992); Kenechi Ohmae, *The Borderless World: Power and Strategy in the Interlinked Economy* (New York: Harper Business, 1990).

5. John Clark, *Worlds Apart: Civil Society and the Battle for Ethical Globalization* (Bloomfield, CT: Kumarian Press, 2003).

6. By the year 2000, we were told, there were ostensibly 120 electoral democracies in place out of 192 countries, of which eighty-five were thought to be full democracies, in the sense that they provide respect for the rule of law, civil and political rights. John Caventa, "Triumph, deficit or contestation? Deepening the 'deepening democracy' debate." IDS Working paper No. 264; and Freedom House, *Democracy's Century: A Survey of Global Political Change in the Twentieth Century.* Washington, DC: Freedom House, 1999.

7. See, among others, Richard Falk, *Predatory Globalization: A Critique* (Cambridge, UK: Polity Press, 1999); Dani Rodrik, *Has Globalization Gone Too Far?* (Washington DC: Institute for International Economics, 1997).

8. Clark, *Worlds Apart*.

9. Stiglitz warned, "If globalization continues to be conducted in the way that it has been in the past, if we continue to fail learning from our mistakes, globalization will not only not succeed in promoting development but will continue to create poverty and instability"; Joseph Stiglitz, *Globalization and Its Discontents* (New York: W. W. Norton, 2002), 248.

10. Alan Blinder, "Free Trade's Great, but Offshoring Rattles Me," *Washington Post*, May 6, 2007.

11. Ibid.

12. Cyrus Bina and Laurie M. Clements, *Beyond Survival: Wage Labor in the Late Twentieth Century* (New York: M. E. Sharpe, 1996).

13. John Tomlinson, *Globalization and Culture* (Cambridge, UK: Polity Press, 1999). Tomlinson argues that cultural identity, properly understood, is much more the *product* of globalization than its victim.

14. Russell R. Dynes and Kathleen J. Tierney, *Disasters, Collective Behavior, and Social Organization* (Newark: University of Delaware Press, 1994).

15. Joseph Schumpeter, *Capitalism, Socialism and Democracy* (New York: Harper, 1942); Michael W. Cox and Richard Alm, "The Churn: The Paradox of Progress," Federal Reserve Bank of Dallas, reprint from 1992 Annual Report, available at http://www.dallasfed.org/fed/annual/1999p/ar92.pdf. See also Katherine Boo, "The Churn: Creative Destruction in a Border Town," *New Yorker*, March 29, 2004, available at http://www.newyorker.com/archive/2004/03/29/040329fa_fact; and Katherine Boo, "The Best Job in Town: The Americanization of Chennai," *New Yorker*, July 5, 2004, 54–69.

16. Thomas Friedman, *The World Is Flat: A Brief History of the Twenty-First Century* (New York: Farrar, Straus & Giroux, 2005).

17. On world citizenship, see Derek Heater, *World Citizenship and Government: Cosmopolitan Ideas in the History of Western Political Thought* (New York: St. Martin's Press, 1996).

18. NBC News/*Wall Street Journal* poll conducted by the polling organizations of Peter Hart (D) and Bill McInturff (R), December 14–17, 2007. Approximately five hundred adults were polled nationwide; the results have a margin of error of ±4 percentage points. See http://www.pollingreport.com/trade.htm.

19. Trish Hallmark, "Americanization of Global Culture," *Global Politician*, April 2007.

20. William McLoughlin, *Revivals, Awakenings and Reform* (Chicago: University of Chicago Press, 1980).

21. Frederick Merk, *Manifest Destiny and Mission in American History* (New York: Knopf, 1963).

22 Amnesty International, 2007 Annual Report. London: Amnesty International, 2007. In the report's forward, Irene Khan writes: "Today far too many leaders are trampling freedom and trumpeting an ever-widening range of fears: fear of being swamped by migrants; fear of "the other" and of losing one's identity; fear of being blown up by terrorists; fear of "rogue states" with weapons of mass destruction. Fear thrives on myopic and cowardly leadership. There are indeed many real causes of fear, but the approach being taken by many world leaders is short-sighted, promulgating policies and strategies that erode the rule of law and human rights, increase inequalities, feed racism and xenophobia, divide and damage communities, and sow the seeds for violence and more conflict. The politics of fear has been made more complex by the emergence of armed groups and big business that commit or condone human rights abuses. Both—in different ways—challenge the power of governments in an increasingly borderless world. Weak governments and ineffective international institutions are unable to hold them accountable, leaving people vulnerable and afraid.

23. Jill Quadagno, "Creating a Capital Investment Welfare State: The New American Exceptionalism," *American Sociological Review* 64, no. 1 (February 1999): 1–11.

24. Nederveen Pieterse, *Globalization and Culture* (Lanham, MD: Rowman & Littlefield, 2003).

25. *The Economist*, special survey on migration, October 31, 2002, p. 50.

26. Stephen Castles and Alastair Davidson, *Citizenship and Migration* (New York: Routledge, 2000).

27. Andrea Cornwall and Vera Schattan Coelho, eds., *Spaces for Change? The Politics of Citizen Participation in New Democratic Arena*, volume 4 of *Claiming Citizenship*, series editor John Gaventa (London: Zed Books, 2004).

28. Kumi Naidoo, World Alliance for Citizen Participation, speech at the World Bank headquarters, Washington, DC, February 10, 2003.

29. Robert D. Putnam, *Making Democracy Work: Civic Traditions in Modern Italy* (Princeton, NJ: Princeton University Press, 1993).

30. The International Fund for Agricultural Development (IFAD), United Nations, International Forum on Remittances, 2007 available at http://www.ifad.org/events/remittances/index.htm.

31. Jonathan Fox, "Binational Citizens: Mexican Migrants Are Challenging Old Ideas about Assimilation." Boston Review, September/October 2006, pp. 26–27.

32. Norma E. Cantu, about Gloria Anzaldua, *Living on the Border: A Wound That Will Not Heal*, Smithsonian Center for Education and Museum Studies, Migrations in History, Borders and Identity.

33. Annie Nakao, "Gloria Anzaldua," obituary, *San Francisco Chronicle*, May 20, 2004.

34. Robert Phillipson, *Linguistic Imperialism* (Oxford: Oxford University Press, 1992).

35. "The Battle of the Books," *Economist*, December 22, 2007.

36. Herbert Marcuse, *One-Dimensional Man*. Boston: Beacon Press, 1991 [1964].

37. Data provided by the Panel Study of Income Dynamics (PSID) and the Federal Reserve Board survey of consumer finances. The PSID, begun in 1968, is a longitudinal study of a representative sample of U.S. individuals (men, women, and children) and the family units in which they reside. It emphasizes the dynamic aspects of economic and demographic behavior, but its content is broad, including sociological and psychological measures. As a consequence of low attrition rates and the success in following young adults as they form their own families and recontact efforts (of those declining an interview in prior years), the sample size has grown from 4,800 families in 1968 to more than 7,000 families in 2001. At the conclusion of 2003 data collection, the PSID will have collected information about more than 65,000 individuals spanning as much as thirty-six years of their lives. The study is conducted at the Survey Research Center, Institute for Social Research, University of Michigan. See also the work of economist Edward N. Wolff, notably Wolff, "Asset Poverty in the United States, 1984–1999: Evidence from the Panel Study of Income Dynamics." *Review of Income and Wealth* 50,4:493–518.

38. Joseph William Singer, "Democratic Values and the American Constitution Society," *Harvard Law & Policy Review Online*, September 18, 2006 available at http://www.hlpronline.com/2006/07/singer_01html.

39. Lant Pritchett, *Let Their People Come:* Breaking the Gridlock on Global Labor Mobility (Washington, DC: Center for Global Development, 2006), p. 18.

PART I

Fragmentation and Transformation of American Society

CHAPTER 1

Capitalism's Churn and Cultural Conflict: How Globalization Has Fractured American Society and Why It Will Be Difficult to Put the Pieces Back Together

Ronnie D. Lipschutz

All societies face recurring threats to their existence, to which they eventually succumb. Yet some societies, even when so threatened, are also capable of postponing their demise by halting and reversing the processes of decline and renewing their vitality and identity. I believe that America can do that and that Americans should recommit themselves to the Anglo-Protestant culture, traditions, and values that for three and a half centuries have been embraced by Americans of all races, ethnicities, and religions, and that have been the source of their liberty, unity, power, prosperity, and moral leadership as a force for good in the world.

—Samuel P. Huntington, *Who Are We?*

For more than thirty-five years, since before Ronald Reagan became president, a *kulturkampf* for social and political hegemony has been raging across the United States. This culture war pits those elites and their followers who see themselves as the guardians of "traditional" norms, values, and hierarchies—social and cultural conservatives, nostalgic Cold Warriors, and pre-millennialist Christians[1]—against a putative cabal of liberals, secular humanists, multiculturalists, and others.[2] Thus, in 1991, a cultural critic on the staff of *Time* wrote:

The customs, beliefs, and principles that have unified the US ... for more than two centuries are being challenged with a ferocity not seen since the Civil War.... Put bluntly: Do Americans still have faith in the vision of their country as a cradle of individual rights and liberties, or must they relinquish the teaching of some of these freedoms to further the goals of the ethnic and social groups to which they belong?[3]

And, in his speech to the 1992 Republican Convention, Pat Buchanan warned:

> My friends, this election is about much more than who gets what. It is about who we are. It is about what we believe. It is about what we stand for as Americans. There is a religious war going on in our country for the soul of America. It is a cultural war, as critical to the kind of nation we will one day be as was the Cold War itself. And in that struggle for the soul of America, Clinton and Clinton are on the other side, and George Bush is on our side. And so, we have to come home, and stand beside him.[4]

Thus were the lines drawn, the war declared, and the battles fought.

While some thought the culture wars would come to an end following September 11, 2001, this was not to be. The invasion of Iraq in 2003, with its strong religious overtones,[5] the reelection of George W. Bush in 2004, vacancies on the nation's Supreme Court in 2005 filled by conservative jurists, and continuing controversies over same-sex marriage, abortion rights, and other such matters have evoked ever fiercer attacks from the Right.[6] But more than this, the terrorist attacks on New York and Washington, as well as the wars that followed, suggested that the American culture wars might be spreading beyond the United States, to other parts of the world. It began to appear as though cultural conflict was also engaging the Catholic Church in Europe and the United States[7] as well as Islam,[8] Hinduism, and even Judaism.

At the beginning of the twenty-first century, the United States and, indeed, the "rest of the world" are experiencing broad and rising cultural and social conflict, in part as a spillover from the U.S. "culture wars." These, in turn, are rooted in recent transformations in modes of production and consumption. In an earlier book, Samuel P. Huntington called such conflicts "the clash of civilizations," but they are better characterized as "clashes within a civilization"—one comprised of various centers of power and weakness organized around particularistic identities, yet deeply linked through a globalized capitalism and the deep and continuing contradictions of modernity. Thus, within the United States, social conflict has broken out between Christian evangelicals and an ill-defined clutch of secular humanist-liberals; in the Catholic and Anglican/Episcopal Church in Europe, the Americas, and Africa between conservatives and modernists; and around the world between neoliberal secularism, on the one hand, and Islamic jihadism, Orthodox Judaism, and ethnocentric Hinduism, on the other. What I argue in this chapter is that there is nothing new about such cultural conflicts. They are, in large part, artifacts of modernity and globalization, of the tendency of capitalist change to destabilize social orders and hierarchies. Such conflicts are especially prominent when the cultural hegemony of a dominant elite is challenged by groups whose rise is linked to economic change and resulting social turmoil. Moreover, they occur repeatedly throughout American history.

The dynamism of capitalism, ongoing power struggles among domestic and transnational social forces, and the actions or inactions of the

American state constantly threaten to undermine established and long-standing hierarchies of power, wealth, and status, along with their ideological justification and the "common sense" they instill in bodies politic. Individual and collective identities are deeply vested in both cultural and materials aspects of daily and social life, and when some part of those identities appears threatened, a collective closing around other parts may arise. In the United States, as we shall see, such periods of disruption are associated with what are generally called "industrial revolutions," and they tend to generate conflicts among elites over changing belief systems, which then diffuse to broader social groups.[9] In the United States, these belief systems have historically been rooted in religion, although social and political elites are not themselves always particularly devout or observant. Thus, the great culture wars of the American past and present have been fought in largely religious terms, even as the sources and symptoms of conflict have been attributable, at least in part, to material transformations across society.

I begin this chapter with a general discussion of the relationship between culture, conflict, and globalization. I argue that, from a historical materialist perspective, capitalism eats away at the foundations of social structures and hierarchies through the "churn" that it generates—in this case, linked to globalization.[10] Churn weakens the "normal" or "commonsense" ideologies and relations that naturalize and justify particular institutionalized forms of domination, social organization, and hegemony. When both beliefs and practices begin to dissolve, the legitimacy of a social order comes under question and challenge. One result is cultural conflict, of the sort we see in America today.

In the second section, I turn to the historical background to American culture wars and the social context within which these struggles have developed and, sometimes, expanded abroad. This context cannot be understood without recalling the religious origins of the United States and the millenarian visions that the Puritans brought to the New England colonies. While these early visions, recapitulated by the neoconservatives writing for the Project for the New American Century, working in the Pentagon, and belonging to various intellectual and activist organizations, are mere fantasies, they have been strongly motivated by the material vagaries of the capitalist economy in which they are embedded. These visions then, in turn, affect material conditions through policies, practices, investments, deployments, constructions, and even wars. Moreover, the visions of the early Puritans continue to inform U.S. ideology, policy, and strategy through the diffusion of American-style democracy and capitalism, which, taken together, offer a global teleology as visionary as anything imagined by the Puritans and their successors, Osama bin Laden and his followers, or, for that matter, decades of development theorists.[11] More to the point, periodic industrial transformations related to cycles of capitalism are strongly correlated with what U.S. historians call "Great Awakenings,"[12] which reflect a widespread, populist revival of religious fervor and institutions, brought on by the uncertainties associated with economic and social changes.

I conclude with some thoughts on the future of America and its culture wars. Given the high costs of the wars in Iraq and Afghanistan, the Bush administration's policies of unilateralism, and growing distrust of the United States abroad, will these culture wars wax or wane in the future? Experience suggests that, as new modes of production and consumption are established and social relations and hierarchies are stabilized, religious fervor also dies down. But global capitalism has become so dynamic that it is not easy to see how such stabilization might come about anytime soon.

One additional note: The arguments presented here are neither exceptionalist nor deterministic, but they do have something to say about the early twenty-first-century state. Many powerful countries have experienced conflict between religious and secular groups, often a by-product of class and social struggles, which have been resolved only through expansionism or war; the United States is not unusual in this regard. And there is no necessary or inevitable connection between such seemingly intractable social conflicts and the destabilizing dynamics of capitalism. Nonetheless, the particular pattern has repeated itself enough times, in enough places, to motivate us to examine it more closely.

CULTURE, CONFLICT, AND GLOBALIZATION

How are culture, conflict, and globalization linked? I define *culture* as that set of beliefs, practices, and material artifacts and infrastructures common to members of a specific group (whose location and dimensions are unspecified), passed from one generation to the next through socialization in the home, education in the schools, propaganda by media and public institutions, consumption of particular goods, and indoctrination through religion. Culture is highly fluid and continually undergoing transformation, even as "traditions" are created and invoked as a means of slowing or halting social change and challenges.

Conflict here specifies significant disagreement among members of a culture over the meanings of foundational beliefs and practices and their consequences, how they should be performed, and what benefits or punishments follow from prescribed and proscribed behaviors. For the most part, conflict is normal and necessary, inasmuch as the constant transformation of culture calls into questions the foundational nature of its ontology and epistemology. At times, however, cultural conflict can open up significant fractures within societies, causing them to fragment.

Finally, for the purposes of this chapter, *globalization* refers to the extension of the capitalist market to more and more sectors of public and private life, reaching even into remote parts of the world that appear quite distant from its conventional workings. Along with the churn characteristic of capitalism (see below), globalization leads to the reorganization and disruption of relations of production, relations of consumption, and social hierarchies and statuses. Globalization, in this sense, is not a new phenomenon. Nor is the social disruption that it engenders.[13]

In examining the relationship between globalization and social change in the United States, I start from the premise that all human societies are constituted by and organized through social relations based on specified rule sets embodied in culture, religion, and law, among other things.[14]

These rule sets explain not only how one should act to succeed but also what constitutes "right order" and "virtuous behavior" (notwithstanding that these rules may be quite unfair, unjust, and even violent). Such rule sets, or "creeds" in Huntington's terms,[15] as noted above are generally taught from birth and communicated at home, in schools and churches, via public rituals, holidays, and commemorations, and in the media. Members of a society acknowledge them as "truths," whether true or not and even if some individuals and groups flatly reject them as a basis for normal social relations. In most cases, the social relations normalized by these rule sets are ordered in an explicit or implicit hierarchy, placing individuals and groups in dominant-subordinate roles on the basis of kinship, descent, contract, wealth, power, office, style, or other attributes read off of appearance, dress, speech, attitude, texts, gender, race, ethnicity, education, or material accoutrements (e.g., cars, swords, cell phones, MP3 players, bling-bling).

In "traditional" societies (ascriptive, in Weberian terms), hierarchies tend to be relatively fixed, and in the absence of mass catastrophes that may destroy them, such as the Black Plague or World War II,[16] the potential for social mobility is limited. Generally speaking, one's place is determined by and at birth, and that is pretty much that. In modern societies, rule sets, practices, and hierarchies are legitimized through what Antonio Gramsci called "hegemony."[17] Hegemony is necessary to a modicum of stability, and it rests on society's consent to and acceptance of the social order—even if, from an "objective" economistic perspective, that order is clearly disadvantageous to large segments of society. Hegemony is to be differentiated from the notion of "false consciousness," in that the former fosters interclass solidarity on the basis of shared social and cultural characteristics, such as religious belief, morality, and identity. People may be fully aware of economic cleavages that separate the rich and poor, but these may matter less than social and cultural similarities and distinctions.[18] Indeed, the mobilization of social forces as *political* actors is much more common than the coming to self-awareness of *class*.

Under conditions of capitalist modernity and growth, as Marx and Engels pointed out, the fixity of rules and social relations cannot be taken as given. As they put it, "All that is solid melts into air."[19] Joseph Schumpeter saw this as one of capitalism's strengths—"creative destruction" was his term—for constant competition ensures that nothing ever remains stagnant for long and that technological and organizational innovation constantly churn the market and society.[20] Churn, however, also causes social turbulence and instability, as older ways of doing things and organizing social and family life are torn apart and reconstituted. This, as we shall see, is central to the generation of cultural conflict.

Without going into greater detail about capitalist transformation and social change,[21] I only note here that the possibility of upward social mobility is one of the most attractive elements of liberal discourse and American capitalism (and it is also essential to capital accumulation). An important element of American social relations and elite hegemony is the deeply held and almost religious notion that the only obstacles to individual "success" are one's own shortcomings, which may be organic, inherited, or learned. The conviction that anyone can succeed by hard work and following the rules is articulated in terms such as *entrepreneurship* and "opportunities" to be seized. American children are often taught that, in the United States, anyone can be president (no one would think to say such a thing in France)[22] and that the success of one's initiatives in the "marketplace of ideas" is a sure path to wealth. In this sense, therefore, life is very much like business: an account of profit and loss.

But this belief is, almost certainly, incorrect. Even the United States, a society with arguably the highest degree of upward (and downward) mobility in the world, is nevertheless characterized by relatively stratified social and racial relations as well as class structures.[23] Moreover, as is widely recognized but rarely admitted, the capacity to "seize" an opportunity, to accumulate wealth, and to move upward in the social hierarchy is not merely a matter of either individual merit or Fortuna.[24] Success breeds success. Those who have wealth are well positioned to acquire more, and they rarely operate in isolation from others who are similarly affluent.[25] The affluent are embedded in webs of social relations with people who are also wealthy and well placed economically and politically, whose families and background are of a particular sort, and who know the ropes (which is why, as Ross Douthat makes clear, going to Harvard is so often a stepping-stone to wealth or public office).[26]

Those lacking such advantages are rarely offered entry into that world.[27] They are, instead, strongly constrained by social hierarchies closely linked to societal divisions of labor that, in turn, are historically related to group (rather than individual) status, attributes, and practices.[28] At the very least, those lower in the economic hierarchy must work all the harder to build the networks of social capital necessary for success. Efforts to remedy disadvantage have been halfhearted, at best.[29] As practiced in the United States, affirmative action—widely criticized as providing unfair advantages to excluded groups—actually seeks to promote *individuals*, and not groups, on the basis of some indicator of merit and behavior.[30] As a racial group, for example, most African Americans remain at the bottom of the American social hierarchy and division of labor,[31] while those who have risen to political and economic prominence constitute a relatively small middle class. Still, the very essence of social stability requires that the possession of power and wealth by some be recognized as legitimate by those who lack these attributes (but who hope they may, someday, be as well-off—thus the enduring appeal of lotteries). Moreover, the established hierarchy must constantly be naturalized through invocation of belief in the possibility of "self-improvement."[32]

Globalization exposes such social relations to relentless attack by the acidic powers of capitalism, as commodification, accumulation, and cultural change reveal the hollowness of what appears to be a stable social order and downsize and eliminate or enhance and improve people's niches in the societal division of labor.[33] This has happened to blue- and white-collar workers in the United States, as parts of the country's industrial base have become less competitive and corporations have outsourced and offshored both manufacturing and services.[34] For reasons having to do with historical racial and ethnic exclusions in certain parts of the United States, as well as pure demographics,[35] the vast majority of downsized blue-collar and middle-management workers are white Protestants.[36] The industrial and corporate reorganizations of the past thirty years have had a significant effect on them, even though minorities tend to be "first fired" and have experienced greater impacts from industrial change.[37] Whatever the numbers say, the "natural order of things" has been upset and "all that is solid melts into air."

This change is especially evident in practices and behaviors that at one time were taboo, such as same-sex marriage, but have become more widely accepted, and as new forms and patterns of livelihood and economic organization undermine the material bases of the more affluent while offering upward mobility to others.[38] In response, those who paint themselves as guardians of "traditional values" warn of the imminent collapse of the social order if people are not disciplined.[39] These elites search for noneconomic sources of the disorder and disrespect that are signs of the coming calamities. Foreigners, communists, gays, adolescents, and progressives, among others, are easy targets, for these are the people most likely to violate or stray from the verities of the past and to exhibit identifiable visible or verbal signs of social heresy. The division of society into those who are "good" and those who are "evil" follows rather easily.

There is a second aspect to globalization's churn, as noted above: it offers possibilities for accumulation and upward mobility to those who are disadvantaged even as it generates new consumer markets directed at those with newly acquired purchasing power and status. Moreover, depending on political and economic conditions at a given time, the disadvantaged may find it possible to acquire economic resources through the very niches in the division of labor to which they have been relegated as a result of a social hierarchy.[40] Improvement in the economic status of members of such groups then spills over into the cultural realm, as the market caters to changing tastes and growing resources.[41] Because these new cultural products differ so greatly from what was previously on offer, they acquire a high degree of visibility and attention and make disadvantaged groups seem more numerous and prominent than they actually are. The rise in the social and economic status of gays and lesbians between 1980 and today and the growing Hispanic/Latino population and flows of migrants from Mexico both illustrate this phenomenon. As a formerly closeted group now possessing rising income, wealth, and social power, gays and lesbians represent a rewarding and rapidly growing market for businesses who cater to their needs and desires, as well as a source of capital for office-seekers and other entrepreneurs.[42] While incomes remain quite low for recent immigrants from Mexico to the United States, consumers from Central and South America constitute an attractive consumer group across the country, estimated to spend more than $600 billion per year.[43]

Even minor cultural changes may come to be interpreted as a challenge to the hegemonic power and privileges of elites and become the basis for political mobilization of those who are linked to elites through religious beliefs and practices. Such groups then seek to restrict or roll back that mobility through rhetorical references to cultural "naturalness,"[44] laws that impose limits on work opportunities and property ownership, or invocations of "natural" law. In some extreme cases, as in the case of Nazi Germany and Rwanda, mobilization can be followed by wholesale genocide. Note, moreover, that even if many members of these groups remain relatively poor and powerless, as in the case of African Americans and Latinos, the upward mobility of the few can come to be seen as a synecdoche of a threat from the subordinate group as a whole (as, apparently, is the case with Huntington).

I should note that, although there is a class character to impacts and consequences of churn, political and social alliances are based generally on cultural relations rather than strictly economic factors. This explains the paradox noted by Thomas Frank in *What's the Matter with Kansas?*—a book that asks why those whose economic interests are so severely eroded by Bush administration policies are, nonetheless, overwhelmingly supporters of the Republican Party.[45] Frank invokes religious solidarity (rather than false consciousness) to account for this phenomenon, and, as we shall see below, this is an important element, although not the only one. Still, in the United States, when culture and economic interests cross swords, so to speak, it is often the former that best explains the odd political coalitions that we often observe.

Finally, it is not necessary that such changes be accepted as problematic by society as a whole. Polling data in the United States suggest that most of the American public is only marginally aware of the culture war, much less engaged in it. Most of those involved are what Samuel Fiorina calls "activists and partisans," that is, those who are either fairly conservative or liberal.[46] While Fiorina regards this division more as a product of electoral competition between Republicans and Democrats seeking to capture voters from the "middle" by convincing them that the rising groups are out of step with the country, there is, as I have argued, a more fundamental matter at stake: hegemony.

Hegemony is, after all, not only about what society takes as "common sense." It also influences how and what policies and programs are legitimated and funded and how and what youth are taught is the "truth." Hegemony even shapes the cultural products delivered by the mass media, which resist at the peril of loss of market share and takeover. Such forms of socialization, in turn, support and legitimate the social order that enables elites to maintain their material and ideological hegemony and assure them that they are the "natural" leaders of society. Clearly, hegemony is a focus of constant political and social struggle, for which it is worth fighting.

GREAT AWAKENINGS AND INDUSTRIAL REVOLUTIONS

In the United States, struggles for hegemony have often been waged in religious terms, manifest in "Great Awakenings" that, in turn, are related to the churn brought about by periodic industrial revolutions. Every fifty or seventy-five years, beginning in the early to middle part of the eighteenth century, the United States has gone through what amounts to a national religious revival, with consequent impacts on culture, economics, politics, and foreign policy. These Great Awakenings occur, in William McLoughlin's words, during "periods of cultural distortion and grave personal stress, when we lose faith in the legitimacy of our norms, the viability of our institutions, and the authority of our leaders in church and state."[47] They are characterized by mass returns to traditional religious practices, religious movements of "purification," and waves of xenophobia and social and political conflict, on the one hand, and by various forms of innovation and syncretism in religious and social beliefs and practices, on the other. These periodic social crises are also associated with peaks in imperialist expansion in pursuit of "Manifest Destiny" or other utopian projects.[48] Expansion is not, however, merely driven by faith; it is also a means of resolving the class and social tensions that arise during such periods. Whether these are cause or effect, each Great Awakening has been paralleled by major economic-industrial transformations (see table 1.1).

Table 1.1.
Great Awakenings and Their Salient Features

Great Awakening	Approximate Dates	Character	Nature of Economic Change
First	1730–1780(?)	Purification movement against Puritanism and individual success, leading to the rise of Congregationalism	Integration of North American colonies into British imperial system
Second	1830–1855	Reaction against Congregationalism and mainline denominations; rise of millennialist and literalist Protestant sects; abolitionism	Penetration of first industrial revolution into U.S. economy; integration through rails and roads
Third	1880–1930	Prairie populism and evangelism; Social Gospel; rise of fundamentalist churches	Corporate monopoly, depressions and currency crisis, farm modernization
Fourth	1975–present	Growth in evangelical, premillennial churches and their expansion into the Third World; reaction against social liberalism	Post-Fordism aka the Information Revolution, outsourcing, downsizing, etc.

NB: This table does not include the original "Great Awakening," which led to the English Civil War during the seventeenth century as well as the Puritan migration to North America.

The First Great Awakening in North America predated the establishment of the United States and is usually dated as beginning around 1730 and continuing for several decades.[49] According to McLoughlin and others, as the descendents of the Puritan settlers became established and prosperous around the turn of the eighteenth century, concerns arose as to the theological implications of material wealth as well as the decrease in membership of the established churches. By 1730, the American colonies were of growing importance to the economic circuits of the British Empire, providing important raw materials and commodities and absorbing large quantities of British manufactures.[50] The result was a new movement of purification. Upward mobility upset traditional religious and social hierarchies, and the religious revival of the period sought to re-instantiate the old ways as a means of disciplining an increasingly disorderly society.

The French and Indian War was an extension of the Seven Years' War in Europe, and by breaking French power in North America, the British victory eliminated barriers to westward expansion across the Alleghenies and into the river valleys of the Midwest. This, in turn, reduced class tensions arising from growing inequalities in wealth in the seaboard colonies. Popular mobilization for war may also have served to resolve the conflicts between the conservative Old Believers and the more religiously progressive Congregationalists. It certainly set the stage for the first stirrings of the American Revolution only thirteen years later.

The Second Great Awakening extended from roughly 1830 to 1850 and played an important role in the coming of the Civil War. This revival came at a time when the First Industrial Revolution was beginning to displace the largely agricultural basis of the Northeastern and mid-Atlantic states.[51] New immigrants from Ireland and other parts of Europe were arriving in the coastal cities, providing cheap labor and generating xenophobic opposition from those who preceded them (recall *The Gangs of New York*). During this period, moreover, the religiously inspired abolitionist movement was gathering steam, adding further fuel to the growing fire. The war with Mexico triggered by U.S. annexation of Texas led to major territorial acquisitions, but it also exacerbated the domestic conflict over slavery. Although the Civil War hardly reduced social tensions, it did open up the South to penetration by Northern capital and the West to settlement.

The Third Great Awakening began during the 1880s and lasted at least until World War I. It developed as manufacturing began to outpace rural production and new sources of grain from other continents entered world markets in competition with American commodities. Millions were thrown off the land and out of work even as the West was populated by settlers enticed through railroad land grants and other attractions. The United States underwent a succession of major depressions, the modern corporation was born, and companies such as Standard Oil consolidated their dominant positions in the national economy. Large numbers of immigrants arrived from Southern and Eastern Europe (many of them Jews), while former slaves sought escape from the South, providing cheap labor for Northeastern industry and exacerbating the unemployment crisis begun by the economic slumps. The culmination of this revival may have come at the Democratic Convention of 1896, when William Jennings Bryan gave his famous "Cross of Gold" speech. Businessmen and scholars of geopolitics alike looked abroad for new markets and sources of raw materials to redress the crisis of overproduction,[52] while China beckoned with its masses waiting to be converted to both Christianity and capitalism. Expansion into Latin America, the Pacific, and Asia began in earnest with the Spanish-American War, even though none of these regions offered the open spaces of earlier times. World War I was more a coda to this period than the main event, however; Woodrow Wilson's crusade to "make the world safe for democracy" marks the launch of the liberal internationalism into which Manifest Destiny was subsumed.

The Fourth Great Awakening began around 1975 (although McLoughlin dates it to the 1960s). Social tensions began to rise in the 1960s as a result of the civil rights movement, activist opposition to the Vietnam War, the rise of the counterculture, and the general decline of political authority.[53] During the 1970s, these tensions were exacerbated by the energy crisis and inflation that struck at the heart of the economic security of the middle class. The crisis of global capitalism during the early 1970s also marked the real beginning of the contemporary industrial revolution, the so-called Information Revolution, also known as post-Fordism.[54] During that period, concerned about the antibusiness tendencies of the new social movements and the social legislation that resulted, conservative members of the business community began to lay conceptual plans for the long Gramscian march to political power through the institutions. Their efforts led, eventually, to the current proliferation of right-wing think tanks, media, foundations, and pundits and the overthrow of the Keynesian consensus and much of the admittedly limited American welfare state.[55]

At the same time, the Nixon administration, pursuing the *realpolitik* proclivities of Henry Kissinger, sought a military balance with both China and the Soviet Union through dual détente, hoping as well to expand the sphere of Western capitalism through the business opportunities that were sure to follow. This offended both the old Cold Warriors and the emerging Christian Right, who viewed the American crusade against communism as central to the country's mission. The election of Ronald Reagan to the presidency rested on a coalition of a fearful middle class, evangelical Christians, and supporters of a new Cold War.[56] Reagan was not especially religious, but he gave voice to the values of those who felt that white Anglo-Protestant hegemony was under threat.[57] During the Reagan administration, the foundation for the global road to neoliberalism was laid down, too. The world went through a major recession—one deliberately triggered by the United States. The Steel Belt began to rust and the American industrial system began its long trek offshore. Large numbers of immigrants from the wars of the periphery arrived in the United States from Latin America, Asia, and other distant parts of the world.

With the collapse of the Soviet Union, the inherent benevolence and triumph of the American Mission seemed to be confirmed,[58] and Cold War constraints on U.S. economic and military expansion vanished. But this very success also posed an existential crisis: without an enemy, what was the mission?

The election of William Jefferson Clinton in 1992 set the stage for the full eruption of the culture war and the eventual cresting of the Fourth Great Awakening, with all of its cultural turbulence. To the Republican coalition, Clinton represented the worst social tendencies of the 1960s. The growing social divergence between the new bourgeoisie of the Information Revolution, which was demographically quite diverse and non-nationalistic, and the old blue- and white-collar "middle class" devoted to family and country fed also into what the Right saw as cultural nihilism. Even though Clinton ran and presided as a "wet" Republican, he and those he symbolized remained the social enemy. This was (and is) especially evident in the "gay wars," beginning with gays in the military and culminating in the post-Clinton struggle over gay marriage. Paradoxically, perhaps, both military service and marriage are profoundly conservative cultural practices, even though they are regarded as anathema by the Right when practiced by gays.

Crucial to the current Great Awakening has been, as noted above, the transition from a material-based to an information-based economy and the latest cycle of capitalist globalization. Knowledge, data, and information are not immaterial goods, as is often claimed, but rather the drivers and products of changes in the ways that "stuff" is made and capital is accumulated. The global reorganization of production following on the commodification of knowledge and data, facilitated by electronic networks and new regulations in the global political economy, have also had impacts on families, households, communities, and entire societies. On the one hand, work has disappeared from many places, undermining stable social relations and long-held verities. On the other hand, consumption patterns have also changed, fostering ever greater individual freedom and identity in the market. Time-honored authority relations have been sundered, and political and social hierarchies have begun to melt away.

As a result, the struggle to maintain the white Protestant hegemony has developed into a political-social-religious coalition encompassing neoconservatives, Christian premillennial dispensationalists, ardent supporters of Israel (both Christian and Jewish), and even conservative members of ethnic and racial minorities.[59] "Family values" is the general code for the social content of this most recent revival. While not easily defined, it includes, among other things, respect for duly constituted authority, fidelity to the patriarchal nuclear family, strictly defined gender roles within the household and without, patriotism, and allegiance to religious strictures.[60] These beliefs and practices are predicated, as noted above, on a vision of social stability rooted in the prosperity and white Anglo-Protestant hegemony of the 1950s, when racial, religious, and ethnic minorities, in particular, had not yet begun to threaten the "natural" order of things.[61]

AWAKENING THE WORLD TO PACIFY THE HOMELAND?

In North America, the first three Great Awakenings were largely domestic affairs (albeit mirrored in Britain and Europe, reacting to both the

Napoleonic Wars and the first industrial revolution).[62] For the most part, however, the effects of American revivalism on the rest of the world were somewhat contained.[63] In recent years, however, borders have been crossed, and, to a growing degree, the culture war has gone abroad and engulfed the rest of the world through the intentional extension and expansion of neoliberal capitalism and U.S. culture. For example, in November 2003, a short letter to the editor appeared in the *New York Times*, written by one Robert K. Elliott of Hastings-on-Hudson, New York. Elliott wrote that "America has two great historical (and historic) projects: to secure the blessings of liberty to our own people and to export liberty to the rest of the world: America the nation and America the ideal."[64] This neo-Hegelian claim is puzzling. Who assigned such world historical projects to "America"? How could Elliott be certain that history *had* assigned these projects to the United States? Was it the United States' spirit or its material success that indicated its selection for this role? And why did Elliott use the term "export" rather than "extend," "offer," or even "impose"?

Such questions lead to the Bush administration's now-discredited plan—whether visionary or fantastic—to disseminate U.S.-style democracy and capitalism in a "New Middle East," beginning with Iraq. Even today, there is no reason to think that such a project could not reach fruition, but on what basis did the United States take on such a monumental and hubristic mission? Washington is in no position to dictate proper behavior to others, and notwithstanding the expenditure of many lives and dollars since 2003, force and punishment have not created a New Middle East. This paradox seems to indicate that *faith* is foundational to the American mission in the world, although it is a peculiar kind of faith.

Nothing in Elliott's letter suggested he was a religious man, even though his argument had a strongly religious cast to it. The terms he used are not necessarily linked to specific institutionalized religions; rather, they are integral to what can be called "American nationalism."[65] Indeed, there is no reason that Elliott need be religious, for his claims echo a long-standing and now secularized notion that the United States should be an exemplar, a "light unto the nations."[66] This Old Testament conceit, adopted by seventeenth-century Puritan immigrants to North America, has informed U.S. relations with the world since then; the idea of "America" as a model to the world and an instrument of God's will, able to hasten the perfection of human society on Earth, is now almost four hundred years old.[67] The Puritans came to build the New Jerusalem; Abraham Lincoln thought America the "last, best hope of mankind"; in his final public words, Woodrow Wilson said, "That we shall prevail is as sure as that God reigns." In his January 2003 State of the Union Address, President George W. Bush proclaimed, "America is a nation with a mission, and that mission comes from our most basic beliefs."[68] Indeed, there is a teleological quality to the American faith in markets and democracy, not far removed from evangelical notions about salvation through good works and belief in Christ.[69]

Even more notionally secular presidents subscribed to such views. In his Farewell Address, George Washington warned the country to "steer clear of permanent alliances, with any portion of the foreign world." While his admonition often has been understood to mean that the United States should maintain a high degree of insularity in foreign affairs, what Washington was most concerned about was keeping clear of the power politics of Europe. Fearful of falling under the control of one or another European power, it seemed prudent for the United States not to put itself in a position in which it might become vulnerable. Washington did not, however, mean to argue that the United States had no role in the world's future; to him, as to most others, the country was a Pacific Republic that stood for a "New Order of the Ages" (*Novus Ordo Seculorum*, as it says on the back of the dollar bill, next to "In God We Trust"). In his view, it was the power of example, not the sword—the rules America lives by and not the ruler under which it lives—that would transform the world. In this, he was simply rephrasing what had been much the conventional wisdom since the first English colonies were established along the Atlantic coast.

The linkage between Protestantism and commerce in the United States was, of course, a focus of Max Weber's essay *The Protestant Ethic and the Spirit of Capitalism* (originally published in 1904–05). Weber was intrigued by the observation that Protestant societies, by and large, were more economically dynamic and expansive than Catholic ones. He attributed this difference to the Calvinist belief in predestination: because one's salvation had been decided by God when the world was created, there was nothing that could be done to change that decision. But the idea that one was either bound for Heaven and Hell ultimately proved too onerous for believers to bear and posed problems of legitimacy and authority for the Puritan elite. Eventually, the Congregationalists and their successors came to define worldly success and benevolence as indicative of salvation and as a good end in itself. In the United States, according to Weber, even this latter concept had gone by the wayside by the nineteenth century. Pointing to the pithy sayings of Benjamin Franklin, Weber noted that a simpler worship of economic accomplishment and a commitment to the hard work needed to reach that goal had become the national religion. Liberty was up to the *individual*. In such a society, people would be too busy pursuing their individual interests to engage in activities that might undermine class and hierarchy, and a constrained form of democracy ensured that the mob could not seize power. No riots, no revolutions, no politics.[70]

These beliefs have not changed dramatically since Franklin's time, and it seems to follow, then, that if the United States has been so successful for so long (more than two hundred years!), it cannot help but stand as an example to the rest of a benighted and heresy-laden world. However, what was mostly rhetoric in the eighteenth century is policy and practice today. Whereas the United States of 1800 had little more than faith on which to pursue this project, by 1900 it possessed the power to go abroad in earnest. That power was put into the service of extending America's economic and political influence, into first northern Mexico and the West Coast, then the Pacific Ocean and Asia, and finally other parts of the world. Indeed, much of the United States' foreign activity since about 1900 can be explained, if not entirely rationalized, as part of a semireligious effort to convert the rest of the world to American-style capitalism (and, perhaps, democracy) in the pursuit of the spiritual salvation inhering in material success.

A century ago, the United States sent missionaries abroad to spread the Gospel of Christ. Today, it sends businesspeople abroad to spread the Gospel of the Market. Whereas "liberty" once connoted freedom from despotic rulers and arbitrary actions, today liberty means choice in the market, unhindered by tariffs, regulations, or other noneconomic restrictions. Salvation can be achieved through the "freedom to choose," as Milton and Rose Friedman put it,[71] and those who would deny individuals such freedom are surely the face of evil in the world.

All of this has been driven by a near-religious faith in the inherent beneficence of the market, constructed in the American image. In the words of George W. Bush, speaking about the Middle East in his 2003 State of the Union Address, "I believe that God has planted in every human heart the desire to live in freedom." The president's statements might simply be dismissed as political rhetoric, an appeal to his evangelical and neoconservative electoral base, but there is more to it than that. First, at the level of "historical structures,"[72] faith in the virtues of American intentions and goals is manifest through the supposed benefits associated with economic liberalism, as suggested above. Second, there is a teleological parallel between the millennialist visions of Christ's return at the End of Days and the neoconservative vision of a New Middle East transformed by an American crusade to bring it markets and democracy. In both cases, a deeply held belief in the *telos* is required—for it is in the mind, and not the body, that salvation begins. Moreover, a New Middle East would give testimony to the virtue of right belief and practice and would demonstrate, at home, that the neoconservative/neoliberal path is the correct one for the country to follow.

What counts most in a culture war is faith—faith in religious and cultural traditions, faith in the inherent goodness of associated social practices, faith in the inevitable triumph of the American Way. The Mission will succeed, according to this teleological view, and any obstacles or manifest failures it might encounter along the way are *tests* of faith, such as those Christ faced in the desert, rather than policy problems. Accepting failure means giving in to evil ("the terrorists win"), and in God's plan for the world, that cannot happen.

The problem here is that the Mission faces an equally powerful and teleological faith: Islam. And just as communism was a product of nineteenth-century Christian liberalism and German Romanticism, political Islam is very much the sibling of Judeo-Christian civilization and modernity. Nor is it at all antithetical to markets or commerce. Failure is unthinkable, yet failure is inevitable.

WHAT NOW FOR THE CULTURE WAR?

Patterns of revivalism and cultural conflict that appear throughout American history and practice may, of course, simply be correlations, artifacts of coincidences among disconnected struggles, structures, and consequences. This is unlikely. There is a set of specific contradictions inherent in the structure and organization of an American-style democratic capitalist society that renders it subject to such periodic culture wars. These contradictions arise between the legitimating functions of the democratic state and the constant erosion of rules and norms due to the churn of capitalism.[73] In some societies, police power and economic control can stabilize the social order (although, as we see repeatedly, even such states are not immune to churn and challenge).[74] Their rule may lack legitimacy, but in the absence of intraclass social struggles, generally manages to maintain itself for some period of time. Capitalist democracies, by contrast, must limit their use of police power in order to maintain the legitimacy of their social choice mechanisms and manage active opposition to domestic distributions of power and authority.[75]

Given that socially dominant groups tend also to hold political power, even in capitalist democracies, it is fairly straightforward to avoid or head off *political* and *social* policies that could lead to radical redistributions of power and wealth and threaten hegemony. Social democracy, in particular, relies on both political mechanisms and redistribution to maintain social hierarchies and "traditional" culture. Libertarian democracies of the type found in the United States eschew such regulatory methods, with considerable cost to longer-term social stability. High rates of economic growth, as well as the disappearance of those forms of regulation that underpinned the welfare state and fostered some limited degree of resource redistribution, have not reduced but rather exacerbated the gap between the better-off and the worse-off. Under such conditions, it is difficult to construct and maintain the social and political coalitions necessary to the acquisition or maintenance of power, and, as seems to have happened to the Democrats' New Deal coalition, they can dissolve if based purely on economic interests rather than the solidarities of social forces and groups.

Thus, the Bush administration's foreign policies can be seen as a response to the socially disruptive character of globalization during the 1980s and 1990s. Parallel to the domestic struggle for hegemony as manifest in the culture war, those policies reflect American efforts to buttress social stability in certain regions and countries while maintaining order at home.[76] Social change within and across societies has led to formation of an odd transnational social movement coalition: the American Christian Right (joined to the Bush administration), the conservative elements in the Catholic Church (supported by Pope John Paul II and, now, Pope Benedict XVI), and governments of selected Muslim countries (invoking the eternal verities of Sharia law).[77] But neoliberal globalization and capitalist churn have also given rise to the global justice movement,[78] as well as the transnational *jihadi* movement (the latter concerned about issues of representation, problems of political corruption, and the unjust exercise of power). This is not to suggest an alliance between the global justice movement and the jihadis, but only to point out that, at the margin, they may actually share some objectives.

Moreover, economic mobility in the United States is at least partly divorced from hierarchy and status, and it poses a challenge to hegemony's "natural order" of things and people, thereby generating various forms of paradoxical *ressentiment*. Such anger and confusion can be mobilized and used to build cultural solidarity against an opponent, reinforce hegemony, and, parenthetically, organize winning political coalitions. Nonetheless, maintaining the conservative "culture war" may prove difficult. Until well into 2008, the Bush administration did not hesitate to play the terrorism card—linked directly to the disorder in Iraq—in order to buttress a socially and culturally conservative agenda and keep the culture wars alive.[79] But other factors suggest problems in the future. For one thing, the white Protestant population in the United States is declining as a percentage of the whole,[80] and a fair fraction of that demographic (perhaps as much as half) remains both liberal and even secular.[81]

Another key problem for the revivalist coalition is exactly that phenomenon which is so central to the culture war: globalization. Cultural conservativism is a form of behavioral regulation, just like any other, and it is also subject to the dynamism of underregulated global capitalism. Religious solidarity around cultural values will not indefinitely survive the growing material gaps between rich and poor. Globalization and U.S. economic policy will continue to exacerbate that gap unless and until Washington institutes an extreme protectionist regime and deploys a truly draconian immigration and travel policy (see the disputes over what to do about China or illegal immigration for examples of intracoalition conflicts). But "Fortress America" would generate such a ferocious depression and decline in the dollar as to permanently wreck the Right (much as happened to the Republican Party as a result of the Great Depression).

Furthermore, culture wars can also produce unanticipated outcomes. The Third Great Awakening pitted farmers and urban labor against Eastern bankers and business, in a context of deepening poverty and growing corporate power and corruption. Christians were active not only in the rising populist movement but also in working for social reform.[82] Progressivism, based on technical expertise and a notion of the "common good," emerged in reaction to both populism *and* corporate excesses of the time and succeeded in dampening social and cultural conflict. The same could well happen again. Between the dying-off of the aging revivalist vanguard and broad acceptance of new mores, practices, and values by younger adults—in another ten or twenty years—the culture wars may fade away. But the social peace that follows is unlikely to last very long. Given capitalism and churn, it never does.

NOTES

1. Didi Herman, "The New Roman Empire: European Envisionings and American Premillenialists." *Journal of American Studies* 34, no. 1 (2000): 23–40.

2. James Davison Hunter, *Culture Wars: The Struggle to Define America* (New York: Basic Books, 1991); Gertrude Himmelfarb, *One Nation, Two Cultures* (New York: Knopf, 1999); Dale McConkey, "Whither Hunter's Culture War? Shifts in Evangelical Morality, 1988–1998," *Sociology of Religion* 62, no. 2 (2001): 149–74; David A. Horowitz, *America's Political Class under Fire: The Twentieth Century's Great Culture War* (New York: Routledge, 2003). It should be noted that not

everyone finds that there is such a culture war under way or that it has become more intense; see, for example, Alan Wolfe, *One Nation, After All: What Middle-Class Americans Really Think About: God, Country, Family, Racism, Welfare, Immigration, Homosexuality, World, the Right, the Left and Each Other* (New York: Viking, 1998); Morris P. Fiorina, with Samuel J. Abrams and Jeremy C. Pope, *Culture War? The Myth of a Polarized America* (New York: Pearson Longman, 2005); and Alan Abramowitz and Kyle Saunders, "Why Can't We All Just Get Along? The Reality of a Polarized America," *Forum* 3, no. 2 (2005).

3. Paul Gray, "Whose America?" *Time*, July 8, 1991, 13.

4. Patrick Buchanan, speech to the Republican National Convention, Houston, August 17, 1992, available at http://www.buchanan.org/pa-92-0817-rnc.html.

5. Michael Northcott, *An Angel Directs the Storm: Apocalyptic Religion and American Empire* (London: I. B. Tauris, 2004).

6. Sean Hannity, *Deliver Us from Evil: Defeating Terrorism, Despotism, and Liberalism* (New York: ReganBooks, 2004); David Frum and Richard Perle, *An End to Evil: How to Win the War on Terror* (New York: Random House, 2003); Ann Coulter, *Treason: Liberal Treachery from the Cold War to the War on Terrorism* (New York: Crown Forum, 2003); Ann Coulter, *How to Talk to a Liberal (If You Must): The World According to Ann Coulter* (New York: Crown Forum, 2004).

7. Garry Wills, "Fringe Government," *New York Review of Books* 52, no. 15 (2005): 46–50.

8. Pew Research Center, "Religion and Politics: Contention and Consensus," July 24, 2003, available at http://pewforum.org/publications/surveys/religion-politics.pdf.

9. George Van Pelt Campbell has made a similar argument, claiming that "globalization undermines moral consensus" through relativization, that is, the "calling into question such things as the definitions, boundaries, categories and conclusions through which they have understood the world and established their identity." But he does not link this process to material or economic change. See George Van Pelt Campbell, "Everything You Know Is Wrong: How Globalization Undermines Moral Consensus," paper presented at the annual meeting of the Association for the Sociology of Religion, San Francisco, August 14, 2004, available at http://hirr.hartsem.edu/sociology/campbell.html.

10. Joseph Schumpeter, *Capitalism, Socialism and Democracy* (New York: Harper, 1942); Michael W. Cox and Richard Alm, "The Churn: The Paradox of Progress," Federal Reserve Bank of Dallas, reprint from 1992 Annual Report, available at http://www.dallasfed.org/fed/annual/1999p/ar92.pdf. See also Katherine Boo, "The Churn: Creative Destruction in a Border Town," *New Yorker*, March 29, 2004, available at http://www.newyorker.com/archive/2004/03/29/040329fa_fact; and Katherine Boo, "The Best Job in Town: The Americanization of Chennai," *New Yorker*, July 5, 2004, 54–69.

11. John Gray, *False Dawn: The Delusions of Global Capitalism* (London: Granta Books, 1998).

12. William McLoughlin, *Revivals, Awakenings and Reform* (Chicago: University of Chicago Press, 1980).

13. See Ronnie D. Lipschutz, *After Authority: War, Peace and Global Politics in the Twenty-First Century* (Albany: State University of New York Press, 2000); and Ronnie D. Lipschutz, with James Rowe, *Globalization, Governmentality and Global Politics: Regulation for the Rest of Us?* (London: Routledge, 2005).

14. I do not want to fall into functionalism here; these are not rule sets that have somehow been consciously and deliberately devised to govern the operation of society.

15. Samuel P. Huntington, *Who Are We? The Challenges to America's National Identity* (New York: Simon & Schuster, 2004).

16. Sandra Halperin, *War and Social Change in Modern Europe: The Great Transformation Revisited* (Cambridge: Cambridge University Press, 2004).

17. Antonio Gramsci, *Selections from the Prison Notebooks*, trans. Quintin Hoare, ed. Geoffrey Nowell (London: Smith, Lawrence, & Wishart, 1971).

18. Thomas Frank, *What's the Matter with Kansas? How Conservatives Won the Heart of America* (New York: Metropolitan Books, 2004); Mark Rupert, *Producing Hegemony: The Politics of Mass Production and American Global Power* (Cambridge: Cambridge University Press, 1995).

19. Karl Marx, Friedrich Engels, and Gareth Steadman Jones, *The Communist Manifesto* New York: Penguin Classics, 2002), p. 223.

20. Schumpeter, *Capitalism, Socialism and Democracy*; Cox and Alm, "The Churn"; Boo, "The Churn."

21. Marshall Berman, *All That Is Solid Melts into Air* (New York: Simon & Schuster, 1982); Ronnie D. Lipschutz, "From 'Culture Wars' to Shooting Wars: Cultural Conflict in the United States," in *The Myth of "Ethnic Conflict": Politics, Economics and "Cultural Violence"*, edited by Beverly Crawford and Ronnie D. Lipschutz, pp. 394–433, (Berkeley: International and Area Studies Press, University of California, 1998); Lipschutz, *After Authority*.

22. Lipschutz, "From 'Culture Wars' to Shooting Wars."

23. Janny Scott and David Leonhardt, "Shadowy Lines That Still Divide," *New York Times*, May 15, 2005, available at http://www.nytimes.com/2005/05/15/national/class/OVERVIEW-FINAL.html. Although the potential for mobility among income quintiles is considerable—more than half of each quintile moved up or down between 1968 and 1991—almost 47 percent of the lowest and 42 percent of the highest quintiles did not move up or down; see Daniel P. McMurrer and Isabel V. Sawhill, "Economic Mobility in the United States," Urban Institute, October 1, 1996, table 2, available at http://www.urban.org/publications/406722.html#tab2.

24. See John Isbister, *Capitalism and Justice: Envisioning Social and Economic Fairness* (Bloomfield, CT: Kumarian Press, 2001); Amartya Sen, *Development as Freedom* (New York: Anchor Books, 1999).

25. Bob Herbert, "The Mobility Myth," *New York Times*, June 6, 2005, available at http://www.nytimes.com/2005/06/06/opinion/06herbert.html.

26. Ross Gregory Douthat, *Privilege: Harvard and the Education of the Ruling Class* (New York: Hyperion, 2005).

27. Isabel Wilkerson, "A Success Story That's Hard to Duplicate," *New York Times*, June 12, 2005, available at http://www.nytimes.com/2005/06/12/national/class/12angelaside-final.html.

28. Chris Tilly and Charles Tilly, "Capitalist Work and Labor Markets," in *The Handbook of Economic Sociology*, edited by Neil J. Smelser and Richard Swedberg, (Princeton, NJ: Princeton University Press, 1994), pp. 218–313.

29. Ira Katznelson, *When Affirmative Action Was White: An Untold History of Racial Inequality in Twentieth-Century America* (New York: W. W. Norton, 2005).

30. Robert Fullinwider, "Affirmative Action," *Stanford Encyclopedia of Philosophy*, 2005, http://plato.stanford.edu/archives/spr2005/entries/affirmative-action.

31. Lee A. Daniels, ed., *The State of Black America, 2005* (New York: National Urban League, 2005).

32. This is why the Bush administration's response to the destruction of New Orleans was attacked so vociferously. Not only was it a dereliction of duty, but it

also exposed to the light of day that social hierarchy so fundamental to American society, yet so naturalized as to be invisible to most. The notion of "self-improvement" is also very Lockean, which should come as no surprise. See the *New York Times* Class Matters series at http://www.nytimes.com/pages/national/class/index.html and the *New York Times* Class Project poll, March 3–14, 2005, especially questions 26–30, available at http://www.nytimes.com/packages/pdf/national/20050515_CLASS_GRAPHIC/classpoll_results.pdf.

33. The British have a marvelous term for this: to be made "redundant."

34. Cox and Alm, "The Churn"; Boo, "The Churn."

35. Diedre A. Royster, *Race and the Invisible Hand: How White Networks Exclude Black Men from Blue-Collar Jobs* (Berkeley: University of California Press, 2003); David Halle and Frank Romo, "The Blue-Collar Working Class: Continuity and Change," in *America at Century's End*, edited by Alan Wolfe, pp. 152–84 (Berkeley: University of California Press, 1991), available at http://content.cdlib.org/xtf/view?docId=ft158004pr&chunk.id=d0e3212&toc.depth=1&toc.id=d0e3212&brand=ucpress. In the latter, table 8.2 indicates that, in 1988, more than 76 percent of blue-collar workers were identified as white Protestants. Thus, to the extent that creative destruction and churn have affected manufacturing in particular, the most likely to be affected were white Protestants.

36. Although precise data are difficult to come by, there are about 125 million self-identified "born-again" or "evangelical" Protestants in the United States (44 percent of the total population), out of 151 million Protestants; see Adherents.com, "Composite U.S. Demographics," http://www.adherents.com/adh_dem.html. Thus, simple demographics would suggest they have been the most affected. There is also strong evidence that conservative Protestants tend to be the highest percentage of the Christian population in the American South, which remains the poorest part of the country, with high unemployment rates, even as the counties in which they live tend to be the more prosperous ones; Association of Religion Data Archives, "U.S. Congregational Membership" maps and reports available at http://www.thearda.com/MapsReports/. Other data also seem to suggest that conservative Protestants are fairly well-off in terms of education and income; Institute for First Amendment Studies, "Survey of Christian Right Activists," 1998, cited at "Christian Fundamentalism Exposed," available at http://www.sullivan-county.com/news/.

37. Sarah Rimer, "A Hometown Feels Less Like Home," *New York Times*, March 6, 1996, available at http://www.nytimes.com/specials/downsize/06down1.html.

38. Fiorina, *Culture War?*, chaps. 4 and 5; Lipschutz, "From 'Culture Wars' to Shooting Wars."

39. Louis Sheldon, "Constitutional Attorney Sees Polygamy as Next Stage of Sexual Revolution," Traditional Values Coalition press release, October 5, 2004, available at http://www.traditionalvalues.org/modules.php?sid=1935; Stanley Kurtz, "Beyond Gay Marriage: The Road to Polyamory," *Weekly Standard*, August 4, 2003, available at http://www.weeklystandard.com/content/public/articles/000/000/002/938xpsxy.asp.

40. Amy Chua, *World on Fire: How Exporting Free Market Democracy Breeds Ethnic Hatred and Global Instability* (New York: Doubleday, 2002).

41. This does not mean that these groups become fabulously wealthy, only that they now make a much greater cultural impression on society at large.

42. Constantine von Hoffman, "Out and About," *CMO*, November 2004.

43. James Lowry, Alex Ulanov, and Thomas Wenrich, "Advancing to the Next Level of Latino Marketing: Strike First, Strike Twice," Boston Consulting Group, 2003, available at http://www.bcg.com/impact_expertise/publications/files/

advancing_latino_marketing_feb2003.pdf; Pluribus Media, "Services: Latino Marketing," http://www.pluribusmedia.com/serv_spanish.htm.

44. Allan C. Carlson and Paul T. Mero, "The Natural Family: A Manifesto," Howard Center for Family, Religion, and Society, 2005, available at http://www.familymanifesto.net.

45. Frank, *What's the Matter with Kansas?*

46. Fiorina, *Culture War?*

47. McLoughlin, *Revivals, Awakenings and Reform*, 2.

48. Frederick Merk, *Manifest Destiny and Mission in American History* (New York: Knopf, 1963).

49. In fact, the English Civil Wars of the seventeenth century can be seen as manifestations of an earlier Great Awakening setting Anglicans and Catholics against the Puritan movement.

50. T. H. Breen, *The Marketplace of Revolution: How Consumer Politics Shaped American Independence* (Oxford: Oxford University Press, 2004).

51. I recognize that not everyone agrees that either the Industrial Revolution or the Great Awakenings actually took place as they are often described. Neither of these *social* phenomena is amenable to easy characterization.

52. Walter LaFeber, *The New Empire: An Interpretation of American Expansion, 1860–1898* (Ithaca, NY: Cornell University Press, 1963); William Appleman Williams, *Empire as a Way of Life* (Oxford: Oxford University Press, 1982).

53. The emergence of these political and social movements and trends is connected to the political economy of the times, but space precludes a detailed discussion here; see Lipschutz, *After Authority.*

54. Rupert, *Producing Hegemony.* See also Lipschutz, *After Authority*, chap. 2.

55. See, e.g., "Attack on the American Free Enterprise System," a memorandum written in 1971 by Lewis F. Powell Jr., who later became an associate justice of the U.S. Supreme Court. The memo is discussed in Lipschutz, *Globalization, Governmentality and Global Politics*, chap. 6, and can be found at http://reclaim democracy.org/corporate_accountability/powell_memo_lewis.html.

56. Robert W. Fogel, *The Fourth Great Awakening and the Future of Egalitarianism* (Chicago: University of Chicago Press, 2000).

57. Paul Kengor, *God and Ronald Reagan: A Spiritual Life* (New York: Regan-Books, 2004).

58. Frances Fukuyama, *The End of History and the Last Man* (Toronto: Free Press, 1992).

59. Premillennial dispensationalists believe that the Second Coming may happen at any time, indicated by "the Rapture." One of the critical signs of Jesus' return and the "End Times" is the reestablishment of Israel; see Herman, "New Roman Empire." Christian support for Israel dovetails nicely with both Jewish concerns and, according to the conventional wisdom, U.S. strategic interests in the Middle East; see Anatol Lieven, *America Right or Wrong: An Anatomy of American Nationalism* (Oxford: Oxford University Press, 2004).

60. It is no small irony, then, that several leaders of this coalition have, over the years, been caught out in infidelity and corruption.

61. Paul M. Weyrich, "Traditional Family Values," *American Daily*, May 4, 2005, available at http://www.americandaily.com/article/7675; Carlson and Mero, "Natural Family."

62. Sandra Halperin, "Religious Revivalism in Nineteenth-Century Europe and the Contemporary Middle East: A Comparison," paper presented at the annual meeting of the American Political Science Association, Washington, DC, September 2–5, 1993.

63. Merk, *Manifest Destiny and Mission*.

64. Robert K. Elliott, "When Bush Talks of Freedom," *New York Times*, November 12, 2003, available at http://nytimes.com.

65. Lieven, *America Right or Wrong*.

66. Ernest Tuveson, *Redeemer Nation: The Idea of America's Millennial Role* (Chicago: University of Chicago Press, 1968).

67. Merk, *Manifest Destiny and Mission*.

68. George W. Bush, State of the Union Address, January 28, 2003, available at http://www.whitehouse.gov/news/releases/2003/01/20030128-19.html.

69. Max Weber, *The Protestant Ethic and the Spirit of Capitalism*, trans. Talcott Parsons (New York: Scribner's, 1958). See also Northcott, *Angel Directs the Storm*.

70. Louis Hartz, *The Liberal Tradition in America* (San Diego: Harvest/HBJ, 1955); Sheldon Wolin, "Fugitive Democracy," in *Democracy and Difference*, edited by Seyla Benhabib, 31–45 (Princeton, NJ: Princeton University Press, 1996).

71. Milton Friedman and Rose Friedman, *Free to Choose* (New York: Harcourt Brace Jovanovich, 1980).

72. Robert Cox, *Production, Power and World Order* (New York: Columbia University Press, 1987).

73. Space precludes a more detailed discussion of the tension between the capitalist state's regulatory and accumulation functions; some of these points are discussed in Lipschutz, *Globalization, Governmentality and Global Politics*.

74. David M. Woodruff, "Power and Prosperity: Outgrowing Communist and Capitalist Dictatorships," *East European Constitutional Review* 10, no. 1 (Winter 2001).

75. Capitalist police states may not be so encumbered by this problem, so long as the bourgeoisie is fully on board, as suggested by the relative economic success of Pinochet's Chile, on the one hand, and the apparent decline of middle-class support for the Saudi monarchy, on the other.

76. *The National Security Strategy of the United States, September 2002* (Washington, DC: The White House, 2002), available at http://www.whitehouse.gov/nsc/nss.pdf; *The National Security Strategy of the United States, March 2006* (Washington, DC: The White House, 2006), available at http://www.whitehouse.gov/nsc/nss/2006/nss2006.pdf.

77. Doris Buss and Didi Herman, *Globalizing Family Values: The Christian Right in International Politics* (Minneapolis: University of Minnesota Press, 2003).

78. Notes from Nowhere, ed., *We Are Everywhere: The Irresistible Rise of Global Anticapitalism* (London: Verso, 2003). I should note that the Third Great Awakening, during the latter part of the nineteenth century, saw the emergence not only of conservative Christianity but also the Social Gospel; see, e.g., Donald K. Gorrell, *The Age of Social Responsibility: The Social Gospel in the Progressive Era, 1900–1920* (Macon, GA: Mercer University Press, 1988).

79. Ronnie D. Lipschutz, "The Clash of Governmentalities: The Fall of the UN Republic and America's Reach for Imperium," *Contemporary Security Policy* 23, no. 2 (December 2002): 214–31.

80. Huntington, *Who Are We?*; Tom W. Smith and Seokho Kim, "The Vanishing Protestant Majority," NORC/University of Chicago, GSS Social Change Report No. 49, July 2004.

81. Fiorina, *Culture War?* Data from 2001 suggest that, while 76 percent (211.5 million) of the American population identifies as "white," only 53 percent (151 million) claim to be Protestant and 44 percent (125.3 million) are "born-again" or "evangelical." Of the latter, only 22 million are "theologically" evangelical; see Adherents.com, "Composite U.S. Demographics."

82. Gorrell, *Age of Social Responsibility*.

CHAPTER 2

Transnational Migrant Networks, Citizenship Rights, and the Future of the Nation-State: The Case of Latin American Migration to the United States

James Cohen

TRANSNATIONAL MIGRATION IN THE AMERICAS: A HUMAN STORY

This chapter is first of all about people struggling to lead decent, and if possible fulfilling, lives under difficult and sometimes very dramatic conditions. It is also about how they can sometimes manage to surmount the worst of their difficulties and even invent new solutions for surviving. Beyond surviving, they sometimes manage to develop complex and innovative networks of social ties, in an era in which globalization has important practical implications for everyone and strategies of creative adaptation are almost a life necessity.

What the following story suggests is that strategies of creative adaptation are not necessarily the monopoly of dominant actors. More and more immigrants to the United States from neighboring countries to the south maintain dense relationships with their home countries and are in a position to act as productive, civic-minded citizens in more than one country. However, the road can sometimes get bumpy for transnational migrants if they are not dominant or highly educated middle-class actors but ordinary working migrants from Mexico (or El Salvador or the Dominican Republic, among other countries).

The main question I ask in this chapter is whether and how the citizenship rights of those who belong by necessity to more than one national space can be respected in a world (and in a region of the world) where national borders are still very much in place—both between national territories and within peoples' minds. What I suggest is that the very notion of citizenship is running up against a new set of problems regarding who belongs, whose rights are recognized, and which rights they can claim. I suggest that the issue is today being forced into the open because of the more nationalist and ethnocentric reflexes of ordinary U.S. citizens and elected officials.

Because I focus on such notions as citizenship and rights and transnationalism, my account of how transnational migrants live is a stylized one: I focus, in their experience, on those facets that pertain most directly to the border-spanning character of their lives as citizens. But it must be said at the outset that the thickest and most remarkable accounts of transnational social networks are told by the migrants themselves. How can one hear their stories? Some researchers have made telling these stories their main job; their work is highly recommended for anyone wishing to better understand the human side of what is examined here.

Peggy Levitt's *The Transnational Villagers* tells the story of the very dense social networks that have sprung up between Miraflores, a town in the Dominican Republic, and Jamaica Plain, a "melting pot" neighborhood in the south of Boston, Massachusetts.[1] Readers learn through the experience of real people about migratory patterns, how resources are shared by migrants with their families back in Miraflores, how families themselves evolve, how gender relations and religious communities change, how education fits into the process, and how homeland politics plays out among emigrants. Levitt puts many individual stories into sociological and historical context, but readers never forget that the lives of human beings are at stake.

Robert C. Smith's *Mexican New York: Transnational Lives of New Immigrants* is a monumental study, conducted over more than fifteen years, of how Mexican immigrants in New York interact with their hometown of Ticuani in the state of Puebla as individuals, as family members, as men and women, as youths and adults, as religious observers, and the like.[2] Others, too, have contributed to the dense, human story of transnational migrants.[3]

These authors' works have the great merit of never idealizing the situation of transnational migrants and never turning them into pure objects or alien "Others." I can only refer readers to their important and highly readable work. For the moment, however, we shall focus more sharply on implications of these transnational lives for the socioeconomic and political environment of the Americas, north and south.

GLOBALIZATION COMES HOME ... TO ROOST

The current crisis of U.S. policy on immigration is a prime example of how "globalization comes home." In other words, its an example of how the problems generated by globalization in its current, neoliberal form— which is not its only conceivable form—may "come home to roost" when a state and those who make its laws are so attached to that form that they are unable to think through its contradictions and instead become trapped in them.

In this section, I examine the terms of the current political crisis surrounding immigration. I suggest that the formulation of policy in this area is limited by narrowly legalistic and nation-centric (not to say nationalist) frames of reference that discourage the formulation of viable, forward-looking policies. Existing policy is thus incapable of taking into account the real logics of mobility of people in the era of neoliberal globalization—and, in the special case of the United States and Mexico, incapable of addressing the social consequences of free trade between two very unequal economies.

In particular, I will show that current policy making overlooks a major development in recent years: the emergence of transnational networks of migrants who organize to improve the lot of their families and their hometowns in several Latin American and Caribbean countries. Policy makers in the United States pay little or no attention to the fact that ordinary working people are increasingly building their lives on the premise of cross-border mobility, belonging and contributing productively to more than one country. Routine border-crossing activity is considered normal for transnational business, political, and artistic elites, but no official recognition has been given to what some have called "globalization from below"[4] or "transnationalism from below."[5]

Researchers, as opposed to policy makers, have indeed paid increasing attention over the past decade to the transnational social ties linking growing numbers of immigrants in the United States to their home countries and villages or, in some cases, to their indigenous groups of origin. These emerging "transnational social fields" and "diasporic" networks, though not an absolute novelty in history, are today recognized by a lively and growing field of transnational migrant studies as significant sociological phenomena that raise major questions about the future of states and nations. Although specialists disagree about many things regarding migrants' transnational networks, most agree that they constitute at least a partial challenge to the territorial basis of nations and to the very sovereignty of states. Yet they refrain from formulating recommendations about how adapt to them and take advantage of the opportunities they offer to promote social development. A further purpose of this paper will thus be to outline some possible policy solutions by which U.S. authorities, instead of ignoring or impeding transnational networks, could create synergies with them, drawing possibly on certain western European experiences that we will briefly examine below.

And yet, however interesting international comparisons might be, it must be recognized at the outset that there is a major U.S. exceptionalism to be accounted for. The very intensity of the current crisis over the regulation of migratory flows may be explained, first of all, by the long (1,900-mile) land border with the United States' neighbor to the south, Mexico. Because of this geographical factor, the spaces of "North" and "South" of the world-system are more extensively interconnected in the Americas than anywhere else. More and more immigrants from Mexico and Central America, as well as countries farther to the south and from the Caribbean, are building lives that span national borders. This raises not only the question of these migrants' "belonging" or "identity"—as they clearly "belong" to more than one national society—but also, crucially, the question of their *rights* as citizens in these respective spaces. The problem of citizenship rights (civil, political, and social) can no longer be framed as a purely national issue; it is now starkly posed in a transnational manner among peoples in the Americas of very unequal social condition. Political choices about how to manage migratory flows from the countries to the south of the United States are inextricably combined with choices about how to deal, if at all, with interregional and class inequalities of a systemic nature—that is, about which rights are to be recognized and which denied.

From the standpoint of those who cross borders and form transnational networks out of material necessity, as well as the advocacy groups who work in their behalf, it may appear eminently rational to envision for the future new, "transnational" forms of political authority that favor migrants' freedom of movement and respect for their basic social rights, whatever side of the border they happen to be on at a given moment. However, such ideas remain well outside the mainstream of political debate within the United States, where the criteria of national sovereignty remain unquestioned. Indeed, national borders maintain such a great symbolic significance that the current crisis over immigration policy is also associated, in the minds of some, with choices about how culturally and linguistically inclusive the nation can and should become. Questions of state sovereignty and national security become tied up with fears about a changing national identity.

It may be that the broad social movement that mobilized millions of migrants and their supporters in the streets in the spring of 2006 brought a little closer to the mainstream the ideas that "no person is illegal" and that the rights of migrants—even those without documents—are worthy of respect in a country that supposedly prides itself on being a "nation of immigrants." However, from the refusal of repressive immigration policies to the formulation of more enlightened and forward-looking ones, there is a step that few have begun to take.

Arguments for policies better adapted to the real patterns of migratory flows and the transnational social spaces they are generating will necessarily relativize the importance of national borders. This does not mean, however, that borders should be treated as a pure construction of the imaginary, or that nation-states should be treated as if they were on the verge of disappearing—a great exaggeration, even if globalization does imply the loss of some aspects of national sovereignty. A future-oriented immigration policy, I suggest, would build on the transnational social networks forged by a growing number of migrants by allowing for greater cross-border mobility in the service of better, more socially conscious economic development in the sending countries.

NEW SOCIOLOGICAL TRENDS IN MIGRATION

As an example of how sociological thought has begun to take into account the importance of transnational migrations for the question of citizenship rights, let us briefly examine the ideas of Stephen Castles, a well-known Australian migrations specialist. Castles asserts that "global-ization undermines many of the core features of the nation-state," agreeing with Manuel Castells that the world is changing from "space of places" to a "space of flows."[6] Although international migrants have by definition always crossed national borders, it has been assumed until now that they would per-manently move from one country to another ("permanent settlement migration") or that they would return home after a period ("temporary labor migration"). In either case, the sovereignty and power of the nation-state was not questioned, but today, Castles writes, "such expectations lose their validity."

This is the case, first of all, because of new developments in information and transport technology that "increase the volume of temporary, repeated and circulatory migration," one manifestation among others of a broad phenomenon of "time-space compression." More and more migrants "orient their lives to two or more societies and develop transnational com-munities and consciousness." Traditional policies of state control and tra-ditional modes of migrant incorporation into society both decline in efficacy. It was long assumed, for example, that immigrants seeking to set-tle permanently in a host country would go through various stages of assimilation and tend over time to "belong" more to that society than to their country of origin. Today, however, "globalization is undermining all the modest of controlling difference premised on territoriality." Because "transnational communities are groups whose identity is not primarily based on attachment to a specific territory," they present a "powerful challenge to traditional ideas of nation-state belonging."

Castles shifts from an analytical to a prescriptive mode when he asserts that, while transmigrants may have "no exclusive loyalty to a specific terri-tory," they nonetheless "need political stability, economic prosperity, and social well-being in their places of residence, just like anybody else." He sees the actors of migrant networks as showing a great capacity to adapt to "multiple social settings" and displaying "cross-cultural competence," adding that "in a mobile world of culturally open societies, such capacities should not be seen as threatening, but, on the contrary, as highly desira-ble." The idea of "primary loyalty to one place" is, in his view, tending toward obsolescence; it is "an icon of old-style nationalism that has little relevance for migrants in a mobile world." Castles does not go so far as to engage in direct policy recommendations, but his commentary leads to the obvious practical conclusion that the kinds of activities in which organized migrants engage nowadays require a different approach to immigration policy than has been offered them up to now.

U.S. IMMIGRATION POLICY IN CRISIS, 2005–2007

The obstacles to achieving new policies should not be underestimated. "Old-style nationalism" may be irrelevant to migrants' needs, but it is still a factor very much to be reckoned with in the U.S. political arena, as abundantly demonstrated by the House of Representatives bill H.R. 4437 (the "Sensenbrenner Bill"), which was passed by a Republican majority in

December 2005. This bill denied any form of legalization to the 10 million to 12 million undocumented people in the United States, proposing instead to radicalize their illegal status and turn them into felons subject to immediate expulsion. In reaction to earlier policies of mass legalization, the term *amnesty* had become, for many legislators, an epithet of scorn and a policy to be resisted at all cost.

H.R. 4437 was conceived in opposition to another approach to immigration, supported by most Democrats in Congress and by the Republican president, according to which a portion of the undocumented would be offered a path to legalization, and labor immigration would be organized through guest-worker programs. This orientation was embodied in the Senate bill S. 2611, adopted amid much turmoil in May 2006. Although a compromise proved impossible between the two versions, especially in an election year, there was visible common ground between the two approaches, in particular in their repressive aspects; both bills called for further militarization of the U.S.-Mexican border, including the further reinforcement of the Border Patrol and the building of barriers along a substantial portion of the border. Both called as well for the expulsion of a significant portion of the undocumented—in the case of the Senate bill, those who have been in the United States for two years or less, and in the House version, all of them.

The more draconian of the two bills struck many immigrants and immigrants' rights groups as so outrageous and so directly threatening to their lives that it sparked an unprecedented wave of street demonstrations, a one-day strike of immigrant labor on May 1, 2006, and the birth of a new immigrants' movement. H.R. 4437 was indeed not so much an example of "globalization coming home" as it was an outright negation of globalization itself—it was a legalistic and nationalistic refusal to recognize the systemic character of abundant migratory flows from South to North.

Although the public language of the bill's backers emphasizes the illegal nature of unauthorized border-crossing, some of them were inspired by ethnocentric and xenophobic "clash-of-civilization" notions, according to which Latinos, seen as a collective threat, are subverting the "true" (Anglo) identity of the nation. Tom Tancredo, Republican representative from the Sixth District of Colorado and leader of the House's Congressional Immigration Reform Caucus, which currently includes more than one hundred members, unabashedly endorses the cultural nationalist ideas of Samuel P. Huntington in *Who Are We?*[7] Huntington's thesis is that the massive presence of Latinos—Mexicans in particular—represents a threat to the very identity of the United States as a nation. (Unlike George W. Bush, these Republicans appeared to have no worries about alienating the Latino vote due to an overly repressive approach to immigration—which is apparently what happened in a spectacular way in the November 2006 midterm elections, when, according to some reports, Republican candidates were opposed by up to 70 percent of Latino voters.)[8] If, as Castles writes, "it is now widely recognized that cross-border population mobility is inextricably linked to the other flows that constitute globalization, and that migration is one of the key forces of social transformation in the contemporary world,"[9] then these restrictionists were acting in denial of globalization itself or in resistance to the change that it brings.

The approach adopted by the Senate was in appearance more moderate, embodying what seemed to many commentators a reasonable legislative compromise, but in its practical implications for immigrants themselves it posed almost as much of a threat. According to the terms of S. 2611 (the Comprehensive Immigration Reform Act or "Hagel-Martínez Bill"), undocumented people who could prove that they have been in the United States for at least five years would have been able to apply for legalization ("earned adjustment") on the condition that they pay a fine and back taxes. Those who had spent between two and five years in the United States were invited to return to their home countries temporarily and apply, with no guarantee of success, for permission to return to the United States through a guest-worker program. Those living in the United States for less than two years would have been urged to return to their home countries within a few months or else face deportation.[10] This bill also provided for the creation of a guest-worker program, or rather the expansion of an existing program (the "H-2A guest-worker program" for agricultural workers), along the lines the Bush administration had been pushing. Such a program would allow for up to 200,000 visas annually, mostly for low-skilled workers. These visas would be valid for three years and could be renewed once.

The Senate bill did not deny the existence of abundant migration, and indeed took some steps toward adapting to it by proposing to legalize a portion of the undocumented and regulate the flow of legal workers through a guest-worker program. Yet it too remained, as we shall see, within the dominant legalistic and nation-centric paradigm. Defenders of this bill bent over backwards to assure their more conservative colleagues that this bill did not call for "amnesty" and indeed required illegal immigrants to "go to the back of the line."

The abundant objections expressed to guest-worker programs by the labor movement were not taken into account (nor were they in subsequent failed attempts, in 2007, to achieve "immigration reform"). One such objection, in the words of labor commentator David Bacon, is that the workers recruited on temporary visas would be "vulnerable to employer pressure, since their visa status would be dependant on their employment." He quotes Ana Avendaño, legal counsel to the AFL-CIO for immigrant affairs, as saying: "This turns jobs which are now held by permanent employees with rights and benefits into jobs filled by temporary, contract employees. It basically takes the jobs of millions of people out of the protections of the New Deal, won by workers decades ago."[11]

Although the two bills were different enough that no compromise was possible between them, both embodied an approach to immigration that treated immigrants purely as subjects of law, abstracting away all their other attributes, including their socioeconomic condition and that of their home countries and regions, as well as the historically determined international division of labor that, over the past five centuries, has divided the world into "central" and "peripheral" spaces (more commonly referred to as "North" and "South"). Legalistic and nation-centric approaches to migration ignore the new reality of transnational migrant networks and transnational social spaces.

The only common ground both houses of Congress were able to find in 2006 was that of repression: on October 26, 2006, President Bush signed a law authorizing the construction of walls along seven hundred miles of the border.[12] This symbolic measure has left a deep impression in the rest of the world.

WHAT TRANSNATIONAL MIGRANT ORGANIZATIONS DO

The literature on transnational migrant networks, which began to appear in the mid-1990s, is by now immense, and it would be futile to try to summarize it all here. My modest ambition is to provide some basic definitions and to look briefly at the different kinds of activities in which such networks typically engage.

The most ordinary action by which migrants support their relatives in the home country is sending money, known as migrant remittances or "migradollars." The economic impact of remittances is immense: in 2006, according to an Inter-American Development Bank report, Latin American migrants sent more than $45 billion in remittances to their home countries.[13] This is an activity in which a clear majority of migrants—over 70 percent—is involved, according to the same source.[14]

However, the kinds of activities usually referred to under the heading of migrant transnationalism are more collective than individual or family-oriented in nature. Three anthropologists who were among the first to observe migrant transnationalism and draw attention to its significance, formulated a definition of the notion that has been often quoted since: "Transmigrants, through their daily activities, forge and sustain multi-stranded social, economic, and political relations that link together their societies of origins and settlement, and through which they create transnational social fields that cross national borders."[15] Similarly, a noted team of sociologists defines *transnational practices* as "the economic, political, and sociocultural occupations and activities that require regular long-term contacts across borders for their success."[16]

At the most basic level of transnational collective activity, immigrants group together by place of origin to form hometown associations that engage in such activities as collecting money to finance local development projects. According to the picture emerging from studies of such networks, this type of pursuit is more typical of Mexican migrant circles than of other groups. In 2006, according to Jonathan Fox, there were at least six hundred such associations registered with Mexican consulates in the United States, with some estimates, he says, reaching two thousand.[17] Although largely concentrated in California, Texas, and Illinois, they cover many other states as well, because Mexican presence in the United States expands far beyond the historic southwestern areas of settlement. According to a study conducted in 2003, the projects supported by these groups concerned above all health and education (60 percent) and infrastructure

(32 percent).[18] The most frequently noted types of projects include projects of town beautification (renovation of the church or the central square), the building of community or youth centers and sports installations, the purchase of sports uniforms, the paving of roads, and installation of irrigation equipment. The projects are usually modest in scale; nearly half of those surveyed in California in 2003 involved amounts less than $5,000; roughly 30 percent were in the $5,000 to $10,000 range.

Most of the towns that boast such associations are located in Mexican states with a long experience of out-migration: Zacatecas primarily (representing roughly a third of the associations found in California), but also Jalisco, Guanajuato, and Michoacán. However, the migration phenomenon is spreading to broader areas of Mexico and may be expected in coming years to give rise to many more associations of this sort.

It is generally recognized that transnational networks are not a majority phenomenon among migrants. According to one estimate, only 250,000 to 500,000 Mexicans take part in hometown associations, out of the ten million or so Mexican migrants present in the United States. However, a survey of recent Mexican migrants in 2005 revealed a higher rate of participation—roughly 14 percent.[19]

Hometown associations do not operate in isolation. They tend to join forces with other such associations of the same state (Federación de Zacatecanos, Federación Californiana de Michocanos, Frente Indígena Oaxaqueño Binacional, Clubes de Jalicenses, etc.). In California alone, twelve of the thirty-two Mexican states boasted such federations in 2003. A typical introductory text on the website of one federation reads:

> The *Federación Californiana de Michoacanos* is an organization of Michoacanos who work for the common good and progress of all immigrants and their native towns as the binational level, promoting education, binational economic development, civic participation, health, and organizational development.[20]

The formation of such federations has much to do, of course, with the efforts of the states in question to institutionalize transnational ties and place them under some form of state control—a subject to which we shall return.

While hometown associations are clearly the main type of transnational migrant organization among Mexicans, studies that extended to other national groups reveal a broad range of types of organizations. A 2005 study conducted by a team of Princeton University researchers led by Alejandro Portes, which included data from an earlier quantitative study, the Comparative Immigrant Entrepreneurship Project, involved transnational migrant organizations created by Mexicans, Dominicans, and Colombians on the East Coast of the United States.[21] This study revealed three major types of organizations, by order of importance:

1. "civic" or "civic/cultural" entities that pursue an agenda of national scope based on several projects in their home country

2. hometown committees whose scope of action is primarily local
3. social agencies that provide health, educational, and other services to immigrants in the United States but which are also engaged in projects in their home country

Civic/cultural organizations make up "the normative form of immigrant transnationalism," emerging "regardless of the origins of the group, how it is received, or where it happens to concentrate." Hometown committees are shown in this study to be associated with a relatively low level of education among immigrants. Social service agencies, also more common among Mexicans than among the two other sample nationalities, are better endowed financially, which reflects the fact that they are more likely than others to receive funds from the cities and states where they are located.

A further observation that emerges from the Princeton study is that organized transnational activities are "more common among better-established, better-educated and wealthier migrants," as these are the ones who have "the wherewithal to involve themselves in frequently complex and demanding cross-border ventures." This remark, the authors note, applies as much to working-class Mexican immigrants as to the typically better-educated immigrants from Colombia, for example.

THE ROLE OF HOME STATES

All observers have noted a growing tendency of home countries, in particular the Mexican federal government and its constituent states, to play an active role in the organizations of transnational migrants and in the channeling of the financial resources they bring back to their countries.[22] At the same time, for the less established migrants, the Mexican government offers several services, including legal defense and health care. Since 2002, it has provided to undocumented persons a form of identification known as the *matrícula consular*, which is of practical help to migrants in need of identification for the purpose of opening a bank account or, in some U.S. states, obtaining a driver's license.

As noted above, the statewide federations of the Mexican hometown associations are one means by which Mexican authorities—both state and federal—exercise some control over migrant activities. There can be benefits in this relationship from the migrants' point of view. As early as 1986, the state of Zacatecas pioneered a program to offer matching funds ("*dos por uno*"), and later double matching funds ("*tres por uno*"), to migrant groups seeking to finance projects in their hometown or area. Other states have followed suit.

The degree of state involvement varies greatly by country and according to immigrants' socioeconomic condition. In the Princeton study, it was found that Mexican immigrants typically form organizations that are "focused on the welfare of mostly rural communities" and with a relatively strong dose of governmental intervention, as compared to Dominicans and Colombians, whose organizations tend to be "broader in scope, more formalized, and more often created by spontaneous grassroots initiative in response to disasters and other national emergencies."

In the cases of Mexico and the Dominican Republic, government departments have been created to manage relations with the expatriate community. The Institute of Mexicans Abroad is a division of the Secretariat of Foreign Relations and includes a Consultative Council made up of 105 elected representatives of immigrant organizations in the United States and Canada, as well as delegates from each of the thirty-two states of the Mexican union. Dominican president Leonel Fernández, himself a longtime resident of New York, following his reelection in 2004, created the position of Secretary of Dominicans Abroad and designed a program—which has yet to be implemented, according to the Princeton study—to "better integrate them into the social and political life of the country."

Both the Dominican Republic and Mexico allow for dual citizenship, and both countries make it possible for expatriates to vote in national elections. Both, as well, have legislators in their national assemblies who live in the United States. Two major Dominican political parties, the Partido Revolucionario Democrático (PRD) and Fernández's own Partido de la Liberación Dominicana (PLD), have hundreds of members and sympathizers in the United States. As for Mexico, it was widely noted that, although several million expatriates are eligible to vote, a remarkably small number actually did so in the hotly contested 2006 presidential election. Some attributed this to the administrative difficulties involved in registering to vote from abroad, but it has clearly raised questions as well about the migrants' own motivation.

In one rather exceptional case, that of the indigenous peoples of the southern Mexican state of Oaxaca, who are numerous in California and have a visible presence in several other states, the solidarity that cements their hometown associations and broader federations is "ethnic" rather than purely geographical. Oaxaca, unlike the rest of Mexico, is divided into a great number of small municipalities, along traditional lines. Under conditions of economic crisis and massive out-migration, many of these villages have been forced to resort to innovative, transnational modes of governance, by which town councils decide, for example, who is authorized to leave for the United States and who is required to return to the hometown for a period of service.[23]

NATIONALIST SUSPICION OF MIGRANT TRANSNATIONALISM

In the abundant sociological and ethnological literature about how transnational migrant networks operate, there is no sense that these networks represent a threat to the cohesion of U.S. society. The only figure of note in the academic world who has voiced strong apprehensions about such networks is Samuel Huntington, who in his 2004 book *Who Are We?* expressed the conviction that Hispanic immigrants in the United States, especially Mexicans, are in danger of undermining the "Anglo-Protestant" identity that, in his view, constitutes the American cultural foundation. Huntington's writings on this subject have been widely criticized as ethnocentric and xenophobic; the renowned Mexican writer and diplomat Carlos Fuentes, for example, referred to him as "the masked racist."[24] I do not wish to dwell here on Huntington's overall argument regarding Hispanics, which has been widely commented on.[25] Here we will concentrate on how Huntington treats the particular subject of transnational—or what he prefers to call "diasporic"—migrant networks.

In a chapter of *Who Are We?* entitled "Merging America with the World," Huntington writes:

> The extensive international involvement of American business, academic, professional, media, nonprofit, and political elites lowered the salience of national identity for those elites, who now increasingly define themselves, their interests, and their identities in terms of transnational and global institutions, networks, and causes.[26]

He is openly disdainful of those "intellectuals, academics, and journalists" he sees as "moralistic" because they are more committed to "humanity" than they are loyal to their nation, just as he is worried by economic elites' exclusive attention to self-interest at the expense of the nation ("Economic transnationalism is rooted in the bourgeoisie," he writes, while "moralistic transnationalism [is rooted] in the intelligentsia"). He goes on to express no small degree of worry about the way in which ordinary migrants form "diasporas"—that is, "cultural communities that cross state boundaries"— while maintaining their homeland state as their "central focus," or so he claims. Diasporas represent in his view a danger to national sovereignty, with the United States having become, in his words, "the world's number one diaspora homeland." This danger is even greater, he asserts, when diasporas are allowed to adopt dual citizenship and thus assume "dual loyalties and dual identities."

Huntington perceives no autonomy whatsoever in the transnational organizational activity of migrants, since, as he sees it, diasporas become mere instruments of their home states. "In today's world," he writes, "domestic ethnic groups are being transformed into transnational diasporas, which homeland states have increasingly seen as the communal and institutional extension of themselves and as a crucial asset of their country." This is even truer when the home countries are "poor [and] overpopulated" and "exert influence through the export of people," because emigrants send billions of dollars in remittances to their home countries. In return they are treated with care by consulates, which act as their protectors—a phenomenon Huntington examines with evident disdain. He is particularly shocked by the phenomenon of the matrícula consular, which provides "certification to illegal Mexican immigrants that they are American residents."

In objecting to those who prefer to defend "humanity" over his view of the U.S. nation, Huntington has the merit of being blunt and straightforward. Yet in factual terms, his understanding of transnational migrant networks suffers from bias. The margin of autonomy that such activities do command—we shall return to this point—is eclipsed in his mind by the strategies and maneuverings of home states. Migrants are portrayed as a diasporic "fifth column." In his nationalistic perspective, countries such as Mexico are seen as purposefully exporting migrants in order to influence U.S. politics from within. The reasons for the poverty and unemployment that reign in Mexico and cause so many to migrate do not concern him, because he implicitly draws boundaries around national economies as well: if each country is responsible for its "own" economy, then only the Mexicans themselves can be blamed for skewed development and poverty within their borders. In other words, Huntington is in complete denial of the systemic factors that make economies interdependent in the era of globalization; his arguments about the U.S. cultural identity as a national attribute to be preserved from alien influence at all costs would begin to break down if he were to admit that there are historic, systemic factors at work in producing large migratory flows from South to North.

Huntington's semiconspiratorial viewpoint about the role of the Mexican and other governments in controlling their diasporas fits with his notorious view that Hispanic migrants to the United States—again, Mexicans in particular—live in cultural and linguistic "enclaves" or worlds apart and can never really become assimilated to U.S. society and its distinctive culture (nor does he appear to want them to). Leaving aside, however, the ethnocentric and nationalistic animus that colors his views, the fatal flaw in his analysis is that transnational migrants are invisible in their role as *citizens*. Since he does not explore in any depth the actual functioning and objectives of such networks, the civic side of what they do remains beyond his perception.

He is not altogether wrong that diasporas can be subject to the control of their home governments. But the reasons for this are not explored; he is content to see them as intruders upon national sovereignty. Huntington fails to note that immigrants to the United States—above all, undocumented immigrants—left to their own devices in a system that recognizes few social rights and offers no basic social services, are driven into the arms of home states that set themselves up as friends and protectors of the migrant. Nor does he pay attention to the role of transnational networks, which, with the aid of funds from their home states in the case of Mexico, contribute, however modestly, to the development of their hometowns and regions. In Huntington's peculiar brand of realism, the power of institutional actors, especially states, by definition takes precedence over that of ordinary working immigrants; only the home states possess true agency in his eyes, while migrants are mere pawns in the game of power.

And yet, according to Alejandro Portes's team of researchers at Princeton, who studied hundreds of transnational migrant organizations and who, as we have seen, are fully aware of the role of home states:

> All empirical evidence indicates that economic, political, and sociocultural activities linking expatriate communities with their countries of origin emerged by initiative of the immigrants themselves, with governments jumping onto the bandwagon only when their importance and economic potential became evident.[27]

Indeed, they note, "many civic, charitable, and cultural transnational organizations remain deeply suspicious of governmental interference which, they fear, may politicize and subvert their original altruistic goals." The example, mentioned above, of the indigenous peoples of Oaxaca and their independent organization, the Oaxacan Indigenous Binational Front (FIOB), simply does not fit into his interpretation.

TOWARD A CIVIC BINATIONALISM?

The role of home states notwithstanding, it is important to understand the forms of civic agency that migrants demonstrate when they become involved in transnational networks. A very different vision from that of Huntington is proposed by political scientist Jonathan Fox in an article aptly entitled "Binational Citizens: Mexican Migrants Are Challenging Old Ideas about Assimilation."[28]

Taking into account the activity of migrants on both sides of the border, and drawing additional inspiration from the movement that emerged in many cities in the spring of 2006, Fox asserts that migrants—in this case, Mexicans—are creating "new ways of becoming American, with membership organizations playing a special role." He notes that, while most migrant organizations began as hometown associations, "many have now developed programs for families in the new communities in the United States." They are coming more and more, in his view, to assume a new sort of "civic binationality"—that is, having "simultaneous membership in Mexican and U.S. society." Contrary to the idea—implicit in Huntington and in more mainstream nation-centric views—that involvement with the home country and incorporation into the receiving society are mutually exclusive, Fox asserts that immigrants' "initial engagement with hometowns abroad spur[s] their active engagement with adopted hometowns in the United States." In other words, far from an enclave effect or an exclusive orientation to the home country, migrants are often engaged in a virtuous cycle by which involvement with the home country stimulates the energies that contribute to more active involvement in the host society.

Fox's analysis coincides with that of Peggy Levitt, in her well-known study of transnational Dominican migrants in the Boston area, of whom she writes:

> They do not shift their loyalties and participatory energies from one country to another. Instead, they are integrated, to varying degrees, into the countries that receive them, at the same that that they remain connected to the countries they leave behind.[29]

Fox traces a definite evolution toward greater involvement by transnational migrants in the affairs of U.S. society. Although few Mexican hometown associations took part in the campaign against California's Proposition 187 in 1994, a decade later they were much more active in a statewide campaign in favor of driver's licenses for the undocumented. He further notes a growing convergence between hometown associations and trade unions, as well as U.S. Latino citizen advocacy groups such as the National Council of La Raza and the Mexican American Legal Defense and Education Fund. The latter group's Los Angeles office now hosts meetings of hometown association organizers and provides them with leadership and media training. There is a growing tendency, Fox observes, for traditional Latino associations and Mexican migrant organizations to "overlap in their issues and sometimes even membership." There remain basic differences in structure and even in orientation; U.S. Latino leaders sometimes express skepticism about whether migrants' associations can really promote civic integration into U.S. society. But the gap, he claims, is narrowing, "as Mexican migrant organizations become increasingly U.S.-focused and Latino organizations increasingly embrace concerns of the growing number of U.S. Latinos who are migrants."

The pressure placed on migrants—most of all on the undocumented—by the draconian H.R. 4437 bill had the effect of throwing millions of them into the streets in spring 2006, causing many observers to comment that they were acting as citizens even though they are deprived of many citizenship rights. Their historic display of civic concern goes beyond opposition to a particularly repressive piece of legislation. Should a compromise ever take shape between the Democrats and the less restrictionist Republicans in Congress, it will most likely involve a guest-worker program that has been rejected in principle by organized labor and by many immigrant advocacy groups. Although it is too early to tell how long the immigrant movement will sustain itself, its convergence with broader forces in U.S. society and the high stakes of the reform make it likely that the civic involvement of migrants in the United States will continue and grow deeper in the coming years.

LESSONS FROM EUROPEAN EXPERIENCE

When compared with certain recent experiences in western Europe, what stands out in the U.S. case is the extent to which migrants, organized or not, are left to their own devices by U.S. federal and state authorities. All levels of government display indifference to migrant-initiated development projects. By contrast, in a few pioneering experiences in western Europe, receiving states have begun to assume an active role in encouraging migrants to learn skills and achieve cross-border mobility in order to contribute, if only modestly, to the development of their home countries.

For a short period (1998–99) under the government of Lionel Jospin, a French government department known as the Interministerial Delegation for Migration and Codevelopment promoted a new type of agreement with sending countries. These agreements provided for support to migrants taking part in development projects or small enterprises. According to Sami Naïr, who was in charge of the delegation, one of the keys to such a policy was to grant open visas to such persons rather than placing restrictions on their ability to return to France for short or even for more extended periods. Unfortunately, the political circumstances under which this experiment was conducted were not conducive to its success.[30]

As Naïr recounts the experience, the French government ceded to the political temptation of instrumentalizing the program by tying its realization to the forced departure of undocumented immigrants, causing the entire program to be discredited through association with repressive policies.

Nonetheless, the delegation managed, during its short life, to sign agreements with three countries: Morocco, Senegal, and Mali. The results were modest, but the vision behind them continues to be promoted today, not just in France but in certain other European countries as well. Naïr points to the example of Spain, which has begun to take initiatives of a similar nature, and to Sweden, which, he says, has set an example for Europe by defining migration as a "development issue" and incorporating it as a key parameter into its policies of cooperation with the countries of the South. This attitude contrasts sharply with that of Great Britain, whose political leaders continue, according to Naïr, to view immigration as just another factor in the world labor market, "to be utilized according to the law of offer and demand." In Germany, he observes, Turkish migrant associations are active in the creation of micro-enterprises in their home country in the absence of any particular support from the German government. Naïr comments:

> The attitude of the OECD [Organization for Economic Cooperation and Development] countries on migration has been changing slowly—too slowly!—from an internal question of economics and security to a question of foreign policy. Immigration ... has, sometimes at least, come to be seen as a matter of cooperation and development.

He is confident in the great potential of migrants in Europe to contribute to the development of their home countries—*if* European governments can rise to the occasion by moving beyond their hesitations and building on a few embryonic but promising experiments.

Other, related experiences deserve attention and, once again, contrast very sharply with the U.S. experience. Today thousands of French citizens, often in collaboration with migrants, take part in local development projects in countries of the South with the backing of French local and regional governments, in schemes referred to under the heading of "decentralized cooperation." Currently nothing of the kind exists in the United States outside the initiatives of a handful of nongovernmental organizations, but it is worth imagining for a moment the benefits both U.S. citizens and the citizens of countries of the South could derive from such initiatives. If such policies were ever to be promoted in the United States, it is certain that the millions of U.S. citizens with families in Latin America and the Caribbean would contribute much energy to their success and bring new meaning to the notion of "civic binationalism."

"TRANSNATIONALISM FROM BELOW": A CHALLENGE TO NATIONAL CITIZENSHIP?

About ten years ago, sociologist Alejandro Portes, in a pioneering article entitled "Globalization from Below: The Rise of Transnational Communities,"[31] advanced the claim that transnational migrant organizations may, in the long run, prove to constitute a kind of revenge of ordinary working people from the South against the effects of "globalization from above." Although "grassroots transnational enterprises are not set up in explicit opposition to the designs of large banks and corporations," he wrote, such activities do "provide examples, incentives, and technical means for common people to attempt a novel and previously unimagined alternative" by which "former immigrant workers are able to imitate the majors." Such activities may tend, over time, Portes claimed, to "weaken a fundamental premise of the hegemony of corporate economic elites and domestic ruling classes"—namely, the premise that "capital is global while labor is local." He admitted, however, that "if, in the long run, transnational enterprise can become an equalizing force, in the short term it can have the opposite effect" because of "growing disparities between sending localities that possess a committee among its migrants abroad and those that do not." Clearly, the emergence of such networks could not be seen as a panacea to the social inequalities generated by transnational corporate capitalism, but Portes nonetheless concluded on an optimistic note, asserting that "capitalist globalization is so broadly based and has generated such momentum as to continuously nourish its grassroots counterpart."

Shortly thereafter, another group of sociologists, including some of Portes's colleagues, published a volume of critical essays under the title *Transnationalism from Below*, in which they openly questioned the notion that migrant transnationalism represented some sort of newfound path to social emancipation.[32] Michael Peter Smith and Luis Eduardo Guarnizo, editors of the volume, took to task certain researchers who, going much further than Portes, chose to see in transnational migrant activity a direct challenge to the nation-state itself. Such scholars, who were in general closer to cultural studies than to the social sciences and economics, brought to the field of transnational studies "a peculiar cultural bent and a distinctive normative, postmodern discursive flavor."[33] They conceived of transnationalism as "something to celebrate, as an expression of a subversive popular resistance 'from below'" thanks to the "cultural hybridity, multi-positional identities, and border-crossing by marginal 'others.'" The transnational practices of migrants came to be depicted as "conscious and successful efforts by ordinary people to escape control and domination 'from above' by capital and the state." They looked to transnational migrant actors as new subjects of social transformation and possibly as bearers of a fundamental challenge to the nation-state.

While there is good reason, as Smith and Guarnizo stressed, to doubt such radical claims, they do contain a grain of truth. As we have seen, the key actors of transnational migrant networks are indeed border-crossers with cultural, linguistic, and political skills that make them among the "hybrid" actors of a new global era. Their new forms of transnational identification make them very different from classic one-way migrants or classic return migrants. And yet Smith and Guarnizo are right to seek to "bring back into focus the enduring asymmetries of domination, inequality, racism, sexism, class conflict, and uneven development in which transnational practices are embedded and which they sometimes even perpetuate."

As for the claim that migrant transnationalism is contributing to the decline of nationalism and to a new "postnational" order, it indeed appears highly exaggerated. Given the political momentum today behind policies of strict, militarized border surveillance, national boundaries are certainly not destined to disappear in the foreseeable future, even if more flexible regimes for managing migratory flows are devised. The question we need to ask is not whether the nation-state is about to disappear, nor whether identification with nations is becoming obsolete, but rather whether it is possible for working people who cross borders on a regular basis to be recognized as *citizens* in the full sense, even though their lives and livelihoods are not confined to a single national space. In other words, we must ask whether citizenship rights sensitive to their situation can be created, legislated, and respected. This question raises, all at once, issues involving class, nation, race/ethnicity, and gender; it cannot be reduced to any of these components, and that is part of the challenge. Without proposing any blueprints or making any major prophetic claims about the future of the nation-state, we can at least ask whether the decoupling of citizenship and nationality may in some form find its way onto the political agenda.[34]

NOTES

1. Peggy Levitt, *The Transnational Villagers* (Berkeley: University of California Press, 2001).

2. Robert C. Smith, *Mexican New York: Transnational Lives of New Immigrants* (Berkeley: University of California Press, 2006).

3. See, for example, Cecilia Menjívar, *Fragmented Ties: Salvadoran Immigrant Networks in America* (Berkeley: University of California Press, 2000). See also Linda Basch, Nina Glick Schiller, and Cristina Szanton Blanc, *Nations Unbound: Transnational Projects, Postcolonial Predicaments, and Deterritorialized Nation-States* (Langhorne, PA: Gordon & Breach, 1994). The authors of this pioneering work do a lot of theorizing about "transnational social fields" in the contemporary world system, but this does not prevent them from approaching the lives of their subjects with an empathy born of close observation of individuals and their subjectivity.

4. Alejandro Portes, "Globalization from Below: The Rise of Transnational Communities," Working Paper WPTC 98-01, Princeton University, 1997.

5. Michael Peter Smith and Luis Eduardo Guarnizo, eds., *Transnationalism from Below* (New Brunswick, NJ: Transaction, 1998).

6. The quotations in this and the following two paragraphs are taken from Stephen Castles, "Migration and Community Formation under Conditions of Globalization," in *Incorporating Diversity: Rethinking Assimilation in a Multicultural Age*, edited by Peter Kivisto, p. 279 (Boulder, CO: Paradigm, 2005).

7. See Michael Crowley, "Border War," *The New Republic* online, www.freerepublic.com/focus/f-news/1366067/posts, March 17, 2005; Tom Barry, "Tom Tancredo: Christian Crusader, Cultural Nationalist, and Iran Freedom Fighter," *Right Web*, International Relations Center, May 24, 2006, http://rightweb.irc-online.org/rw/3281.html.

8. Roberto Lovato, "Latino Backlash Could Doom GOP," November 17, 2006, http://www.alternet.org/story/44257.

9. Castles, "Migration and Community Formation," 277.

10. For a detailed and critical examination of the legalization provisions of the Hagel-Martínez bill, see the Center for Human Rights and Constitutional Law, "Analysis of the legalization provisions of the Senate 'compromise' on immigration reform: a flawed, inadequate, anti-worker proposal" (April 10, 2006), available at www.nilc.org.

11. David Bacon, "No Bill Is Better," Pacific News Service, May 25, 2006.

12. Michael A. Fletcher and Jonathan Weisman, "Bush Signs Bill Authorizing 700-Mile Fence for Border," *Washington Post*, October 27, 2006. More than twenty Democratic senators (of the forty-five then in office) and over fifty Democratic representatives (out of about two hundred) had voted for the measure, demonstrating that the repressive approach to border management is not a Republican monopoly.

13. Inter-American Development Bank, "Remittances from the U.S. to Latin America, 2006," http://www.iadb.org/mif/remittances/usa/ranking2006b.cfm.

14. Alejandro Portes, Luis Guarnizo, and Patricia Landolt, "The Study of Transnationalism: Pitfalls and Promise of an Emergent Field," *Ethnic and Racial Studies* 22, no. 2 (1999): 217–37.

15. Basch, Schiller, and Szanton Blanc, *Nations Unbound*, 6.

16. Portes, Guarnizo, and Landolt, "Study of Transnationalism," 8.

17. Jonathan Fox, "Binational Citizens: Mexican Migrants Are Challenging Old Ideas about Assimilation," *Boston Review*, September–October 2006, available at http://bostonreview.net/BR31.5/fox.php.

18. Manuel Orozco and Michelle Lapointe, *Mexican Hometown Associations and Their Development Opportunities*, report commissioned by the U.S. Agency for International Development, Inter-American Dialogue Research Series on Remittances No. 3, cited in Emmanuelle Le Texier, "Associations et comités de village mexicains de Californie," *Revue européenne des Migrations internationales* 20, no. 3 (2004): 163–77.

19. Fox, "Binational Citizens," quoting an article from the *Sacramento Bee*.

20. See http://www.fecademi.org/quienes_somos.html.

21. Alejandro Portes, Cristina Escobar, and Aleandria Walton Radford, "Immigrant Transnational Organizations and Development: A Comparative Study," CMD Working Paper No. 05-07, Princeton University, August 2005. The unattributed quotes in the following paragraphs are from this paper.

22. The information in the following paragraphs regarding the role of home states in transnational migrant activities is taken from Portes, Escobar, and Radford, "Immigrant Transnational Organizations."

23. See Michael Kearney and Federico Besserer, "Oaxacan Municipal Governance in Transnational Context," in *Indigenous Mexican Migrants in the United States*, edited by Jonathan Fox and Gaspar Rivera-Salgado (San Diego: Center for U.S.-Mexican Studies and Center for Comparative Immigration Studies, University of California, San Diego, 2004), 449–66.

24. "El racista enmascarado," *El País*, March 23, 2004.

25. Andrew Hacker, "Patriot Games," *New York Review of Books* 51, no. 11 (June 24, 2004); Alan Wolfe, "Native Son: Samuel Huntington Defends the Homeland," *Foreign Affairs* (May–June 2004): 120–25; James Cohen, "Les Hispaniques, un nouveau 'péril' pour les Etats-Unis?" in *Les Latinos aux USA*, edited by J. Cohen and A. Tréguer, p. 15–27 (Paris: IHEAL-CREDAL, 2004).

26. The quotations in this paragraph and the next are taken from Samuel P. Huntington, *Who Are We? The Challenges to America's National Identity* (New York: Simon & Schuster, 2004), chap. 10.

27. Portes, Escobar, and Radford, "Immigrant Transnational Organizations."

28. Quotations and information in the next few paragraphs are taken from Fox, "Binational Citizens." In fact, Fox's work in this area is much more extensive. See also, for example, his "Unpacking 'Transnational Citizenship,'" *Annual Review of Political Science* (2005): 171–205, and "Mapping Mexican Migrant Civil Society," paper presented at "Mexican Migrant Civic and Political Participation," Woodrow Wilson International Center for Scholars, Princeton University, November 2005, as well as Fox and Rivera-Salgado, *Indigenous Mexican Migrants*.

29. Levitt, *Transnational Villagers*, 5.

30. Information and quotations in this and the following paragraphs are taken from Sami Naïr, *L'immigration est une chance. Entre la peur et la raison* (Paris: Editions du Seuil, 2007), 173–218.

31. The quotations that follow are from Portes, "Globalization from Below."

32. See Luis Eduardo Guarnizo and Michael Peter Smith, "The Locations of Transnationalism," in Smith and Guarnizo, *Transnationalism from Below*. The quotations that follow are from this volume.

33. Homi Bhabha and Arjun Appadurai are among the authors singled out for criticism. Alejandro Portes is also mentioned in this regard, but as I argue here, his interpretation of transnational migrant networks has little to do with the "postmodern," cultural-studies approach justly criticized by Smith and Guarnizo.

34. This question is raised with great clarity in Linda Bosniak, "Denationalizing Citizenship," in *Citizenship Today: Perspectives and Practices*, edited by T. Alexander Aleinikoff and Douglas Klusmeyer, 237–52 (Washington, DC: Carnegie Endowment for International Peace, 2001).

CHAPTER 3

From Mother Africa to Blacks with Accents: Diaspora and African American Studies in the United States

Tyler Stovall

The people

Had forfeited the confidence of the government

And could win it back only

By redoubled efforts. Would it not be easier

In that case for the government

To dissolve the people

And elect another?

—Bertolt Brecht, "The Solution"

For African Americans, globalization has always been a double-edged sword. In many ways, it has served as a means of empowerment. From the exiles who sought freedom in Liberia, Paris, and elsewhere abroad to Malcolm X's call on black Americans to see themselves as part of a global majority rather than a national minority, blacks have often seen escape from the United States, in one form or another, as a solution to their oppression.[1] At the same time, arguably no other culture in the world today has had the global impact of African American music and performance.[2] In contrast, however, the impact of globalization on American domestic life has often proved problematic. Not only have African Americans frequently found themselves in a losing competition with immigrants, both historically and currently, but the neoliberal philosophy that underlies much of current globalist thinking has often forestalled progressive strategies to address the economic underdevelopment of black neighborhoods.[3]

In this chapter, I wish to address this ambivalence by looking at the history of ideas of African diaspora in the United States. Scholars of African American life ever since W. E. B. Du Bois have opted for a global perspective on the black condition in the United States. More recently, spurred on by the work of black British scholars such as Stuart Hall, Paul Gilroy, and Hazel Carby, among many others, diasporic theories have taken the field of black studies in America by storm; department after department has rebaptized itself with names like "African American and African Diaspora Studies."[4] In 2005, the Museum of the African Diaspora (MOAD) opened its doors in San Francisco, the least black of all major American cities.[5] As far as African American intellectuals are concerned, therefore, globalization has clearly carried the day.

In discussing the history of black diasporic thought in the United States, I wish to focus on both a shift in emphasis and a paradox. A central theme of, and initial motivation behind, the diasporic perspective has always been an assertion of the link between Africa and the descendants of the African slave trade, a belief in particular that African culture was not destroyed in the New World but remained a central feature of black cultures in the Americas. While links between the African continent and the diaspora have remained an important feature of what Gilroy has termed the "Black Atlantic," interest has in many cases shifted to an exploration of the diversity of the diaspora itself and to the interactions between different diasporic populations.[6] At the same time, one can discern a tendency, at least in the United States, not only to privilege the study of black communities and experiences outside this country but also at times to exclude African Americans from a working definition of *diaspora*. The very phrase "African American *and* African diaspora studies" suggests this. Or, to offer another example, at a recent MOAD conference, the organizer and museum director claimed to a mostly black audience that studies of the diaspora are important because "the diaspora is coming to you," citing as evidence a recent celebrated *New York Times* article, which noted that recent immigration from Africa to the United States was greater on a yearly basis than the transfer of African slaves here during the height of the Middle Passage. The idea that the African American attendees at the conference were also part of the African diaspora did not figure into his analysis.[7]

Again, I would emphasize that such trends are not universal nor even hegemonic. Much of African diasporic intellectual production still centers around relationships to Africa, and many scholars continue to promote diasporic interpretations of the black experience in the United States.[8] Nonetheless, this tendency to see diaspora as a counterpoint to American rather than African black life is pronounced enough to merit comment. This essay will explore the reasons for this shift and its implications for both African American studies and black America in general. Although these reasons are numerous, of primary importance is both African diaspora theory's heritage of postmodern anti-essentialism, a desire to redress the traditional overwhelming focus of African American studies on black life in the United States, and perhaps most important, the changing composition of the African American community and the impact of those changes on the very meaning of blackness in American life today. The increasing diversity of America's black communities is sure to become a major theme of black life in the twenty-first century, and exploring debates over definitions of diaspora will hopefully provide one way of illuminating these changes.

DIASPORA AND AFRICAN AMERICAN STUDIES IN THE UNITED STATES

From its beginnings, the theory of African diaspora as articulated in the United States centered on the idea that a certain fundamental unity characterized the black communities and cultures of the Atlantic basin, and that unity rested upon the African origins of black civilization. As early as 1910, amateur anthropologist Harry Johnston argued in *The Negro in the New World* that blacks in the Americas were fundamentally African in character and culture.[9] In 1915, W. E. B. Du Bois published *The Negro*, which gave a positive, if romanticized, view of Africa and underscored its significance for African American culture.[10] In 1941, Melville Herskovits stated this position more forcefully in his seminal book *The Myth of the Negro Past*, which made the case that African cultures had largely survived the Middle Passage and continued to shape black culture in the United States.[11] The notion that American blacks were largely African also had a major impact on the writers, artists, and musicians of the Harlem Renaissance, who saw in African music and sculpture in particular a vital source of heritage and creative inspiration. The idea of a return to Africa, either literally or symbolically, became a mass movement under the leadership of Marcus Garvey.

This position, of course, did not go unchallenged: much of black America's artistic and cultural establishment viewed the avant-garde of the Harlem Renaissance with undisguised hostility, and E. Franklin Frazier flatly rejected Herskovits's claims of African cultural survivals, emphasizing instead the novelty and distinctly American character of the black experience in the United States.[12]

The term *African diaspora* first became widely used in the 1960s and 1970s.[13] In a series of articles, historian George Shepperson underscored the centrality of the Atlantic slave trade to black identity in the New World, arguing for their continuing links both to the mother continent and around the Atlantic basin to each other.[14] This idea of black Atlantic cultures as a transnational community united by a common relationship to the African continent became a defining feature of this first wave of African diaspora studies. One of the most distinguished representatives of this school of thought is historian Joseph Harris. In his 1992 study *Global Dimensions of the African Diaspora*, he defined his approach in the following terms:

> The African diaspora concept subsumes the following: the global dispersion (voluntary and involuntary) of Africans throughout history, the emergence

of a cultural identity abroad based on origin and social condition, and the psychological or physical return to the homeland, Africa. Thus viewed, the African diaspora assumes the character of a dynamic, continuous, and complex phenomenon stretching across time, geography, class, and gender.[15]

An insistence on the African roots of African American culture achieved great popularity among both academics and activists in the 1960s and 1970s; the invention of the African American holiday Kwanzaa by Ron Karenga in 1966 is one of its most enduring legacies.[16] At the same time, many challenged some of the basic assumptions of this perspective. One criticism, made especially by scholars of the African continent, charged that diasporic thought tended to reify the idea of "Africa," reducing a complex and diverse region to a one-dimensional assemblage of a few essential cultural traits.[17] Another related problem was the image of African culture as essentially unchanging, an image unfortunately not so far removed from the European colonial stereotype that non-Western societies were bereft of history. In their 1992 study *The Birth of African American Culture*, Sidney Mintz and Richard Price argued that discontinuity as much as continuity typified the African cultural presence in the New World, and that blacks had invented their own cultures by drawing from a variety of African, European, and Native American practices.[18]

At the same time, the politics of cultural nationalism provoked other challenges to standard diasporic conceptions. The emphasis on unity, both political and cultural, that had so characterized African American communities in struggle during the era of civil rights and Black Power became increasingly viewed as a straightjacket of enforced conformity by some at the end of the twentieth century. A new school of black feminist thought criticized the sexist tendencies of many black movement leaders, as well as the general silencing of women's voices as part of nationalist agendas.[19] By the 1980s and 1990s, the nationalist consensus had come under fire by queer theorists, postmodernists, and a variety of others who came together to emphasize the diversity of the black condition in the United States and abroad.[20] In part a reflection of the decline of de jure segregation and racial terror in America, which opened new doors to African Americans and thus rendered such diversity more possible, this new insistence also represented a turning away from narrow conceptions of African heritage. The rise of Afrocentrism, which viewed black Americans as purely and simply African and reduced the slave experience to a minor blip in the otherwise glorious history of black kings and queens, represented for some the kind of mystical fallacies that could arise from diasporic thinking and prompted its critics to search for new ways of conceptualizing black identity in the modern era.[21]

Thus were born contemporary philosophies of the African diaspora. Current interpretations of black diasporic thought draw heavily upon postmodern philosophies and methodologies, and while scholars from many different disciplines have contributed to this approach, those working in literary and cultural studies have tended to set the tone—in contrast to the social science orientation of much of the earlier diasporic school.

If there is one theme that dominates current African diasporic thought, it is *diversity*, in particular the diverse meanings of blackness across different times and places. Feminist and queer theory in particular have undermined traditional notions of a single black community, exploring the fissures within African American life as a complement and challenge to nationalist emphases on black versus white dualities. Against nationalist essentialism, the new diasporic theory has asserted the absence of certainties, fixed boundaries, or settled definitions of race or culture. As Stuart Hall put it in 1990:

> Diaspora does not refer us to those scattered tribes whose identity can only be secured in relationship to some sacred homeland to which they must at all cost return.... The diaspora experience as I intend it is defined not by essence or purity, but by the recognition of necessary heterogeneity and diversity; by a conception of "identity" which lives with and through, not despite, difference; by hybridity. Diasporic identities are those which are constantly producing and reproducing themselves anew, through transformation and difference.[22]

A key aspect of the new diasporic thought has been a shift in the meanings of geographical interchange. While the issue of African survivals in the New World and the relationship between Africa and the West in general have remained important, they have to a certain extent been superseded by a concern for the various levels of interaction between different black communities throughout the Atlantic basin and beyond. Current diasporic thought generally rejects the idea of an essential African culture against which all black communities must be judged, in favor of a more egalitarian evaluation of different black communities on their own terms.[23] Paul Gilroy's notion of the black Atlantic as an interactive historical unit has been adopted by many, instead of more traditional bilateral images of the relationship between Africa and her children. Moreover, the very notion of the transatlantic slave trade as the center of global black life has come under critical scrutiny. The recent boom in studies of black Europe has brought attention to a region that not only historically had a very small population of African descent but also did not, for the most part, practice slavery on its territory; most black Europeans are free migrants and their descendants, from both Africa and the Americas.[24] Some scholars have also challenged the Atlantic focus of diasporic scholarship by considering the example of black communities in the Indian and Pacific Ocean basins.[25] Diasporic theory's emphasis on diversity has often had the effect of stripping Africa of its centrality to global black life by calling into question the very notion of centrality.

Two other major themes suffuse current thinking about the geographical diversity of the African diaspora. The first is a strong emphasis on transnationalism and the deconstruction of traditional national communities and boundaries. Scholars have long studied issues such as migration, cultural diffusion, and international cooperation and conflict that involve regional or global interchanges, but in recent years some have focused on the global experiences of nonstate actors, reconceptualizing international relationships both as formative for individuals and communities in the modern world and as challenging the centrality of nation-states to modernity.[26] Among students of the African diaspora, one result has been a celebration of those who travel, seen as not only forging links between different diasporic communities but also, in effect, constituting themselves a paradigmatic diasporic space.

The second theme is a focus on the experience of travel and displacement itself. Gilroy's *Black Atlantic* deploys the image of the ship as a metaphor for diaspora, reconfiguring a traditional icon of the horrors of the slave trade into a symbol of unbounded horizons and endless possibilities. In a similar vein, in her recent study of black Liverpool, *Dropping Anchor, Setting Sail*, Jacqueline Nassy Brown counterposes that city's history as a cosmopolitan port with its centrality to the slave trade.[27] In these readings, the idea of travel complements the trauma of the Middle Passage and the loss of Africa with the creation of a new, decentered diasporic world.

It is perhaps no accident that many of the new postmodern conceptions of the African diaspora have been pioneered by British scholars of Caribbean descent.[28] It would be hard to conceive of a world region more appropriate to theories of diaspora than the Caribbean: a scattered series of islands of diverse linguistic and colonial heritages whose populations have been shaped not only by the Atlantic slave trade but by migration from Europe and South and East Asia as well, not to mention considerable emigration *to* Europe, North America, and even Africa. Not for nothing did Edouard Glissant regard diversity and hybridity as the essence of Caribbean identity in his *Caribbean Discourse*. This struggle with issues of blackness and diaspora has in fact been a *leitmotiv* of Francophone Caribbean literary theory, from the *negritude* of Aimé Césaire and Léon Damas to the *antillanité* of Glissant and the *créolité* of Raphaël Confiant and Patrick Chamoiseau.[29] However, I would argue that black British writers such as Hall, Gilroy, Carby, and many others have had a greater impact not just because of their own individual brilliance but also thanks to the large size (the largest in Europe) of Britain's black community and its ability to enter into dialogue with black communities in the United States, themselves shaped by a long history of Caribbean immigration.[30] In a sense, therefore, diasporic theories have formed a template for a new sense of black British and Anglophone Caribbean identity.

One aspect of this identity, and of the diasporic project as a whole, has been a criticism of what has been termed "African American exceptionalism."[31] The idea that peoples of African descent in the United States constitute the world's (or at least the diaspora's) paradigmatic black community derives from several factors, including the tremendous vibrancy of African American culture; the violent segregation of postemancipation American life, which forced blacks to develop an unprecedented network of social and cultural institutions; and the global reach of American power as a whole in the twentieth century. In general, African Americans have often been a leading example of an unassimilable racial minority in an advanced liberal capitalist democracy. They are certainly not the only one, however, and the rise of postcolonial populations in Europe during the late twentieth century in particular has undergirded the diasporic conviction that blackness has many faces. If Africa can no longer be considered the source of all original black culture, then neither can America be treated as the essential diasporic experience.

A NEW BLACK AMERICA

We are now positioned to explore more fully a central tenet of this chapter: that current thinking about the African diaspora tends to focus upon black experiences outside both Africa and the United States, diminishing the importance of, if not altogether excluding, the latter. As I noted earlier, this is just a tendency, not a hegemonic practice. In particular, black Americans who travel outside the United States, as political exiles, missionaries, or musicians on tour, remain very much a part of the diasporic project. Nonetheless, one can often find indications of a contrast between black Americans and diasporic Africans. For example, writing in the *African Studies Review*, Judith Byfield notes:

> In the United States, cities like New York have become home to significant numbers of Nigerians, Ethiopians, and Senegalese as well as Jamaicans, Haitians, and Dominicans. All can be claimed as part of the African diaspora, but their relationship to Africa, to each other, and to black Americans is mediated by national and ethnic identities, gender, and class. Together they have forged multinational, multiethnic urban black communities of overlapping diasporas with both shared and competing interests.[32]

Byfield's conceptualization of contemporary black diasporas in America highlights a fundamental development around which I wish to conclude this essay. Diasporic theory's interest in diversity is not just a matter of looking beyond the boundaries of the United States, but is also driven by the increasingly polyglot nature of America's black population. The number of American blacks whose ancestors did not come to the United States as slaves has grown markedly since the late twentieth century. This is especially true of African immigrants, but there have also been new waves of migration from the Caribbean to America, especially to Florida and the Eastern Seaboard. The United States census of 2000 revealed that 6 percent of America's black population was foreign born. More than 40 percent of those had come to the United States since 1990 (73 percent since 1980). Of these, 60 percent came from the Caribbean and 25 percent from sub-Saharan Africa. The African population in the United States doubled during the 1990s, reaching some 600,000 individuals by the early twenty-first century.[33]

The diversity of black America has increased in other ways as well. The relative decline of social taboos against interracial relationships has produced a significant new mixed-race population in the United States, heralded by the decision of the federal government to allow individuals to check more than one racial category on the 2000 census.[34] Between 1990 and 2000, for example, the percentage of blacks married interracially increased from 8.4 to 12.6 percent, and on the 2000 census, 4.2 percent of those with non-Hispanic African ancestry identified as multiracial.[35] Concurrently, the numbers of black children adopted into white families has also increased. Since Congress passed the Multiethnic Placement Act in 1994, transracial placements of black orphans have increased sharply, from 14 percent of all such placements in 1998 to 26 percent in 2004.[36] Increasingly, we seem to be witnessing the Creolization of not just the black American population but of America as a whole.

As historians are fond of saying about globalization (and basically everything else), there is very little new under the sun. America has long had a diverse black population; as Philip Kasinitz noted in his 1994 study *Caribbean New York*, the percentage of black New Yorkers of Caribbean ancestry was no greater in the 1990s than in the 1920s. What has shifted is less the statistical demography of the African American population and more the social and political context in which it is interpreted. The increasing emphasis on African American diversity both derives from and feeds into current diasporic theory. It also reflects a new climate of racial tolerance where people of African ancestry have greater latitude to choose different identities. For example, America has always had mixed-race people, but in the past, they were either regarded as black or else passed surreptitiously for white. Such choices still exist, of course, but there is also today an assertive mixed-race community that claims its own distinct hybrid identity.[37]

At the same time, the new emphasis on the diversity of blacks in the United States conforms to other, more negative representations of African American life. The tendency of many diaspora theorists and other postmodern scholars to romanticize the idea of hybridity tends to mask the fact that Creole societies have generally been hierarchical and inegalitarian, marked by supple but powerful limitations based upon interactions of race, class, and gender.[38] Diasporic views of black diversity have operated both to broaden and to narrow the meaning of *African American*: while the black population is viewed as more cosmopolitan than ever, the term *African American* is seen as linked specifically to those whose ancestors (all or most of whose ancestors) came to America in shackles. One paradox of this is the tendency to use the term to refer specifically to those with no immediate ties to Africa and not to those born there. How else can one understand *Time* columnist Joe Klein's description of a certain popular senator from Illinois as "African and American, as opposed to African American."[39]

This, of course, brings us to the fascinating case of Barack Obama, whose ubiquitous presence in the American media today includes being featured alongside his wife on the cover of *Ebony* magazine as "America's next First Couple?"[40] Senator Obama has made no secret of his identification as a black American; he has not, for example, sought to portray himself as mixed race. At the same time, he has skillfully deployed his father's status as a black immigrant to appeal to mainstream America and implicitly to distinguish himself from traditional American notions of blackness. There is a very complex history of American discourses and popular attitudes toward immigration, and even today, immigrants are often viewed negatively.[41] However, when one counterposes immigrant against slave origins and racialized identity, the former becomes more palatable, indeed more American. As a recent article in *U.S. News and World Report* put it in appraising Obama's appeal, "He identifies himself more with the immigrant's experience widely shared by countless millions of Americans than with the heritage of slavery and African American oppression that has been shared by prominent black politicians at the national level."[42] The case of Barack Obama illustrates both the cosmopolitan possibilities and the limits to acceptability of blackness in contemporary America, and further suggests that the two are intimately related.

This becomes evident when one considers the ardor with which many white commentators generally indifferent (at best) to black concerns have rushed to embrace Obama. Fellow senator Joseph R. Biden Jr. in launching his own presidential bid, touched off a firestorm of protests when he complimented Obama as "the first mainstream African American who is articulate and bright and clean and a nice-looking guy."[43] In attacking the refusal of the Reverend Al Sharpton to endorse Obama, conservative syndicated columnist Kathleen Parker wrote:

> Though of African descent via his Kenyan father, Obama is half white and is not descended of slaves. He doesn't share that heritage, nor did he pay his dues in the civil-rights movement.
>
> In fact, Obama has made clear that he is a new generation of American black. He doesn't have to genuflect to the civil-rights period, nor is he tethered to a heritage that seems at times to hold others hostage.
>
> It is precisely Obama's ability to address America's broader needs—black and white, red and blue—that makes him accessible and acceptable (and nonthreatening) to whites weary of the burden of the nation's racist past.
>
> He is, in other words, that next generation history has been waiting for.[44]

Biden's remarks and Parker's article share not just a positive view of Obama but also a tendency to praise him in contradistinction to those of more traditional black ancestry. Biden's use of the term "mainstream" is particularly interesting: at a time when some questioned the ability of Obama to represent black America, he implied that his fellow senator belonged to the political mainstream—not of African Americans, but of white Americans. This tendency to embrace Obama as a "good Negro" recalled not only colonial narratives of "good" versus "bad" natives but also more recent efforts by American conservatives to create a pliant black leadership and impose it upon the African American community as a whole.[45]

Precisely because so many whites rushed to praise Senator Obama, many blacks reacted to his presidential campaign with some hesitation. Prominent scholar Stanley Crouch rejected the idea that Obama is "one of us," and author Debra J. Dickerson similarly questioned his black identity:

> I've got nothing but love for the brother, but we don't have anything in common.... His father was African. His mother was a white woman. He

grew up with white grandparents. Now, I'm willing to adopt him.... He married black. He acts black. But there's a lot of distance between black Africans and African Americans.[46]

The unwillingness of some African Americans immediately to embrace Barack Obama as one of their own prompted a number of heated reactions, which at times did not stop short of accusing blacks of racism. In a curious paradox, those who made such arguments often both championed new, more diverse ideas of blackness in America and at the same time upheld the traditional, much-criticized "one-drop rule," according to which anyone with any discernable African ancestry is black and only black.[47] Sociologist Orlando Patterson condemned this ambivalence about Senator Obama's presidential candidacy as "the new black nativism":

> Obama is being rejected because many black Americans don't consider him one of their own and may even feel threatened by what he embodies.
> So just what is the nature of black American identity today? Historically, the defining characteristic has been any person born in America who is of African ancestry, however remote. This is the infamous one-drop rule, invented and imposed by white racists until the middle of the twentieth century. As with so many other areas of ethno-racial relations, African Americans turned this racist doctrine to their own ends.... What for whites was a means of exclusion was transformed by blacks into a glorious principle of inclusion. The absurdity of defining someone as black who to all appearances was white was turned on its head by blacks who used the one-drop rule to enlarge both the black group and its leadership with light-skinned persons who, elsewhere in the Americas, would never dream of identifying with blacks....
> In recent years, however, this tradition has been eroded by a thickened form of black identity that, sadly, mirrors some of the worst aspects of American white identity and racism. A streak of nativism rears its ugly head. To be black American, in this view, one's ancestors must have been not simply slaves but American slaves.[48]

Such criticisms of black American attitudes to Barack Obama, and more broadly to the issue of black diversity in the United States, miss the point in several respects. Most obviously and paradoxically, they tend to label blacks as racist for refusing to vote on grounds of racial solidarity. They also leave unexplored the reasons why so many whites have been so enthusiastic about Obama and what that enthusiasm reveals about contemporary white views of African American life. As noted above, I contend that it is precisely this enthusiasm that gives many black Americans pause when it comes to the presidential candidacy of Senator Obama. If whites love Obama because around him they do not have to feel guilty about slavery and segregation, what does that say about their willingness to confront America's racist past and its contemporary legacies? Most importantly for the purposes of this essay, the arguments of Patterson and others fail to account for the diversity of black life in contemporary America and the extent to which that diversity calls into question the idea that all blacks have similar experiences. Patterson's romanticized view of the inclusiveness enforced by the one-drop rule not only fails to mention the history of tensions between native-born blacks and Caribbean immigrants in American life but also leaves unexplored the ways in which different groups of blacks conceive of their racial identity in different ways in contemporary America.

In short, the case of Barack Obama illustrates, at the level of presidential politics, the ways in which the idea of a newly diverse black population has been developed in contrast to traditional ideas about African American life. Representing both African immigration and mixed-race identity, Obama symbolizes a diasporic view of African American life that parallels, from within the United States, challenges to the hegemonic role of black Americans in global conceptualizations of blackness. His prominence also highlights the importance of black diversity in America and some of the political implications of that diversity.

The Obama example also raises the question of intersections between diversity and social status among different black communities in the United States.[49] A walk through black immigrant neighborhoods like Washington Heights or the South Bronx in New York, or Little Haiti in Miami, would quickly divest anyone of the notion that their inhabitants constitute a social elite. At the same time, black immigrants have frequently done better than native-born African Americans (and for that matter many American whites) in educational and professional endeavors. A June 2004 *New York Times* article noted that the majority of black students at Harvard University are the children of either immigrants or biracial couples, for example.[50] In researching the ethnic and racial attitudes of the children of black immigrants in New York, sociologist Mary C. Waters found that the more upwardly mobile and successful were more likely to identify as West Indian, whereas those less well-off tended to view themselves more as black Americans. Whereas the new black diversity offers a broader range of choices of racial identity, these choices may also be pegged to new class and status hierarchies.[51]

Distinctions between immigrant and native-born blacks are hardly the only fault lines in contemporary African American society. Gender is at least as significant, if not more so: some elite universities have black population ratios that are three-to-one female, for example. Nonetheless, the increasing diversity of black America and its championing by theorists of diaspora has profound implications for the nature of blackness in the twenty-first century. Both theory and demography suggest a refutation of the one-drop rule and a redefinition of who is (and is not) black in the United States. This process fits into broader trends in American society and the place of race therein. A broad consensus exists among historians that race is central to American life and that the nature of racial identity, inclusion, and exclusion has changed over time. In particular, historians of "whiteness" have argued that being white is a social, not a biological or even phenotypical, characteristic and have pointed to the success of European immigrants in changing their status from nonwhite to white as a part of their integration into American society.[52] More recently, some scholars have argued that what applied to Irish, Italian, and Jewish immigrants in the nineteenth and early twentieth centuries may apply to Asian and Latino immigrants today—that they may be undergoing similar processes of acculturation that enable them in effect to claim white status.[53]

Of course, whiteness cannot exist without blackness, and a central tenet of whiteness theory claims that immigrant successes have come at the expense of African Americans, condemned by their history to serve as the template of the racialized Other in the United States. From this perspective, the increasing integration of immigrants into contemporary society may not translate into the decline of racial difference in general, but on the contrary may simply reinforce the exclusion of blacks from the mainstream of American life. As one author puts it, "Paradoxically, America can become more multicultural without becoming less racist."[54]

If this is so, where does this leave black immigrants? One possibility is a kind of flight from blackness: if whiteness is a social category that can be claimed by Latinos and Asians, why cannot some blacks claim it as well? Those most in a position to do so are precisely those who have traditionally stood on the margins of black life in America: immigrants and those of mixed racial heritage. Several scholars have noted a tendency among Afro-Caribbean and African immigrants to distinguish themselves from native-born African Americans as a way of escaping the traditional stigma associated with black skin in the United States. As historian Eric Foner has observed: "Historically every immigrant group has jumped over native-born blacks.... The final irony would be if African immigrants did it too."[55] The rise of a mixed-race movement (of those with both black and white ancestry) that claims an identity distinct from that of African Americans also fits into this trend.[56] To the extent that members of both groups, and their descendants, are able to achieve greater integration into American society, this suggests less the rise of a hybrid African American population and more a new Creolization of America, in which the black/white divide is replace by a hierarchical continuum that relegates blacks without claims to immigrant or mixed-race status to the margins of society. As sociologist Herbert Gans argues:

> If current trends persist, today's multiracial hierarchy could be replaced by what I think of as a dual or bimodal one consisting of "nonblack" and "black" population categories, with a third, "residual," category for the groups that do not, or do not yet, fit into the basic dualism.
>
> More important, this hierarchy may be based not just on color or other visible bodily features, but also on a distinction between undeserving and deserving, or stigmatized and respectable, races. The hierarchy is new only insofar as the old white–nonwhite dichotomy may be replaced by a nonblack–black one, but it is hardly new for blacks, who are likely to remain at the bottom once again.[57]

At the same time, the desire of both immigrant blacks and those of mixed-race ancestry to assert distinct identities has often constituted a response to a perceived rejection by mainstream African American communities. Just as the emphasis on the global diaspora in part reflects a challenge to the idea of the black American experience as a normative standard of blackness, so does the assertion of diasporic diversity in the United States call into question traditions of black identity at home. Black immigrants and mixed-race individuals have frequently experienced having their status as blacks called into question by both whites and African Americans. As one professor of Egyptian origin noted:

> White Americans ... perhaps following the dictum of "divide and conquer," imply, in veiled conversation, that we Africans and Caribbeans are different from African Americans. In the minds of many, we are cut from a better cloth and should keep away from the "black sheep" of our own race. Our accent is foreign to Black as well as White America and our religions are not limited to the dominant religion of Black America (i.e., Christianity). These linguistic and religious differences have been used to separate us from members of our own race of African Americans. If we are too successful and live in nice White neighborhoods, then we are accused by African Americans of betraying our race, being "Black Bourgeois" and wanting to be White. For White neighbors, we are safe because we are Blacks from Africa and the Caribbean, not from the South or Brooklyn and, to their stereotypic way of thinking, we do not do drugs or alcohol or have big late night parties. To African Americans, we remain outsiders even when our experience and expertise are needed.[58]

Such testimonies underscore the fact that the heart of the diasporic project, both domestically and globally, has always been to render ideas of blackness and black community as inclusive as possible. The rise of a more diverse black population in America has resulted from significant improvements in the nation's racial climate, most notably the increasing acceptance of interracial relationships and the decline of racism in immigration policy. Yet the fact that such changes could both promote greater tolerance and at the same time create new racial hierarchies (with more than a passing resemblance to the old) testifies eloquently to the enduring significance of race in American life.

To conclude, the emphasis on diasporic and global perspectives has been a centerpiece of scholarship by and about blacks in the United States for several decades. The rise of a postmodern school of diaspora studies has emphasized more supple and cosmopolitan conceptions of blackness, rejecting essentialism in favor of interchange and hybridity. It has moved away from the idea of Africa as the original fount of black culture, and at the same time has challenged the belief that African Americans represent the gold standard of blacks as racialized minority communities.

As I have tried to show in this chapter, such a position is intimately connected to a new emphasis on the diversity of black populations in the United States and has both positive and negative aspects. It, of course, provides a much more sophisticated understanding not just of blackness but also of race and American identity in general. At the same time, in the context of America's continuing inability to construct a truly multiracial society or to deal conclusively with its own history as a slaveholding republic, it offers the possibility of rendering invisible those aspects of black life most difficult to integrate into standard popular narratives of American history. In this case, globalization offers both individuals and societies the ability to choose the racial communities with which they are most comfortable. If one does not like the black community inherited from the past, one can, as Bertolt Brecht suggested more than fifty years ago, simply choose another.[59]

NOTES

1. Malcolm X, with Alex Haley, *The Autobiography of Malcolm X* (New York: Ballantine Books, 1999). See also Adi Hakim and Marika Sherwood, *Pan African History: Political Figures from Africa and the Diaspora since 1787* (New York: Routledge, 2003); James A. Tyner, *The Geography of Malcolm X: Black Radicalism and the Remaking of American Space* (New York: Routledge, 2006).

2. See, for example, Uta Poiger, *Jazz, Rock, and Rebels: Cold War Politics and American Culture in a Divided Germany* (Berkeley: University of California Press, 2000); and Brenda Gayle Plummer, *Rising Wind: Black Americans and U.S. Foreign Affairs, 1935–1968* (Chapel Hill: University of North Carolina Press, 1996); Mary L. Dudziak, *Cold War Civil Rights: Race and the Image of American Democracy* (Princeton: Princeton University Press, 2000); Tyler Stovall, *Paris Noir: African Americans in the City of Light* (Boston: Houghton Mifflin, 1996); Penny Von Eschen, *Race against Empire: Black Americans and Anticolonialism, 1937–1957* (Ithaca, NY: Cornell University Press, 1997); and *Satchmo Blows Up the World: Jazz Ambassadors Play the Cold War* (Cambridge, MA: Harvard University Press, 2004).

3. On blacks and immigration, see Steven Shulman, ed., *The Impact of Immigration on African Americans* (New Brunswick, NJ: Transaction, 2004); Daniel S. Hammermesh and Frank D. Bean, eds., *Help or Hindrance: The Economic Implications for African Americans* (New York: Russell Sage Foundation, 1998); and Roger Waldinger, *Still the Promised City: African-Americans and New Immigrants in Postindustrial New York* (Cambridge, MA: Harvard University Press, 1996). On blacks and globalization, see Clarence Lusane, *Race in the Global Era: African Americans at the Crossroads* (Boston: South End Press, 1997); Cecilia Conrad et al., eds., *African Americans in the U.S. Economy* (Lanham, MD: Rowman & Littlefield, 2005).

4. Three examples include the Department of African American and African Diaspora Studies at Indiana University, the Program in African American and Diaspora Studies at Vanderbilt University, and the Program in African, African American, and Diaspora Studies at Wheaton College.

5. "Tasked with Turning the Tide," *San Francisco Chronicle*, April 15, 2007. It is perhaps no accident that a city with such small black representation should choose to create as a symbol of black culture an institution focusing on diaspora. See Albert Broussard, *Black San Francisco: The Struggle for Racial Equality in the West, 1900–1954* (Lawrence: University Press of Kansas, 1993); Douglas Henry Daniels, *Pioneer Urbanites: A Social and Cultural History of Black San Francisco* (Philadelphia: Temple University Press, 1980).

6. Paul Gilroy, *The Black Atlantic: Modernity and Double Consciousness* (Cambridge, MA: Harvard University Press, 1993); John Cullen Gruesser, *Confluences: Postcolonialism, African American Literary Studies, and the Black Atlantic* (Athens: University of Georgia Press, 2005).

7. "Paris Is Burning" conference, Museum of the African Diaspora, San Francisco, May 2006.

8. Earl Lewis, "To Turn as on a Pivot: Writing African Americans into a History of Overlapping Diasporas," *American Historical Review* (June 1995) 765–87; Larry Ross, *African American Jazz in the Diaspora* (Lewiston, NY: E. Mellen, 2003); Heike Raphael-Hernandez, ed., *Blackening Europe: The African American Presence* (New York: Routledge, 2004).

9. Harry Johnston, *The Negro in the New World* (New York: Macmillan, 1910).

10. W. E. B. Du Bois, *The Negro* (1915; New York: Oxford University Press, 2007).

11. Melville Herskovits, *The Myth of the Negro Past* (New York: Harper, 1941).

12. Jerry Gershenhorn, *Melville J. Herskovits and the Racial Politics of Knowledge* (Lincoln: University of Nebraska Press, 2004); Anthony M. Platt, *E. Franklin Frazier Reconsidered* (New Brunswick, NJ: Rutgers University Press, 1991).

13. As Stéphane Dufoix notes, the term had already been used by some in this connection earlier, especially in making links between Jewish and black history; Stéphane Dufoix, *Diasporas* (Paris: Presses Universitaires de France, 2003).

14. George Shepperson, "'Pan-Africanism and Pan-Africanism': Some Historical Notes," *Phylon* 23, no. 4 (1962) 346–58; "The African Diaspora—or the African Abroad," *African Forum* 2 (1976) 76–93; "The Afro-American Contribution to African Studies," *Journal of American Studies* 8, no. 3 (1975) 281–303.

15. Joseph Harris, ed., *Global Dimensions of the African Diaspora* (Washington, DC: Howard University Press, 1993), 3–4, cited in Dwayne E. Williams, "Rethinking the African Diaspora: A Comparative Look at Race and Identity in a Transatlantic Community, 1878–1921," in *Crossing Boundaries: Comparative History of Black People in Diaspora*, edited by Darlene Clark Hine and Jacqueline McLeod (Bloomington: Indiana University Press, 1999), 108.

16. M. Ron Karenga, *Kwanzaa: Origin, Concepts, Practice* (San Diego: Kawaida, 1977); Keith Mayes, "'A Holiday of Our Own': Kwanzaa, Cultural Nationalism, and the Promotion of a Black Power Holiday, 1966–1985," in *The Black Power Movement: Rethinking the Civil Rights–Black Power Era*, edited by Peniel E. Joseph, 229–50 (New York: Routledge, 2006); William Van Deburg, *New Day in Babylon: The Black Power Movement and American Culture, 1965–1975* (Chicago: University of Chicago Press, 1992).

17. Frederick Cooper, "Race, Ideology, and the Perils of Comparative History," *American Historical Review* 101, no. 4 (1996); Paul Lovejoy, "The African Diaspora: Revisionist Interpretations of Ethnicity, Culture, and Religion under Slavery," *Studies in the World History of Slavery, Abolition and Emancipation* 2, no. 1 (1997).

18. *The Birth of African-American Culture: An Anthropological Perspective* (Boston: Beacon Press, 1992).

19. Patricia Hill Collins, *From Black Power to Hip Hop: Racism, Nationalism, and Feminism* (Philadelphia: Temple University Press, 2006); Beverly Guy-Sheftall, ed., *Words of Fire: An Anthology of African American Feminist Thought* (New York: W. W. Norton, 1995).

20. See Gilroy, *Black Atlantic*, on this point.

21. Molefi Kete Asante, *The Afrocentric Idea* (Philadelphia: Temple University Press, 1998); Stephen Howe, *Afrocentrism: Mythical Pasts and Imagined Homes* (London: Verso, 1998); Algernon Austin, *Achieving Blackness: Race, Black Nationalism, and Afrocentrism in the Twentieth Century* (New York: New York University Press, 2006).

22. Stuart Hall, "Cultural Identity and Diaspora," in *Identity: Community, Culture, Difference*, edited by Jonathan Rutherford (London: Lawrence & Wishart, 1990), 235.

23. Tiffany Ruby Patterson and Robin D. G. Kelley, "Unfinished Migrations: Reflections on the African Diaspora and the Making of the Modern World," *African Studies Review* 43, no. 1 (April 2000) 11–45; Sidney J. LeMelle and Robin D. G. Kelley, eds., *Imagining Home: Class, Culture, and Nationalism in the African Diaspora* (London: Verso, 1994).

24. Examples of this rapidly growing literature include Allison Blakely, *Blacks in the Dutch World* (Bloomington: Indiana University Press, 2003); Sue Peabody, *"There Are No Slaves in France": The Political Economy of Race and Slavery in the Ancien Regime* (New York: Oxford University Press, 2006); Gretchen Gerzina, *Black London: Life before Emancipation* (New Brunswick, NJ: Rutgers University Press, 1995); James Winders, *Paris Africain* (New York: Palgrave Macmillan, 2006); Tyler Stovall, "Race and the Making of the Nation: Blacks in Modern France," in *Diasporic Africa: A Reader*, edited by Michael A. Gomez 200–18 (New York: New York University Press, 2006).

25. Joseph Harris, *The African Presence in Asia: Consequences of the East African Slave Trade* (Evanston, IL: Northwestern University Press, 1971); Heidi Carolyn Feldman, *Black Rhythms of Peru: Reviving African Musical Heritage in the Black Pacific* (Middletown, CT: Wesleyan University Press, 2006).

26. Arjun Appadurai, *Modernity at Large: Cultural Dimensions of Globalization* (Minneapolis: University of Minnesota Press, 1996); Saskia Sassen, *Globalization and Its Discontents* (New York: New Press, 1998); Aihwa Ong, *Flexible Citizenship: The Cultural Logics of Transnationalism* (Durham, NC: Duke University Press, 1999); Steven Weber, ed., *Globalization and the European Political Economy* (New York: Columbia University Press, 2001); Linda Basch, Nina Glick Schiller, and Christina Szanton Blanc, *Nations Unbound: Transnational Projects, Postcolonial Predicaments, and Deterritorialized Nation-States*. Langhorne, PA: Gordon & Breach, 1994); Robin Cohen and Steven Vertovec, eds., *Migration, Diaspora, and Transnationalism* (Northampton, UK: Edward Elgar, 1999).

27. Jacqueline Nassy Brown, *Dropping Anchor, Setting Sail: Geographies of Race in Black Liverpool* (Princeton, NJ: Princeton University Press, 2005).

28. Houston A. Baker Jr., Manthia Diawara, and Ruth H. Lindeborg, *Black British Cultural Studies: A Reader* (Chicago: University of Chicago Press, 1996).

29. Edouard Glissant, *Caribbean Discourse: Selected Essays*, translated by J. Michael Dash (Charlottesville: University Press of Virginia, 1989); Jean Bernabé, Patrick Chamoiseau, and Raphaël Confiant, *Eloge de la creolité* (Paris: Gallimard, 1989); Maryse Condé and Madelaine Cottenot-Hage, *Penser la creolité* (Paris: Karthala, 1995); Shireen K. Lewis, *Race, Culture, and Identity: Francophone West African and Caribbean Literature and Theory from Negritude to Creolité* (Lanham, MD: Lexington Books, 2006).

30. On Caribbean immigrants in Britain, see, among others, Peter Fryer, *Staying Power: The History of Black People in Britain* (London: Pluto Press, 1984); Laura Tabili, *We Ask for British Justice: Workers and Racial Difference in Late Imperial Britain* (Ithaca, NY: Cornell University Press, 1994).

31. Ch. Didier Gondola, "'But I Ain't African, I'm American!': Black American Exiles and the Construction of Racial Identities in Twentieth-Century France," in *Blackening Europe: The African American Presence*, edited by Heike Raphael-Hernandez, 201–16 (New York: Routledge, 2004).

32. Judith Byfield, "Rethinking the African Diaspora," *African Studies Review* 43, no. 1 (April 2000): 6.

33. Jesse D. McKinnon and Claudette E. Bennett, *We the People: Blacks in the United States* (Washington, DC: U.S. Department of Commerce, 2005); "More Africans Enter United States than in Days of Slavery," *New York Times*, February 21, 2005.

34. David Hollinger, *Postethnic America: Beyond Multiculturalism* (New York: Basic Books, 1995); Jennifer D. Lee and Frank D. Bean, "America's Changing Color Lines: Immigration, Race/Ethnicity, and Multiracial Identification," *Annual Review of Sociology* 30 (2004) 221–42; Joel Perlmann and Mary C. Waters, eds., *The New Race Question: How the Census Counts Multiracial Individuals* (New York: Russell Sage, 2002).

35. Jennifer Lee, Frank D. Bean, Jeanne Batalova, and Sabeen Sandhu, "Immigration and the Black-White Color Line in the United States," in *The Impact of Immigration on African Americans*, edited by Steven Shulman (New Brunswick, NJ: Transaction, 2004), 38–41.

36. "Breaking through Adoption's Racial Barriers," *New York Times*, August 17, 2006; Randall Kennedy, *Interracial Intimacies: Sex, Marriage, Identity and Adoption* (New York: Vintage, 2004); Barbara Rothman, *Weaving a Family: Untangling Race and Adoption* (Boston: Beacon, 2005).

37. Naomi Zack, ed., *American Mixed Race: The Culture of Microdiversity* (Lanham, MD: Rowman & Littlefield, 1995); Jon Michael Spencer, *The New Colored People: The Mixed Race Movement in America* (New York: New York University Press, 1997); Kathleen Korgen, *From Black to Biracial: Transforming Racial Identity among Americans* (Westport, CT: Praeger, 1998); David L. Brunsma, ed., *Mixed Messages: Multiracial Identities in the "Color-blind" Era* (Boulder, CO: Lynne Rienner, 2006); Carol Camper, ed., *Miscegenation Blues: Voices of Mixed Race Women* (Toronto: Sister Vision, 1994).

38. Avtah Brah and Annie E. Coombes, eds., *Hybridity and Its Discontents: Politics, Science, Culture* (London: Routledge, 2000); Marwan Kraidy, *Hybridity, or the Cultural Logic of Globalization* (Philadelphia: Temple University Press, 2005); Pnina Werbner and Tariq Modood, eds., *Debating Cultural Hybridity: Multicultural Identities and the Politics of Anti-racism* (London: Zed Books, 1997).

39. Joe Klein, "Why Barack Obama Could Be the Next President," *Time*, October 23, 2006.

40. Lynne Norment, "The Hottest Couple in America," *Ebony*, February 2007.

41. For example, see Tamar Jacoby, ed., *Reinventing the Melting Pot: The New Immigrants and What It Means to Be American* (New York: Basic Books, 2003).

42. Kenneth T. Walsh, "Talkin' 'bout My Generation," *U.S. News and World Report*, December 31, 2006.

43. Rachel L. Swarns, "So Far, Obama Can't Take Black Vote for Granted," *New York Times*, February 2, 2007.

44. Kathleen Parker, "From Selma to Obama," *San Francisco Chronicle*, March 5, 2007.

45. Eugene Robinson, "Tokenism, Not Diversity, Marked GOP," *San Francisco Chronicle*, November 14, 2006; Gayle T. Tate and Lewis A. Randolph, eds., *Dimensions of Black Conservatism in the United States: Made in America* (New York: Palgrave, 2002); Manning Marable, "Black Conservatives," in *Speaking Truth to Power: Essays on Race, Resistance, and Radicalism*, 62–68 (Boulder, CO: Westview Press, 1996).

46. Swarns, "So Far."

47. For example, no one argued that Obama should be regarded as white (or for that matter even mixed-race), even though one could make a good case, on both biological and cultural grounds, for doing so. I argue that this reveals not

just the strength of traditional views of race in American society but also a tremendous political and emotional investment in being able to point to Obama as a desirable black candidate for president. On the history of the one-drop rule, see David Hollinger, *Cosmopolitanism and Solidarity: Studies in Ethnoracial, Religious, and Professional Affiliation in the United States* (Madison: University of Wisconsin Press, 2006).

48. Orlando Patterson, "The New Black Nativism," *Time*, February 8, 2007. The issue of distinguishing between those blacks whose ancestors came to America as slaves and those enslaved elsewhere (many Africans and virtually all Caribbean immigrants) is an important one. I would defend this distinction, not because American slavery was worse than elsewhere (many historians argue the contrary), but because those enslaved elsewhere came to America as free immigrants and can easily be integrated into a discourse, so popular in American life, of fleeing oppression elsewhere to find freedom here. By contrast, those whose ancestors were American slaves hardly fit the mold of America as the Land of the Free. Moreover, there is the question of America's responsibility for slavery practiced upon its territory. This issue has surfaced in particular in debates over the question of reparations for African Americans. See Ronald P. Salzberger and Mary C. Turck, eds., *Reparations for Slavery: A Reader* (Lanham, MD: Rowman & Littlefield, 2004), and Alfred Brophy, *Reparations: Pro and Con* (New York: Oxford University Press, 2006).

49. For example, Patterson and others have argued that one source of black reluctance to endorse Senator Obama springs from the perception that he is too middle class, and thus too white. Given that Sharpton and the Reverend Jesse Jackson Jr. have had no problem endorsing politicians such as Julian Bond, former Virginia governor Douglas Wilder, and many others who are every bit as middle class, this argument strikes me as off the mark. However, it does highlight a perceived link between black diversity and social class that is significant. See Patterson, "New Black Nativism."

50. See Shilpa Banerji, "Black Immigrant Study Puts Spotlight Back on Affirmative Action Debate," *Diverse Issues in Higher Education*, February 22, 2007.

51. Mary C. Waters, "Ethnic and Racial Identities of Second-Generation Black Immigrants in New York City," in *The New Second Generation*, edited by Alejandro Portes, 171–96 (New York: Russell Sage Foundation, 1996).

52. David Roediger, *The Wages of Whiteness* (New York: Verso, 1991); Noel Ignatiev, *How the Irish Became White* (New York: Routledge, 1995); Karen Brodkin, *How Jews Became White Folks and What That Says about Race in America* (New Brunswick, NJ: Rutgers University Press, 1998).

53. Frank D. Bean and Gillian Sevens, *America's Newcomers and the Dynamics of Diversity* (New York: Russell Sage Foundation, 2003); Gerald D. Jaynes, ed., *Immigration and Race: New Challenges for American Democracy* (New York: Russell Sage Foundation, 2000); Mia Tuan, *Forever Foreigners or Honorary Whites? The Asian Ethnic Experience Today* (New Brunswick, NJ: Rutgers University Press, 1998).

54. Steven Shulman, ed., *The Impact of Immigration on African Americans* (New Brunswick, NJ: Transaction, 2004), xi.

55. *New York Times*, "More Africans Enter United States."

56. As Katya Gibel Azoulay has noted, "Instituting 'multiracial' as an alternative to unscientific homogenous race categories or hyphenated pseudoethnic classifications threatens to resurrect the ghosts of color-based divisions within the Black community, never entirely erased even during the era of Black Power and Black Consciousness"; Katya Gibel Azoulay, *Black, Jewish, and Interracial: It's Not the*

Color of Your Skin, but the Race of Your Kin, and Other Myths of Identity (Durham, NC: Duke University Press, 1997), 5.

57. Herbert J. Gans, "The Possibility of a New Racial Hierarchy in the Twenty-First-Century United States," in *The Cultural Territory of Race: Black and White Boundaries*, edited by Michèle Lamont (Chicago: University of Chicago Press, 1999), 371.

58. Mohammed Aman, foreword to *Foreign-Born African Americans: Silenced Voices in the Discourse on Race*, edited by Festus E. Obiakor and Patrick A. Grant (New York: Nova Science, 2002), xiii.

59. Bertolt Brecht, *Poems 1913–1956*, eds. John Willett and Ralph Manheim (London: Methven, 1976), 440.

CHAPTER 4

Racial Politics and Racial Theory in the Twenty-First-Century United States

Howard Winant

In a time when the racial ideology of "color blindness" has achieved vast popular currency, yet manifest disparities in what Max Weber called "life-chances" persist along racial lines, how do U.S. citizens of various racial identities manage the disparate and contradictory meanings of race?

W. E. B. Du Bois famously identified "double consciousness" as a feature of black identity: "One ever feels his [sic] twoness—an American, a Negro; two warring souls, two thoughts, two unreconciled strivings; two warring ideals in one dark body, whose dogged strength alone keeps it from being torn asunder."[1] Double consciousness was a problem both of theory and practice. Like other issues in pragmatist thought, it was based in the concept of *self-reflective action*.[2]

The great merit of pragmatism—this uniquely American body of philosophical thought—is its attentiveness to agency-in-context, which can be seen as remarkably democratic. In repudiating Cartesian mind-world dualism and insisting, from the work of Charles Sanders Peirce onward, that the sentient mind always finds itself already in the social world, pragmatism already had brought a hefty dose of materialism to philosophy by the 1870s. In recognizing the complexities of the social structuring of the self, pragmatism developed the basic template of social psychology by the 1920s.[3] In George Herbert Mead's view, and in many ways in the views of William James and Peirce as well, human beings possess self-directed sensibilities that they deploy in myriad social interactions, mindful of the social contexts in which they are situated. Creating and managing one's own self occurs under a formidable series of constraints, to be sure; it is a sporadic, and never completed, process, and it involves internalizing a great deal of the outside world, the "Others." Yet some basic aspect of this process involves the recognition of an "I": never completely present, this nominative aspect of the self is still "in charge," managing, navigating not only in the social world but also in the inner, inculturated, socialized world within the head and heart of each individual.[4]

The democratic implications, the democratic potentialities, of this framework are significant. At its most open, this perspective urges the political agency of all human subjects; it grants "voice"—or the possibility of achieving it—to each individual, the lowly as well as the elite.[5] In fact, it rejects the usual elitism of social science and political philosophy—that the masses of humans are politically disengaged, indeed almost entirely so. C. Wright Mills famously declared in *White Collar*:

> We are now in a situation in which many who are disengaged from prevailing allegiances have not acquired new ones, and so are distracted from and inattentive to political concerns of any kind. They are strangers to politics. They are not radical, not liberal, not conservative, not reactionary; they are inactionary; they are out of it. If we accept the Greeks' definition of the idiot as a privatized man, then we must conclude that the US citizenry is now largely composed of idiots.[6]

Despite the attractions of such a perspective today—when reality TV, Fox News, *American Idol*, and *Project Runway* dominate the airwaves in a U.S. version of the "bread and circuses" atmosphere of the Roman Empire, I argue against this view here, specifically rejecting it in respect to racial matters. I suggest that race is operating in a far more engaged way—that for Americans it is far more "present," so to speak, than the comments by Mills would imply.

Hence a return to pragmatist social and political theory. At the level of experience and identity (the "microsocial") and at the level of collective action, states, and social structures (the "macrosocial"), we should apply a pragmatist perspective to the task of understanding the contradictions of race and racism that beset the United States today. The approach to be adopted has a long tradition, going back to the work of Du Bois and Alain Locke; it is deeply grounded in the work of Peirce and William James, and it continues into the present epoch through the Chicago tradition in sociology, the symbolic interactionism of Herbert Blumer and radical racial pragmatism of Cornel West, critical race theory,[7] and racial formation theory.[8] Social structurally, politically, and indeed experientially, the race concept is in crisis today. A good deal of energy goes into navigating its contradictions, I submit. This is an effort that is political with both a small and a large "*p*": race still structures the national political (big "*P*") arena, operating in the electoral arena, with respect to the welfare state, immigration, and innumerable other issues. At the same time race shapes *the politics of the social*, the politics of the personal. The amount of everyday attention drawn to racial matters is itself a product of the post–World War II racial crisis and the wave of racial reforms enacted in the 1960s.[9]

DOUBLE CONSCIOUSNESS AND PRAGMATISM

What was "double consciousness" in 1903, when *Souls* appeared? At the turn of the twentieth century, racial theory was still immured in biologistic approaches to race—social Darwinist, Spencerian, and so on. The world-system was at the apogee of colonialism or, should I say, at its nadir: in the Congo, Putumayo, the Rand, "orientalism," and the Raj. The British-French encounter at Fashoda and the Congress of Berlin were still recent events. In the United States, the *Plessy* decision (1896) and Booker T. Washington's capitulation to Jim Crow in the Atlanta Exposition speech (1895) expressed the state of official "race relations." At the level of everyday life, the United States was a racial dictatorship, a despotic regime especially (but not only) in the South, where 88 percent of black people lived in 1903. The southern Negro of whom Du Bois was writing in 1903 was greatly constrained by this situation, forced to live within a submissive and defensive racial consciousness. In a flat-out racial dictatorship, subordination was a life-or-death matter: one risked one's life by speaking out of turn or offending a white, no matter how ignorant or illiterate that white might be.

This was the atmosphere to which Du Bois's pragmatism, his concepts of "the veil" and "double consciousness," were addressed. Black Americans had to "navigate" just to survive. But how to do so? Of course, for many there was little contact with whites, mercifully little chance to incur the displeasure and possible violence of the "ruling race." But most black people could not avoid whites entirely. In their work—in the fields and the domestic service that were the allotted toil of many—in the public space of street or store, even under conditions of the most intense segregation, it was inevitable to encounter whites.

What were the rules of interracial engagement, so to speak? Always remove one's hat in the presence of a white, never speak unless spoken to, step off the sidewalk (if there was a sidewalk) into the muddy street when a white passed, never use the white person's given name, only "sir," or "ma'am." Always defer. Of course, the rules of white supremacist etiquette were not so consistent, not so knowable, as this may imply; much was arbitrary, unpredictable, cranky.[10] But not to follow the rules, not to defer, was to be "uppity," to risk the most severe sanction. To know the rules meant to think like a white, to see one's black self through (hypothetical) white eyes, to anticipate the expectations of whites. It meant, in short, to "introject" whiteness into one's black self.[11] But naturally one remained a black American: one's "I"—to invoke the pragmatist model of the self developed by Mead in the 1920s and 1930s—was not whitened.[12] Even one's "me"—the self one presents to others in Mead's conceptualization—remained fully black. It was the "generalized other"—the socialized and regulated self, the ruled self—that was penetrated by white supremacy and white power.

By internalizing whiteness, one collaborated with this contamination of the self. But this dualism was not merely capitulation; it was also strategic. It was contradictory, unresolved, creative, and intelligent, and simultaneously debilitating. One might subordinate oneself, but one also lived to tell the tale; one survived by knowing whites intimately.[13] And although I have placed Du Bois's conception in the framework of Mead, let me note that Du Bois produced the "double consciousness" model decades before Mead's theory of the self appeared.[14]

This contradiction, this dialectic of racial doubling, cannot be resolved by a higher synthesis. No Hegelian *aufhebung* will reconcile the "unreconciled strivings" of which Du Bois speaks. Thus, by necessity, Du Bois's archetypal Negro/American was engaged in self-reflective racial action—struggling not only with a despotic and segregated society but with his (or her) *internally* unintegrated self in the Jim Crow America of 1900. After all, the Reconstruction amendments and civil rights laws of the 1870s, and indeed most of the political legacy of Reconstruction, had been wiped out. The racial order in turn-of-the-twentieth-century America (especially in the South) was based on debt peonage: an improved and modernized version of slavery.

As an advocate of political engagement with this state of affairs—as an opponent of Booker T. Washington's resignation before the monolith of white supremacy (and later as an opponent of Marcus Garvey's refusal to engage the national political complex of Jim Crow), Du Bois saw in double consciousness not only a micro-level or tacit and experientially oriented politics of race, something merely defensive or survival oriented. No, he also saw in it a potential macro-level politics of race that both sought inclusion, equality, and full rights of citizenship (especially the franchise) and simultaneously upheld a collective black identity, a self-determinist and quasi-"nationalist" politics.[15] In his combination of radical democracy and socialism, on the one hand, and pan-Africanism and advocacy of collective economic development and education, on the other, Du Bois addresses double consciousness as an eminently political, social movement-oriented, collective phenomenon.[16]

So Du Bois's work on double consciousness and the veil and his insistence on the centrality of a political understanding of race and on the importance of political activism in combating racial injustice were the key axes of his radical pragmatism. He was followed by Alain Locke, another monumental race theorist—a Harvard Ph.D., Rhodes scholar, and committed pragmatist—who in 1916 delivered a series of prescient lectures on race theory at Howard University[17] and went on to play a major role in the Harlem Renaissance and black intellectual life more generally. Then, at the University of Chicago from the late 1920s on, pragmatist analyses of race and discrimination (the word *racism* did not yet exist) were developed by sociologists led by Robert Park and his students (who included E. Franklin Frazier, Charles S. Johnson, Oliver C. Cox, and numerous other illustrious sociologists of race). Still later, Herbert Blumer, a student of Mead's at Chicago, studied the dynamics of prejudice and discrimination using a social psychological approach based in pragmatist insights. Space is not available here to address all these contributions, but it is worth noting that the tradition of radical activist scholarship on race, founded in good measure by Du Bois and continued (or rediscovered) in the "Chicago School" of sociology, has maintained its influence down to today.[18]

DOUBLE CONSCIOUSNESS IN THE POST–CIVIL RIGHTS ERA

Fast forward to the present. A century after the publication of *Souls*, North Americans face different versions of these dualities and contradictions. We are embarked on the racial journey of the "post–civil rights era," the supposedly color-blind age of the twenty-first century. If in 1900 African Americans were struggling both to be "race men" (or "race women") and to exercise their democratic rights as fully fledged American citizens under the Thirteenth, Fourteenth, and Fifteenth Amendments, today in 2006 similar dilemmas confront North Americans where race is concerned.

It is not just black people that confront these dilemmas. The enormous post–World War II racial "break" with the business-as-usual system of American apartheid has disrupted all racial identities, just as it interrupted a political system fundamentally premised on the exclusion of racial minorities.[19] Spurred by the civil rights movement and its allies and institutionalized by the reforms in state racial policy achieved during the 1960s, double consciousness ceased to be largely a "black thing." It became a societywide thing as individuals of all racial identities, as well as institutions with remodeled racial constituencies, practices, and personnel, sought to operate in a racially reformed "lifeworld."

Of course, the civil rights upsurge and reforms it achieved, monumental as they were, were also and necessarily inadequate to the Herculean task of transforming the system of white supremacy that was a fundamental component of the sociopolitical structure of the United States. Therefore racial dualism—double consciousness, the veil, the whole apparatus of structural racism—survived alongside the new racial reforms. Reform was not revolution; it was an uneven and vulnerable political process, subject to reversals of various types, and in some areas—notably residential segregation[20] and the distribution of wealth[21]—remarkably impervious to political pressure. Rather than undertaking the substantive task of redistribution, rather than forthrightly addressing the "dream" (Dr. King's dream, let's say) that the United States would break definitively with its history of racial despotism and embrace a thoroughgoing racial democracy, reform was accompanied by reaction. Repressive policies underwrote it in significant ways: law-and-order rhetoric poured forth as an effective right-wing "code" for perpetuating racism; imprisonment rates shot up for blacks and browns; racial profiling became a fine art. Shepherded by the New Right, anchored in the "Southern strategy," rationalized by neoconservative racial policy that equated the ephemeral problem of "reverse discrimination" with the deeply embedded legacy of structural racism, the dream reverted to a nightmare. Reform is not revolution.

Thus all American individuals, all institutions, all political organizations, and all state agencies found themselves—and still find themselves today—on the horns of a racial dilemma. What is the new meaning of racial identity? How should state racial policy be understood? What patterns of inclusion and exclusion should now prevail? This dilemma, this ongoing crisis—a term famously defined by Antonio Gramsci as a situation in which "the old is dying but the new cannot be born"[22]—continues to describe racial conditions in the post–civil rights era today.

Under these conditions, racial identity continues to embody "unreconciled strivings." Let's think realistically: let's acknowledge the fact that in the twenty-first century *all* Americans must still navigate between the Scylla of ongoing racial inequality[23] and ubiquitous racialization, on the one hand, and the Charybdis of a hegemonic racial ideology of color blindness, on the other. Under such conditions, how could conflicting and contradictory notions of racial identity possibly be avoided? Conscious or unconscious, acknowledged or denied, the racial organization of everyday life is omnipresent: where we live, what work we do, what we eat and what we wear, the language we speak and the idioms we use, the TV channels we watch—in short, nearly every aspect of our daily lives is shaped in crucial ways by race. Such a list of activities could be extended indefinitely. To be without racial identity is impossible in the United States.[24]

Of course, however segmented we are, there is still a national society, a single economy and political system, an overarching national culture. The concept of double consciousness always acknowledged this: "an *American*, a Negro." The veil was always about this: divided within our society, we are also divided within ourselves, held together by our "dogged strength alone."

These characterizations can no longer be applied only to blacks. Today, in the twenty-first century, in the post–civil rights era, half a century after the postwar racial break, they depict the unresolved racial situations in which all Americans find themselves, albeit in very different ways. Today we are all beset by double consciousness, in ways that of course vary tremendously with our racially framed "group position" (as Blumer called it).

Consider some of the key unresolved racial questions that the nation faces: the significance of race (declining or increasing?), the interpretation of racial equality (color-blind or race-conscious?), the institutionalization of racial justice (reverse discrimination or affirmative action?), and the very categories—black, white, Latino/Hispanic, Asian American, and Native American—employed to classify racial groups. These were all called into question as the nation emerged from the civil rights movement "victory" of the mid-1960s. These racial signifiers all remain ambiguous or contradictory today. On the one hand, we cannot escape the racial labels that U.S. society comprehensively assigns to all within it; this has been the fate of Americans since Europeans arrived on these shores. On the other hand, we cannot identify unproblematically or unself-consciously with these designations either, for they are riven—as we ourselves are fissured—to an unprecedented extent by the conflicts and contradictions posed by the political struggles of the past decades. Such is double consciousness in the twenty-first century.

How do these conflicts and contradictions shape the various racial identities available today? With apologies for the necessarily schematic character of the following remarks, I will now survey the contemporary racial "politics of identity." By noting the uncertainties and inconsistencies, the shoals of racial indeterminacy through which all the main racially categorized groups—and the individuals within them—must navigate their fragile craft of racial identity, I seek to emphasize not only the continuity of double consciousness but the ongoing relevance of racial pragmatism. My claim here is that no less as groups than as individuals, no less in twenty-first-century civil society than in the post-civil-rights-era racial state, we must exercise the self-reflective action, the situated creativity,[25] that is the core insight of pragmatism, in order to operate in a racialized world.

DOUBLE CONSCIOUSNESS FOR ALL

With these conditions in mind, let us explore the operations of double consciousness, focusing on the varied circumstances that the main racially defined groups confront in the United States today.[26]

Black Double Consciousness

Forty years after the ambiguous victory of the civil rights movement, what does it mean to be "black"? The decline of the organized black movement in the 1970s, and the wholesale assaults against the welfare state initiated by Ronald Reagan during the 1980s, sharply increased divisions along class and gender lines in the black community.

The divergent experiences of the black elite and the black poor—experiences far more distant from each other than they were in the days of official segregation—undermine the fundamental black nationalist principle of a unitary racial identity. Yet blackness is so salient to everyday experiences of recognition (or misrecognition) that virtually every black person, including every middle-class black, can recall numerous incidents of "profiling," not only by the police but by white civilians: the well-dressed black lawyer handed a coat to check or a bag of garbage to take out at a fancy party in Beverly Hills or on the Upper East Side, the black woman in an evening gown who is given a tip by a white matron in the ladies' room at the opera—such stories are endless.

Divisions along gender lines have also grown sharper, as recent writing by leading black feminists suggests.[27] This pattern may be attributed to many causal factors: heightened rates of imprisonment and ongoing state harassment of black men,[28] differentials in mobility across gender lines,[29] and cultural conflicts[30] all play their part, such that black men's and black women's experiences probably diverge more significantly today than at any other moment since slavery days.

Divisions of class have meant that, in the upper strata of the black community, a portion of the ideal of substantive equality[31] has indeed been achieved—though in the United States, no black person can ever believe her- or himself to be beyond the reach of white supremacy. Meanwhile, the desolation of the poor increases steadily, fueled in part by the very claim that equality (formal equality, that is) has been attained, that we are now a color-blind society, and the like. Such rhetoric attributes black poverty to defects in black motivation, intelligence,[32] or family structure—a strategy of victim-blaming that often takes aim at "underclass" blacks, low-income black women in particular.[33]

Black double consciousness today is not what it was a century ago. In 1903, the duality took the form of noncitizen (black) versus citizen (internalized white). It was framed by the violence and despotism that was the racism of the era. In the twenty-first century, racial despotism is far from eliminated, as is evidenced most notably by the disaster visited upon New Orleans blacks, not by Hurricane Katrina but by the U.S. government in the storm's aftermath.[34] Yet it has unquestionably been ameliorated, especially at the upper levels of the racial stratification hierarchy. The existence of a substantial black middle class, the increased availability of professional white-collar employment, the proliferation of black suburbs,[35] all undermine linkages to traditional white supremacy. The incorporation of black (and allied) movement demands and personnel into the law and the state (as elected officials, notably), all facilitated the transition to a post–civil rights era. These developments also deprived racially based movements for social justice of their momentum and dismissed their radical and redistributive demands in favor of brokered—and mainstream political—compromises.[36]

But the hard fact of black double consciousness remains. The divisions within the black community, and hence within black identity, have always been complex. On the one hand, the emergence of diverse and even conflicting voices in the black community is welcome, for it reflects real changes in the direction of mobility and democratization. On the other hand, the persistence of glaring racial inequality—that is, of an ongoing dimension of white supremacy and racism that pervades the entire society—demands a level of concerted action that division and discord tend to preclude. The legendary political adroitness of the black voter (whose bloc voting for Democrats is but the present stage of long tradition of astute bloc voting behavior)[37] and the well-documented Republican efforts in 2000 and 2004 to suppress black voting testify to the limits of the moderate reforms that initiated the present post–civil rights epoch. Racial dualism and double consciousness persist in the black community, with all their attendant requirements for pragmatist personal and political navigation.

Other "Others"

In the twenty-first century, what does it mean to be "yellow" or "brown"? Before the success of civil rights (and particularly immigration) reforms in the mid-1960s, racialized groups of Asian and Latin American origin experienced very high levels of exclusion and intolerance. After the passage of the Immigration and Nationality Reform Act of 1965 (a major civil rights reform in its own right),[38] these communities began to grow rapidly. Previously isolated in enclaves based on language and national origin, Koreans, Filipinos, Japanese, and Chinese underwent a new "pan-ethnic" racializing process from the late 1960s onward, emerging as "Asian Americans."[39] Accompanying these shifts was significant upward mobility for some—though by no means all—sectors of Asian America.

Similar shifts overtook Mexicans, Puerto Ricans, Central Americans, and even Cubans as the "Latino" and "Hispanic" categories were popularized.[40] For example, the destruction of formal segregation in Texas had a profound impact on Mexican–Americans there.[41] Segregation of Latinos in the upper- and middle-economic strata decreased rapidly across the country (far more rapidly than that of comparable black income earners),[42] and some Latino groups achieved or consolidated solid middle-class status (notably Cubans and to some extent Dominicans). The *barrios*, however, continued to be plagued by immigrant bashing and high levels of poverty that can only be seen as racially organized. The new nativism espoused by Samuel P. Huntington[43] and practiced by various vigilante groups, both on the U.S.-Mexico border and nationwide, has been matched by something unprecedented: the emergence of a mass movement for immigrants' rights. The expanding U.S. Latino/Hispanic population, its degree of political organization, and the very meaning of Latino identity are up for grabs in this conjuncture: How do people see social mobility taking place (assimilationist vs. group-based/nationalist)? To what extent and in what ways do they experience pan-ethnicity? What are their emerging patterns of political adherence (culturally conservative/Republican vs. pro-labor and civil rights-oriented/Democratic)?

Thus, for both Asian Americans and Latinos, contemporary racial identity is fraught with contradictions. Apart from long-standing antagonisms among particular groups—for example, Cubans and Puerto Ricans, or Koreans and Japanese—significant class- and gender-based conflicts exist as well. Tendencies among long-established residents to disparage and sometimes exploit immigrants who are "fresh off the boat," or for group ties to attenuate as social mobility increases, suggest the centrality of class in immigrant life.[44] The liberating possibilities encountered by immigrating women, and their greater proclivity to settle in the United States rather than to return to their countries of origin, suggest the centrality of gender in immigrant life.[45]

Not unlike blacks, Asian Americans and Latinos often find themselves caught between the past and the future. Old forms of racism have resurfaced to confront them, as in the renewed enthusiasm for immigrant bashing and the recurrent waves of anti-Japanese and anti-Chinese paranoia. Discrimination has reappeared, sometimes with regard to new issues, as in controversies over Asian admissions to elite universities.[46] Yet at the same time, the newly pan-ethnicized identities of Asian Americans and Latinos have brought them face-to-face with challenges that are quite distinct from anything confronted in the past. Some examples of these challenges are the dubious gift of neoconservative support (Asians as the "model minority," for example), the antagonism of blacks,[47] and the tendencies toward dilution of specific ethnic/national identities in pan-ethnic/racialized categories created by a combination of "lumping" and political exigency. Often more successful and accepted than in the past, but subject to new antagonisms and new doubts about their status, Asian Americans and Latinos experience their own distinctive forms of double consciousness today.

Native Americans, too, face the question of shifting—and riven—racial identities today. There is ample evidence to indicate that, in the postwar period, Indian nations and individuals as well have come face-to-face with racial dualism. For one thing, the old logic of despoliation still applies: environmental destruction and land rape, neglect, poverty, and cultural assault continue to take their toll. Yet a new activism, evident in struggles over casino wealth, in a profound cultural reemergence, and in strategic political activity, especially in areas where the concentration of Indian voters can swing races (South Dakota, most notably) is also under way. Today Indians have developed techniques for fighting in the courts, for asserting treaty rights, and indeed for regaining a modicum of economic and political control over their tribal destinies that would have been unthinkable a generation ago.[48]

White Double Consciousness

What does it now mean to be white? In the past, white identity (and particularly white male identity) was "normalized"; "Otherness" was elsewhere: among "people of color" and to some extent women. All these were marked by their identities, but under conditions of virtually unchallenged white supremacy, whites (especially white men) were different.

The idea of white privilege, although somewhat unidimensional, captures not only the core meaning of racist practice but also the peculiar Otherness of whites. In the post–civil rights era, color blindness has become a staple of neoconservatism and the political right; not coincidentally, white voters, notably white men, have turned right in great numbers, while voters of color and women across the racial spectrum tend to vote for the Democrats (i.e., the center-left). Color-blind racial ideology protects and validates whites, shepherding their normalized racial identity from the old Jim Crow days to the present postreform era.

In the old days, "white egalitarianism"[49] and "*herrenvolk* Republicanism"[50] were the political price elites had to pay to secure mass electoral support; indeed, that was the organizing principle of nineteenth-century U.S. politics and culture. Only whites (only white men) were full citizens; only they were fully formed individuals. In terms of race and gender, their identities were, so to speak, transparent, which is what we mean by the term *normalized*.

Of course, for a long time, many whites partook of an ethnic Otherness that placed them in an ambiguous relationship with both established white Anglo-Saxon Protestant elites and with racially defined minorities. Although it was romanticized by certain neoconservatives,[51] by the 1960s, white ethnicity was in serious decline. Large-scale European immigration had become a thing of the past. While urban ethnic enclaves continued to exist in many major cities, suburbanization and gentrification had taken their toll. Communal forms of white ethnic identity had been eroded by outmarriage and by heterogeneous contact in schools, workplaces, neighborhoods, and religious settings.[52] White ethnics, white workers, were incorporated en masse into the broad middle class, beginning with the New Deal and culminating after World War II.[53]

Nor were alternative collective identities, other forms of solidarity, readily available to whites. Class-based identities had always been weak in the

United States, and they were particularly debilitated in the wake of the Red-baiting period of the late 1940s and 1950s, the same moment in which the black movement was gathering strength. What remained was the "imagined community" of white racial nationalism: the United States as a "white man's country," and, of course, a considerable, psychologically driven, quasi-fascist ultraright.[54] It was this ideological construct of whiteness, already deeply problematic in a thoroughly modernized, advanced industrial society, that the black movement confronted in the post–World War II period.

Detached from their forebears' ethnicities, unable to see themselves as part of a potentially majoritarian working class with larger social justice interests, and unable to revert to the discredited white supremacy of an earlier period, most whites were ripe for conversion to neoconservative racial ideology after the civil rights victory in the mid-1960s. Efforts on the part of Martin Luther King Jr., Bayard Rustin, and even the Black Panther Party to forge multiracial alliances for large-scale redistributive policies and other forms of substantive social justice never had a serious chance in the national political arena.

Instead, neoconservative and New Right politicians, initiated by the George Wallace campaigns of the mid-1960s, appealed to white workers on the basis of their residual commitments to racial "status honor."[55] Wallace, and Richard Nixon in his "Southern strategy," invoked the powerful remnants of white supremacy and white privilege. Since white identities could no longer be overtly depicted as superior, they were now presented in coded fashion as a beleaguered American individualism, as the "silent majority," as the hallmarks of a noble tradition now unfairly put upon by unworthy challengers. The racial reaction begun by Wallace and consummated by Reagan, which resurrected twentieth-century Republicanism from the oblivion to which the New Deal had supposedly consigned it, was thus a fairly direct descendant of the "white labor republicanism" that had shaped the U.S. working class along racial lines more than a century earlier.

In this fashion from the late 1960s on, white identity was reinterpreted, rearticulated in a dualistic fashion: on the one hand, egalitarian, and on the other hand privileged; on the one hand, individualistic and color-blind, and on the other hand, normalized and white. With Reagan's election in 1980, the process reached its peak. A class policy of regressive redistribution was adopted; working-class incomes, stagnant since the mid-1970s, continued to drop in real terms as profits soared. Neoconservative racial ideology—with its commitment to formal racial equality and its professions of color blindness—now proved particularly useful: it served to organize and rationalize white working-class resentments against declining living standards. To hear Republicans (and some Democrats) tell it, the problems faced by white workers did not derive from corporate greed for ever-greater profits, nor from deindustrialization and the "downsizing" of workforces; rather, their troubles emanated from the welfare state, which expropriated the taxes of the productive citizens who "played by the rules" and "went to work each day" in order to subsidize unproductive and parasitic welfare queens and career criminals "who didn't want to work."

RADICAL RACIAL PRAGMATISM

What are the implications of the Duboisian concept of double consciousness for contemporary U.S. racial politics? In the early twenty-first century, U.S. racial conditions are quite different from what they were a century earlier, when Du Bois boldly announced that the color line would be "the problem of the century." Most notably the rise and fall of the civil rights movement and its allies, the adoption (in limited but still significant versions) of democratic racial reforms during the 1960s, and the deformation of those gains under the misleading banner of color blindness have combined to create a confused and contradictory racial politics today. As a result, racial identities—*all* racial identities—are now beset by uncertainty and anxiety.

The simultaneous avowal and disavowal of racial politics shapes (and debilitates) political language and strategic thinking: in electoral politics, rhetorics of national and community identity, and visions of equality and social justice. It undercuts social movements oriented to racial equality, redistribution, and the strengthening of the welfare state. This is what characterizes the post–civil rights era: the once-powerful wave of race-based mobilization and state-based efforts at racial reform is now receding into the past, leaving in its wake an uneasy post–civil rights combination of greater racial mobility and tolerance, on the one hand, and a reformed and reconsolidated system of racial inequality, on the other.

This chapter has concentrated on the effects of the post–World War II racial break on the panorama of racial identities now available: the peculiar list of colors—black, white, brown, red, and yellow. I have emphasized the relevance of Duboisian double consciousness to the disruption of those identities that occurred during and after the break. But double consciousness, as noted, is just the most familiar and accessible dimension of the radical racial pragmatism pioneered by Du Bois and later developed by Locke and the Chicago School. This approach to issues of race and racism holds enormous promise for us today, as we seek to move beyond the inadequate reforms of the civil rights era.

Pragmatist concepts of self and society center on the core idea of *self-reflective action*. Keep double consciousness in mind here. Think of the racialized self as a tentative synthesis combining both an ascriptive identity and the powers of conscious self-activity. At the microsocial level, this approach presumes that each racial self engages in a certain amount of sociopolitical navigation, as noted. This action takes place in everyday life and in political life, and it requires what might be called racial "antennae," or racial "intelligence." It links or articulates the racial conditions of everyday life with those of the overall social structure. Does A perceive B's use of a race-inflected term ("Yo, nigga"; "Hey, white boy") as a gesture of solidarity or antagonism? Does C see a racially designated group ("Latin@s Unidos para la Gente") or a group not racially designated ("Planned Parenthood of Los Angeles County") as including her, or not?

Similar questions apply to the actions of a racialized collectivity as to the racialized self. Consider some movement organizations as examples: in the height of a political campaign (say, in Birmingham, 1963) a movement group can navigate, synthesizing opposing viewpoints and actions, choosing a path. Under less mobilized, less electrifying circumstances, collective action is much less possible; only divided and improvised responses to a given situation, only individual gestures, or perhaps no more than silence and confusion, are available. States, too, confront varied conditions of action (state action is by definition collective action): Can a clear racial policy be framed and implemented? Is repression or reform indicated? At the macrosocial level as well, then, this approach suggests that a certain room to maneuver is available to movements and states, obviously depending to varying extent on political circumstances.

From this standpoint, the crucial problem of "structural racism" can also be seen as a historically situated phenomenon. Just as individual circumstances require self-reflective action in respect to racial identification and racially oriented action—and just as strategic political situations shape the potentialities and limits of the collective action of movements and states—so too does social structure sometimes become amenable to alteration. While recognizing the accumulated weight of past racist practices as the core component of structural racism—the way the legacy of slavery has been "unwilling to die,"[56] the way racially unequal distribution of resources in the past has structured continuing inequality and injustice in the present,[57] and so on—structural racism should be seen as a processual, not a permanent and fixed, feature of U.S. society. Of course, opportunities to overhaul the racist system systematically *tout court* are very rare: as Du Bois argued, these constitute revolutionary moments.[58] But these moments do indeed arise, notably when the racial regime *becomes too dependent upon the cooperation of its subordinated "Others."*[59] Questioning the subtext of stasis and pessimism visible in many analyses of structural racism[60] leads me to suggest that the idea be opened up somewhat: to the "accumulated legacy of injustice" argument, let us add something more pragmatist and processual. Structural racism can then be seen as the variable outcome of a multilayered conflict in which the weight of despotic racial traditions and practices confronts the counterweight of democratic accomplishments: past and present collective action driven by "freedom dreams."[61]

What is different about this approach from those of such illustrious predecessors as Du Bois, Locke, and Blumer? Without question, they invented the first truly social theory of race, breaking with biologistic understandings (at first by degrees, but ultimately quite comprehensively). Led by Du Bois and Locke, and then recapitulating Du Bois's insights later at Chicago, these thinkers and activists also pioneered the first fully political theories of race and racism. Du Bois's advocacy of democratic opposition to racial despotism in the United States and beyond, his insistence on political struggle against Booker T. Washington's quietism and Marcus Garvey's refusal to engage U.S. national politics, his intrepid and systematic portrayal of the U.S. Civil War as a second American revolution and an anti-imperialist drama, and his rejection of the assimilationism/separatism binary, all set the standard for radical racial pragmatism.

Du Bois's idea of double consciousness and his lifelong invocation of the veil as a metaphor for (what we now call) racism also highlighted the experiential dimensions of racial oppression and race-consciousness. In this area of racial theory—the zone where micro- and macro-level relationships intersect—Du Bois's pioneering work was highly influential on the other luminaries I have named: Blumer developed the symbolic interactionist approach and applied it to race and racism issues, influenced not only by Mead but also by Du Bois. Locke explored "culture contacts," ethnonationalism, and racialization (another word that—like *racism*—did not yet exist when he was writing). Here were the principal axes of a radical pragmatist theory of race and racism.

So again, what is different, and what is new, in what I'm suggesting here? What can we say today about racial politics that Du Bois was not already saying a century ago? It is an insistence on inclusion, on the politics of the social, on *radical democracy*, that distinguishes us today from these luminous ancestors.

For all Du Bois's democratic affinities, he was an avowed elitist, seeking to empower his "talented tenth" to uplift the race. For all his pragmatist understanding of the dilemmas of black identity—"two warring ideals in one dark body" and so on—he did not recognize that self-reflective political action, "situated creativity," could flow from double consciousness; he did not trust that the ordinary "Negro," the woman or man of the "masses," could be relied upon to navigate in the choppy waters of ordinary American racism. Blumer's understanding of prejudice as *performance*, as the "collective process through which a sense of group position is formed,"[62] though tremendously attentive to experiential issues— "feelings" of superiority, difference, privilege, and fear—did not view the individual experiencing these feelings as capable of reflecting upon them, "checking herself" so to speak, or consciously reinterpreting or acting upon their meaning. She is a mere vessel for the (racist) society's assignment of "group position."

Without dismissing the validity of such positions, it is important to move beyond them. To be sure, the Duboisian Southern Negroes in 1903 were greatly constrained by their situation, forced to live within a submissive and defensive racial consciousness.[63] Something similar is true for the feelings Blumer anatomizes: They were virtually ubiquitous among whites in the 1950s; they were the inculcated products of a ferocious, comprehensive, and largely unquestioned structural racism.[64]

I do not suggest that Du Bois saw African Americans as passive and depoliticized social actors; indeed, his argument that they engaged in a "general strike" during the Civil War, as well as his innumerable other insights, should make that clear.[65] Instead I want to urge that *even in highly oppressive conditions, self-reflective action is under way*. Politically, this "situated creativity" is potentially democratic and self-emancipatory, though also constrained by the historical and structural conditions in which it is operating. Even the near-absolute despotism of racial slavery did not entirely extirpate this capability for self-reflective action.[66] Supposedly submissive black consciousness has given rise to a lot of resistance; it effectively subverted and sabotaged racial oppression, through humor, language, and an extensive network of underground opposition.[67]

Nor do I think Blumer classified late-1950s whites as uniformly prejudiced; their numbers, of course, included antiracist activists as well. Gunnar Myrdal's "dilemma" was fundamentally about the contradiction within whiteness, after all: he charged that American democracy and white supremacism were fundamentally incompatible.[68]

In criticizing these indispensable works, I seek to highlight the core pragmatist insight into racial politics: its fundamentally social character, its rootedness in the intelligence and awareness, however situationally constrained, of the actor. This viewpoint, while never entirely absent from the pragmatist political toolkit, only regained its prominence with the ascendance of the civil rights movement, the "new social movements" of the 1960s, and the politicization of the social ("the personal is political") during that period. Not only were the democratic gains made in the United States by the black movement and its allies at their core social achievements, but so were the political advances toward equality, social justice, and inclusion accomplished in the United States by "new social movements" of various types—second-wave feminism, gay liberation, and indeed the environmentalist and antiwar movements.[69]

All the new social movements were subject to "rearticulation";[70] indeed, all confronted their virtual mirror images in the mobilizations that arose to counter them from the political right. Yet even their containment, even their confrontations with the various "backlash" phenomena of the past few decades, revealed both the permanence and the contradictions of the "politicization of the social." While it is not possible here to explore so extensive a theme, it is worthwhile noting that, in the United States at least, it was the long-delayed eruption of racial subjectivity and self-awareness into the mainstream political arena that set off this transformation, shaping both the democratic and antidemocratic social movements that today dominate American politics.

The post–civil rights era formula of color blindness cannot succeed in dissipating racial conflicts; only an overarching effort at social reconstruction could even begin to tackle such a task. Confronted with the limits of color blindness, and daunted by the enormity of structural racism, we could easily succumb to despair. But to recognize the many obstacles that still confront the dream of racial democracy, equality, and justice is also to recognize the enormous achievements of the movement for racial justice over the latter half of the twentieth century: the movement made race and racism a public matter, a social fact in the Durkheimian sense. Movements may experience setbacks, the reforms for which they fought may be revealed as inadequate, and many of their leaders may be co-opted or eliminated, but racial subjectivity and self-awareness, unresolved and conflictual both within the individual psyche and the body politic, endures.

Radical pragmatism suggests that we see politics as an everyday creative practice, that we understand self-reflective action as an everyday matter. Such an approach enables a new interpretation of race and racism. Let us, then, think about race and racism, as well as a wide range of other political themes, as *everyday encounters between despotic and democratic practices*, in which individuals and groups, confronted by state power and entrenched privilege but not entirely limited by those obstacles, make choices and locate themselves over and over in a constant "reconstruction" of everyday life.

NOTES

An earlier version of this paper was presented at the annual meetings of American Political Science Association, Philadelphia, 2006. Some of the material in the section "Double Consciousness for All" appeared earlier in Howard Winant, "Racial Dualism at Century's End," in *The New Politics of Race: Globalism, Difference, Justice* (Minneapolis: University of Minnesota Press, 2004).

1. W. E. B. Du Bois, *The Souls of Black Folk* (1903; New York: Penguin, 1989), 5.

2. See Cornel West, *The American Evasion of Philosophy: A Genealogy of Pragmatism* (Madison: University of Wisconsin Press, 1989); Hans Joas, *The Creativity of Action*, translated by Jeremy Gaines and Paul Keast (Chicago: University of Chicago Press, 1996); Louis Menand, ed., *Pragmatism: A Reader* (New York: Vintage Books, 1997); Morris Dickstein, ed., *The Revival of Pragmatism: New Essays on Social Thought, Law, and Culture* (Durham, NC: Duke University Press, 1999). The earlier literature in pragmatist sociology remains relevant as well; most basically, see George Herbert Mead, *Mind, Self and Society from the Standpoint of a Social Behaviorist* (1934; Chicago: University of Chicago Press, 1967), and Herbert Blumer, *Symbolic Interactionism: Perspective and Method* (Englewood Cliffs, NJ: Prentice-Hall, 1969).

3. Mead, *Mind, Self and Society*.

4. This crude summation denies Mead his due as a complex sociological theorist and philosopher of mind. It also glosses over the vast literature that has developed in this area. For a sampling of other key work, see Robert S. Perinbanayagam, *Signifying Acts: Structure and Meaning in Everyday Life* (Carbondale: Southern Illinois University Press, 1985); Richard Rorty, *Consequences of Pragmatism: Essays, 1972–1980* (Minneapolis: University of Minnesota Press, 1982); Blumer, Herbert. "Race Prejudice as a Sense of Group Position." In *Pacific Sociological Review*, Vol. 1, no. 1 (Spring, 1958); and Joseph Margolis, *Reinventing Pragmatism: American Philosophy at the End of the Twentieth Century* (Ithaca, NY: Cornell University Press, 2002). For a valuable treatment of the contradictions of the political subject, see Judith Butler, *The Psychic Life of Power: Theories in Subjection* (Stanford, CA: Stanford University Press, 1997).

5. This notion of "voice"—that is, political voice—has some overlap with Hirschman's idea, though it is obviously more general and philosophical. In the absence of an adequate discussion, let's equate the two in a tentative fashion. See Albert O. Hirschman, *Exit, Voice, and Loyalty: Responses to Decline in Firms, Organizations, and States* (Cambridge, MA: Harvard University Press, 1970).

6. C. Wright Mills, *White Collar: The American Middle Class* (1951; New York: Oxford University Press, 2002), 328.

7. Kimberlé Crenshaw et al., eds., *Critical Race Theory: The Key Writings That Formed the Movement* (New York: New Press, 1995); Richard Delgado and Jean Stefancic, *Critical Race Theory: An Introduction* (New York: New York University Press, 2001).

8. Michael Omi and Howard Winant, *Racial Formation in the United States: From the 1960s to the 1990s*, 2nd ed. (New York: Routledge, 1994).

9. There is, of course, ongoing work in the social sciences that seeks to address similar problems: notably through work on racial attitudes from an empirical standpoint; see Howard Schuman et al., *Racial Attitudes in America: Trends and Interpretations*, rev. ed. (Cambridge, MA: Harvard University Press, 1997); Jennifer L. Hochschild, *Facing Up to the American Dream: Race, Class, and the Soul of the Nation* (Princeton, NJ: Princeton University Press, 1995); and Michael C. Dawson, *Black Visions: The Roots of Contemporary African-American Political Ideologies* (Chicago: University of Chicago Press, 2001). Others concentrate on political attitudes among contemporary African Americans or on white-black comparisons; see Bob Blauner, *Black Lives, White Lives: Three Decades of Race Relations in America* (Berkeley: University of California Press, 1989). Yet the question of "double consciousness" does not in general preoccupy these authors (with the exception of Dawson, who is quite attentive to the Duboisian legacy).

10. David R. Roediger, *Black on White: Black Writers on What It Means to Be White* (New York: Schocken, 1999).

11. This use of the Freudian term is not entirely improper. A significant amount of psychological (and political) literature has been devoted to "internalized racism" (see, for example, Suzanne Lipsky, *Internalized Racism* [Seattle: Rational Island, 1987]). Fanon's insights on these dynamics—the views of a psychoanalyst well acquainted with Freud's theory of "the mechanisms of defense"—remain relevant; see Frantz Fanon, *Black Skin, White Masks*, translated by Charles Lam Markmann (1952; New York: Grove, 1967).

12. Mead, *Mind, Self and Society.*

13. Consider the links between this account and that of subalternity theory with its "weapons of the weak," subversive knowledges, and "hidden transcripts." See, respectively, James C. Scott, *Domination and the Arts of Resistance: Hidden Transcripts* (New Haven, CT: Yale University Press, 1990); Homi K. Bhabha, *The Location of Culture* (New York: Routledge, 1994); and Robin D. G. Kelley, *Race Rebels: Culture, Politics, and the Black Working Class* (New York: Free Press, 1994).

14. Du Bois's pragmatism drew most centrally on William James's framework of verification through practice; see William James, *Pragmatism: A New Name for Some Old Ways of Thinking* (New York: Longmans Green, 1907). The dualistic model has also been linked to Du Bois's German-derived romanticism; see Adolph Reed, *W. E. B. Du Bois and American Political Thought: Fabianism and the Color Line* (New York: Oxford University Press, 1997). In my view, Reed is improperly dismissive of the double consciousness concept.

15. Although space does not permit the full development of this argument here, it is a well-established framework in all the major assessments of Du Bois's unfolding politics. See Lewis, David Levering. *W. E. B. Du Bois: Biography of a Race.* New York: Henry Holt, 1993; Manning Marable, *W. E. B. Du Bois: Black Radical Democrat* (Boston: Twayne/G. K. Hall, 1986), and Gerald Horne and Mary Young, *W. E. B. Du Bois: An Encyclopedia* (Westport, CT: Greenwood Press, 2001). See also Howard Winant, "Dialectics of the Veil," in *The New Politics of Race: Globalism, Difference, Justice* (Minneapolis: University of Minnesota Press, 2004).

16. See especially W. E. B. Du Bois, *Black Reconstruction: An Essay toward a History of the Part Which Black Folk Played in the Attempt to Reconstruct Democracy in America, 1860–1880* (1935; New York: Atheneum, 1977), and his nearly simultaneously written essay, "A Negro Nation within the Nation," in *W. E. B.*

Du Bois: A Reader, edited by David Levering Lewis (New York: Henry Holt, 1995).

17. "Race Contacts and Interracial Relations: Lectures on the Theory and Practice of Race" was not published in book form until 1992. Locke, Alain Leroy. *Race Contacts and Interracial Relations: Lectures on the Theory and Practice of Race*. Jeffrey C. Stewart, ed. Washington DC: Howard University Press, 1992. See also the essays in Leonard Harris, ed., *The Critical Pragmatism of Alain Locke* (Lanham, MD: Rowman & Littlefield, 1999), notably Nancy Fraser, "Another Pragmatism: Alain Locke, Critical 'Race' Theory, and the Politics of Culture."

18. "The trouble with the standard account of American sociology's birth is that it happened not at the University of Chicago in the 1920s, but at the University of Pennsylvania in the 1890s; rather than being led by a group of classically influenced white men, it was directed by W. E. B. Du Bois, a German-trained African American with a Ph.D. from Harvard. His 1899 study, *The Philadelphia Negro*, anticipated in every way the program of theory and research that later became known as the Chicago School. Although not generally recognized as such, it represented the first true example of American social scientific research, preceding the work of Park and Burgess by at least two decades. Were it not for the short-sighted racism of Penn's faculty and administration, which refused to acknowledge the presence—let alone the accomplishments—of a black man or to offer him a faculty appointment, the maturation of the discipline might have been advanced by two decades and be known to posterity as the Pennsylvania School of Sociology. Instead, Du Bois went on to a distinguished career as a public intellectual, activist, and journalist, and the University of Chicago, not the University of Pennsylvania, came to dominate the field." (Elijah Anderson and Douglas S. Massey, "The Sociology of Race in the United States," in *Problem of the Century: Racial Stratification in the United States*, edited by Elijah Anderson and Douglas S. Massey [New York: Russell Sage Foundation, 2001], 3–4).

19. This racial break was a global transformation, not merely an American one. It was the overdetermined outcome of the upheavals of World War II, the massive migrations that occurred during and after the war, the upsurge of anticolonial movements, the onset of the Cold War, and numerous other world-historical shifts. For a comparative historical analysis, see Howard Winant, *The World Is a Ghetto: Race and Democracy since World War II* (New York: Basic Books, 2001).

20. Douglas S. Massey and Nancy A. Denton, *American Apartheid: Segregation and the Making of the Underclass* (Cambridge, MA: Harvard University Press, 1993).

21. Melvin L. Oliver and Thomas M. Shapiro, *Black Wealth, White Wealth: A New Perspective on Racial Inequality*, 2nd ed. (New York : Routledge, 2006).

22. Antonio Gramsci, *Selections from the Prison Notebooks*, edited by Quinton Hoare and Geoffrey Nowell-Smith (New York: International, 1971), 276.

23. This is not the place to inventory the ongoing conditions or racial inequality in the contemporary United States, but for good overview material, see Alice O'Connor, Chris Tilly, and Lawrence Bobo, eds., *Urban Inequality: Evidence from Four Cities* (New York: Russell Sage Foundation, 2001), and Michael Brown et al., *White-Washing Race: The Myth of a Colorblind Society* (Berkeley: University of California Press, 2003). For data on residential segregation, see John Iceland and Daniel H. Weinberg, with Erika Steinmetz, "Racial and Ethnic Residential Segregation in the United States, 1980–2000," U.S. Bureau of the Census Special Report (Washington, DC: GPO, 2002); Douglas S. Massey, "Residential Segregation and Neighborhood Conditions in U.S. Metropolitan Areas," in *America Becoming: Racial Trends and Their Consequences*, edited by Neil J. Smelser,

William Julius Wilson, and Faith Mitchell, vol. 1 (Washington DC: National Academies Press, 2001); and Massey and Denton, *American Apartheid*. For data on incarceration, see Mark Mauer, *Race to Incarcerate*, 2nd ed. (New York: New Press, 2006). For data on educational segregation, see Orfield, Gary. "Schools More Separate: Consequences of a Decade of Resegregation." 2001. Working Paper: Harvard Civil Rights Project, 124 Mt. Auburn St. Cambridge, MA 02138. For data on workplace segregation, see Judith Hellerstein and David Neumark, "Workplace Segregation in the United States: Race, Ethnicity, and Skill," National Bureau of Economic Research Working Paper No. 11599, Cambridge, MA, September 2005. For data on black-white economic inequality, see Oliver and Shapiro, *Black Wealth*. For data on racial attitudes, see Lawrence Bobo, "Racial Attitudes and Relations at the Close of the Twentieth Century," in Smelser, Wilson, and Faith, *America Becoming*; Dawson, *Black Visions*; and Donald R. Kinder and Lynn W. Sanders, *Divided by Color: Racial Politics and Democratic Ideals* (Chicago: University of Chicago Press, 1996).

24. Omi and Winant, *Racial Formation*, 59–60.

25. Joas, *Creativity of Action*.

26. The Big Five (the black, brown, yellow, red, and white racial categories) comprise the current list of U.S. racial categories. More groups could, of course, be included—for example, those of Middle Eastern and South Asian descent (whether Arab or not, whether Muslim or not) who are hesitantly and tentatively experiencing a new pan-ethnicized raciality in the wake of 9/11 and the emergence of Islamophobia in the West; see Fred Halliday, "Islamophobia Reconsidered," *Ethnic and Racial Studies* 22, no. 5 (September 1999), and Salah D. Hassan, "Arabs, Race and the Post–September 11 National Security State," *Middle East Report* 224 (Fall 2002).

27. Patricia Hill Collins, *From Black Power to Hip Hop: Racism, Nationalism, and Feminism* (Philadelphia: Temple University Press, 2006); Barbara Smith, ed., *Home Girls: A Black Feminist Anthology*, rev. ed. (New Brunswick, NJ: Rutgers University Press, 2000).

28. Angela Y. Davis and Cassandra Shaylor, "Race, Gender, and the Prison Industrial Complex: California and Beyond," *Meridians* 2, no. 1 (2001); Ruth Wilson Gilmore, *Golden Gulag: Prisons, Surplus, Crisis, and Opposition in Globalizing California* (Berkeley: University of California Press, 2007).

29. Robert M. Hauser, "Intergenerational Economic Mobility in the United States: Measures, Differentials, and Trends," Center for Demography and Ecology Working Paper No. 98-12, Department of Sociology, University of Wisconsin–Madison, June 1998.

30. Tricia Rose, *Longing to Tell: Black Women Talk about Sexuality and Intimacy* (New York: Farrar, Straus & Giroux, 2003).

31. Relative improvements in *income* inequality at the higher end of the racial stratification system are not reflected in *wealth* distribution by race; median white net worth now exceeds median black net worth by a factor of twelve; see Oliver and Shapiro, *Black Wealth*.

32. Richard Herrnstein and Charles Murray, *The Bell Curve: Intelligence and Class Structure in American Life* (New York: Free Press, 1994).

33. Ange-Marie Hancock, *The Politics of Disgust: The Public Identity of the "Welfare Queen"* (New York: New York University Press, 2004); Dorothy Roberts, *Killing the Black Body: Race, Reproduction, and the Meaning of Liberty* (New York: Pantheon, 1997).

34. "Katrina: Unmasking Race, Poverty, and Politics in the Twenty-First Century," *Du Bois Review* 3, no. 1 (Spring 2006); Chester Hartman and Gregory D.

Squires, eds., *There Is No Such Thing as a Natural Disaster* (New York: Routledge, 2006).

35. Mary Pattillo-McCoy, *Black Picket Fences: Privilege and Peril among the Black Middle Class* (Chicago: University of Chicago Press, 1999).

36. Robert C. Lieberman, *Shaping Race Policy: The United States in Comparative Perspective* (Princeton, NJ: Princeton University Press, 2005).

37. See Nancy J. Weiss, *Farewell to the Party of Lincoln: Black Politics in the Age of FDR* (Princeton, NJ: Princeton University Press, 1983).

38. The Immigration and Nationality Act of 1965 amended the 1924 and 1952 Immigration Acts to abolish quota systems based on national origins, to afford visas for the reunification of immediate family members (spouses, children, parents), and for persons with special occupational skills, abilities, or training (needed in the United States).

39. Dina Okamoto, "Toward a Theory of Panethnicity: Explaining Asian American Collective Action," *American Sociological Review* 68, no. 6 (December 2003); Yen Le Espiritu, *Asian American Panethnicity: Bridging Institutions and Identities* (Philadelphia: Temple University Press, 1992). *Pan-ethnicity* is the product of "linking" and "bridging" tendencies that synthesize disparate ethnic (i.e., culturally or nationally defined) groups into racially defined ones. This process—which may also be characterized as "racial lumping"—is necessarily uneven and contradictory; it operates across intergroup antagonisms that can sometimes be quite severe and is often driven by external pressures, including the "ocularity" of racism and periodic onsets of nativism and xenophobia on the part of ruling groups and the state. Hence, pan-ethnicity can be understood, at least in the U.S. context and perhaps more generally, as an unstable combination of centripetal and centrifugal forces.

40. Nicholas De Genova, *Working the Boundaries: Race, Space, and "Illegality" in Mexican Chicago* (Durham, NC: Duke University Press, 2005); Marcelo M. Suarez-Orozco and Mariela Paez, eds., *Latinos: Remaking America* (Berkeley: University of California Press, 2002).

41. Neil Foley, *The White Scourge: Mexicans, Blacks, and Poor Whites in Texas Cotton Culture* (Berkeley: University of California Press, 1997); Montejano, David. *Anglos and Mexicans in the Making of Modern Texas, 1836–1986.* Austin: University of Texas Press, 1987.

42. Lisa García Bedolla, *Fluid Borders: Latino Power, Identity, and Politics in Los Angeles* (Berkeley: University of California Press, 2005).

43. Samuel P. Huntington, *Who Are We? The Challenges to America's National Identity* (New York: Simon & Schuster, 2004). See Sanchez's early diagnosis in George J. Sanchez, "Face the Nation: Race, Immigration, and the Rise of Nativism in Late Twentieth-Century America," *International Migration Review* 31, no. 4 (Winter 1997).

44. Michael Jones-Correa, "Bringing Outsiders In: Questions of Immigrant Incorporation," paper prepared for the Conference on the Politics of Democratic Inclusion, University of Notre Dame, October 17–19, 2002, available at http://www.nd.edu/~amdemoc/Jones-Correa.pdf; Alejandro Portes and Rubén G. Rumbaut, *Immigrant America: A Portrait*, 2nd ed. (Berkeley: University of California Press, 1996); Pei-te Lien, M. Margaret Conway, and Janelle Wong, *The Politics of Asian Americans: Diversity and Community* (New York: Routledge, 2004).

45. Vicki Ruiz, *From Out of the Shadows: Mexican Women in Twentieth-Century America* (New York: Oxford University Press, 1998); Grasmuck, Sherri, and Patricia Pessar. *Between Two Islands: Dominican International Migration.* Berkeley: University of California Press, 1991.

46. Takagi, Dana Y. *The Retreat from Race: Asian American Admissions and Racial Politics.* New Brunswick, NJ: Rutgers University Press, 1993.

47. Clair Jean Kim, *Bitter Fruit: The Politics of Black-Korean Conflict in New York City* (New Haven, CT: Yale University Press, 2003).

48. Eva Garroutte, *Real Indians: Identity and the Survival of Native America* (Berkeley: University of California Press, 2003); Lawrence Bobo and Mia Tuan, *Prejudice in Politics: Group Position, Public Opinion and the Wisconsin Treaty Rights Dispute* (Cambridge, MA: Harvard University Press, 2006); Duane Champagne, *Social Change and Cultural Continuity among Native Nations* (Lanham, MD: Altamira, 2007); Joanne Nagel, *American Indian Ethnic Renewal: Red Power and the Resurgence of Identity and Culture* (New York: Oxford University Press, 1995); Stephen E. Cornell and Joseph Kalt, "Where Does Economic Development Really Come From? Constitutional Rule among the Modern Sioux and Apache," Working Paper R93-30, John F. Kennedy School of Government, Harvard University, 1993.

49. Alexander Saxton, *The Rise and Fall of the White Republic: Class Politics and Mass Culture in Nineteenth-Century America* (New York: Verso, 1990).

50. Roediger, David R. *The Wages of Whiteness: Race and the Making of the American Working Class.* New York: Verso, 1991.

51. Michael Novak, *The Rise of the Unmeltable Ethnics: Politics and Culture in the Seventies* (New York: Macmillan, 1972).

52. Richard D. Alba, *Ethnic Identity: The Transformation of White America* (New Haven, CT: Yale University Press, 1990); Mary C. Waters, *Ethnic Options: Choosing Identities in America* (Berkeley: University of California Press, 1990).

53. Ira Katznelson, *When Affirmative Action Was White: An Untold History of Racial Inequality in Twentieth-Century America* (New York: Norton, 2005).

54. Ronald W. Walters, *Pan-Africanism in the African Diaspora: An Analysis of Modern Afrocentric Political Movements* (Detroit: Wayne State University Press, 1995); Carol M. Swain, *The New White Nationalism in America: Its Challenge to Integration* (New York: Cambridge University Press, 2003); Kathleen Blee, *Inside Organized Racism: Women in the Hate Movement* (Berkeley: University of California Press, 2003); Carolyn Gallaher, *On the Fault Line: Race, Class and the American Patriot Movement* (Lanham, MD: Rowman & Littlefield, 2003).

55. Mark Gerson, *The Neoconservative Vision: From the Cold War to the Culture Wars* (Lanham, MD: Madison Books, 1996); Thomas Byrne Edsall, with Mary Edsall, *Chain Reaction: The Impact of Race, Rights, and Taxes on American Politics*, rev. ed. (New York: Norton, 1992).

56. William O. Douglas, concurring: *Jones v. Mayer Co.*, 392 U.S. 409 (1968); Joe R. Feagin, *Racist America: Roots, Current Realities, and Future Reparations* (New York: Routledge, 2000). On the continuity of nativism/white racial nationalism, see Peter Brimelow, *Alien Nation: Common Sense about America's Immigration Disaster* (New York: Harper, 1996); Chip Berlet and Matthew N. Lyons, *Right-Wing Populism in America: Too Close for Comfort* (New York: Guilford, 2000); and Huntington, *Who Are We?*

57. Oliver and Shapiro, *Black Wealth.*

58. Du Bois, *Black Reconstruction.*

59. Winant, "Dialectics of the Veil," 209–10.

60. David Wellman, *Portraits of White Racism*, 2nd ed. (New York: Cambridge University Press, 1993); Stephen Steinberg, *Turning Back: The Retreat from Racial Justice in American Thought and Policy* (Boston: Beacon, 1995).

61. Robin D. G. Kelley, *Freedom Dreams: The Black Radical Imagination* (Boston: Beacon, 2002).

62. Blumer, "Race Prejudice as a Sense of Group Position," 7.

63. And yes, those constraints certainly persist today, although with more flexibility and room to maneuver.

64. Indeed, many of the leading pragmatist thinkers, though "progressive" in their politics, were creatures of their times. If not active racists, they were fairly oblivious to race. Race was not a challenging political issue for Mead in the 1920s when the lectures that were to become *Mind, Self, and Society* were first presented. Nor did it intrude on John Dewey's democratic ideal—the New England town meeting—a setting notable for its racial homogeneity.

65. Du Bois, *Black Reconstruction*, chap. 4.

66. Space is not available for an adequate discussion of these ideas, which reference (among many other themes) debates on totalitarianism and the dehumanizing characteristics of slavery; see Hannah Arendt, *The Origins of Totalitarianism*, 2nd ed. (New York: Meridian, 1958), and Zygmunt Bauman, *Modernity and the Holocaust* (Ithaca, NY: Cornell University Press, 2000). See also the once-famous debate on U.S. racial slavery between Kenneth Stampp and Stanley Elkins: Kenneth M. Stampp, *The Peculiar Institution: Slavery in the Antebellum South* (New York: Knopf, 1956); Stanley M. Elkins, *Slavery: A Problem in American Institutional and Intellectual Life* (New York: Grosset & Dunlap, 1963). In addition, see Orlando Patterson, *Slavery and Social Death* (Cambridge, MA: Harvard University Press, 1982).

67. Kelley, Robin D.G. *Yo Mama's Disfunktional! Fighting the Culture Wars in Urban America*. Boston: Beacon Press, 1997; Smitherman, Geneva. *Black Talk: Words and Phrases from the Hood to the Amen Corner*, 2nd Ed. Boston: Houghton Mifflin, 2000; Kochman, Thomas. *Rappin' and Stylin' Out: Communication in Urban Black America*. Urbana: University of Illinois Press, 1972.

68. Gunnar Myrdal, *An American Dilemma: The Negro Problem and Modern Democracy* (1944; New York: Harper & Row, 1962). Numerous other examples could be cited. Consider Robert K. Merton's well-known article "Discrimination and the American Creed" (in *Discrimination and the National Welfare*, edited by Robert W. MacIver [New York: Harper, 1949]), which sought to revise Myrdal in important ways. Here Merton distinguishes between prejudice and discrimination, depicting a U.S. white population already uneasy, at least in part, about the comprehensive racism that had been largely taken for granted over the entire history of white rule in North America.

69. Alberto Melucci, *Nomads of the Present: Social Movements and Individual Needs in Contemporary Society* (Philadelphia: Temple University Press, 1989); M. G. Guigni, "Was It Worth the Effort? The Outcomes and Consequences of Social Movements," *Annual Review of Sociology* 24 (1988); Enrique Larana, Hank Johnston, and Joseph R. Gusfield, eds., *New Social Movements: From Ideology to Identity* (Philadelphia: Temple University Press, 1994).

70. Chantal Mouffe and Ernesto Laclau, *Hegemony and Socialist Strategy: Towards a Radical Democratic Politics*, translated by Winston Moore and Paul Cammack (London: Verso, 1985).

PART II

Globalization and Fears

CHAPTER 5

Globalization, Race, and the Politics of Fear in the United States

Andrew L. Barlow

A TALE OF TWO COUNTRIES: 9/11 AND 3/11

Two cases—the United States after September 11, 2001, and Spain after March 11, 2004—demonstrate how differently Western countries can respond to terrorist attacks. The predominant American response was to depict the events of 9/11 as "the day everything changed," "the first major attack on American soil," an unprovoked assault on "the American people" engineered by "religious fanatics" (later, "Muslim fascists") driven by their hatred for the "modern values" for which America stands. Describing 9/11 as an attack on the values and people of the United States, the president's declaration of war on a singular enemy ("the terrorists") completed the framing of terrorism in nationalistic, us-versus-them terms. U.S. policy in the context of the Global War on Terrorism entailed pursuing military interventions, curtailing domestic civil liberties, undermining human rights regimes, and hardening borders—both for travelers and immigrants—which reversed political trends toward greater global cooperation and openness and declining militarism.[1]

The Spanish response to the 2004 Madrid bombings was markedly different. The attack took place just three days before national elections. Initially portrayed by Prime Minister Jose Maria Aznar as an attack by the Basque terrorist group ETA, the bombers were soon discovered to have been a group of Muslim fundamentalists. The electorate's reaction to Aznar's deception was swift: on March 14, 2004, his conservative government was defeated. Voters clearly linked the Madrid bombing with Aznar's decision to participate in the U.S.-led invasion and occupation of Iraq.

Furthermore, the bombing was not seen as a unique and inexplicable event, but one that was understood against the backdrop of history: the terrorism of the Spanish Civil War, World War II, and the widespread targeting of civilians by both sides in the fifty-year Basque separatist conflict. Rather than provoking an outcry for national revenge, the predominant Spanish response to the Madrid bombings led to a new search for international cooperation to deal with the long-standing and multifaceted problem of terrorism. Not surprisingly, the immediate consequence of the 2004 national election was the new government's decision to withdraw Spanish troops from the occupation of Iraq.

The Spanish response to terrorism—viewing the attacks in a historical context that made such attacks less singular, if still tragic and reprehensible—was far more typical than the American response. After the London subway bombing in July 2005, opinion polls showed a deepening public reaction against the government of Prime Minister Tony Blair and its participation in the war in Iraq. Like Madrid residents, Londoners were quick to contextualize the attack with previous acts of terror, including the German blitzkrieg and the Irish Republican Army and British bombings of the previous thirty years. Japanese reaction to the 1995 poison gas attack on the Tokyo subways was similar. Indeed, after the 9/11 attacks, Yumi Kikuchi, a Japanese peace activist, organized the Global Peace Campaign, which placed a full-page ad in the *New York Times* urging the United States not to react in nationalist terms but to view the terrorist attacks as an international human rights violation plaguing many countries and requiring global cooperation to remedy.[2]

Whether compared with other nations' understandings or on its own terms, the U.S. war on terrorism can be critiqued as an altogether inaccurate way of framing the problem of terrorism. First, the framework is based on a historical and isolationist understanding of the United States, one that denies the role of U.S. government policy in creating at least some of the conditions for terrorist attacks. Also missing in this narrative is the long history of American governmental terrorism against Native Americans, African Americans, and peoples in Latin America, the Caribbean, and the Pacific islands, as well as in Southeast Asia, Central Asia, and Africa in the late twentieth century.[3] Second, the historically accepted definition of *war* (as an international armed conflict) does not even correspond to a global problem defined by a military tactic (terrorism) committed by many different groups, let alone to a nation-state. Third, the framework of the Global War on Terrorism pits the "good" United States against an unspecified "evil," a vague descriptor typically understood to mean Muslim people everywhere in the world, an ambiguity that fosters racism and religious radicalism.

As Central Intelligence Agency estimates reveal, the war on terrorism has been an abysmal failure at suppressing even the specific terrorist networks that the United States claims as its targets. But, despite these fundamental flaws, the remarkable fact is that the war on terrorism has successfully created a politics of fear that for years has garnered the willing cooperation of a majority of American citizens with policies that are based on wholesale falsehoods, ignore world opinion, curtail Americans' democratic rights, and have harmed most Americans' economic well-being.

Certainly, this is not the first time politicians have relied on a politics of fear to gain consent for their policies. American politics has been dominated by such a tactic before, including Ronald Reagan's War on Drugs campaign of 1986–88, Richard Nixon's Silent Majority campaign of 1968, the anticommunist campaign of the 1940s and 1950s, the xenophobic efforts to restrict immigration in the 1920s, and the racism of agrarian populism in the late nineteenth century.[4] Indeed, xenophobic political campaigns can be traced back to the founding of the United States, and to the establishment of the North American colonies before that.[5]

Much of the existing literature on the politics of the fear in the United States attributes it to the right wing of the Republican party and focuses on describing the network of right-wing organizations and the political strategy that they elaborated in the 1970s and 1980s, winning Congress and the White House in 1994 and 2000, respectively.[6] These studies have documented the remarkably disciplined and well-financed process by which the New Right emerged from the ashes of the 1964 Barry Goldwater campaign and methodically built an impressive political apparatus of think tanks, foundations, and media outlets, along with a network of operatives that supported political candidates who embraced their ideology.

The rise of the New Right and its successful deployment of a politics of fear, however, raise significant sociological questions that go beyond these accounts of institutional and policy development. Why did American politicians of both major political parties adopt this political strategy while those in other countries, including European nations that have recently experienced terrorist attacks, rejected it? Why were most U.S. citizens predisposed to accept the narrative of the war on terrorism initially, while citizens of other countries that have experienced terrorist attacks were more likely to reject such nationalist and exceptionalist rhetoric? In order to answer these questions, it will not suffice to discuss the American Right's political strategy or organizational capacity. It becomes necessary to explain why U.S. politicians of both parties—who, with the exception of one member of Congress, voted to authorize the USA Patriot Act and overwhelmingly supported the invasion and initial occupation of Iraq—were predisposed to accept this frame, and it also becomes necessary to explain why a sizable portion of the public has been willing to accept it.

The American readiness to accept the politics of fear thus requires two interactive levels of analysis. First, to account for politicians' predisposition to rely on fear-based politics, it is necessary to explain the opportunities and constraints that operate on policy makers and legislators—that is, in the realm of state power. Second, to explain public sentiment, it is necessary to analyze the conditions of civil society that incline people to accept the politics of fear. In this chapter, I will argue that the American predisposition toward a politics of fear—both among policy makers and the public—can best be understood in the context of the new challenges posed by globalization, manifested in an increasingly unstable social

arrangement characterized by a historically weak state and a strong, historically rooted tendency toward nationalism and racism.

GLOBALIZATION AND STATE POWER

We are now in the early period of a new—but certainly not the first—
stage of globalization. This era is marked by the development of new
information-processing technologies, such as the World Wide Web,
computers, and microminiaturization. The social impact of these new technologies, so well described by Manuel Castells, Anthony Giddens, and
others, has been to reduce the significance of time and space in people's
lives.[7] That is, the new technologies have enabled the creation of social
networks that span the globe and communication across these networks
that is virtually unrestricted by time. Globalization in this sense has created
a new reality in which people everywhere potentially share new cosmopolitan connections and a new global culture. But this image of globalization,
recently trumpeted by Thomas Friedman, is misleading.[8]

The crucial fact missing from this glowing assessment is that the development of the new technologies is taking place in a unipolar, capitalist
world in which the processes of globalization are producing and are dominated by gigantic pools of capital, referred to as *transnational corporations*
(TNCs). These TNCs are capable of dominating local and national markets
and can rapidly shift investments anywhere that profitable conditions arise.

The creation of global connections driven by TNCs, which can be
termed *market globalization*, has two distinctive features. First, it engenders a new division of labor, generating millions of high-paying jobs in the
knowledge service sector centered in the most-developed countries
(MDCs), but eliminating entry-level jobs that might provide access to
middle-class wages, rupturing previous expectations about wages, benefits,
and job security. Second, the TNCs and international financial institutions
(e.g., the International Monetary Fund and World Bank) that are the chief
architects of the global economy are putting significant pressure on governments at all levels (local and national) to deregulate businesses and to
cut taxes on the wealthy as well as on corporations. The result of these
two trends is a vast increase in inequality of incomes and asset ownership,
with the rich getting richer and the poor poorer within the MDCs and
less-developed countries (LDCs) alike.

Perhaps most importantly, the capacity of TNCs to rapidly shift investments without regard for time and space has significantly altered the role
of the state in society. Deregulation pressures on governments are a result
of the real threat that TNCs will react to "adverse business climates" by
moving their investments elsewhere. The relative fluidity of capital, as
compared to the fixed investments of the industrial era, places state actors
in a difficult new role in their relationship to corporate investors. During
the post–World War II era, marked by rapidly growing economies and
profits, political elites were able to create a type of state that sought to
assure social stability through regulatory mechanisms and redistributive
social policies. Politics in that era tended toward what Joel Kreiger

has termed a "growth coalition" approach, where economic expansion enabled state actors to offer something to everyone.[9] Politics was not, and needed not be, a zero-sum game. During this era of the so-called welfare state, the degree to which the state came to penetrate the economy and civil society varied considerably across countries, but all MDCs had strong regulatory and redistributive states.

The weakest of these welfare states was the United States. As Rick Fantasia and Kim Voss explain, the weakness of the American welfare state in the mid-twentieth century was not so much a function of the lack of civic participation or labor organizing as it was the strength of capitalism in a society with a historically weak state.[10] Certainly, the weakness of the American state was also the product of the fatal compromise between slavery and freedom that marked the first seventy-six years of its history and of the states' rights doctrine supporting the Jim Crow system of legal racism for the next hundred years.[11] Finally, the U.S. position as the sole country to emerge from World War II as an economic and military superpower deformed the development of the welfare state. In a peacetime era in which at times as much as 15 percent of the gross domestic product was diverted to military expenditures, the capacity of the American state to undertake massive social programs was qualitatively undermined.[12]

The dynamics of globalization have undermined welfare states in every MDC, but nowhere else as thoroughly as in the United States. Since the late 1970s, when "fiscal crises" shaped urban politics for the first time, governments at every level—local, state, and national—have abandoned policies aimed at regulating and redistributing capital.[13] Successor policies have included eliminating trade barriers aimed at protecting many national industries, cutting taxes for corporations and wealthy individuals, gutting regulatory regimes (such as the Food and Drug Administration and the Occupational Safety and Health Administration), and launching an all-out assault on redistributive social problems, symbolized by the termination of welfare and the institutionalization of "workfare" in 1996.[14] Together, these policies replaced the welfare state with a new type of state, aimed at fostering and maximizing the private accumulation of wealth.[15]

The "capital investment state," as Jill Quadagno terms it, together with the vast inequalities of the globalized economy, provide a highly restricted space within which politicians can maneuver. Securing the consent of the governed is far easier when economic opportunities are expanding and when the government can increase social spending and entitlement programs. In the era of the welfare state, it was possible for skilled politicians to create win-win situations, in which gains for one group did not have to be at the expense of another group. Indeed, the civil rights movement's success at building a multiclass, multiracial coalition in the 1960s and 1970s was possible for precisely this reason. In the era of globalization, politicians must practice their art in an environment marked by rapidly growing economic inequality and severe restrictions on public expenditures on social programs.

The restricted political options in this era of globalization go a long way toward explaining the tendency of politicians to manufacture a politics of fear as a way to gain the consent of the governed. Absent the expanding economy and tax base that provides them with the capacity to rule by building universalistic "growth coalitions," politicians are far more likely to turn to the art of dividing people, securing electoral support from one segment of the population by turning them against other groups. The politics of fear replaces the welfare state's politics of universal benefit because the economic and social conditions of market globalization as they are manifest in the United States today produce a sense that a win by one group can come only at the expense of another group. Claiming to "defend the interests" of a discrete section of the electorate against imagined "outsider attacks" by "evil people," politicians can justify actions that might otherwise be seen as morally unacceptable to protect the interests of the people deemed to be "politically relevant."

The long history of the racialization of American society itself provides a strong basis for interest group identity and politics to take on a racialized form. That is, the fact that in American society physical characteristics have long been given social significance for the purpose of privileging some (those termed "white") and oppressing others (those termed various people "of color") lends itself in the present era to the defense of white peoples' "way of life." The identification of the suburbs with race, for example, is itself a product of both open Jim Crow housing policies and the dynamics of racial discrimination in the housing market in the present.[16] For decades, politicians have fed the white, middle-class suburbanites feeling the decentering effects of job restructuring and cuts in government services a steady diet of racialized explanations for their malaise. Black criminals, illegal immigrants, and terrorists have become familiar characters of the American political landscape, providing a reassuringly simply physical representation of the disorienting effects of globalization, along with a simple set of remedial policies to address peoples' concerns: mass imprisonment, a wall between the United States and Mexico, and war against "the terrorists" have become the political coins of the realm.[17]

Racialized politics of fear does more than foster intergroup conflict. It also provides politicians aligned with corporate interests desiring a less regulated and taxed business environment with a powerful weapon to undermine welfare-state policies and programs. The dismantling of welfare-state apparatuses also weakens the capacity of other state actors to offer an alternative, more universalistic model of governance, one that offers the middle class a more expansive sense of interest and identity.[18]

The creation of the American welfare state, after an early history of white privilege, was in large measure bound up with the civil rights movement in the 1960s and 1970s. Many programs that benefited whites as well as people of color were enacted as a response to civil rights demands.[19] The efforts to dismantle the welfare state in the 1980s and afterward were often carefully crafted as an assault not on still-popular universal entitlement programs, but on civil rights programs such as affirmative action and school integration. The New Right reframed what had once been seen as programs to help create opportunity for all into selfish efforts to protect undeserving minorities' "special interests."[20] This assault on civil rights went far beyond dismantling protections for minorities: critics of affirmative action and school integration offered "free market" solutions to replace programs they critiqued as "government intrusion" into "private choices." The attack on the gains of the civil rights movement was thus a core component of the larger campaign for the "private accumulation state" model.

The opportunity for a particular form of politics that utilizes fear to achieve its ends is thus created in an economic context marked by growing inequality, social destabilization, and increasing restrictions on the capacity of the state to intervene on behalf of social justice and stability.[21] In a world of market globalization, this form of politics is also likely to celebrate the market as the most just arbiter of social utility and to link the assault on the welfare state with a celebration of the virtues of markets. In short, the politics of fear is likely to be a right-wing political ideology.

GLOBALIZATION AND CIVIL SOCIETY

Politicians may be predisposed to govern through a racialized politics of fear in the political and economic context of the United States in the global era. But this tendency does not explain the receptivity of the citizens who consent to this form of politics. An analysis of the conditions of American civil society is thus required to explain the consent of the governed to policies that a decade ago were unthinkable.

The concept of "decentering," explored by Saskia Sassen, helps explain people's receptivity to fear-based politics.[22] In general, Sassen observes, emergent global arrangements often bump up against, and run over, pre-existing local and national social arrangements.[23] In the United States, the growth of economic inequality and the declining capacity of the state to intervene have threatened the old social order—that is, the middle class. The irony of market globalization, then, is that rather than creating more cosmopolitanism and global connections between people, globalization in its current form is creating conditions in which people feel threatened and retreat from one another. The most salient feature of this epoch is not the "flat world" depicted by Friedman, but the polarized world, in which people retreat from one another and gravitate toward coherent but isolating nationalism, ethnic group identification, and religious fundamentalism rather than larger frames of reference. In an era in which technologies connect people in new ways to one another, people often seek the safety of the local over the global in the face of growing inequality and declining state interventions. Globalization is "decentering" social life by adding an often-dissonant global dimension to preexisting national and local ways in which social life is structured.

In this context, fear is effective as a tool for governance because, by creating an external enemy, politicians provide people who are decentered with a sense of group membership. A prerequisite to knowing who is "us" is to know who is *not* "us"—that is, who is "them." By offering up a dangerous external enemy at a time when people's sense of belonging is destabilized, the politics of fear confirms their understanding of themselves and their relationship to others they see as being "like them" and to the world around them.[24] People's receptivity to fear-based politics rests on four specific social conditions:

1. They are more likely to be open to fear-based politics when they feel that the dominant social order is destabilized.
2. They are more likely to accept fear-based politics when they perceive that other, more inclusive options do not fulfill their self-interest and they turn inward for social support.
3. They are more likely to accept fear-based politics when ignorant of those characterized as the enemy, knowing little but the images created by purveyors of the politics of fear.
4. They are more likely to accept fear-based politics when the Other is perceived as nonhuman, a project that is most completely achieved by racializing the other.

Let us now turn to a more in-depth look at each of these conditions as they appear in the U.S. context.

The Destabilization of the Middle-Class Social Order

The current policies of free-market globalization are destabilizing the middle-class social order of the United States. The "middle-class social order" is a political regime and an ideological construct in which social stability (and social peace) is created by promising Americans the likelihood of home ownership and a job with sufficient disposable income to purchase specific status symbols, at first the automobile and the television set, and later the cell phone and computer.[25] The middle-class social order was created in the 1940s and 1950s, when the post–World War II economic boom enabled American businesses to enter into a new type of labor agreement that promised workers increasing wages and benefits as the economy expanded. This social order was also the creation of government programs, most notably the G.I. Bill, which subsidized both mortgages on new homes and the costs of higher education.

Globalization is undermining this middle-class social order in a number of ways. As discussed above, the new division of labor and the TNCs' mounting pressure on labor and welfare states have produced a rapidly widening gap between the economic haves and have-nots in the United States. Those who live outside the global metropolises are experiencing a net loss of middle-class jobs (mostly unionized manufacturing jobs), and within the global cities, widening income and wealth gaps are depriving millions of home ownership, disposable income, and other middle-class "privileges."[26] A growing portion of middle-class Americans are forced to go into deeper debt to maintain private home ownership and to pay privately for services that used to be entitlements or corporation-paid benefits. Meanwhile, most American workers are compelled to put in more hours to maintain their standard of living, with the average family now working fifteen weeks a year more than in 1975 for the same basic standard of living.[27] It is hardly surprising, then, that a May 2006 Pew Research Center survey reported that a majority of Americans are now pessimistic about the next generation's chances of having a higher standard of living than today's adults when they grow up.[28]

Globalization has also brought other destabilizing trends. The reorganization of cities has threatened and reshuffled the old suburban/urban distinction, as former "bedroom communities" become major attractors of businesses, with growing population densities, rising crime rates, traffic jams, and air pollution. Meanwhile, urban cores, including former ghettoes, are becoming gentrified and increasingly white. As well, the rapid growth in immigration has transformed many parts of the United States, especially the Upper Midwest and the Southeast, bringing a far greater Latino presence and cultural influence than ever before.

The politics of fear finds resonance especially among those who feel dislocated by globalization—which, in the United States, is predominantly suburban white people. The discontent of the white middle class increased significantly in the late 1970s and 1980s. The massive defection of middle-class blue-collar workers from the Democratic Party in the Reagan years was driven by the fear of overseas job loss. The gravitation of residents of new suburbs and exurbs to right-wing politics in the 1994 Republican sweep of Congress was spurred by the promise of tax relief and strong anticrime (especially drug crime) measures, a political program that brilliantly provided middle-class voters with a way of framing their discontents and a way to recapture their aspirations for the "good old days."

The Collapse of the Welfare State and the Shrinking Scope of Social Responsibility

A second factor spurring the increasing acceptance of the politics of fear is a sense that alternative ways of addressing social problems through expanding opportunities are not working and that people can best gain control over their lives by walling themselves off from others. In this way, the politics of fear both resonates with and helps create a narrower, smaller social world in which people can place their trust.[29]

The middle-class arrangement itself has had conflicting ideological frames. On the one hand, the middle class tends to separate people by focusing their priorities on owning property and consumption activities. Middle-class life is centered within the home, creating an inward tendency that literally walls off broader notions of community and society. Even the middle class's public activities often take place in corporate-created places—malls, bowling leagues, and the like—where individuals interact with the institutional setting, not with one another. This critique of the middle-class social order was the subject of much public discussion in the early 1950s, as the mass middle-class social order was coming into its own, especially in the powerful writing of Lewis Mumford. David Riesman's classic *The Lonely Crowd* threw a spotlight on the social and psychological isolation of middle-class individuals in mass society as well.[30]

On the other hand, the middle class is a product of government policy, and in the era of the welfare state, sizable majorities of the middle class embraced the ideology of social inclusion. As a reflection of this impulse, the middle class experienced significant conflict *against* individualism and consumerism. The ideal of social inclusion was linked to the ideology of the middle class in *Brown v. Board of Education* (1954), for example, in which the U.S. Supreme Court struck down legal segregation of schools because educational opportunity was seen as the gateway to all other opportunities in the middle-class society.

The ideal of social inclusion was also expressed through protest politics. Many middle-class youths (the "hippies") in the 1960s undertook a cultural rebellion against the propertied and consumptionist notions of those in their own social stratum and participated in two massive social movements (the civil rights and anti–Vietnam War movements) that expressed the values of inclusion and social justice. It is not incidental that these social movements took place in a time of long-term economic growth and the expansion of the welfare state's scope. The availability of government support for expansive (and expensive) social programs aimed at raising marginalized people into the middle-class order encouraged both official policy and protest politics.[31]

In this context, middle-class public discourse from the 1950s well into the 1970s supported broad notions of state action and citizen responsibility, a sentiment captured by John F. Kennedy's often-repeated 1961 inaugural speech line, "Ask not what your country can do for you, but what you can do for your country." In that era, in part because of pressure from the civil rights movement, politicians and citizens alike came to largely accept the premise that it was possible to simultaneously expand opportunities for the middle class as a whole, engage in a War on Poverty, and undertake affirmative action to secure the civil rights of minorities, women, and people with disabilities.

But in the mid-1970s, this expansive view of the responsibilities and entitlements of the middle class rapidly shifted. As corporations joined the white middle-class flight to the suburbs, fiscal crises gripped a host of American cities in 1975, presaging a new era in which politicians argued that government could no longer afford expensive social programs.[32] Supreme Court decisions such as *Milliken v. Bradley* (1974) insulated the suburbs from claims of responsibility for urban problems, and *Bakke v. U.C. Regents* (1978) signaled the end of the era of expanding civil rights by accepting the idea that white men needed the same Fourteenth Amendment protections from discrimination as people of color and women.

The collapse of the high-wage, unionized blue-collar jobs in the smokestack industries, along with a short but severe recession in 1974–75, brought to the fore both the growing economic insecurity and pessimism of the middle class and the declining power of organized labor to protect workers. The declining membership in labor unions, combined with Reagan's all-out assault on organized labor in the air traffic controllers' strike, signaled the end of the long era in which organized labor spoke for and to all workers. Unions were now just another "special interest group," and the middle class increasingly saw private savings rather than collective action as the only way to achieve economic security. The passage of the first property tax caps in California in 1979 heralded the end of middle-class support for unrestrained government programs. By the end of that decade, Jimmy Carter's commitment to the welfare-state model seemed anachronistic to white suburbanites, and Reagan's assault on the welfare state was broadly popular, even in many Democratic Party strongholds.

The unleashing of market forces and growing constraints on government interventions in the global era ushered in a new set of conditions that were highly unfavorable to the continuation of a political regime based on the premise that everyone benefits from inclusive policies. And, waiting in the wings as the new pro-market conditions emerged was a political movement ready to present the increasingly discontent middle class with a coherent ideology that would transform American culture and politics. As many writers have observed, the right-wing political culture naturalizes market forces (and with it, the growing wealth of the top fifth of the population) by blaming politicians, the poor, minorities, and immigrants for the ills of society and glorifying the supposed efficiency and rationality of the market.[33] In the 1980s and 1990s, the Keynesian framework of the previous half-century was seemingly undone. Many analysts have explained the remarkable rise of the Right as the result of sophisticated organizing: the careful process by which neoconservatives built an infrastructure of think tanks and foundations and placed its ideologues in key academic posts; the organization of Christian fundamentalists into a political force; and the skilled development of messages that played on voters' fears.[34] However, while the Right certainly was well organized, this factor cannot alone, or even in the main, explain its political successes.

The willingness of many middle-class whites to support the welfare-state model had been premised on a set of socioeconomic conditions that rapidly faded in the 1980s, undermined by the impersonal economic forces of globalization that at the time were only dimly perceived. As Jean Hardisty accurately observes, the economic dynamics of the last thirty years presented a unique opportunity for the Right to succeed.[35] But the success of the Right was not simply due to the articulation of its ideology with these economic conditions. Under the same economic conditions—the elimination of many high-wage jobs, cuts in the "social wage" of government and corporate benefits, and so forth—it is possible to imagine a very different response: workers threatened with loss of wages, benefits, and job security mobilizing politically in favor of social democratic and socialist politics.[36]

In order to explain the gravitation of sizable majorities of the middle class to support for right-wing politics, including policies that were directly counter to their long-term economic interests, we must examine another feature of the middle-class social order that had been in place from its origins, a factor that was strengthened by the crisis of the middle class in the 1980s and 1990s: the middle-class defense of racial privilege.

Structural Racism and Middle-Class Ideology

From its beginnings in the 1940s, the mass middle-class social order was a racial project. The social programs that supported mass private home ownership and college attendance as the gateway to respectability, such as the G.I. Bill, were racially segregated programs.[37] When suburbs became the site of mass-produced housing in the late 1940s and 1950s, racial segregation was legal and widely practiced by developers, mortgage lenders, and the federal government itself. Thus, the middle class was in its origins a racially privileged group.

The importance of racial segregation as a form of privileging was not lost on anyone, as was revealed by the rapidly rising property values of initially inexpensive suburban tract homes and the massive white flight from urban cores. Racial privilege was further structured into the day-to-day lives of suburban residents by the growing importance of higher education for high-paying jobs, a linkage that overwhelmingly benefited whites because of the historic barriers minorities had faced to getting a high school education, and by the suburban tax base that supported public education. After the mid-1960s, the elimination of Jim Crow housing laws did little to change the patterns of racial privilege and segregation that had been put in place over the previous generation.[38] Even after the passage of the Fair Housing Act of 1968, rising housing prices put the suburbs out of reach of most people of color, and the linkage of higher education with jobs became a real obstacle to minorities' access to the higher-paying jobs that might allow them to afford suburban housing.

In short, even after the end of Jim Crow, the suburbs remained white without legal segregation because white privilege was now deeply embedded (structured) into the reciprocal social arrangements of jobs, housing, and education.[39] The new racial system was especially effective because it operated without the need for an explicit racist ideology: racial segregation and privilege were now maintained by impersonal forces. Who could afford the price of suburban housing, who did well in school, and who was qualified for jobs now seemingly were just neutral facts. Racism was now invisible to those who chose not to see it, as segregation was maintained by impersonal social forces, not government policy or individual action as had been the case in the Jim Crow and slave eras.[40]

The civil rights movement's efforts to break down the racial barriers of suburbs, jobs, and education spawned some of the most vicious fights of the 1970s and 1980s.[41] As the demands for civil rights matured in the mid-1960s into efforts to redistribute real resources like public education, housing, and jobs, Martin Luther King Jr., among others, decried the desertion of the civil rights movement by the majority of whites.[42] And, in 1968, Richard Nixon proclaimed his Southern Strategy, which sought to bring whites from the historically Democratic South into the Republican Party. But the early skirmishes in the war for the white middle class did not rebound in the Right's favor. Despite determined efforts in the 1970s and 1980s to end school desegregation efforts and to stop affirmative action initiatives in higher education and employment, these programs continued to expand and were even strengthened into the early 1990s.[43] However, while government and tepid popular support for desegregation continued, the Right was making strong headway in realigning the electorate, starting in the Deep South, steeped in its history of racist, antilabor, and pro-military politics.

During the 1980s and 1990s, the Right fully deployed explicit racial messages to stoke white middle-class antipathy toward the welfare-state elites: unscrupulous politicians were trying to take away what was rightfully the birthright of the (white) middle class—seats in selective universities, access to professional and managerial jobs, and so forth—to hand them over to undeserving minorities. In place of government efforts to expand opportunity through economic regulation and redistribution of scarce resources, the Right offered up the free market and the ideology of meritocracy as the perfect solutions to every problem. But, as many commentators have observed, it seemed far-fetched to think that working people in worsening economic situations would believe that what worked for the wealthy (the private accumulation of capital) would benefit them as well. The reason for this unholy class alliance cannot be found in the facts of economic restructuring, but in the response to it: the development of a culture of fear, in which people experiencing the dislocations of globalization seek safety by trusting in no one but "our own," where "our own" were defined in thinly veiled racial terms.

The construction of the image of besieged, self-determining individuals who must struggle for scarce resources against political elites, minorities, and the larger world around them gained real traction in the 1990s, as sizable portions of the middle class—especially those outside the global cities on the two coasts—experienced real downward mobility pressures due to economic restructuring and cuts in government subsidies (especially in education). The art of right-wing politics was to render invisible (or at least, inconsequential) the fact that pro-free-market policies overwhelmingly benefit the rich by focusing middle-class voters' attention on the threats to their way of life: arrogant and incompetent political elites, minorities, and the murky and frightening world that lay outside the U.S. borders.

A steady diet of racialized campaigns against "the Other" was also offered up: the black criminal of the War on Drugs (1986–98),[44] the black welfare queens and pimps abusing welfare (1994),[45] the incompetent minority "affirmative action babies" (1996),[46] and the undeserving "illegal aliens" (1994–2006).[47] And, of course, the attacks of September 11, 2001, offered a qualitatively more powerful opportunity to create a remarkably homogeneous image of American identity and interests, captured by the vague post-9/11 slogan (ironically taken without acknowledgment from the labor movement of the 1930s) "United We Stand."

The success of these ideological projects required that their targets buy just one premise: that people were having what was rightfully theirs taken away from them unjustly. This premise was easy for many whites to accept: the fact that the formation of the suburbs, and whites' privileged access to property and other forms of wealth, had been protected by Jim Crow laws disappeared in the never-discussed prehistory of the middle class, who imagine that they and their forbears had produced their own wealth and property by their own hard work alone. Indeed, suburbanites not only saw the disparities between their lifestyles and those of inner-city residents but *exaggerated* them—imagining the cities as pathological places inhabited by gangs of drug dealers.[48] Faced with the prospect of declining wages and benefits and cuts in social services, many whites responded to the challenge by seeking to insulate themselves from the poor and minorities—anyone who might make a claim on social resources—to save their lifestyles from the threats posed by globalization, by any means necessary.

Perhaps most importantly, the right-wing project has a dynamic and logic of its own. That is, once people accept the basic premise that their (just) way of life is under (unjust) attack (by evil and nonwhite criminals, immigrants, or terrorists), they then tend to withdraw support for social programs that are promotive of opportunity for all. When inclusive programs are undermined, the Right can then point to the failure of these programs as further evidence of the corruption of politicians, immoral minorities, and the like.

Nowhere has this logic been demonstrated more completely than in the assault on equal opportunity in public education. During the 1980s, the self-styled "tax revolt" led to a radical reduction in per-capita student spending in most states. In response, wealthier (and whiter) school districts began to fund their own public schools with separate parcel taxes and bond issues. In many multiracial urban areas, whites withdrew from public schools altogether. In the 1990s, urban public schools came under attack from the Right for failing their students—with no reference, of course, to the underlying funding problems. Finally, the No Child Left Behind Act of 2003 codified this attack, by threatening "failing schools" with closure without addressing the underlying inequities that made schools fail in the first place. It is small wonder that the dropout rate of minority youth is now growing faster than ever relative to those of whites.[49] And, as an additional by-product of this assault, the United States continues to fall further and further behind the other MDCs in science and math competence, as well as basic literacy. With an increasingly uneducated population, the Right has become further emboldened, charging that scientific theory is just a matter of opinion and that Christian fundamentalist dogma is better able to explain such things as the origins of the universe or the evolution of life on Earth.[50]

In sum, American culture has become increasingly defined by efforts to appease displaced white middle-class voters' fears by creating powerful ideological notions of who is entitled to and who is not entitled to the wealth of America. The process of group formation based on the narrative of white people under attack has been quite successful, as suggested by the willingness of the majority of whites to support the American invasion of and occupation of Iraq despite the strong evidence that these policies were and are based on false and illegitimate premises.

After bearing witness to the rise of fear-based politics for the previous two decades, many of its harshest critics despair for the future. Thomas

Frank concludes his pathbreaking book, *What's the Matter with Kansas?*, this way:

> As a social system, the backlash *works*.... This arrangement should be the envy of every ruling class in the world. Not only can it be pushed much, much further, but it is fairly certain that it will be so pushed. All the incentives point that way, as do the never-examined cultural requirements of modern capitalism. Why shouldn't our culture just get worse and worse, if making it worse will only cause the people who worsen it to grow wealthier and wealthier?[51]

Indeed, the politics of fear have no boundaries set by human nature, as the studies of the Holocaust have so powerfully demonstrated.[52] Fortunately, there are other possibilities for the future in which this downward, de-civilizing cycle, this race to the bottom, may very well be broken.

GLOBAL DESTABILIZATION AND THE POTENTIAL FOR THE REEMERGENCE OF A POLITICS OF INCLUSION

Globalization is creating a new social reality. Looked at from the top, the new global arrangements are opening up new avenues for wealth creation, modernization, and liberal democratic reforms. But looked at from the bottom—the vantage point of at least 80 percent of humanity—the most significant feature of the new era of globalization is not the new social connections that are being forged, but the destabilization of all pre-existing social arrangements in the face of growing inequality and the erosion of governmental supports.

Thus far, this chapter has focused on the ways in which the destabilization of the middle-class social order and the fear-based responses to it reshaped the American political and cultural landscape. But there is another possibility nascent within the new global arrangements: the potential for a new politics of inclusion. This potential rests on two factors: first, the growing costs of social destabilization for TNCs and political elites, and second, the growing political capacity of people (both globally and within the United States) who are clearly not benefiting from market globalization. These two factors, I believe, have the potential to give rise to a new politics in the United States, one akin to that already emerging in Latin America and Asia today.

The destabilizing factors today are quite significant and are growing increasingly severe. They include:

- The radical American project for dominating the world through military means, called the Global War on Terrorism, which is undermining international law, multilateral arrangements, and efforts to achieve regional peace agreements and nuclear nonproliferation.
- The weakening of nation-states, especially in the LDCs, and the resultant emergence of increasing ethnic and religious forms of organization and conflicts.

- The destabilization of the world's ecology.
- Rapidly growing inequality and the erosion of the middle classes within most nations and all of the MDCs.

These factors together comprise a significant challenge to social stability everywhere on the planet, including within the United States. But even more, they provide a powerful incentive for a realignment of global politics, one that just might temper free-market globalization in favor of social justice.

The hope for such a political response can be derived from the seminal work of Karl Polanyi, who explored the process by which market capitalism emerged in England in the sixteenth and seventeenth centuries.[53] Polanyi's thesis was that markets do not a society make. The new capitalist system in England, he showed, did not just create a new society; the new entrepreneurial class needed to adapt to existing social arrangements because market exchange requires social stability as its basic precondition. Consequently, early capitalists were compelled to negotiate with semifeudal political elites, artisan and workers' organizations, and others about the terms on which they would be allowed to earn profits. This observation about the importance of social stability for market relationships may hold true in the future as well as the past: the destabilization of international law, international politics, national governments, and social orders does not benefit investors.[54] In the future, as social orders erode (or collapse), it may well be necessary for the currently unchallenged masters of the universe to negotiate with those that are already feeling the bite of market globalization.

In this destabilized climate, political movements of those who are left at the margins of the global economy are even now gathering momentum throughout the world. The rise of new political regimes in the South (e.g., in Brazil, Venezuela, and Bolivia) and the concomitant collapse of the Free Trade Agreement of the Americas makes manifest the growing desire of the world's majority to regulate global markets in the interests of social justice for the poor. And the political fate of the Bush and Blair administrations is certainly demonstrating to all thoughtful observers that support for destabilizing policies brings ruin to political elites who delude themselves that they can act with impunity against the interests of the world's majority.

Within the United States, there is some reason to expect that what Evans terms "counter-hegemonic global politics" is already beginning. Globalization is bringing tens of millions of immigrants from LDCs into the United States, where the large majority of them is incorporated into the low-wage service and manufacturing sectors of the U.S. economy. As we have seen, most of these new immigrants, and many of the nonwhite descendants of previous generations of immigrants as well, are increasingly subjected to the brunt of the politics of fear, treated as racially inferior people aptly termed by Mae Ngai "impossible subjects," ineligible for citizenship or even basic social services.[55]

But there is another side to the story: these immigrants are forming new communities at the center of the global metropolises, in which people are forging important social networks.[56] The sudden appearance of the largest demonstrations in the history of the United States in February– May 2006 in response to such treatment may well be a harbinger of the new politics of the global era. Another important example of the new politics may be seen in the emergence of a newly energized labor movement, one that is cognizant of the need to organize those working in the new jobs of the global economy, especially immigrants.[57] The new labor movement, to some extent, is also engaging in efforts at transnational labor organizing, especially with Canadian and Mexican labor unions.[58]

These new impulses are still at the margins of American politics. But an important question is whether these social movements can provide a new way of framing the problems of the middle class in such a way that it reorients the political debate about the basis for social order in the United States. The movement for immigrant rights, for example, might succeed in forcing a larger discussion of the many ways that TNCs try to force down wages and benefits for American workers. Whether or not these movements will succeed at moving into the center of American politics will depend on whether or not they succeed in developing frames of reference that convince middle-class whites of their shared interests with people of color.

In other words, the United States is still faced with the same challenges it faced in previous eras. There is no chance for a new politics that saves the middle class from the race to the bottom that is not simultaneously a politics of inclusion for all people of different races, colors, nationality statuses, religions, genders, and sexual orientations. In the era of the welfare state, we saw that the middle class was willing to tolerate and at times even support the demands of the civil rights movement for the inclusion of people of color at a time of expanding economic opportunities in the unique post–World War II economic boom. In this era, the white middle class will have to come to the politics of inclusion through a different route, one that recognizes that there will be no social stability in any country, let alone throughout the world, if there remains a growing chasm between the haves and the have-nots. Clearly, the United States is not yet at this point. But as the crises of globalization continue to deepen, the opportunities to articulate a new politics of inclusion based on a socially just vision of globalization will continue to appear with increasing urgency. While there can be no certainty that people will ultimately choose inclusion over fear, it does seem certain that the demands for inclusive social justice—and the dreadful consequences of continuing to ignore these demands—will become increasingly compelling in the coming decades.

NOTES

1. Edward Said, "Thoughts about America," *Counterpunch*, March 5, 2002.

2. "Can America Help Lead the World to Peace and Justice?" *New York Times*, October 9, 2001. For an excellent overview of other Japanese reactions, see Ueda Yasuo, "The Response to 9/11 in Japanese Publishing," *Japanese Book News* 41 (2003): 4–20.

3. For an excellent account of the ways that U.S. and Soviet foreign policy created the terrorist organization that attacked the USS *Cole* in Yemen, see Mahmood Mamdani, *Good Muslim, Bad Muslim: America, the Cold War, and the Roots of Terrorism* (New York: Pantheon, 2004).

4. On the War on Drugs, see Craig Reinarman and Harry G. Levine, eds., *Crack in America: Demon Drug and Social Justice* (Berkeley: University of California Press, 1997). On populism and racism, see C. Vann Woodward, *Tom Watson: Agrarian Rebel* (New York: Macmillan, 1938). In his social history of the organization of California into the United States in the late nineteenth century, *Racial Fault Lines* (Berkeley: University of California Press, 1994), Tomas Almaguer carefully delineates the use of external enemies to cohere internal consent.

5. Benjamin Franklin, for example, warned the Pennsylvania colony in 1751, "Why should the Palatine boors be suffered to swarm into our settlements, and by herding together, establish their language and manners, to the exclusion of ours? Why should Pennsylvania, founded by the English, become a colony of aliens, who will shortly be so numerous as to Germanize us, instead of our Anglifying them?"; quoted in Stephen Steinberg, *The Ethnic Myth* (New York: Atheneum, 1981), 19.

6. Manuel G. Gonzalez and Richard Delgado, *The Politics of Fear* (Boulder, CO: Paradigm, 2006); Lee Cokorinos, *The Assault on Diversity* (New York: Institute for Democratic Studies, 2000).

7. Manuel Castells, *The Rise of the Networked Society* (Oxford, UK: Blackwell, 1996); Anthony Giddens, *The Consequences of Modernity* (Cambridge, UK: Polity Press, 1990).

8. Thomas Friedman, *The World Is Flat* (New York: Farrar, Straus & Giroux, 2006).

9. Joel Krieger, *Reagan, Thatcher and the Politics of Decline* (London: Polity Press, 1986).

10. Rick Fantasia and Kim Voss, *Hard Work: Remaking the American Labor Movement* (Berkeley: University of California Press, 2005).

11. Derrick Bell, *And We Are Not Saved* (New York: Basic Books, 1987).

12. Mike Davis, *Prisoners of the American Dream* (London, Verso, 1999); Martin Luther King Jr., *Where Do We Go from Here: Chaos or Community?* (Boston: Beacon Press, 1967).

13. James O'Connor, *The Fiscal Crisis of the State* (New Brunswick, NJ: Transaction, 2002).

14. Andrew L. Barlow, "Reframing the Welfare Debate: Advocating for the Poor in the 1990s," *Hastings Women's Law Review* 7, no. 2 (Summer 1996): 205–11.

15. Jill Quadagno, "Creating a Capital Investment Welfare State: The New American Exceptionalism," *American Sociological Review* 64, no. 1 (February 1999): 1–11.

16. Nancy A. Denton and Douglas S. Massey, *American Apartheid: Segregation and the Making of the Underclass* (Cambridge, MA: Harvard University Press, 1993).

17. William J. Chambliss, "Crime Control and Ethnic Minorities: Legitimizing Racial Oppression by Creating Moral Panics," in *Ethnicity, Race and Crime: Perspectives across Time and Place*, edited by Darnell F. Hawkins (Albany: State University of New York Press, 1995).

18. Henry Giroux, "Democracy and the Politics of Terrorism: Community, Fear, and the Suppression of Dissent," *Critical Methodologies* 2, no. 3 (2002): 334–42.

19. Jill Quadagno, *The Color of Welfare: How Racism Undermined the War on Poverty* (New York: Oxford University Press, 1994); Bell, *And We Are Not Saved*, esp. chap. 2.

20. Cokorinos, *Assault on Diversity*.

21. Paul Chevigny, "The Populism of Fear: Politics of Crime in the Americas," *Punishment & Society* 5, no. 1 (2004): 77–96.

22. Saskia Sassen, *Globalization and Its Discontents* (New York: New Press, 1998).

23. Arundhati Roy makes the same observation about India in *Power Politics* (Boston: West End Press, 2002).

24. On the general theory of boundaries and group formation, see Frank Parkin, *Marxism and Class Theory: A Bourgeois Critique* (New York: Columbia University Press, 1979).

25. Davis, *Prisoners of the American Dream*.

26. Harold Kerbo, *Social Stratification and Inequality*, 5th ed. (New York: McGraw-Hill, 2005).

27. Lawrence Mishel, Jared Bernstein, and John Schmitt, *The State of Working America, 1998–1999* (Washington, DC: Economic Policy Institute, 1999).

28. Pew Research Center, "Once Again, the Future Ain't What It Used to Be," May 2, 2006.

29. On the shrinking scope of trust and intimacy, see Robert Putnam, *Bowling Alone* (New York: Simon & Schuster, 2000).

30. Lewis Mumford, *The City in History* (New York: Harcourt, Brace & World, 1961); David Riesman, *The Lonely Crowd* (New Haven, CT: Yale University Press, 1950).

31. Doug McAdam, *Political Processes and the Development of Black Insurgency* (Chicago: University of Chicago Press, 1982).

32. O'Connor, *Fiscal Crisis of the State*.

33. Thomas Frank, *What's the Matter with Kansas?* (New York: Owl Books, 2004).

34. Amy E. Ansell, *Unraveling the Right: The New Conservatism in American Thought and Politics* (Boulder, CO: Westview Press, 1998).

35. Jean Hardisty, *Mobilizing Resentment* (Boston: Beacon Press, 1999), esp. pp. 30–36.

36. This contrast is explored in Thomas 2004.

37. David L. Kirp, John P. Dwyer, and Larry A. Rosenthal, *Our Town: Race, Housing and the Soul of Suburbia* (New Brunswick, NJ: Rutgers University Press, 1995).

38. Denton and Massey, *American Apartheid*.

39. Andrew L. Barlow, *Between Fear and Hope: Globalization and Race in the United States* (Lanham, MD: Rowman & Littlefield, 2003), esp. chap. 4.

40. Michael K. Brown, Martin Carnoy, Elliot Currie, Troy Duster, Marjorie M. Schultz, and David Wellman, *Whitewashing Race: The Myth of a Color-Blind Society* (Berkeley: University of California Press, 2003).

41. Kirp, Dwyer, and Rosenthal, *Our Town*; Quadagno, *Color of Welfare*.

42. King, *Where Do We Go from Here?*

43. For example, when the U.S. Supreme Court issued a series of rulings aimed at gutting the legal support for affirmative action programs in 1989, the Congress immediately passed, and President George H. W. Bush signed, the Civil Rights Act of 1991, reversing much of the damage done by these rulings.

44. Reinarman and Levine, *Crack in America*.

45. Barlow, "Reframing the Welfare Debate."

46. Brown et al., *Whitewashing Race*.

47. Cokorinos, *Assault on Diversity*.

48. This image was delivered regularly to mass audiences in movies (e.g., *New Jack City*, 1991) and gangsta rap, which became dominant in hip-hop after the release of NWA's *Straight Outta Compton* (1988).

49. Institute for Democracy, Education, and Access (IDEA), University of California, Los Angeles, *Fifty Years after* Brown: *California's Opportunity Gap* (Los Angeles: IDEA, 2004).

50. Chris Mooney, *The Republican War on Science* (New York: Basic Books, 2005).

51. Frank, *What's the Matter with Kansas?*, 249–50.

52. Primo Levi, in particular, explores the "banality" of the Holocaust in *Survival in Auschwitz: The Nazi Assault on Humanity* (New York: Collier, 1993).

53. Karl Polanyi, *The Great Transformation* (Boston: Beacon Press, 1944).

54. Peter Evans, "Counter-hegemonic Globalization: Transnational Social Movements in the Contemporary Global Economy," in *Handbook of Political Sociology*, edited by Thomas Janoski, Alexander Mitchell, and Mildred Schwartz (Cambridge: Cambridge University Press, 2005). Evans points out that even economists closely associated with global finance, such as Sachs and Stiglitz, raise the same cautions about unfettered market globalization.

55. Mae Ngai, *Impossible Subjects: Illegal Aliens and the Making of Modern America* (Princeton, NJ: Princeton University Press, 2005).

56. Robert Putnam, in "E Pluribus Unum: Diversity and Community in the 21st Century," *Scandinavian Political Studies* 30, no. 2 (2007), argues that immigrants suffer from isolation and the loss of connection in the short run and develop new social capital in the medium run.

57. Fantasia and Voss, *Hard Work*.

58. Tamara Kay, "Labor Transnationalism and Global Governance: The Impact of NAFTA on Transnational Labor Relations in North America," *American Journal of Sociology* 111, no. 3 (November 2005): 715–56.

CHAPTER 6

Un-American Gothic: The Fear of Globalization in Popular Culture

Paul A. Cantor

Many critics of globalization discuss the process as if it involved only the Americanization of the globe. Given the United States' position as the only global superpower today, this view is understandable, especially because American military might undergirds various forms of political, economic, and cultural influence as well. To see Coca-Cola, McDonald's, KFC, and other U.S. brand names wherever one travels around the world today can easily lead one to believe that the Earth is rapidly being made over into a gigantic American strip mall.

But if one looks at a typical American strip mall these days, one might begin to form the opposite impression. It might very well contain a Jamaican restaurant, a Mexican grocery, a Tae Kwan Do academy, a Chinese acupuncture clinic, and perhaps even a Buddhist or a Baha'i temple. As recently as twenty years ago, if you went into a restaurant in, say, South Dakota and asked for wine, the waiter would likely have stared at you in disbelief. Today the chances are that even a semi-upscale restaurant in the backwaters of America will have a wine list, perhaps featuring bottles from France and maybe from as far away as Australia and South Africa, chosen on the basis of the latest recommendations from the *Wine Advocate* or the *Wine Spectator*. The globalization of the American palate may seem like a trivial development, but it is no more so than the burgeoning worldwide taste for Big Macs and fries.

In short, if we are what we eat, the globalization of America is proceeding apace with the Americanization of the globe. And that means that Americans are developing the same anxieties about globalization that people all over the world are experiencing. The globalization of the United

States has occurred so rapidly and included such extensive and deep changes that it has unsettled and unnerved the American people. This unease has been mirrored in American popular culture in some obvious and not-so-obvious ways. In this chapter, I discuss the way that fears about immigration and the porousness of U.S. borders have surfaced in American television programs, reflecting a deep-seated concern that the very integrity of American identity is being eroded. These fears often take the form of nightmare images of alien invasions and alien-human hybrids—the birth of a mode in popular culture that might be called Un-American Gothic.

To many, it looks as if America and Americans have conquered the world, and U.S. popular culture sometimes reflects this sense of triumph. But many television programs do not give the impression that Americans feel that they are sitting on top of the world. Rather, they seem to live in fear that sinister forces somewhere out there in the world are about to conquer them. The seemingly paradoxical experience of the conqueror feeling conquered is by no means unprecedented in world history. Indeed, it seems to be integral to the experience of empire, as the example of Rome illustrates.

Ancient Rome dominated the Mediterranean world in many ways more fully than the United States dominates the globe today. Where today local natives may cringe at the sight of a McDonald's going up in their neighborhood, Gauls or Judeans would have balked at the sudden appearance of a Roman amphitheater in their midst. With its military, political, and economic power, Rome projected its cultural influence more forcefully and self-confidently than the United States ever has. The Romans openly proclaimed themselves to be conquerors and forced people all around the world they ruled to acknowledge them as masters.

But even as Rome entered its imperial age, some of its best thinkers began to feel uneasy about maintaining their Roman identity intact. Virgil's *Aeneid* celebrates the imperial triumphs of Augustus Caesar, but in its portrait of his great rival, Mark Antony, it suggests that a Roman conqueror might succumb to the very forces he thought he had conquered. Toward the end of Book VIII, Virgil portrays an Egyptianized Antony, overwhelmed by oriental forces, seduced by the Egyptian queen Cleopatra, and linked up with the bestial gods of the East:

>   And facing them, just come
> From conquering the peoples of the dawn,
> From the red shores of the Erythraean Sea—
> Together with barbaric riches, varied
> Arms—is Antonius. He bring with him
> Egypt and every power of the East
> And farthest Bactria; and—shamefully—
> Behind him follows his Egyptian wife. . . .
>   . . . Every kind of monster
> God—and the barking god, Anubis, too—
> Stands ready to cast shafts against Minerva
> And Venus and at Neptune.[1]

Antony's story illustrates the cultural contradictions of empire: campaigning in foreign lands exposes the conqueror to alien ways of life, which may end up subverting his attachment to his own people. Military victory may thus turn into cultural defeat.

Moreover, as Roman armies marched into lands all around the Mediterranean, foreigners from those same lands poured back into the city of Rome, attracted to the center of empire and eager to embrace Roman citizenship for all it was worth. All this explains how a good-size Egyptian pyramid came to be built in downtown Rome by a man named Cestius, who evidently felt it would be fashionable to go to his grave like a pharaoh. The pyramid of Cestius is an early example of what is jokingly referred to in postcolonial studies as the "Empire Strikes Back" motif. As if in anticipatory revenge for all those alien amphitheaters Rome was to go on to construct around the Mediterranean, the imperial metropolis got an Egyptian pyramid that stands to this day as part of its Aurelian walls—an eternal monument to the way Rome was orientalized even as it tried to Romanize the world around it.

Rome as a distinct community dissolved into the vastness of its own empire. Once a neatly walled-in city with its horizons narrowly focused on war and the warrior virtues, Rome turned into an imperial cosmopolis embracing a wide range of ways of life and cultural options. To be a Roman in the age of the Empire was something very different from being a Roman in the early days of the Republic.[2] Among other transformations, Rome eventually metamorphosed into a Christian community, the ultimate example of how the subjugated East ended up conquering the seemingly dominant West in the ancient world.

The history of Rome lays bare the inexorable logic of empire: unlimited military expansion is inevitably linked to unlimited immigration from the imperial frontiers. The price an empire pays for trying to extend its control over the whole world is to have to absorb a sampling of the whole world's population within its borders. The imperial state necessarily becomes a multinational community, or at least a multiethnic one, and thus has trouble maintaining its traditional communal identity. The history of the British Empire tells the same tale as the Roman, culminating in the image of an orientalized London—the Londonstan that Salman Rushdie has presented brilliantly in novels such as *The Satanic Verses*. In one of the most imaginative passages in the book, Rushdie has his hero Gibreel Farishta fantasize about the results of a tropicalized and therefore totally transformed London:

> Institution of a national siesta, ... higher-quality popular music.... Improved street-life, outrageously colored flowers.... better cricketers; higher emphasis on ball-control among professional footballers, the traditional and soulless English commitment to "high workrate" having been rendered obsolete by the heat. Religious fervor, political ferment.... No more British reserve; hot-water bottles to be banished forever, replaced in the fetid nights by the making of slow and odorous love.... Spicier food.[3]

Having chosen Imperial Rome as a model for their own empire, the British ended up with a similar experience, as they came to watch citizens in the homeland adopting the manners and mores of their formerly colonized subjects in India.

The United States has not pursued empire as directly or openly as Rome or Great Britain did, but it has ended up exercising a kind of global hegemony nevertheless and is having to face the domestic consequences in ways that closely resemble the earlier Roman and British experiences. The pressures of immigration, especially of Hispanic peoples, have become acute in the United States, straining medical, educational, welfare, and other resources and leading many Americans to feel that their way of life is fundamentally under attack. The United States has dealt with several immigration crises in its history, but in the larger context of an overall globalization of America, the current situation seems to be especially disturbing to people around the country. In economic terms, Americans are especially concerned that domestic jobs are being outsourced to foreign shores, while jobs that remain at home are being taken by illegal immigrants. As a result, immigration has become a heated political issue in the United States, with many people calling for the government to close its borders, especially with Mexico, to immigrants of any kind. The ongoing and contentious debate over bilingualism in the United States is only one cultural reflection of these concerns. Whatever one's attitude to the rights and wrongs of immigration may be, it is a simple fact that the American people are deeply troubled by the issue.

It is hardly surprising, then, that in the past decade or so fears about immigration have begun to feature prominently in American popular culture. The best example is the popular Fox science-fiction series *The X-Files*, which aired from 1993 to 2002. *The X-Files* is especially significant because of the way it relates the problem of immigration to the problem of globalization and links both to what might be termed the larger problem of empire. At its science-fiction/conspiracy-theory core, *The X-Files* presents as dark a picture of globalization as has ever appeared in American popular culture—indeed a paranoid nightmare of globalizing forces run amok and riding roughshod over American traditions and institutions.

The premise of the series is that alien beings plan to invade and colonize the Earth. They have entered into a conspiracy with a shadowy syndicate of political and business leaders from around the globe to help prepare for the alien takeover, which among other things involves the creation of alien-human hybrids. The hero and heroine of the series are two FBI agents, Fox Mulder and Dana Scully, who gradually learn that the pillars of the American regime—the FBI itself, the Department of Justice, the Congress, the presidency—are not what they seem. Those who appear to be in charge turn out to be just taking orders—puppets manipulated from behind the scene by members of the syndicate, who are working for—although at times against—the aliens. The sources of the syndicate's power are kept vague, but it is obviously international in character, associated with multinational corporations and multinational organizations, including the United Nations. What is clear in *The X-Files* is that the United States and its government are no longer in control of their own destiny.

To explain how this loss of control came about, *The X-Files* offers a revisionist history of America since World War II, which suggests that in its quest for global power, the United States, much like the Roman Empire, became the mirror image of the forces it was trying to contain and combat. The history emerged in bits and pieces over the course of several seasons, but chronologically arranged, it basically begins with the end of World War II when, according to the series, the United States used captured German and Japanese scientists to pursue the agenda of its own military-industrial complex. *The X-Files* presents this development as a Faustian bargain in which, for the sake of power, America joined up with the very forces it had been fighting against as the embodiment of evil in the world. The series takes a similar view of the Cold War. Several episodes point to covert links between American and Russian science and technology. The way *The X-Files* ties all this together is to link the German, Japanese, Russian, and American scientists to experiments involving alien-human hybrids.

In short, the whole invasion/conspiracy plot connecting the aliens, the syndicate, and the U.S. government symbolizes the way that America's military and imperial aspirations led to its being caught up in a system of international power relations in which it came to resemble the enemies against whom it claimed to be defining and defending itself. *The X-Files* suggests that to a large extent the United States created this system, but eventually it became a prisoner of its own creation, subject to the dictates of an amoral and inhuman science, whose unbridled use in totalitarian regimes it had condemned. In *The X-Files*, the way the United States gradually becomes assimilated to its supposed opposites is the heart of the problematic of empire and the most sinister aspect of globalization.

The X-Files thus represents a kind of cultural backlash against globalization, especially the globalization of America, in the 1990s. For decades, Americans had felt confident that their country was projecting its power outward into the world and in a way that was unequivocally good—a confidence reflected in popular culture in series such as the original *Star Trek* (1966–69), in which American democratic institutions were being spread not just around the globe but throughout the whole galaxy.[4] But in *The X-Files*, the American Empire appears to be imploding, as alien forces unleashed in the course of imperial expansion now strike back, subverting and replacing the duly constituted government of the United States. This fictionalized situation mirrored an increasing sense among Americans in the 1990s that they were no longer sure who was running their lives—their own government and institutions or mysterious forces from beyond their borders.

In the 1990s, a number of theorists from different fields developed a thesis that came to be known as "the end of the nation-state."[5] They argued that after centuries of being the dominant political institution, at least in the West, the nation-state in the late twentieth century was losing ground to all sorts of alternative forms of economic, cultural, and even political organizations—from supranational organizations like the European Union to economic trading areas like that created by the North American Free Trade Agreement (NAFTA) to newly emerging economic and cultural units like the Pacific Rim to the increasing power and independence of multinational corporations. These developments all have positive aspects, especially in economic terms, and many of the "end of the nation-state" theorists hail them as the wave of the future. But from the traditional perspective of the nation-state and the patriotism it seeks to spawn, all these developments appear to be subverting its authority and hence look sinister. In a variety of ways—some literal, some figurative—*The X-Files* makes reference to all the "end of the nation-state" phenomena, especially the way that economic and cultural forces no longer respect national borders.

The X-Files became famous for offering a remarkably negative portrait of the American government, but really its point is that the government is no longer *American* in any meaningful sense. It has been taken over by alien forces and no longer represents the will of the American people. In particular, *The X-Files* shows the traditional civil liberties of the American people being taken away by a global technocracy. The projected triumph of the aliens is linked to an Orwellian and even Foucauldian vision of an administered world gone global, in which institutions, including hospitals, clinics, schools, laboratories, research facilities, prisons, asylums, nursing homes, orphanages, and corporations, compile information about human beings in order to exercise control over them. In *The X-Files*, an inhuman—and un-American—science becomes the instrument of global power.

The X-Files went on to link these fears about globalization with fears about immigration. The series rests on a fundamental pun on the word *alien*. In science-fiction terms, the word, of course, refers to extraterrestrial beings: the little green—or, in this case, gray—men, of whom we get tantalizing glimpses in many episodes. But *The X-Files* also uses *alien* in the sense we mean when we speak of "illegal aliens." Several episodes deal with the plight of foreigners who have entered the United States under suspicious circumstances, either illegally or just surreptitiously. In all cases, *The X-Files* stresses the fact that the immigrants are racially or at least ethnically distinct from the American mainstream, and yet usually their goal—and often their threat—is to blend into that mainstream.

Immigrants in *The X-Files* include African Americans, Mexican Americans, and Chinese Americans, as well as figures from Eastern Europe and India.[6] The typical immigrant in *The X-Files* is presented as a hybrid figure, half American and half something else. Here is the most important link between the alien as extraterrestrial and the alien as immigrant. The extraterrestrial aliens also frequently appear as hybrids, half human and half something else. Indeed the issue of hybridity becomes central in *The X-Files* and links up with anxieties about globalization. The hybrid is at once a monster and "just like us." One of the chief concerns about the immigrant aliens and the extraterrestrial aliens in *The X-Files* is that they may be able to pass for ordinary Americans, blending right into society and thus able to carry out whatever nefarious schemes they may have in mind. But at the same time, *The X-Files* presents that hybridity as monstrous, a mixing together of what is meant to be kept apart. Episodes are often devoted to forcing one form of alien or another to come out of its shell, either literally or figuratively, and reveal its truly alien—and hence monstrous—character.

Fears about immigration in *The X-Files* are thus the mirror image of fears about globalization, and the show in effect explores the immigration problems of an imperial regime. Once again, we see how the logic of empire produces a multinational community at home, rife with the potential for ethnic and cultural strife. In both immigration and globalization, something non-American and even un-American is taking over America, usually by masquerading as American while standing for principles that are alien to the United States. The immigrants in *The X-Files* are all associated with traditional ways of life native to their home countries, customs quite alien to the American way of life. The illegal aliens typically practice voodoo, witchcraft, or other forms of magic quite foreign to the enlightened world of contemporary America. Their supernatural powers hark back to the pre-Enlightenment past, when religion ruled society. Scully and Mulder typically have to use all the resources of modern science to meet the challenge the old-time religion poses to modern America. Yet Mulder has a great interest in and respect for the occult, and the triumph of scientific modernity over traditional beliefs is often presented negatively in the series (for example, *The X-Files* displays a great admiration for the traditional religious beliefs and practices of Native Americans).

Indeed, in its portrayal of the clash between American modernity and foreign ways rooted in the past, *The X-Files* often seems to be lamenting the destruction of traditional ways of life around the world (another negative consequence of globalization). In the manner of many horror movies, the show is often quite sympathetic to the "monsters" it portrays, dwelling on the difficulty anyone who is different will inevitably have adjusting to the mainstream of society and its limited sense of what is "human." *The X-Files* often seems to be suggesting that monstrousness is in the eye of the beholder, and that society actually creates the monsters it then seeks to expel from its ranks. Reflecting the confusion of the American people themselves, the show seems unable to decide whether the United States should open or close its borders. At many points, *The X-Files* appears to celebrate ethnic and other forms of difference and to fear nothing more than the homogenization of humanity in a global state (symbolized by the experiments with cloning and other unnatural forms of reproduction throughout the series). But at the same time, *The X-Files* displays an overwhelming tendency to gothicize difference, to present the alien as truly monstrous and incompatible with the normal—and normative—American way of life.

The X-Files thus presents globalization as a process that affects all nations, including the one that appears to be exercising global hegemony. Although the imperial center thinks that it is exercising control over the periphery, through processes such as immigration the imperial frontier reacts back upon the center, threatening in a process of cultural blowback to blur the distinction between colonizer and colonized.

For a television show, *The X-Files* develops a surprisingly sophisticated understanding of globalization, one that seems very relevant to the world situation today. Yet some have argued that *The X-Files* is dated, a relic of the 1990s, made obsolete by the events of 9/11, which pundits at the time supposed would turn the American people from skeptics about their government into believers in it as their protector (as did in fact happen to a large extent, at least initially).[7] But it seems odd to dismiss the continuing relevance of a show that, in retrospect, has proved to be so prophetic. In an eerily accurate prediction of 9/11, the pilot episode of the *X-Files* spinoff *The Lone Gunmen*, which aired on March 4, 2001, deals with a terrorist attempt to pilot a commercial airliner into the World Trade Center. In general, at a time when most people were still thinking that threats to America would continue to come from foreign nations, *The X-Files* was already suggesting that in the future they would become more amorphous and hence more difficult to deal with. The central image of a foreign threat in *The X-Files* is an infection, with an unidentifiable source, an unknown cure, and the ability to spread unchecked in any direction. *The X-Files* offered an early warning about the emergence of the threat of terrorism, particularly bioterrorism, as one of the most negative consequences of globalization.

As if in recognition of the continuing relevance of *The X-Files*, the fall 2005 television season might have been dubbed "The Return of Scully and Mulder." No fewer than six debuting shows in one way or another drew upon the Fox series as a predecessor: *Bones, Supernatural, The Night Stalker, Invasion, Threshold,* and *Surface.*[8] Some of these shows involved personnel who had worked on *The X-Files*, and they all referred to it, either in their actual scripts or in their publicity material. For example, in the opening episodes of both *Bones* and *Supernatural*, one character turns to his partner and says, "If you're Scully, I'm Mulder."

Three of these shows—*Invasion, Threshold,* and *Surface*—are especially relevant to our purposes because they carry on the cultural work of *The X-Files* and explore the same thematic material. Although post-9/11 popular culture was supposed to become uniformly patriotic, these shows revived the political paranoia of *The X-Files*, dealing with government conspiracies and cover-ups, and chronicling the erosion of civil liberties in the United States. Above all, they portray the American government spying on its own people and imprisoning and interrogating them in a less than fully constitutional manner.[9] Moreover, the three titles all point to the issue of borders and the frightening possibility of their being violated.

The shows are in fact remarkably similar in conception, suggesting that they somehow reflect significant concerns of the American people. *Invasion* deals with a monster hurricane that hits the east coast of Florida and brings with it some kind of alien force that takes possession of people's bodies (or rather recreates them), turning them into alien-human hybrids. *Threshold* deals with an alien force that descends upon a ship at sea, turning its crew into alien-human hybrids, who then try to spread the "infection" throughout the U.S. population. *Surface* deals with strange hybrid creatures that suddenly appear in the ocean and go on to threaten the mainland United States in a giant tsunami that overwhelms the Mid-Atlantic coast.

Because these shows did not make it beyond a first season—*Threshold* did not even complete one full season—it is difficult to interpret any of them without knowing where they were headed.[10] After the first season of *The X-Files*, for example, we knew virtually nothing about the conspiracy between the aliens and the syndicate. In fact, we were not even sure if the aliens really existed and were not just figments of Mulder's hyperactive imagination. But even in their brief runs, the three television series offer interesting material for analysis, especially because they tend to reinforce each other, as well as to hark back to *The X-Files* in the way they reflect anxieties about the porousness of U.S. borders and the threat of immigration to the integrity of the American way of life.

It is certainly interesting to find three shows simultaneously returning to the theme of hybridity, and all present it as something monstrous. *Invasion* even jokes about bringing up the issue. At one point, when the hero of the series uses the term *hybrid* with one of the aliens, he replies: "I heard that's what you're calling us. It's very trendy."[11] It is rare that a term that is fashionable in literary criticism becomes fashionable in American television, but it happens here. The three shows seem all to be concerned about the fact that Americans no longer have a simple and straightforward identity. They are becoming hybrids, and the new admixture is a foreign or an alien element that makes them fundamentally different from what they were before and poses a threat to the continuation of their way of life as Americans.[12]

It is particularly interesting that in all three shows the alien threat is associated with and comes up out of the ocean. This motif is already developed in *The X-Files*, in which a number of episodes deal with ship's crews infected at sea and the mysterious alien "black oil" being transported by oceangoing vessels. In the typical science-fiction movie or television show in the 1950s or 1960s, alien threats tended to come from the sky—most famously, of course, in flying saucers. This motif obviously reflected Cold War anxieties about nuclear weapons, strategic bombers, intercontinental ballistic missiles, and the space race between the United States and the Soviet Union. During the Cold War, Americans had a great deal to worry about—above all, nuclear annihilation—but at least they were confident that they knew who their enemies were.

Threats from the sky seem to suggest "at least we'll see them coming." But threats from the ocean are harder to pinpoint and identify. They seem just to well up and can hit at any time and any place; moreover, in *Invasion* and *Surface*, they masquerade as natural disasters. The shift from invasion from the sky to invasion from the ocean seems to register a change in Americans' perception of the world, a recognition of the way the rules of the international game changed in the 1990s: "We didn't know where the real threat was coming from. We thought it was from one nation, the USSR, but now we see that it's something more complicated. Something is coming across our borders and we don't know what, where, or when." I am perhaps formulating this point too explicitly, but it does seem significant that *Invasion*, *Threshold*, and *Surface* all suggest that, whatever the threat to the United States may be, it can no longer be simply identified as a fleet of invading spaceships but is something much more nebulous and harder to spot. In a globalized world, where national borders no longer have the same force, an invasion may easily be confused with more benign or natural processes.[13]

Moreover, in American mythology, the ocean has always been identified as the route of immigration. Today, more people may come to the United States by plane than by boat, but the image of immigration in popular culture is still the tired, the hungry, the huddled masses yearning to breathe free docking at Ellis Island in New York Harbor. The aliens landing in flying saucers in science-fiction movies of the 1950s looked more like an invading army than huddled immigrants. By contrast, alien creatures washing up on our shores come closer to the immigrant archetype—another reason why the ocean may figure so prominently in *Invasion*, *Threshold*, and *Surface*.

Of the three, *Invasion* is the one that most systematically confronts the issue of immigration. Since it is also by far the best of the three artistically and the one that most fully harks back to *The X-Files*, I will concentrate on *Invasion* for the rest of this essay, with occasional references to the other two shows.

Because *Invasion* is set in southern Florida, in the area of the city of Homestead and Everglades National Park, it is easy for the series to bring up the issue of immigration. The opening shot in the pilot episode features a Hispanic woman with her son, and at many points during the series we hear Spanish spoken (the hero is a Cuban refugee). A scene deleted from the broadcast pilot but available on the DVD version features a Hispanic policewoman trying to get an old man to seek shelter from the coming hurricane. Refusing her help, he tells her, "You go, Gomez—go back to Havana." She denies that she is an immigrant: "I'm not Cuban, Earl. I'm from Pensacola. Pensacola, Florida." When he replies, "Pensacola, my ass. You're a damn alien" (1), the show humorously introduces the same pun on which *The X-Files* is based. Throughout *Invasion*, we hear of aliens in the sense of extraterrestrials and aliens in the sense of immigrants, illegal or otherwise, and often characters turn out to be aliens in both senses at once. Given the Florida setting, it is natural for Cuba and Cubans to come up often in the series, but it also contains references to countries in Central America (Honduras), the Caribbean (Haiti), and South America (Venezuela and Brazil).

For one plot reason or another, the show keeps picturing what look like and in fact are refugee camps, either on the mainland or in the Florida Keys. The rising tide of the hurricane brings a flood of refugees to the shores of Florida, who must be dealt with and who quickly strain the combined resources of local and federal authorities. *Invasion* was well into production before Hurricane Katrina struck the Gulf Coast, but what was a disaster for New Orleans was a stroke of good fortune for the TV series, which seemed extremely timely when it debuted on September 21, just a few weeks after Katrina devastated New Orleans on August 29. The show made excellent use of the political controversy surrounding Katrina. The fourth episode, "Alpha Male," features a substantial and pointed debate over the way the government dealt with the hurricane disaster, which closely echoes the actual complaints made by the American public, especially about the Federal Emergency Management Agency's inadequate and inept response (FEMA is referred to negatively in episode 19). Residents of the town complain bitterly to the sheriff about the quarantine he has imposed—which, as they insist, keeps out the very help they need to rebuild their lives.

Like *The X-Files*, *Invasion* displays a strong antigovernment streak, and it eventually reveals the federal government, and above all the military, to be mixed up in the alien invasion, or at least to be trying to cover it up. *Invasion* strongly suggests that ordinary Americans do not want their shores invaded by aliens, while the federal government is indifferent to their concerns and perhaps is even aiding the aliens for its own dark purposes. At one point, the military is shown experimenting on the aliens to discover and presumably exploit their superpowers—a plot development reminiscent of the story of the government supersoldiers in the final seasons of *The X-Files*.

One of the clearest indications that *Invasion* is dealing with American anxieties about immigration is the extraordinary fertility of the aliens. The women whose bodies have been taken over by the aliens do not just have babies, they evidently have litters. As the first season drew to its conclusion, the show increasingly focused on the situation of a number of hybrid women who had become pregnant and were facing the prospect of an uncertain and extremely painful childbirth. Unfortunately, the series ended without clarifying what exactly the alien births would involve, but it is clear that they would be multiple, and the show strongly suggests that the aliens are indifferent to the fate of the mothers and care only about the propagation of their own species. One of the standard fears about immigrants is that they reproduce rapidly and without restraint. This anxiety goes to the heart of the fundamental fear that the immigrant population will displace the mainstream population by overwhelming it numerically. Alien pregnancy turned out to be the most Gothic element in *Invasion*. In the best horror-movie tradition, à la *Rosemary's Baby* (1968), it takes a legitimate fear women experience ("Will my baby be normal?") and gothicizes it with monstrous images of grotesquely distended, pulsating bellies and the sonogram-promise of abnormally multiple births.

The larger issue of alien-human hybridity in *Invasion* gets very complicated. When a human drowns or otherwise ends up in ocean waters, he or she may be taken over by one of the alien beings (more precisely, the original human body is discarded, while the alien makes a kind of clone of it). In terms of outward appearance, the resulting alien-human hybrid is indistinguishable from the original, although blood tests and other medical indicators can discriminate a hybrid from a real human being. But more significantly, subtle psychological changes point to the difference between the new hybrid and the old human. For example, early on, the young daughter of a hybridized woman intuitively senses that her mother is no longer the same person. Indeed, the most pronounced changes brought about by hybridization occur in women, who begin to lose interest in their children and sometimes cease to care about them at all. One young hybridized mother abandons her baby and refuses even to acknowledge that it is hers.

Whatever the invasion may ultimately be, it chiefly seems to constitute a threat to the nuclear family. This motif ties in with the central plot line of *Invasion*, which centers on a broken family, or rather two families. The hero, a park ranger named Russell Varon, is divorced and has remarried a woman named Larkin Groves. His ex-wife Mariel, a medical doctor, is now married to Tom Underlay, the town's sheriff (both of whom, as it turns out, have been hybridized). Mariel's two children with Russell, Jesse and Rose, are now chauffeured back and forth between the two households in a variety of SUVs, getting lost in transit with alarming frequency. Sheriff Underlay has a daughter named Kira from a previous marriage, and Larkin is newly pregnant with Russell's child. All this may sound like a soap opera, but only because it is. Take away the science-fiction trappings and *Invasion* is a good old-fashioned soap opera about divorce, remarriage, sexual jealousy, broken families, custody of the kids, and all the emotional mayhem that results. Mariel sums it all up when she tells her son, "Divorce sucks, Jesse" (7).

Indeed, the emotional core of *Invasion* is the trauma of a broken family for all concerned, and the characters are constantly struggling to protect their families from external forces that threaten to tear them apart. They are repeatedly faced with situations in which they must choose between protecting their families and performing their professional duties (as sheriff, park ranger, doctor, or, more generally, savior of the world). What does all this have to do with globalization? The suggestion seems to be something like this: the increasing complexity of the modern globalized world makes increasing demands upon the time and energy of modern professionals, forcing them to neglect their families. The force with which Hurricane Eve slams into the Florida coast may be a symbol for the impact of the global on the local. People can no longer pay sufficient attention to their immediate and local concerns—their families and their neighborhoods—because they are distracted by all sorts of global concerns that demand their attention.

In *Invasion*, the pressing need to deal with what amounts to an immigration crisis—the flood of refugees into southern Florida—prevents the main characters from adequately dealing with a number of personal and family crises they are facing. In the midst of all the hurricane-induced chaos, the children repeatedly complain that they have been abandoned by their parents. As Jesse says at one point, "So, basically, we have no parents now" (18). *Invasion* reflects Americans' fears that, with their new concern with global issues—saving the world—they are losing sight of what is right before their eyes and closest to their hearts: their own families. Russell speaks for all the central characters in the series when he says of the crisis around him, "I care about how this affects my family" (2). Later, when he is asked if he is ever going to tell the world what he knows about the invasion, Russell replies, "When I know it's not going to hurt my kids" (11). Larkin, who is a TV journalist, concludes a live report with this observation about what she has learned from the hurricane experience: "What's really important is family and the people we love" (13).

The tension between the global and the local, specifically the threat to the nuclear family, is common to all the shows discussed. *The X-Files* developed into a chronicle of three dysfunctional nuclear families—the Mulders, the Scullys, and the Spenders (the family of the infamous Cigarette-Smoking Man).[14] Episodes work out so that involvement in the alien conspiracy forces people to sacrifice members of their family, and, particularly in the later seasons, the series explores the ways in which Mulder's and Scully's careers prevent them from having families of their own. In *Threshold*, the absence of families, normal or otherwise, is striking. The cast of characters is a rather unattractive crew of emotional and even sexual misfits who seem incapable of and uninterested in having families. The youngest (and most sympathetic) member of the *Threshold* team is engaged to a woman—later we learn that he has secretly married her—but his commitment to fighting the alien invasion prevents him from having a normal relation with her and almost costs him his life (or his human identity). The plot of *Surface* also involves several broken families and custody battles. To carry on her crusade against the alien creatures, the heroine must break off contact with her children, while the hero, in his obsessive quest for the creatures, ends up with his wife demanding a divorce.

The pattern in these series is extraordinarily consistent (for the record, *Bones*, *Supernatural*, and *The Night Stalker* all deal in one way or another with broken families, as well). The main thing that gets sacrificed in response to global threats is the nuclear family and above all the children, who are left to fend for themselves while their parents go off, either to conspire with or fight against an alien invasion. If *Invasion* and these other shows offer any insight into the American psyche, its great fear at the moment is that the integrity of the American home and the nuclear family is being threatened. And this threat is somehow linked to America's increasing global commitments.

Alien-human hybridity has many other meanings in *Invasion*—so many that one might call it overdetermined as a symbol. When hybrids begin to take over the local high school, the show, following in the tradition of *Buffy the Vampire Slayer* (1997–2003), makes something Gothic out of normal adolescent anxieties. The teenage hybrids behave like bullies, form cliques that exclude the remaining humans, and generally act like jerks—more precisely, jocks. In one scene, we see the high school hybrids on a basketball court, performing perfectly as a team, able to pass around the ball without dropping it even though they have their eyes shut. This is one of the many respects in which the hybrids develop abilities superior to those of normal human beings. More generally, they experience a much deeper community spirit, which comes at the expense of their sense of individuality.

Perhaps *Invasion* is harking back to some of the antitotalitarian science-fiction allegories of the 1950s. It seems to owe a great deal to *Invasion of the Body Snatchers* (1956) and indeed pays homage to that classic movie with its many references to "pod people" in episode 9 (which also contains a mention of "body-snatched people"). Critics have interpreted this film in different ways, but one obvious reading views it as a Cold War parable of a communist takeover of America.[15] The pod people think the same way, feel the same way, and act the same way—all contrary to the spirit of American individualism. With specific references to Cuba, the Bay of Pigs, and Fidel Castro in *Invasion*, it might be interpreted as an anticommunist allegory.

But in many ways, the hybrids seem more fascist than communist. They are associated with the local police force—Sheriff Underlay is one of their leaders—and they become linked up with the U.S. military and form their own paramilitary group. There is one pointed reference to Nazism in the series, when Jesse says, "I feel like I'm in occupied France, the trains are rolling, and nobody's doing anything to stop them" (19). Perhaps *Invasion* is exploring the possibility of homegrown fascism in the United States. But in the end, whether the show is attacking left-wing or right-wing totalitarianism may be immaterial. What is important is that it is anti-government in general and more specifically anti-authoritarian. The show seems to lament the way the hurricane and the invasion behind it become an excuse for a massive increase in local and federal government intrusion into the lives of ordinary citizens in Florida. Perhaps the hurricane-invasion can be read as a symbol, not of immigration, but of the new terrorist threat in post-9/11 America (these two sources of anxiety are, of course, related). Although *Invasion* focuses on Hispanic characters and the Latin American world, there are a few pointed references to Iraq in the series, including a strange moment when Russell learns of the two hybrid leaders: "If Underlay is Saddam, Szura is Zarkawi" (13).

If terrorism is at issue in *Invasion*, then the series may be suggesting that the United States has overreacted and sacrificed its fundamental liberties in the course of trying to protect them. The show seems to be responding negatively to the increasing militarization of American society since 9/11, particularly the use of the military in civilian situations. Episode 21 offers a very negative portrait of security control by the military, with a particularly ugly scene included in the DVD version that conjures up all the nastiness of airport security measures these days (including cute little Rose having her pet cat taken away from her by a heartless soldier). In episode 22, Russell says bitterly, "When it comes to national security, we're pretty good about justifying anything." Terrorism seems to be even more central to *Threshold*, and the issue of the sacrifice of civil liberties keeps coming up in that show, although most of the time it seems to endorse the choice of security over liberty.[16] The stance of *Invasion* seems more libertarian, but one must remember that the military forces in episode 21 are in fact hybrids masquerading as the U.S. Army and in the end the real Air Force comes to the rescue of the endangered humans. Perhaps the show is suggesting that our government is protecting us against alien terrorists after all.

On the other hand, in support of the libertarian reading, *Invasion* repeatedly presents negatively the way the hybrids band together to assert their authority and form various kinds of goon squads. Several scenes portray the hybrids coming together in a local church with a priest who is himself hybridized, and again the show seems to be criticizing the group-think of this community and the way they gang up on outsiders, which is to say, normal human beings. But it is not clear that *Invasion* is attacking organized religion as a force for evil in the United States. The priest insists that the group is simply using his church building as a meeting place and that he is not conducting religious services or in any way serving in his capacity as a priest with them. Rather than religious services, the meetings in the church seem more like a support group with a twelve-step program. The hybrids refer to themselves as "survivors," give testimony to their survival experiences, and encourage each other's personal growth as if they were members of "Aliens Anonymous." Perhaps the show is criticizing New Age movements and the whole ideology of self-help and self-development, which, among other things, leads people to turn their backs on their families, especially their children, in the name of self-actualization.

All this may sound confusing, and perhaps the show is itself confused on these issues, but then again perhaps the confusion is the point. *Invasion* may be portraying the confusion that results from the globalization of America. We begin with a typical American small town, with typical small-town values, chiefly a premium on traditional family values. This tightly knit community is suddenly invaded by a wide range of new ideological and religious possibilities, as well as new varieties of people, who challenge its self-definition. We witness all the strains these new developments place on the small town, as it tries to rebuild itself and reform its sense of community. The remaining humans increasingly come to feel that their way of life is fundamentally threatened, and they try to find ways to fight back against what they view as a hostile takeover of their homeland.

At the most general level, *Invasion* is about social change and whether people are going to resist it or embrace it. For example, in episode 9, Underlay says of his wife Mariel: "She doesn't exactly embrace change.... She's afraid of letting go of the past." Thus we see the same Gothic dynamic at work we observed in *The X-Files*. The hybrids are passing as normal human beings, and that helps them gradually extend their control over society and remake it, especially given their allies in high places and, above all, their links to the military. But although they look like humans, we keep getting hints that the hybrids are monstrous and will destroy the America we know. They are abnormally attracted to water and can survive underneath it for prolonged periods of time, they give birth in an alien way, and indeed in one of the final revelations we get in the series, we learn that the hybrid women must give birth in water. At many points, *Invasion* gives the impression that the very survival of the human species is at stake and that a failure to stop the alien invasion will mean the extermination of humanity. If we are to associate the invasion with the globalization of America and all the changes it involves, then *Invasion* gives almost as negative a portrait of the process as *The X-Files* does.

But in its concluding episode, *Invasion* offers a twist on this dark vision. Faced with the prospect of a number of hybrid women giving birth, Mariel Underlay insists on saving their lives and helping them—partly because she is a doctor, partly because she is a woman, and partly because she is a hybrid herself (and pregnant, too). She even succeeds in getting her ex-husband and confirmed alien fighter, Russell Varon, to assist the process and help the pregnant hybrids to the water. This plot development reflects a fundamental ambiguity in the way the aliens are presented in *Invasion*. Most of the time, the hybrids are pictured as monsters and treated as deeply un-American, specifically in their collectivist attitudes. But just as happens in *The X-Files*, *Invasion* at times treats the aliens quite sympathetically. It even raises the possibility that they may be the legitimate next stage in human evolution (this idea comes up in *Threshold*, too). The series is filled with references to Darwin and evolutionary language, with phrases like "survival of the fittest" and "Cambrian Explosion" appearing frequently and episodes entitled "Unnatural Selection" (5), "Origin of Species" (10), and "Re-Evolution" (18). Larkin's brother, Dave, describes the situation vis-à-vis aliens this way: "like we're the Neanderthals and they're us" (18).

In certain physical and mental respects, the hybrids certainly are improvements over the human species. They heal from wounds much faster, for example, and are even able to regenerate limbs. Tom Underlay as leader of the hybrids becomes an increasingly sympathetic figure over the course of the season. Played brilliantly by William Fichtner, he starts out as a sinister figure—the seeming villain of the show—poised in opposition to Varon as the hero. But as we learn more about his past history, we come to empathize with Underlay's plight as a hybrid, and in the last episodes he joins up with Varon to fight a renegade group among the hybrids, led by Szura, and thus becomes a kind of hero himself. We will never know where *Invasion* was heading ultimately in its treatment of the hybrids, but it is clear than even in its one completed season, it went from treating them as pure monsters—the "pod people"—to considering the possibility that they might have a good side and perhaps even represent the future of humanity.

This ambiguity is evident in the rhetoric of the show. At times, *Invasion* could not have been more xenophobic in its language, as characters basically voice versions of the traditional attitude that "the only good alien is a dead alien." But at other times, the rhetoric of *Invasion* becomes distinctly multicultural in spirit. Sometimes the hybrids are allowed to speak eloquently of their right to be different and, paradoxically, to be treated as human beings. In the final episode, for example, when Mariel defends the pregnant hybrids' right to give birth, she says: "Whatever's inside them may be different, but it doesn't mean that it's bad. And it doesn't mean that it's dangerous—it's just different" (22). This defense of difference was a recurring motif in the series. Earlier Dave—who is fully human—says, "Just because something is different doesn't necessarily make it bad" (10), and Underlay echoes this phrasing when he says, "Just because someone's different doesn't make them a monster" (14). Perhaps Jesse puts it best when he speaks for teenagers everywhere: "Weird's cool" (11).

Like *The X-Files*, *Invasion* is deeply suspicious of hybridity, but it tries to remain open to the possibility that hybridity, as an alternative to homogeneity, may be something good. Both shows generally tend to gothicize difference, but they have their moments of celebrating it, as well. In this ambiguity, they perhaps reflect something about the American people—they may be anxious and even frightened about globalization, but at the same time, they appear to be eager to embrace what might be its good aspects. The way *The X-Files* and *Invasion* give a remarkably complex and nuanced view of globalization, and try to air both sides of the issue, suggests that occasionally the American people get the television programs they deserve. And even when they are at their most fantastic, television shows may point to the reality—sometimes the frightening reality—with which we live.

NOTES

1. Virgil, *The Aeneid*, translated by Allen Mandelbaum (New York: Bantam Dell, 2004), Book VIII, lines 888–95, 908–11.

2. I discuss this contrast as Shakespeare presents it in his Roman plays in Paul A. Cantor, *Shakespeare's Rome: Republic and Empire* (Ithaca, NY: Cornell University Press, 1976). As often happens, Shakespeare anticipates the great problems of later ages. In particular, *Antony and Cleopatra* is in effect a study of globalization, and Shakespeare explores the connection between the pursuit of empire and the loss of cultural identity.

3. Salman Rushdie, *The Satanic Verses* (New York: Viking Penguin, 1988), 355.

4. For a discussion of the galactic politics of *Star Trek*, see the chapter on the series in Paul A. Cantor, *Gilligan Unbound: Pop Culture in the Age of Globalization* (Lanham, MD: Rowman & Littlefield, 2001), 35–64.

5. See, for example, Kenichi Ohmae, *The End of the Nation-State: The Rise of Regional Economies* (New York: Free Press, 1995); Jean-Marie Guéhenno, *The End of the Nation-State*, translated by Victoria Elliott (Minneapolis: University of Minnesota Press, 1995); and Martin van Creveld, *The Rise and Decline of the State* (Cambridge: Cambridge University Press, 1999).

6. I discuss in great detail the theme of immigration in *The X-Files* and analyze at length the treatment of these different ethnic groups in the chapter on the series in Cantor, *Gilligan Unbound*, 122–48.

7. See, for example, Andrew Stuttaford, "The Ex-Files: Mulder and Scully's Exit," *National Review Online*, May 17, 2002, http://www.nationalreview.com/stuttaford/stuttaford051702.asp.

8. Matt Roush links together all of these shows (except *Bones*) and compares them to *The X-Files* in "Scared Yet? Rating TV's New Creepshows," *TV Guide*, October 24, 2005.

9. These shows may not be quite as paranoid about the government as *The X-Files* was, but then again, *The X-Files* set a high standard of political paranoia. *Invasion* and *Surface* seem on the whole to take a dim view of the American government. *Threshold* seems to be largely pro-government, but only because its premise is that a set of experts has in effect taken over the federal government in a time of crisis and institutions such as Congress are no longer in control. In fact, *Threshold*, much like the series *24*, suggests that the normal operations of the federal government, including bureaucratic standard operating procedures and congressional oversight, can only get in the way of dealing with today's crises. If *Threshold* is pro-government, it is not in favor of anything recognizable as traditional American government. It is telling that in one episode, the *Threshold* team gets authorization to have blown out of the sky a plane carrying a U.S. senator because they have evidence that he has become hybridized into an alien. So much for congressional oversight as far as this series is concerned. For more on this issue, see note 16.

10. It might be argued that the fact that these three shows all failed calls into question my claim that they reflected the mood of the American people. Here we get into the extremely murky question of why a given TV show succeeds or fails. The ideational or ideological content of a show is rarely, if ever, the decisive factor in whether it makes it or not. Television is an entertainment medium, and entertainment values are usually the most important factor in an audience's reaction to a show.

Stuttaford, in "The Ex-Files," argues that the events of 9/11 were responsible for the demise of *The X-Files* in the spring of 2002, because the country was no longer in the mood for its political paranoia. As with many arguments about television, this is a classic case of the fallacy of *post hoc, ergo propter hoc* reasoning (and it also fails to explain why the show is still extremely popular in syndication). The 2001–2002 season was *The X-Files'* ninth, an exceptionally long run for any series, and hence the show had probably run its course with or without 9/11. Moreover, problems with retaining its two stars, David Duchovny and Gillian Anderson, after the seventh season left the show's creators unable to plan out whole seasons in advance as they had done so well in the past, and led to a decline in quality in the eighth and ninth seasons (to his credit, Stuttaford acknowledges the importance of the Duchovny problem in the decline of *The X-Files*).

Entertainment considerations such as these are more likely to explain the cancellation of *Invasion*, *Threshold*, and *Surface* than their failure to get in sync with the Zeitgeist. *Surface* was simply a silly show and deserved to be canceled. *Threshold* had an intriguing premise and solid production values, but its characters were largely unlikable and the show committed a cardinal sin in television terms—it failed to develop any sexual tension between its female lead and any of the male leads (one of the keys to the success of *The X-Files* was the audience becoming fascinated by the possibility of a romance between Mulder and Scully). I cannot point to any artistic faults in *Invasion*, and I believe that it deserved to be renewed. In fact, ABC did not cancel the show until the last possible moment. Sometimes the success or failure of a given show is simply a matter of luck.

The two *X-Files* clones that did make it into a second season, *Bones* and *Supernatural*, have less of the ideational contents of their model and more of its entertainment values. Both shows stress sheer horror values—the "grisly corpse of the week" motif—and both draw more than *Invasion*, *Threshold*, or *Surface* did on sheer star power. Moreover, *Bones* and *Supernatural* succeeded in developing a chemistry on screen between their leads. *Supernatural* is a classic on-the-road buddy story, featuring two extremely handsome young brothers. *Bones* copies the *X-Files* formula exactly, with the underlying sexual tension between its male and female leads at the center of its audience appeal.

The 2005–2006 season offered us probably as close as we will ever come to a controlled experiment in television programming. With several shows imitating various aspects of *The X-Files*, we have some evidence for the claim that entertainment value trumps ideational content when success on television is at stake. The shows that imitated the more superficial aspects of *The X-Files* did better than those that drew upon its deeper content. But a controlled experiment by television standards hardly meets the criteria of real science, and I offer this conclusion as highly tentative. I do, however, feel justified in concluding that the mere fact that a show was canceled does not justify inferring that its ideational content was responsible and therefore that it was out of touch with the American people. Other factors may have been responsible for the cancellation. In any case, even though *Invasion*, *Threshold*, and *Surface* ultimately failed, like any prime-time network programs, they were watched with interest by millions of viewers and thus probably did, to some extent, reflect the concerns of the American people.

As a footnote to this footnote, I can add the fact that in their second seasons, both *Bones* and *Supernatural* have begun to interject an element of *X-Files*-type political paranoia, with episodes involving FBI and other governmental malfeasance and cover-ups.

11. I have transcribed all quotations from *Invasion* from the DVD version and will cite them simply by episode number. This line is from episode 14; in the future, I will place the number of the episode in parentheses in the text. Later in the series, *Invasion* plays with "hybridity" again when the same character says, pointing at a street full of aliens: "They're hybrids—the people, not the cars" (19).

12. *Surface* does not pursue this theme as clearly as the other two shows. Its hybrid creatures are not extraterrestrial, but have been created by scientists working for a mysterious corporation. The teenage hero of the series, Miles, raises one of the hybrid creatures from an aquatic egg, and as a result, they become very attached to each other. After being bitten by his pet, "Nim" (short for Nimrod), Miles begins to assimilate the creature's alien nature, developing some of its superpowers. In this plot motif, *Surface* begins to parallel *Invasion* and *Threshold* and thus can be reasonably categorized with them.

13. To make a point, I have exaggerated the difference between contemporary TV shows and earlier popular culture. Threats from the ocean occasionally appear in 1950s and 1960s popular culture, for example, in the movie *It Came from Beneath the Sea* (1955). By the same token, a sort of spaceship does appear in *Threshold* and the alien creatures in *Invasion* drop from a stormy sky as bright lights. Nevertheless, the fundamental reorientation in spatial symbolism I discuss in this paragraph does seem to be occurring in recent popular culture. *Invasion* at times insists that the aliens are not in fact extraterrestrial, but may be somehow native to the Earth. In a globalized world, it is harder to trace a threat to a clearly foreign source.

This reorientation is strikingly evident in Steven Spielberg's 2005 remake of the classic *War of the Worlds* story. In contrast to what happens in all earlier versions, in Spielberg's the Martians do not suddenly appear in spaceships. Rather, it turns out that they have already buried their war machines in American soil, and they simply pop up to wreak destruction (in the area of New York City). This reworking of the story seems to reflect new fears about terrorist sleeper cells—the enemy is already in our midst, and we just don't know it. For an insightful discussion of fears of terrorism in recent popular culture, including Spielberg's *War of the Worlds*, see Michael Valdez Moses, "Blockbuster Wars: Revenge of the Zeitgeist," *Reason Online*, September 30, 2005, http://www.reason.com/news/show/32973.html.

14. I discuss the crisis of the nuclear family in *The X-Files* in Cantor, *Gilligan Unbound*, 204–11.

15. See, for example, Richard A. Schwartz, *Cold War Culture: Media and the Arts, 1945–1990* (New York: Checkmark, 1998), 151.

16. Writing in *TV Guide* ("Threshold of a Hit," November 7, 2005), Craig Tomashoff says of the *Threshold* team, "They're not above squashing a civil liberty or two." He then compares the show to *The X-Files* and goes on to quote Brannon Braga, its executive producer, doing the same thing: "In *The X-Files*, the government conspiracy was the shadowy enemy. In our show, the heroes *are* the conspiracy." This quotation seems to mark a post-9/11 change in attitude toward covert government activities in *Threshold*. Charles Dutton, one of the actors in the series, describes it as "playing into what's happening in this country today with Homeland Security and the Patriot Act." Tomashoff continues: "And when aliens attempt to infect our food supply in an upcoming episode, Braga notes, there is definitely 'a parallel to the terrorist threat that strikes a primal fear.'" By contrast, when a high-ranking military official in *Invasion* says, "I promise, we're all patriots here" (8), the show appears to be treating the remark skeptically.

CHAPTER 7

Cultural Globalization and American Culture: The Availability of Foreign Cultural Goods in the United States

Diana Crane and Susanne Janssen[1]

Cultural exchanges among countries have increased to such an extent since World War II that a case has been made for the existence of a "cultural world-system,"[2] in which many different forms of culture are circulating. One indication that the level of cultural globalization is increasing is a steady rise in the numbers of foreign countries mentioned in press reports on the arts and culture in elite newspapers in four Western countries (France, Germany, the Netherlands, and the United States). Between 1955 and 2005, the number of countries represented has increased by 50 percent.

The genres of culture that are being transmitted from one country to another can be characterized in various ways. They include the arts—visual art, theater, literature, classical music, and so forth—and popular entertainment such as film, popular literature, pop music, and television. These forms of culture transmit symbols and values that embody various aspects of national cultures. Some cultural goods convey aesthetic values that are primarily meaningful to people with special training in the arts; others contribute to a nation's historical heritage, its "cultural memory"; and still others can be understood by almost anyone because they convey what it means to live in a particular place at a particular time, "a structure of feeling," as a culture theorist once put it.[3]

Why is the transmission of these types of culture important? On the one hand, such cultural exchanges may contribute to the richness and cultural diversity of national cultures. On the other hand, these cultural "imports" may have negative consequences if they replace indigenous cultures with products that are shallow and superficial and that are disseminated to many other countries at the same time. The threat of the emergence of a homogenous global culture consisting of Hollywood blockbusters (*Spiderman*, *Titanic*), American television series (*Bonanza*, *The Bold and the Beautiful*), and American best-sellers (*The Secret History*, *The Da Vinci Code*) has frequently been discussed.

Countries vary in their capacity to produce cultural "exports." These variations are related to the ways in which cultural products are created. While we tend to think of cultural creation in terms of the cliché of the solitary artist, in fact a great deal of cultural creation takes place in cultural or creative industries. The term *cultural industry* originally referred to clusters of very large firms, usually oligopolies, in which popular entertainment such as film, music, and television were produced. Recently, it has been defined more broadly to include "advertising, marketing, broadcasting, film industries, the Internet industry, the music industries, print and electronic publishing, video, and computer games."[4] Theater and the making, exhibition, and sale of artworks are considered "peripheral" cultural industries that lack the industrial form of production and reproduction.

A somewhat broader term, *creative industry*, is sometimes applied to both popular entertainment and the arts. *Creative industries* have been defined as "those industries which have their origin in individual creativity, skill, and talent, and which have a potential for wealth and job creation through the generation and exploitation of intellectual property."[5] They include advertising, architecture, the art and antiques market, crafts, design, designer fashion, film and video, interactive leisure software, music, the performing arts, publishing, software and computer games, television, and radio.

Substantial claims have been made for the economic importance of creative industries. For example, Richard Florida argues that these industries have "produced most of our economic growth over the late twentieth century." He suggests that the creative sector of the U.S. economy accounts for 30 percent of employment and nearly half of total wages and salaries in the United States.[6] Steven Tepper claims that art and culture are now considered to be engines of economic growth and development in "creative cities," "creative clusters," and "creative economies."[7]

However, leaving aside the successful Indian and Egyptian film industries, the economic benefits of creative industries are largely confined to the advanced, postindustrial economies of Europe, North America, and Japan. They are virtually nonexistent in the post-Socialist economies of Eastern Europe, the rapidly modernizing Asian economies, and the premodern economies in underdeveloped regions such as Africa.[8] Consequently, the cultural products of these latter countries are not widely disseminated in the postindustrial economies—though the modernizing economies provide markets for some types of cultural products from the advanced countries, particularly film and popular music.

National governments attempt to influence the production and dissemination of cultural products. The rationale for this type of activity is, in part, "to find, serve, and nurture a sense of belonging through educational institutions and cultural industries."[9] According to Justin Lewis and Toby Miller:

> Cultural policies are a means of governance, of formatting public collective subjectivity.... Some of this is done in the name of maintaining culture, to preserve ways of being a person. It can also be managed in terms of economic development generating new modes of expression. The former tend to invoke cultural hierarchies—such as those bound up in glorifying the history of Western civilization. The latter tend to embrace developments in the social technology of culture in ways that talk about the need for a citizenry to have available the latest and the best, whether it is a compact disk or an Internet hook-up.[10]

European countries have generally developed explicit cultural policies that attempt to encourage the production and dissemination of the arts rather than popular entertainment. Mario d'Angelo and Paul Vespérini write:

> The "who am I" of a nation is plainly revealed in its cultural policy through activities that have an impact on its image and that are more or less coherent over time ... the image one wants to give of oneself as well as the image that emerges from the representation, more or less idealized, that one has of oneself.[11]

The concern among European countries with regard to popular entertainment is more likely to involve the use of quotas to prevent or inhibit cultural "imports" that might compete with or overwhelm indigenous cultures. The U.S. government has a minimal policy toward the arts and an inexplicit, almost invisible, policy toward the protection of its cultural industries.

In this chapter, we will examine the availability of different genres of foreign cultural goods in the United States. If foreign cultural goods are not available, their impact is likely to be small. The literature on cultural globalization warns about the hegemonic role of American culture in global media and the threat of "Americanization" of other cultures,[12] but there has been little discussion of the role of foreign cultures in American culture. However, there are indications that the United States may actually be less open to foreign cultural goods than many other countries at comparable levels of economic development.

The availability of foreign cultural goods in the United States can be assessed by considering the level of attention to foreign products in press coverage of the arts and culture. We will analyze this issue using statistics concerning the extent of coverage of foreign arts and culture in a major American newspaper, the *New York Times*, in comparison with analogous coverage in comparable European newspapers. These data will be interpreted using several theoretical approaches.

KEY FACTORS IN THE INTERNATIONAL DISSEMINATION OF CULTURAL GOODS

In this section, we consider four types of explanations for variation in levels of dissemination of cultural goods in different countries. The first focuses on characteristics of countries that influence the receptivity of their population to foreign cultural goods. The second addresses characteristics of culture industries that influence production of cultural goods and receptivity toward foreign cultural goods. The third centers on cultural and trade policies that influence the dissemination of cultural goods. The fourth examines variations among cultural genres that influence the dissemination of cultural goods.

Determinants of a Country's Receptivity to Foreign Cultural Goods

Demography (Size and Diversity)

The size of a country's population is known to be associated with its receptiveness to foreign cultural products. For a variety of reasons, large countries tend to maintain fewer transnational, cultural relations than small countries. Relative to their size, the latter tend to import more cultural goods than larger countries.[13] To start with, Peter Blau's theorem operates here: the smaller the group, the more important the exchanges between groups.[14] Second, countries with large home markets profit in their cultural production from economic advantages of scale that small countries have to do without. Particularly in capital-intensive sectors, small countries depend more on foreign markets and in turn mean less to these foreign countries. Third, elites in small countries tend, out of status considerations, to focus on elite cultural producers in large countries who have substantial influence outside their own borders. Fourth, the cultural diversity of large countries may reduce their incentive to seek cultural diversity outside their own borders. Other factors being equal, the above suggests that the United States would be less receptive to foreign cultural goods than smaller and more homogenous Western European countries.

Economic Development

Economic development increases a country's capacity to produce cultural goods that can be disseminated to and from other countries. One of the consequences of the increasing wealth of developing countries, particularly in Asia, has been an enormous expansion in the amount of film and television fiction being produced.[15] The extent to which these films reach American audiences will be discussed below.

Regional Proximity

Regional proximity is another variable that affects the dissemination of cultural goods. Countries are more likely to exchange cultural products with their neighbors than with more distant countries. This finding can be explained by the fact that regional proximity is often associated with cultural proximity, which facilitates the reception of cultural goods. In the case of the United States, cultural goods are more likely to be exported to its neighbors than imported from them. Both its neighbors (Canada and Mexico) have much smaller populations, which in turn affects the quantity of cultural goods these countries produce and, in the case of Mexico and part of Canada, different languages are spoken.

Cultural Proximity and Diversity

Under what conditions are foreign cultural goods meaningful to audiences? The cultural proximity of the material is a major factor.[16] Audiences tend to prefer cultural goods, such as films and television programs, that are produced in their own language and using their own national and local cultures. Among foreign cultural goods, they tend to prefer those that have been produced within cultures that are similar historically, ethnically, religiously, linguistically, and geographically. There may even be a kind of "resistance" to foreign cultural goods if audiences perceive them as lacking cultural proximity. However, perceptions of cultural and linguistic similarities tend to change over time as specific cultures change in relation to others, reflecting the complexity of cultural identities.

Ironically, the worldwide diffusion of American cultural goods, such as film and popular music, has given American products a kind of pseudo proximity or familiarity to many members of foreign audiences. Even items of clothing such as jeans and T-shirts, and drinks and food like Coca-Cola and hamburgers, have cultural implications. When audiences are willing to consume cultural goods from cultures that are very different from their own, it is likely to be the result of a desire to have some experience of cultures that are perceived as being more "modern" or "advanced" in certain ways than their own.[17]

There are two principal interpretations of the impact of cultural goods on audiences. Some media specialists have conceptualized audience behavior as largely *passive*. Long-term exposure to foreign cultural influences (particularly American) has been shown to have pervasive effects on attitudes, values, and tastes in other countries.[18] Other theorists conceptualize audience behavior as *active*. According to this approach, members of the audience select cultural goods that are meaningful to them and reinterpret them in terms of their own culture.[19] From the perspective of the "active" consumer, foreign cultural influences in the United States would be likely to expand and enrich the cultural repertoires of many Americans.

During the period examined by this study, 1955–2005, the characteristics of audiences for American culture changed considerably. In the first two decades, cultural tastes varied by social class. Audiences for high culture and popular culture drew from different social class strata.[20] The audience for high culture was interested in certain aspects of foreign high culture. By the 1990s, the audience for some forms of high culture had been significantly reduced, while the audience for popular culture had become highly differentiated into niche audiences representing lifestyles that varied within and across social classes. These audiences selected cultural fare from a variety of offerings within genres—such as popular music, television fiction, and film—in which American cultural industries were preeminent.

Social class continued to influence cultural tastes, but in a very different way.[21] Studies suggest that better-educated consumers are likely to be "omnivores" who sample many different types of culture and are presumably receptive to foreign cultural goods. Less-educated consumers are more likely to be "univores" who concentrate their attention on a particular cultural genre and are probably less receptive to foreign cultural goods.

Because of the enormous size of the United States and historical differences in the characteristics and geographic dispersion of immigrants and settlers, local regional cultures have been, and remain, diverse.[22] At the same time, social and political factors are decreasing the availability and visibility of foreign cultures.[23] In the previous century, immigration contributed substantially to cultural diversity. The influx of Hispanic immigrants in recent decades has had a considerable impact on the cultures of American states located near the Mexican border. In these regions, a second language, Spanish, is widely spoken. However, the aftermath of 9/11 has led to heightened government security measures that impedes the entry of foreign artists, performers, writers, and students through widespread denial of visas.[24] What's more, the U.S. Congress has debated legislation that would terminate illegal immigration across the Mexican border, expel illegal immigrants already in the United States, and reduce legal immigration from Mexico and other Latin American countries.

Language

Previous studies have shown that countries are less likely to import cultural products in languages other than their own.[25] This finding suggests that cultural goods from foreign Anglophone cultures will be more likely to be widely available in the United States than those from non-Anglophone countries. Less than 5 percent of all books published in the United States are translations.[26] One explanation for the low level of translation is the dominance of the English language throughout the world.[27] On a global scale, books are primarily translated *from* English rather than *into* English.

Cultural Industries, Media Imperialism, and the Dissemination of Cultural Goods

According to Robert McChesney and other proponents of the media imperialism approach, global mergers and joint ventures among media companies have led to control by a small number of companies over the content of the media at the national and international levels.[28] Douglas Kellner states that mergers of major entertainment and information conglomerates have produced "the most extensive concentration and conglomeration of information and entertainment industries in history."[29] The effects of this type of cultural domination—reflecting the attitudes and values of Western, particularly American, capitalist societies—are viewed as extremely pervasive and as leading to the homogenization of global culture.

This thesis has been challenged by some authors as being overly deterministic and as neglecting the impact of other sources of media content.[30] Based on the seeming success of Third World television productions, notably telenovelas, the possibility of "reverse cultural imperialism" has been discussed. However, recent studies of the popularity of the telenovela in different markets[31] and of the continuing success of American television fiction in the European market[32] have cast doubt on the viability of that thesis. A rare example that does support the thesis of reverse cultural imperialism is the domination of the video game industry by Japanese animators, whose cultural goods are heavily consumed by American children and adolescents.

An alternative outcome of media imperialism is the homogenization of American culture. Control by media conglomerates over cultural distribution systems in the United States may have led to a kind of media imperialistic hegemony in America, impeded the dissemination of foreign cultural goods in the United States, and narrowed the cultural choices available to American consumers. One example of this phenomenon is television fiction. While a great deal of attention has been paid to American leadership in exported television, there has been little discussion of the extent and impact of imported television in the United States.

American television networks have generally incorporated negligible amounts of foreign programming.[33] Only very recently has network television been available in any language other than English. American network television has been described as being "informally closed" to television from other cultures; the industry claims that the American audience rejects foreign programming on the basis of its inferior quality, unfamiliar settings, and slow pace. Yet while the United States has generally accused other countries of being protectionist toward cultural imports, practices that protect its own cultural industries may not be recognized. Richard Nielsen suggests that cultural-economic nationalism may play a role: "Trade in some products and services is being restricted because they are considered foreign threats to the domestic culture."[34] Denise Bielby and C. Lee Harrington state: "any imported series or concept competes with a network's ownership stake in its own shows and in keeping them on the air as long as possible to sell them to the domestic (and international) syndication market."[35]

Cultural diversity in the form of programming from other countries is most likely to appear on public television, which constitutes a very small segment of the American television industry, and on cable networks. Two large Spanish-language cable networks primarily show telenovelas produced in Latin America. The success of the telenovela with American audiences is due to several factors relevant for the introduction of other forms of foreign content: the existence of a sizable audience poorly served by existing programs (in this case, Hispanics), the availability of large amounts of fiction material from abroad compatible with the interests of that audience, and declining audiences for a specific genre (for example, soap opera). The diminishing audience for soap operas has led the networks to introduce changes in their series to make the episodes more attractive to the Hispanic audience.

Studies of the American film industry suggest that tight control over distribution networks in the United States by American media conglomerates limits the domestic distribution of foreign films. More foreign films are being shown in some parts of the country, but, with few exceptions, they do not reach sizable audiences. Similarly, American publishing houses increasingly belong to large media conglomerates that are profit oriented and may therefore be reluctant to publish books by foreign authors that might have limited appeal to American audiences.

Cultural and Trade Policies

In an increasingly turbulent environment for the international transmission of cultural goods, national cultural policies are necessary to provide guidelines for the protection of cultural heritage and for the management of cultural industries. In many countries, centuries-old cultural forms, an important aspect of a country's cultural heritage, are threatened. Cultural policies can stipulate strategies for preserving, protecting, and rejuvenating these cultural forms and for altering and transforming them for global consumption.[36]

National cultural policies can also determine the appropriate level of government subsidies and investment in genres that face highly competitive international markets and, in some cases, dwindling national markets. Such policies can also indicate ways of increasing private financing and investment in the production of cultural goods and can encourage transnational cooperation in the form of international co-productions, joint exhibitions, and festivals that reduce expenses and increase international marketability.

National governments vary in the importance they attribute to cultural policy. In France and the Netherlands, cultural policy is an important function of the national government.[37] In Germany and the United States, national cultural policy emerges from decisions made by thousands of actors at the state and local level. A recent study indicates that a huge number of American arts organizations, largely nonprofit and supported with private funds, flourish in a relatively unregulated policy environment, providing some cultural diversity inside the country—in comparison with a relatively homogenous popular culture that is disseminated both internally and externally.[38] The role of governments in setting cultural policy is increasingly difficult because of the external impacts of globalization and the development of regional governments, such as the European Union, and internal tensions between national and local governments and between insufficiently funded arts organizations and powerful cultural industries.[39]

A major issue in cultural policy is the extent to which cultural goods, particularly film and popular music, should be treated like other types of goods or should be given a special status in the market. In its negotiations with other countries, the U.S. government has insisted that there should be no restrictions on imports of cultural goods. American economic policy emphasizes the importance of free trade and unhindered flows of goods across national borders. The United States has strongly resisted the idea of a "cultural exception" to free trade that has been supported by, among others, France and Canada[40] and was recently endorsed by the United Nations Educational, Scientific, and Cultural Organization (UNESCO).[41] In 2001, UNESCO adopted a Universal Declaration on Cultural Diversity that recognized "the specificity of cultural goods and services which, as vectors of identity, values, and meaning, must not be treated as mere commodities or consumer goods."[42] The debate over the cultural exception has not yet been resolved. The outcome will have important implications for the future of cultural globalization.[43]

Variation by Cultural Genre

Cultural genres vary in the ease with which artifacts in those genres may be disseminated internationally. Music is one of the easiest types of cultural goods to disseminate widely and rapidly; literature, because of language differences, disseminates less easily. The development of global markets for certain types of cultural goods, such as avant-garde art and fashion,[44] has accelerated dissemination of such goods beyond national boundaries.

The extent to which a country excels in the production of a specific genre tends to negatively affect its receptivity to foreign cultural goods in that genre.[45] This is another reason why the United States, one of the world's largest producers of fiction films,[46] is less likely to import theatrical films than other countries at comparable levels of economic development. As we have seen, this is also the case for television fiction, of which the United States is the largest global producer.[47] American producers also have an advantage in these genres because they have created distinctive aesthetic styles that dominate these genres and that are often emulated elsewhere.[48]

A similar phenomenon is seen in the genre of popular music, where the United States, along with Great Britain, is a major producer of rock music and its offshoots. Again, the United States dominates the market not only quantitatively but also in terms of a specific aesthetic of pop music that has been accepted as the norm worldwide.[49] Instead of being perceived as a form of cultural imperialism, American rock music has been widely accepted because it expresses rebellion against oppressive cultures and authoritarian regimes while at the same time offering possibilities for the expression of "cultural uniqueness" and diversity in other countries.

Conversely, in certain genres, foreign cultural goods have a significant impact on American culture, because these genres originated in other countries and have accumulated and retain enormous symbolic value in American culture. The European musical and artistic canons fit this description. These works are well represented in the repertoires of American symphony orchestras[50] and in American art museums. Traditions underlying American dance and theater also originated in Europe.

However, consumption of some of these types of cultural goods tends to be low,[51] while there is also evidence that interest in these genres is waning among younger cohorts, in particular among people with a college degree.[52] This declining interest is visible in all genres with a "preponderantly Euro-American character" (classical music, ballet, and theater), whereas jazz, with its close ties to the African American community, and art museums, which represent works and objects from many cultures and traditions, gained in popularity. According to Paul DiMaggio and Toqir Mukhtar, this development may thus be related to societal trends toward multiculturalism and greater inclusiveness, as well as to the rise of visual culture.

The above discussion shows how the relative importance of cultural genres changes over time. At present, new types of cultural goods are displacing older ones and are changing the ways consumers use cultural goods. Video games are now more profitable than film and popular music. Consumers are inventing new types of genres on the Internet that permit them to exercise greater control over their cultural environment. They have access to new opportunities for creating cultural goods and for disseminating them. This suggests that the American environment for the import of cultural goods is continually changing. The public may be more or less receptive to foreign cultural goods in different time periods.

To summarize, American aesthetic styles dominate several genres that complement one another: film, music, and television fiction. This situation has increased the influence of American culture and possibly its hegemony in other countries at certain periods. At the same time, America's dominance in these genres decreases its receptivity to foreign cultural goods in those genres. Some European countries have created aesthetic styles that have dominated other genres—for example, classical music (Germany) and visual arts (France). In these genres, the United States is more likely to import foreign culture. Among Anglophone countries, the United Kingdom has been an important source of aesthetic styles in literary fiction. Here, too, the United States is likely to import foreign culture. Differences in national origins of genres have implications for the extent to which foreign cultural items created within those genres will be marketable in the United States.

MEDIA ATTENTION AND AMERICANS' EXPOSURE TO FOREIGN CULTURE: METHOD AND DATA

Media attention to foreign arts and culture is an indication of their availability for consumption in a specific country and of the level of that country's exposure to foreign culture. We examine coverage of foreign arts and culture in the United States in comparison with three European countries. More specifically, we analyze:

1. the amount of newspaper coverage allocated to foreign arts and culture actors
2. the representation of countries and regions in arts and culture coverage
3. the extent of international coverage of various cultural genres

Content Analysis

Our data are taken from a comprehensive, quantitative content analysis[53] of arts and culture journalism in American, Dutch, French, and German newspapers in four sample years: 1955, 1975, 1995, and 2005.[54] The analysis covered nine main categories of cultural artifacts: classical music, popular music, theater, dance, fiction books, visual arts, film, television fiction, and applied arts.

Our case selection was based on several criteria. First, because only a limited number of newspapers per country could be included in the content analysis, newspapers targeting the political, intellectual, and cultural elite were chosen; these elites determine to a considerable degree whether and how all sorts of subjects are discussed within the media and the wider community, and they fulfill a key role in processes of cultural valorization.[55] Second, as this research is aimed at tracing diachronic and synchronic variations in journalistic attention to foreign and domestic arts and culture, the focus was on daily newspapers with a national or supraregional distribution (as opposed to regional and metropolitan newspapers, which by definition are primarily focused on local news). A third selection criterion was that the chosen newspapers had appeared during the entire research period.

Because application of the above criteria still produced too many newspaper titles, we decided to select for each country two newspapers having on average the largest paid circulation in the research period (see table 7.1). The data for the United States that are analyzed in this chapter are taken from the *New York Times*.

The nature and extent of cultural information provided in a newspaper not only differs each weekday but is also subject to seasonal influences. To generalize about the total coverage of arts and culture in each reference year, the sample must contain proportional numbers of editions from each weekday and season. Therefore, the following sampling method was used: for each day of the week, a random edition from each quarter was selected, resulting in four constructed weeks—that is, twenty-eight editions (including Sunday editions) per reference year for the *New York Times*, and twenty-four editions per year for each of six European newspaper titles. Sampling efficiency studies have shown that, as a rule, two constructed weeks provide a reliable image of the size and composition of newspaper coverage during a whole year.[56] Our sample included four constructed weeks (688 editions in total)—with the larger number of articles boosting the total reliability of and the level of detail in the analysis.

Table 7.1.
Selected Newspapers per Country and Their Circulation in 1955 and 1995

	Founded	1955	1995
New York Times[a]	1851	555,726	1,122,277
Le Monde[b]	1944	166,000	379,089
Le Figaro[b]	1854	384,000	391,533
Frankfurter Allgemeine Zeitung[c]	1949	145,475	391,220
Süddeutsche Zeitung[d]	1945	188,081	396,746
N.R.C./NRC Handelsblad[e]	1844	109,471	267,000
de Volkskrant[e]	1919	149,501	359,000

Sources:

[a] *The World Almanac and Book of Facts 1956* (New York: New York, World Telegram, 1956).

[b] Jean-Marie Charon, *La presse quotidienne* (Paris: La Découverte, 1996); Paul Murschetz, "State Support for the Press in Europe: A Critical Appraisal." *European Journal of Communication* 13, 3 (1998): 291–313. European Institute for the Media, 1997), 71–114. Circulation figures pertain to 1960 instead of 1955.

[c] FAZ Media Service.

[d] IVW-Circulation Figures Süddeutsche Zeitung (first quarter of the year).

[e] Frank van Vree, *De metamorfose van een dagblad: Een journalistieke geschiedenis van de Volkskrant* (Amsterdam: Meulenhoff, 1996); Frank Huysmans, Jos de Haan, and Andries van den Broek, *Achter de schermen: Een kwart eeuw lezen, luisteren,kijken en internetten* (The Hague: SCP, 2004), 41. The *NRC Handelsblad* is the result of a merger of the *Nieuwe Rotterdamse Courant (N.R.C.)* and the *Algemeen Handelsblad* in 1970. For the period prior to that, the *N.R.C.* was coded.

The data collection was not restricted to arts and culture sections or lifestyle supplements. We screened the whole newspaper for all types of articles on culture with at least ten lines, including reviews, background articles, news bulletins, interviews, and columns. In the case of articles that reviewed more than one item (e.g., several movies or novels), a separate registration form was filled out for each item.

Measurement

The primary measure of the *international focus* of arts and culture was the share of "foreign" actor-items within the total supply of arts and culture items. All items were classified as either a "foreign" or a "domestic" actor-item based on the country of location of the principal actor(s) reviewed (i.e., the countries in which the main actor[s] had their professional base at the time of publication). Actors included any individual or group directly associated with a cultural item—for example, the director, producer, or actors in a film; the conductor or musicians in an orchestra; and so on.

Using the data on the country location of the principal actor(s), we specified the *direction and composition of the international orientation* by looking at (1) the specific countries covered in the international reports and (2) the diversity of countries covered in reports.

RECEPTIVITY OF THE PRESS TO FOREIGN ARTS AND CULTURE IN THE UNITED STATES AND EUROPE

Level of Attention to Foreign Actors in Press Coverage of Arts and Culture

In comparison with its European counterparts, the *New York Times* published substantially fewer items about foreign actors in its coverage of arts and culture (see table 7.2). Surprisingly, this was true during all four sample years (1955, 1975, 1995, and 2005). The percentage of items devoted to foreign actors in the *New York Times* increased slightly in 1995 but returned to its previous level in 2005. Dutch and German newspapers devoted substantially higher percentages of items to foreign actors throughout the period, and these figures increased in 1995 and 2005. The share of foreign actors in French newspapers was only slightly higher than that in the *New York Times* in 1955 and 1975, but increased substantially in 1995 and 2005.

These data suggest that before cultural globalization became a widespread phenomenon, the *New York Times* focused largely on domestic arts and culture and paid less attention to foreign content. What is more remarkable is that this tendency did not change with increasing levels of cultural globalization. A slight decline in attention to foreign actors occurred in 2005, possibly as a result of 9/11. In any case, the isolationism that has frequently characterized American foreign policy appears to have had a counterpart in international coverage of arts and culture by the country's leading newspaper.[57] One would expect that coverage of foreign arts and culture in other American papers would be substantially lower.

Representation of Foreign Countries in Press Coverage of Arts and Culture

Another indication of the cultural orientation of the press (and indirectly the level of foreign cultural exposure of its readers) is the number of

Table 7.2.
Percentage of Items Devoted to Foreign Actors in Newspaper Arts and Culture Coverage by Country, 1955–2005

	1955	1975	1995	2005
United States	26.0	25.7	30.0	26.2
France	29.1	31.8	44.1	49.5
Germany	44.5	50.0	55.2	57.6
Netherlands	46.4	45.2	51.5	52.2

Table 7.3.
Representation of Countries in the Arts and Culture Coverage of the *New York Times*, 1955–2005
(percentage of items per country and total number of countries represented)

1955	%	1975	%	1995	%	2005	%
1. US	74.0	1. US	74.3	1. US	70.0	1. US	73.8
2. UK	7.1	2. UK	6.5	2. UK	7.7	2. UK	7.1
3. France	4.0	3. USSR/Russia	3.3	3. France	3.7	3. France	2.0
4. Italy	2.0	4. France	2.9	4. Italy	2.2	4. Germany	2.0
5. West Germany	1.9	5. Italy	1.8	5. Canada	1.5	5. Canada	1.1
6. USSR/Russia	1.2	6. West Germany	1.7	6. Russia/USSR	1.2	6. Italy	1.0
7. Canada	1.0	7. Austria	0.5	7. Germany	1.0	7. Australia	0.8
8. Spain	0.9	8. Canada	0.5	8. Japan	0.7	8. Japan	0.8
9. Austria	0.9	9. Israel	0.5	9. Australia	0.6	9. China	0.6
10. Japan	0.7	10. Japan	0.5	10. South Africa	0.6	10. Spain	0.6
11. Poland	0.5	11. Netherlands	0.5	11. Spain	0.6	11. Ireland	0.5
12. Belgium	0.4	12. Brazil	0.4	12. Austria	0.4	12. Mexico	0.5
13. Switzerland	0.4	13. Philippines	0.3	13. India	0.4	13. Netherlands	0.5
14. Australia	0.3	14. Sweden	0.4	14. Netherlands	0.4	14. Austria	0.4
15. Denmark	0.3	15. Puerto Rico	0.4	15. Norway	0.4	15. Denmark	0.4
16. Hungary	0.3	16. Australia	0.3	16. Poland	0.3	16. Russia/USSR	0.4

17. Ireland	0.3
18. Netherlands	0.3
Other countries (20) < 0.3	38
Number of Countries Represented	
N=1,481 / missing 70	

17. Ireland	0.3
18. Norway	0.3
19. Switzerland	0.3
Other countries (17) < 0.3	36
Number of Countries Represented	
N=758 / missing 28	

17. China	0.3
18. Czech Republic	0.3
Other countries (27) < 0.3	45
Number of Countries Represented	
N=894 / missing 32	

17. Switzerland	0.4
18. Finland	0.3
19. India	0.3
20. Norway	0.3
21. South Africa	0.3
22. Sweden	0.3
Other countries (31) < 0.3	53
Number of Countries Represented	
N=1,032 / missing 62	

countries represented in its arts and culture coverage. Representation of foreign countries in the arts and culture coverage of the *New York Times* has changed very little since 1955, when approximately a quarter of all items were devoted to foreign actors (see table 7.3). This figure increased slightly in 1995 but recovered its previous level in 2005. However, the total number of countries represented has increased substantially (by 39 percent), from thirty-eight to fifty-three. Presumably, this increase is an indication of growing cultural globalization, although the impact of approximately half the countries is so small that it has to be considered peripheral.[58]

Overall, there has been a substantial change by region in the proportion of coverage in the *New York Times* devoted to foreign actors (see table 7.4). The proportion of European actors declined but remained very high (67 percent), while the proportion of Asian and African actors increased slightly. Throughout the period, other regions, such as Africa and the Middle East, were represented minimally or not at all. These data suggest that the United States is primarily oriented toward its own culture and secondarily toward certain European countries.

Cultural proximity is a useful concept for understanding these figures.[59] In all four sample years, cultural items from the United Kingdom, a major Anglophone country, were the most highly represented on these lists. Three Western European countries—France, Italy, and Germany—consistently provided more cultural items than most other countries. Again, the notion of cultural proximity is relevant. Large numbers of immigrants from Germany and Italy settled in the United States in the nineteenth and early twentieth centuries. Their descendants constitute ethnic groups that are still distinctly identifiable today. France has had a significant impact on American traditions in the fine arts and in applied arts, such as fashion and

Table 7.4.
Representation of Regions in the Foreign Arts and Culture Coverage of the
New York Times, **1955–2005** (percentage of items per region)*

	1955	1975	1995	2005
Western Europe	78.4	62.7	63.9	66.0
Europe (Other)	9.7	14.0	9.0	4.7
North America	4.0	8.8	7.8	4.3
Latin America	1.9	5.2	3.9	7.0
Asia	4.6	7.3	7.8	10.9
Africa	0.3	0.5	5.1	3.1
Oceania	1.1	1.6	2.4	3.9
Various countries across the world	3.6	1.0	4.9	5.2
N	*385*	*195*	*268*	*270*

Note: Domestic coverage is not included in this table.

gastronomy. A U.S. neighbor that is also a largely Anglophone country, Canada, ranked substantially higher on these lists than its other neighbor, Mexico, which is not an Anglophone country and which attained an important rank on these lists only in 2005.

Although the European newspapers paid considerably more attention to foreign arts and culture than the *New York Times*, on average their coverage of arts and culture did not include substantially more countries (see table 7.5). However, almost twice as many countries provided substantial amounts of cultural items (at least 1 percent) on these lists than was the case for the United States.

The proportion of items dealing with domestic arts and culture in the three European countries was substantially lower than in the United States and declined steadily during the period under study (the comparable American figures remained virtually unchanged during this period— compare tables 7.5 and 7.3).

The countries most heavily represented in the European newspapers were Western European countries. The findings for the three European countries appear to be the result of a previously documented tendency for newspapers to cover arts and cultural events in neighboring countries, which is another example of cultural proximity.[60] Most European countries are neighbors of one or more of these three countries and share historical and cultural traditions that have lasted for several centuries.

In 1995 and 2005, the proportion of the arts and cultural coverage in these European papers that was devoted to the United States substantially increased. This percentage was almost twice as large in 1995 and 2005 compared to 1955 and 1975, suggesting that the impact of American culture in these countries was increasing.

Variations by Genre in Press Coverage of Arts and Culture

Additional insight into the role of foreign arts and culture in American culture may be obtained by examining differences in the representation of foreign actors by cultural genre. We will focus on the most important genres according to our data set: popular music, classical music, theater, fiction books, visual arts, film, and television fiction. In each of these genres, the presence of foreign actors in the *New York Times* varied significantly in terms of the national or regional origins of a particular genre and the extent to which American cultural goods have influenced the development of the genre.

The percentage of items devoted to foreign actors varied by genre in each of the four sample years (see table 7.6), but on the whole, attention to foreign actors was highest in classical music and lowest in popular music, television fiction, and theater. These figures were remarkably stable over the entire period. By contrast, in the three European countries, coverage given to foreign actors in most genres increased substantially in 1995 and 2005 in comparison with 1955 and 1975, indicating a growing impact of globalization on these genres in these countries. This was not the case for the *New York Times*, which shows no significant rise in its

Table 7.5.

Representation of Countries in the Arts and Culture Coverage of European Newspapers, 1955–2005 (mean percentage of items per country and average number of countries represented in French, German, and Dutch newspapers)

1955	%	1975	%	1995	%	2005	%
1. Home country	*60.0*	*1. Home country*	*57.6*	*1. Home country*	*49.7*	*1. Home country*	*46.9*
2. France	11.4	2. US	8.7	2. US	14.6	2. US	14.8
3. US	7.3	3. France	5.4	3. UK	7.2	3. UK	6.1
4. Italy	3.9	4. UK	4.8	4. France	5.4	4. France	5.1
5. UK	3.8	5. Italy	4.3	5. Germany	4.4	5. Germany	3.0
6. West Germany	3.0	6. West Germany	3.0	6. Italy	3.1	6. Italy	3.5
7. Austria	2.4	7. Austria	2.5	7. Austria	2.3	7. Belgium	2.0
8. USSR/Russia	1.7	8. USSR/Russia	2.3	8. Spain	1.3	8. Austria	1.8
9. Spain	1.4	9. Belgium	1.1	9. Belgium	1.2	9. Switzerland	1.5
10. Denmark	0.9	10. Spain	1.1	10. Russia/USSR	1.2	10. Russia/USSR	1.6
11. Switzerland	0.9	11. East Germany	1.0	11. Switzerland	1.1	11. Japan	1.2
12. East Germany	0.9	12. Switzerland	0.8	12. Canada	1.0	12. Spain	1.2
13. Belgium	0.5	13. Netherlands	0.8	13. Netherlands	0.5	13. Netherlands	0.9
14. Netherlands	0.5	14. Hungary	0.5	14. Yugoslavia etc.	0.5	14. Canada	0.7
15. Hungary	0.4	15. Sweden	0.5	15. Australia	0.5	15. Poland	0.7
		16. Czechoslovakia	0.4	16. Denmark	0.4	16. China	0.6

17. Norway	0.5
18. South Africa	0.5
19. South Korea etc.	0.5
20. Mexico	0.4
21. Sweden	0.4
22. Denmark	0.3
23. Estonia etc.	0.3
24. Ireland	0.3
25. Turkey	0.3

Number of Countries Represented 51

N = 3,482 / missing 156

17. Poland	0.4
18. Japan	0.3
19. Ireland	0.3
20. Sweden	0.3

Number of Countries Represented 50

N = 3,289 / missing 112

17. Denmark	0.4
18. Japan	0.4
19. Poland	0.4
20. Canada	0.3
21. Greece	0.3
22. Yugoslavia	0.3

Number of Countries Represented 35

N = 2,134 / missing 106

Number of Countries Represented 25

N = 1,554 / missing 86

147

Table 7.6.
Percentage of Items Devoted to Foreign Actors in the *New York Times* by
Genre, 1955–2005

	1955	1975	1995	2005	N
Popular Music	19.0	17.5	19.4	15.2	376
Classical Music	47.8	30.2	32.7	42.7	603
Theater	13.5	25.8	15.7	12.2	588
Fiction Books	29.2	25.0	33.8	24.3	621
Visual Arts	29.8	33.8	35.4	27.4	394
Film	14.4	33.8	34.8	34.5	702
Television Fiction	6.4	9.7	19.0	12.3	253

attention to foreign actors, except in its coverage of film (between 1955 and 1975) and classical music (between 1995 and 2005).

Music

The level of attention to foreign popular music was found to be much lower for the *New York Times* than for the European newspapers. In 2005, 15 percent of all popular music items in the *New York Times* dealt with foreign music, as opposed to the 56 percent, 69 percent, and 76 percent in the French, Dutch, and German papers, respectively (see table 7.7A). Insofar as the *New York Times* did pay much attention to popular music from other countries, it favored British and Irish artists, who received 40 percent of all items on foreign actors. Sales figures also indicate that little foreign popular music is distributed in the United States in comparison with the three European countries (see table 7.8).

Compared to popular music, sales figures for classical music are much lower in all countries. However, in the latter genre the representation of international musicians is considerably higher, as proved to be the case in the extent of coverage given to foreign classical music actors in the *New York Times* (see table 7.7B), which, in most sample years, did not differ significantly from that in the papers of the three European countries.

Here, it should be taken into account that several categories of actors may be featured in newspaper stories on classical music, such as composers, conductors, performers, and various others involved in the production, distribution, and reception of music. Out of all the principal actors reviewed in the classical music items in the 2005 editions of the *New York Times*, 51 percent were performers, 21 percent were conductors, 18 percent were composers, and 10 percent were other actors. The international focus of the *New York Times* was particularly strong in the case of composers, who for the most part (76 percent) originated in Europe, especially Germany. Nonetheless, the musical conductors (44 percent) and performers (36 percent) who were reviewed in the *New York Times* also often originated in other countries, in particular Germany, the United Kingdom, and Italy.

Table 7.7.
Percentage of Newspaper Items Devoted to Foreign Actors by Genre and
Country, 1955–2005

A. Popular Music	1955	1975	1995	2005
United States	19.0	17.5	19.4	15.2
France	29.6	31.8	64.0	54.6
Germany	37.5	66.7	74.4	75.5
The Netherlands	23.1	62.0	70.9	68.8
B. Classical Music	1955	1975	1995	2005
United States	47.8	30.2	32.7	42.7
France	45.1	33.7	57.6	51.1
Germany	40.0	53.1	52.5	48.2
The Netherlands	39.8	45.4	51.5	61.2
C. Theater	1955	1975	1995	2005
United States	13.5	25.8	15.7	12.2
France	15.0	20.2	22.7	27.0
Germany	48.0	48.5	41.5	39.3
The Netherlands	35.6	40.0	29.4	23.0
D. Fiction Books	1955	1975	1995	2005
United States	29.2	25.0	33.8	24.3
France	19.4	36.2	38.3	48.1
Germany	52.2	47.3	54.5	60.0
The Netherlands	50.6	53.0	53.1	48.6
E. Visual Arts	1955	1975	1995	2005
United States	29.8	33.8	35.4	27.4
France	14.5	33.6	43.6	53.6
Germany	37.3	48.0	53.8	59.3
The Netherlands	37.0	26.8	47.3	48.1
F. Film	1955	1975	1995	2005
United States	14.4	33.8	34.8	34.5
France	50.6	41.8	55.8	61.8
Germany	47.9	77.0	80.9	73.2
The Netherlands	84.1	71.8	73.8	72.5
G. Television Fiction	1955	1975	1995	2005
United States	6.4	9.7	19.0	12.3
France	—	6.3	19.1	30.8
Germany	—	20.4	22.2	20.0
The Netherlands	—	26.5	58.3	26.7

Table 7.8.

A. Distribution of Music by Genre and National Origin by Country, 1998 (percentages)

	Domestic Popular	International Popular	Classical
United States	91	5	4
France	44	46	10
Germany	43	47	10
The Netherlands	27	64	9

Source: UNESCO, *World Culture Report* (Paris: UNESCO, 2000), table 5, pp. 310–11.

B. Number and Percentage of Translations in the National Literary Book Production by Country, 1995 (includes reprints)

	Total Number of Literary Book Publications[a]	Number of Translations[b]	Percentage of Translations
United States	11,537	639	6
France	10,545	4,923	36
Germany	13,571	3,710	35
The Netherlands	2,950	—	58

Sources:

[a] UNESCO Book Production Statistics, 1995–1999.

[b] For France, Germany, and the United States: *Index Translationem.* Paris, UNESCO, available at databases.unesco.org/xtrans/xtra-form.shtml; for the Netherlands, Jacques Mélitz, *English-Language Dominance, Literature and Welfare* (London: Centre for Economic Policy Research, 1999), 39.

C. Film Production, Film Imports, and Market Share of Domestic Films by Country, 1994-1998

	Share of Imported films within Total Number of Films Distributed[a]	Average Number of Films Produced per Year, including Co-productions	Market Share of Domestic Films
United States	42%	706[b]	92.3%[f]
France	56%	113[c]	34.3%[g]
Germany	62%	78[d]	14.3%[h]
The Netherlands	91%	29[e]	4.7%[e]

Sources:

[a] UNESCO, *World Culture Report* (Paris: UNESCO, 2000), table 4, pp. 304–7. *Note:* The data do not indicate an average for all the years in the period 1994–98 but refer to any one of the years in this period.

Table 7.8. C (*continued*)

ᵇYearly average for 1995–98. *U.S. Entertainment Industry Marketing Statistics, 2005*, 12, http://www.mpaa.org/05%20Economic%20Review.pdf

ᶜCentre national de la cinématographie (CNC): http://www.cnc.fr/Site/Template/T3.aspx?SELECTID=1040&ID=402&t=2

ᵈYearly average for 1996–98. SPIO: http://www.spio.de/index.asp?SeitID=24

ᵉNFC, *Annual Report 2001*, 27: http://www.nfcstatistiek.nl/jv01.pdf

ᶠShare in 1999. *Focus 2000. World Film Market Film Trends* (Strasbourg European Audiovisual Observatory, 2000), 10, http://www.obs.coe.int/online_publication/reports/focus2000.pdf

ᵍEuropean Audiovisual Observatory: http://www.obs.coe.int/oea_publ/eurocine/00001439.html

ʰYearly average for 1995–97. European Audiovisual Observatory: http://www.obs.-coe.int/oea_publ/eurocine/00001448.html

The difference in international focus of the *New York Times*'s popular and classical music coverage seems to reflect the importance of American contributions to popular music as well as the origins of classical music and its present-day practitioners in German and other European cultures.

Theater

In each of the four sample countries, theater coverage was one of the least international forms of arts journalism (see table 7.7C). Obviously, theater is very locally based, strongly dependent on language, and difficult to commodify or record, which hampers international dissemination. However, in comparison with the European papers, theater coverage in the *New York Times* had a much stronger national focus: in 2005, only 12 percent of all items concerned foreign actors. This may be partly due to the fact that the American genre has evolved along different lines from its European counterpart. According to Emma John, European theater is more concerned with social and political issues than is American theater, which emphasizes the family and individual solutions to its problems.[61]

When foreign actors did receive attention in the *New York Times*, it involved mostly actors from the United Kingdom and other Anglophone countries (73 percent). Almost half (47 percent) of the principal actors reviewed in the 2005 editions of the *New York Times* were performers, 14 percent were directors, 27 percent were playwrights, and 10 percent were other actors. The international focus of the *New York Times* was lowest in the case of performers, 9 percent of whom originated in another country; of the directors and playwrights, respectively 25 percent and 19 percent came from another English-speaking country.

Fiction Books

Although the *New York Times* continued to devote a substantial amount of attention to foreign literature (accounting for about a quarter of all items on fiction books in 2005), its level of international coverage remained far below that in the European papers (see table 7.7D). If we look at the foreign countries represented in the *New York Times*, the effect of shared language is particularly clear here: the majority of international items (82 percent) concern literary actors from the United Kingdom (55 percent) and other Anglophone countries (27 percent).

Very few foreign-language books are translated in the United States (see table 7.8B). In 2004, less than 5 percent (4,982 titles) of all published books were translations, ranging from literary novels to self-help books and travel guides. Given the size of the U.S. market, this figure is very low: it is less than half of the 12,197 translations reported in Italy and only four hundred more than the number of translations reported in the Czech Republic.[62] In the field of literature, even fewer foreign works are making their way to American readers. A National Endowment for the Arts study in 1999 showed that only 3 percent (197 titles) of the fiction and poetry published in the United States that year were translations— contrasting sharply with other countries, where the figure can be almost 60 percent (cf. table 7.8B).

A recent study examined how many contemporary novels from various countries had been translated between 2000 and 2006, revealing how underrepresented all foreign-language books in fact are in the United States.[63] Looking at French-, German-, and Dutch-language novels only, we find that fifty-two novels from France, thirty-six from Germany, Austria, and Switzerland, and nineteen from the Netherlands were translated in the United States during this six-year period. This represents a yearly average of 8.7 for France, 6.0 for the German-speaking countries, and 3.2 for the Netherlands and Flanders—many of which were books originally published several years previously. Considering the numbers of contemporary works of fiction that are coming out in those countries every year, these average numbers are very low.

These low numbers are reflected in the best-seller lists of *Publisher's Weekly* or Nielsen, which carry hardly any books by foreign authors. In 2004, only *One Hundred Years of Solitude* by Gabriel García Márquez and *The Kite Runner* by Khaled Hosseini made it to the list of best-selling trade paperback fiction.[64]

Visual Arts

In the visual arts, the importance of the United States clearly changed during the period under study. The contemporary visual art world has become increasingly centered in the United States, replacing France.[65] According to the German "Kunstkompass" for 2004, almost a third of the hundred most renowned, living contemporary artists were American; the remainder consisted of German (27), British (7), French (4), Italian (3), and Swiss (3) artists, with other nationalities sharing the few remaining places. Since 2004, Bruce Nauman has been the highest-ranking contemporary American artist on the list; in the previous year, it was Andy

Warhol. The United States also headed the list of countries represented at the 2005 Basel Art Fair with a delegation of 63 galleries out of 274. Moreover, if we look at the nationalities of artists represented at the world's major museums and centers of contemporary art, the United States appears to be well ahead of other countries.[66]

Although the share of foreign cultural items in the *New York Times* fine arts coverage has remained fairly substantial (almost 30 percent in 2005), it is much lower than in the European papers, which devoted 50 to 60 percent of their visual arts coverage to foreign arts items (see table 7.7E). Visual artists and other visual arts actors from the United Kingdom were most likely to receive attention in the *New York Times* (6 percent), followed by German and French artists (4 percent each).

A similar picture is found if we look at the nationalities represented in the contemporary art galleries at the Museum of Modern Art in New York. In 2005, the majority of contemporary artists were American (63 percent), followed by artists from the United Kingdom (6 percent) and Germany and France (4 percent each). Although the big "international" contemporary art collections in Europe also tend to favor domestic artists, the United States seems particularly active in championing its national artists.

Film

The case of film seems less clear-cut, because, since the 1970s, a substantial proportion of items about film in the *New York Times* has been devoted to foreign actors. Nonetheless, this proportion is much lower than in the European press (see table 7.7F), and again America's leading position in a genre appears to be inversely related to its international orientation in this genre. Considering the representation of various countries in the international film coverage of the *New York Times* in 2005, we find that six countries—the United Kingdom, France, Spain, China, Japan, and Hong Kong—attracted almost three-quarters of all foreign-movie items.

In the past decades, film production in the above and other countries has expanded considerably, but Hollywood continues to dominate the international film market. Statistics on imports of feature films by country demonstrate clearly the overwhelming global dominance of American film.[67] In most countries, the United States is the major country of origin for imported films. On average, imported films accounted for 86 percent of the total number of films distributed in 1994–98.[68]

But although the percentage of imported films in the United States is considerable, their market share is much lower (see table 7.8C). *Variety*'s lists of the fifty top-grossing films in the United States in 2000[69] and 2005[70] did not include a single foreign film. A few of these films were co-productions between American and foreign companies. Excluding co-productions, the share of the U.S. film market represented by films made in Europe and other parts of the world was 5.5 percent in 2005,[71] indicating that the United States, as Johanne Brunet and Galina Gornostaeva put it, "remains a strong, impenetrable, and unattainable market for foreign productions."[72] The most successful foreign film of 2006 was *Kung Fu Hustle* at $17.1 million—making it the 116th biggest release; a mere ten foreign-language films broke $1 million, which led the reporters of *Newsweek* to conclude:

> Gone are the days when there was a guaranteed audience for a Kurosawa or Truffaut, when Claude Lelouch's *A Man and a Woman* could stay in one theater for two years. Who are the marquee directors now? Almodovar. Maybe Zhang Yimou, but only when he makes action movies such as *Hero*.[73]

Television Fiction

Both in the United States and European countries, the coverage given to television fiction in 1995 and 2005 was strongly focused on domestic actors compared to most other genres (see table 7.7G). But in comparison with the European papers, coverage in the *New York Times* had a much stronger national focus: in 2005, only 12 percent of all items concerned foreign actors. Three-quarters of these international items involved actors from the United Kingdom.

For European countries, the European Audiovisual Observatory, among others, provides detailed data on the share of domestic and foreign fiction in national television programming, as well as the market share of foreign imports. In 2000, American fiction (film and TV fiction) had a share of almost 70 percent in the fiction programs transmitted by 101 European Union networks.[74] Unfortunately, comparable data are lacking for the United States, but both the share of foreign programming (film and TV fiction) on American television and the share of imported television on the U.S. market are undoubtedly very low, and in both cases most foreign products in all likelihood originate in the United Kingdom. The European Audiovisual Observatory estimated the receipts for European audiovisual exports (i.e., both film and television) to North America at $827 million in 2000, of which British companies took the lion's share ($691 million). Europe's deficit in the balance of audiovisual trade with North America was estimated at $8.2 billion that year.[75]

In each of the above genres, attention to foreign actors was, with few exceptions, lower in the *New York Times* than in the press in the other three countries.[76] The international orientation of the *New York Times* was particularly low (again compared to the European papers) in genres in which the United States dominated the international marketplace: film, popular music, television fiction, and (in the later years) visual arts. This confirms that a leading international position in the production of a genre reduces the receptivity to foreign products in this genre. However, even in genres in which U.S. dominance was less salient—such as literature and theater—coverage was far more national in focus in the *New York Times* than in the European newspapers. This overall national/local orientation may be connected with a more general centralized position: if one is in the center, there is no need to look far. Of course, one could also argue that the United States, and especially New York, also has gained an increasingly central position in the literary field as well as the performing arts.

Moreover, in almost every genre, international coverage in the *New York Times* was primarily focused on actors originating in the United Kingdom and other Anglophone countries—except for classical music, in which Germany and Italy were the best-represented foreign countries.

CONCLUSION

In this chapter, we have used press coverage of arts and culture in the *New York Times* as an indicator of American exposure to foreign cultural influences. Comparisons with similar data for three European countries between 1955 and 2005 suggest that Americans have been relatively less exposed to foreign cultural influences. This conclusion is modified partially by variations in levels of attention to foreign cultural actors in different genres. By contrast, it appears that the influence of American arts and culture in other countries has steadily increased during this period. On the basis of these data, American culture as a whole appeared to be substantially more influential than any other culture during the second half of this period.

These data suggest that, in the global arena, cultural genres function like languages. A country whose native tongue is a dominant language, such as English, translates fewer books published in countries with nondominant languages than those countries translate from publications of countries using dominant languages.[77] Similarly, America's dominance in several leading cultural genres, reinforced by the dominant position of its global media companies, restricts the amount of culture it imports in those genres. Ironically, the United States contributes enormously to cultural globalization through the dissemination of its own cultural goods, but remains relatively isolated from global influences itself. This isolation seems partly to be the result of powerful media industries that tend to protect their own markets. It may also reflect a resistance to foreign cultural influences on the part of a population that has been accustomed to cultural goods that reflect a high level of cultural proximity.

At the present time, the American public is highly fragmented into a large number of "niche" audiences, each of which represents a relatively small proportion of the population. Consequently, the influence of foreign cultural goods on the American public is likely to be highly specific and probably limited.

NOTES

1. This chapter is based on data collected for the VICI [Innovational Research Incentives Scheme] project, Cultural Classification Systems in Transition (http://www.fhk.eur.nl/onderzoek/viciproject/), subsidized by the Netherlands Organization for Scientific Research (NWO, project 277-45-001), and is part of more

extensive, comparative research on the internationalization of journalism on art and culture, undertaken by Susanne Janssen in close cooperation with Giselinde Kuipers and Marc Verboord.

2. Abraham de Swaan, "De sociologische studie van de transnationale samenleving," *Amsterdams Sociologisch Tijdschrift* 22, no. 1 (1995): 16–35.

3. Raymond Williams, *Marxism and Literature* (London: Oxford University Press, 1977).

4. David Hesmondhalgh, *The Cultural Industries* (London: Sage, 2002).

5. Department for Culture, Media, and Sport (DCMS), United Kingdom, "Creative Industries" section, available at http://www.culture.gov.uk/creative_industries.

6. Richard Florida, *The Flight of the Creative Class* (New York: Harper Business, 2005), 26–27.

7. Steven Tepper, "Creative Assets and the Changing Economy," *Journal of Arts Management, Law and Society* 32 (2002): 159–68.

8. Tomic-Koludrovic and Petric, "Creative Industries in Transition."

9. Justin Lewis and Toby Miller, eds., *Critical Cultural Policy Studies: A Reader* (Malden, MA: Blackwell, 2003), 2.

10. Ibid.

11. Mario d'Angelo and Paul Vespérini, *Politiques culturelles en Europe: Une approche comparative* (Strasbourg: Editions du Conseil de l'Europe, 1998), 26.

12. Ulrich Beck, Natan Sznaider, and Rainer Winter, eds., *Global America? The Cultural Consequences of Globalization* (Liverpool, UK: Liverpool University Press, 2003).

13. Johan Heilbron, "Mondialisering en transnationaal verkeer," *Amsterdams Sociologisch Tijdschrift* 22, no. 1 (1995): 162–80.

14. Peter M. Blau, *Inequality and Heterogeneity: A Primitive Theory of Social Structure* (New York: Free Press, 1977), 19–44, 248–55.

15. John Sinclair, Elizabeth Jacka, and Stuart Cunningham, eds., *New Patterns in Global Television* (New York: Oxford University Press, 1996).

16. Antonio C. La Pastina and Joseph D. Straubhaar, "Multiple Proximities between Television Genres and Audiences," *Gazette* 67 (2005): 273.

17. La Pastina and Straubhaar, "Multiple Proximities," 276.

18. Richard Kuisel, "Debating Americanization: The case of France," in Beck, Sznaider, and Winter, *Global America?*, 95–113.

19. Gerard Delanty, "Consumption, Modernity, and Japanese Cultural Identity: The Limits of Americanization," in Beck, Sznaider, and Winter, *Global America?*, 114–33; Koichi Iwabuchi, "From Western Gaze to Global Gaze: Japanese Cultural Presence in Asia," in *Global Culture: Media, Arts, Policy, and Globalization*, edited by Diana Crane, Nobuko Kawashima, and Ken'ichi Kawasaki, 256–73 (New York: Routledge, 2002).

20. Herbert J. Gans, *Popular Culture and High Culture: An Analysis of Taste* (New York: Basic Books, 1977).

21. Richard A. Peterson, "Problems in Comparative Research: The Example of Omnivorousness," *Poetics* 33 (2005): 253–87.

22. Wendy Griswold and Nathan Wright, "Cowboys, Locals, and the Dynamic Endurance of Regionalism," *American Journal of Sociology* 109 (2004): 1411–51.

23. Richard Florida, *Flight of the Creative Class*; Emma John, "Un-American Beauties," *New Statesman*, August 7, 2006, 32–34.

24. Corine Lesnes, "L'Amérique se méfie aussi de la musique," *Le Monde*, April 21, 2006.

25. Johan Heilbron, "Towards a Sociology of Translation: Book Translations as a Cultural World-System," *European Journal of Social Theory* 2 (1999): 429–44.

26. Ibid., 439. Between 1994 and 1996, 1,721 translations were published in the United States, as compared to 6,542 in France, 9,931 in Germany, and 4,561 in the Netherlands; see UNESCO, *World Culture Report: Cultural Diversity, Conflict and Pluralism* (Paris: UNESCO, 2000): 374–75.

27. Abraham de Swaan, *Words of the World: The Global Language System* (Cambridge, UK: Polity Press, 2001).

28. Robert McChesney, *Rich Media, Poor Democracy* (Urbana: University of Illinois Press, 1999).

29. Douglas Kellner, "New Technologies, the Welfare State, and the Prospects for Democratization," in *Communication, Citizenship, and Social Policy,* edited by A. Calabrese and J. C. Burgelman, 239–56 (New York: Rowman & Littlefield, 1999).

30. Peter Golding and Phil Harris, eds., *Beyond Cultural Imperialism: Globalization, Communication and the New International Order.* London, Sage, 1997; Sinclair, Jacka, and Cunningham, *New Patterns in Global Television.*

31. Daniël Biltereyst and Philippe Meers, "The International Telenovela Debate and the Contra-flow Argument: A Reappraisal," *Media, Culture and Society* 22 (2000): 393–413.

32. Els de Bens and Hedwig de Smaele, "The Inflow of American Television Fiction on European Broadcasting Channels Revisited," *European Journal of Communication* 16 (2001): 51–76.

33. Denise D. Bielby and C. Lee Harrington, "Opening America? The Telenovelaization of U.S. Soap Operas," *Television and New Media* 6 (2005): 383–99.

34. Richard P. Nielsen, "Cultural-Economic Nationalism and International Trade Policy," *Academy of Management Review* 4 (1979): 449–52.

35. Bielby and Harrington, "Opening America?" 394.

36. Diana Crane, "Culture and Globalization: Theoretical Models and Emerging Trends," in Crane, Kawashima, and Kawasaki, *Global Culture*, 1–25.

37. Philippe Poirrier, *Les politiques culturelles en France* (Paris: Documentation française, 2002); *Cultural Policy in the Netherlands* (The Hague: Dutch Ministry of Education, Culture and Science, 2006).

38. Frédéric Martel, *De la culture en Amérique* (Paris: Gallimard, 2006).

39. Poirrier, *Politiques culturelles.*

40. Mary E. Footer and Christoph Beat Graber, "Trade Liberalization and Cultural Policy," *Journal of International Economic Law* 3 (2000): 115–44.

41. Garry Neil, "Assessing the Effectiveness of UNESCO's New Convention on Cultural Diversity," *Global Media and Communication* 2 (2006): 257–62.

42. This point of view was codified in an international Convention on the Protection and Promotion of the Diversity of Cultural Contents and Artistic Expressions, adopted by the General Conference of UNESCO in October 2005.

43. Neil, "Assessing the Effectiveness."

44. Alain Quemin, *Le rôle des pays prescripteurs sur le marché et dans le monde d'art contemporain* (Paris: Ministère des Affaires Etrangères, 2001); Susanne Janssen, "Fashion Reporting in Cross-national Perspective, 1955–2005," *Poetics* 34 (2006): 383–406.

45. Heilbron, "Mondialisering en transnationaal verkeer."

46. UNESCO, *World Culture Report*, 305–6.

47. Bielby and Harrington, "Opening America?" 384. The report *Building a Global Audience: British Television in Overseas Markets* (London: Department of Culture, Media and Sport, 1999) estimates that 85 percent of all children's programming, 81 percent of television movies, and close to 75 percent of dramatic television programs sold in the global television market are of U.S. origin.

48. Alexander Hicks and Velina Petrova, "*Auteur* Discourse and the Cultural Consecration of American Films," *Poetics* 34 (2006): 180–203.

49. Motti Regev, "'Rockization': diversity within similarity in world popular music," in Beck, Sznaider, and Winter, *Global America?*, 222–34.

50. Timothy J. Dowd et al., "Organizing the Musical Canon: The Repertoires of the Major U.S. Symphony Orchestras, 1969," *Poetics* 30 (2002): 35–61; Samuel Gilmore, "Tradition and Novelty in Concert Programming," *Sociological Forum* 8 (1993): 221–42.

51. According to UNESCO, in 1998, classical music accounted for less than 5 percent of sales of music in the United States (*World Culture Report*, 310). Martel notes that in 2002, only 12 percent of the population had attended at least one concert of classical music and at least one theatrical performance; only 10 percent had attended a dance performance (*De la culture en Amérique*, 505).

52. Paul DiMaggio and Toqir Mukhtar, "Arts Participation as Cultural Capital in the United States: Signs of Decline?" *Poetics* 34 (2004): 162–94.

53. Kimberly A. Neuendorf, *The Content Analysis Guidebook* (Thousand Oaks, CA: Sage, 2002).

54. Susanne Janssen, *Cultural Classification Systems in Transition: The Social Valuation of Cultural Goods in France, Germany, the Netherlands and the United States, 1955–2005*, Erasmus University, Rotterdam, 2002, available at http://www.fhk.eur.nl/onderzoek/viciproject/.

55. For example, in the fall of 2006, two-thirds of the readers (68 percent) of the *New York Times* had university diplomas, compared to 25 percent in the U.S. population as a whole; see http://www.nytimes.whsites.net/mediakit/docs/readership/MRI_high_quality_demos.pdf.

56. Daniel Riffe and Charles F. Aust, "The Effectiveness of Random, Consecutive Day and Constructed Week Samples in Newspaper Content Analysis," *Journalism Quarterly* (Vol. 70, 1993): 133–39.

57. According to the *Globalization Index 2006*, the United States occupied a modest forty-first position in the rankings in political globalization, as measured by such factors as participation in treaties, peacekeeping, government transfers, and membership of international organizations; see http://www.globalpolicy.org/globaliz/econ/2006/11globindex.pdf.

58. Representation in the arts and culture coverage of the *New York Times* was less than 0.3 percent for 53 percent of the countries in 1955, 47 percent in 1975, 60 percent in 1995, and 58 percent in 2005.

59. La Pastina and Straubhaar, "Multiple Proximities."

60. Joseph D. Straubhaar, "Beyond Media Imperialism: Asymmetrical Interdependence and Cultural Proximity," *Critical Studies in Mass Communication* 81 (1991): 39–59.

61. John, "Un-American Beauties," 32–34.

62. "The Non-English Patient," *Culture Report* 1 (2007), http://www.signandsight.com/service/1029.html.

63. John O'Brien, "Translations, Part 5," *Context* 19 (2006), available at http://www.dalkeyarchive.com/article/show/172.

64. *The World Almanac*, (New York: World Almanac Books, 2006), 274.

65. Raymonde Moulin, *Le marché de l'art: Mondialisation et nouvelle technologies* (Paris: Flammarion, 2000); Alain Quemin, "Globalization and Mixing in the Visual Arts," *International Sociology* 21, no. 4 (2006): 522–50.

66. Quemin, "Globalization and Mixing."

67. UNESCO, *World Culture Report*, table 4.

68. For the most part, countries for which data were not available in this table had low levels of economic development and literacy.

69. *The World Almanac, 2002* (New York: World Almanac Books), 267.

70. European Audiovisual Observatory, *Focus 2006: World Film Market Trends*, 39, available at http://www.obs.coe.int/online_publication/reports/focus2006.pdf.

71. Ibid., 36.

72. Johanne Brunet and Galina Gornostaeva, "Working Title Films, Independent Producer: Internationalization of the Film Industry." *International Journal of Arts Management* 9 (2006): 60–69.

73. "Lost in Translation," *Newsweek*, February 27, 2006.

74. European Audiovisual Observatory, press release, April 9, 2002, http://www.obs.coe.int/about/oea/pr/desequilibre.html.

75. Ibid.

76. The exceptions were primarily in French newspapers in 1955 and 1975.

77. Heilbron, "Mondialisering en transnationaal verkeer."

PART III

Globalization as a Source of Creativity
and Innovation in Civil Society

CHAPTER 8

Art on the Borderline

Tirza True Latimer

With the emergence of the term *globalization* over the last decade or so to describe the technology-driven conquest of territorial barriers to trade, tourism, and communication, emphasis has shifted from the "international" to the "transnational" and finally to the "global" in the rhetoric of politicians, business executives, economists, and generals. In the arts, a similar shift has taken place. Until recently, when Americans evoked the "art world," they usually meant New York and perhaps a few cities in Western Europe. Over the past decade or so, however, the art market, as well as sites of artistic production and exhibition, has migrated away from traditional centers such as Paris and New York. Indeed, the list of cities hosting prestigious biennial art exhibitions and commercial art fairs grows longer and less Western every year. The phrase *art world* today takes virtually the entire planet into its sweep. This highly multicultural scene makes the national pavilions that configure the landscape of the venerable Venice Biennale seem somewhat arbitrary, almost quaint. Indeed, talking about art-making—or diplomacy, warfare, or commerce—as events transpiring between nations no longer seems equal to the task of explaining either contemporary creative dynamics or global relations. Today's planetary flow of ideas, creative energy, bodies, and information produces new communities and configurations that cannot be adequately explained by traditional theories of political science centered on relations among and within nation-states.[1]

Against the backdrop of a global system that appears to undermine the authority of nations per se, national borders figure ever more prominently in the news, as debates about territorial integrity, national security, cultural cohesion, and even ethnic purity erupt on multiple frontiers around the world. Of course, borders have traditionally borne the symbolic burden of distinguishing "us" from "them," those on the other side of the divide. The us-them logic of the borderline generates a false effect of unity within national boundaries and stigmatizes those beyond the bounds as aliens—a branding that in turn makes vigorous defense of the dividing line itself appear crucial. How then do the forces of globalization enter into this scenario? Why does the organizing framework of the nation still hold such sway? Why do national borders flare up incessantly as symbolic flashpoints?

In recent years, U.S. border zones—because of the cultural questions they raise and the conflicts they mobilize—have drawn the focus not only of politicians, free-trade lobbyists, human rights advocates, anti-immigrationists, border police, and the media but also of many artists, particularly those with Mexican and Latin American ties or sympathies. These artists share a commitment to practices that extend artistic concern beyond the production of aesthetic objects, into work that self-consciously aims to raise social awareness and advocate for social justice. Such artists consider themselves to be alternately peacemakers or troublemakers, intellectuals or educators, but above all, instigators of social change.[2]

In the 1980s, a cluster of colleges and universities in the southwestern United States began to offer students the opportunity to pursue "border studies" as a new major, making the claim that the U.S./Mexico frontier would become the focus of global attention because, "as the interconnectedness between peoples, groups, and countries spreads throughout the world," the region's solutions to its cultural and economic problems forecast what is to become of borders everywhere.[3] This theme of the borderland as a zone of connectedness, a model of intercultural vitality, recurs in the creative initiatives of the artists, writers, curators, and educators I will discuss below. The premise is striking, in that it stands in stark contrast to media representations of the border—particularly the El Paso del Norte and San Diego frontiers, which cut across two densely populated binational metroplexes—as zones of perpetual conflict.

That borders are culturally active sites—or, more precisely, that creative activity transpires at boundaries, where one consciousness, one point of view, encounters another—is by now a commonplace observation. The early twentieth-century Russian philosopher and literary critic Mikhail Bakhtin, for one, famously wrote: "A cultural domain has no inner territory. It is located entirely upon boundaries; boundaries intersect it everywhere.... Every cultural act lives essentially on the boundaries, and it derives its seriousness and significance from this fact."[4] This image of culture as a terrain shot through with borders—lines with the power to shift and change the lay of the land the way that fault lines do—has had a profound impact upon certain contemporary artistic practices, inspiring new genres of literature, public art, and performance art.

Gloria Anzaldúa, whose writings interlace English and Spanish into a language of cultural emancipation, exemplifies a generation of artist-activists committed to inventing new vocabularies for talking about, and thus thinking differently about, the borderlands. Anzaldúa calls for a "new mestiza"—an individual who is acutely aware of conflicting and meshing identities and who uses her borderland perspective to challenge the binaries that pattern Western thought, particularly with respect to identity. (*Mestizo* and *mestiza* were first used in the Spanish Empire to designate people of mixed European and Amerindian ancestry living in Latin America.) Anzaldúa, whose family has occupied the multicultural El Paso region for six generations, destigmatizes mixed-race identity by proudly embracing the mestiza not as the shameful human residue of colonization but as a new kind of social subject, possessed of multiple cultural attributes, thriving on the borderline. She activates the borderline—traditional trope of the us-them binary—as a site of complex and compound creative vision.[5]

Anzaldúa's revalorization of border cultures reverberates with particular force within the field of border studies (which she helped to found). The practices of artists who transgress the border that has separated canonical Euro-American art of the modern era, as a set of rarefied aesthetic practices, from the rough-and-tumble domain of politics have contributed to this project of revision (or, better yet, this project of re-envisioning). Below, I will introduce several highly politicized artistic initiatives that explore the borderland as a geopolitical site, a terrain of cultural possibility, and/or a metaphor.

The Border Art Workshop/Taller de Arte Fronterizo (BAW/TAF) has labored since its inception in 1984 to reimagine and reimage the border as a shared corridor, where the terms of identity, community, and culture are incessantly negotiated but never resolved. BAW/TAF has strong ties to the Centro Cultural de la Raza in San Diego's Balboa Park, a Chicano/Chicana arts and educational center founded in 1971.[6] Several of BAW/TAF's early members—performance artist Guillermo Gómez-Peña, for one—contributed to raising public interest in the borderlands and border cultures as subjects of art, literature, political action, and community study. Founded as "a multinational conduit that serves to address issues we are confronted with while existing in a region where two countries meet," the actions staged by BAW/TAF evolved, like the preoccupations of border studies majors in American colleges, from a U.S.-Mexico border-specific focus to engage with a much wider field of interrelated concepts and concerns.[7] The stretch of frontier where BAW/TAF staged its early demonstrations marked not only the border between the United States and Mexico but also, symbolically, the fence separating U.S. citizens from their neighbors in Central and South America. This border also served as a line of scrimmage between the corporate values that the members of BAW/TAF disavowed and the interests of the indigenous American populations they supported all up and down the Americas.

From the beginning, participating artists expressed an interest in addressing "the social tensions that the Mexican-American border creates, while asking us to imagine a world in which this international boundary has been erased."[8] This kind of work, which sets in motion intellectual, psychological, and/or political processes and does not necessarily result in the creation of material art objects, has been described by analysts of contemporary artist trends as "social practice," "relational aesthetics," or "new genre" public art.[9] As one of the group's members, Emily Hicks, explains, BAW/TAF "is dedicated to creating art and conditions for the viewing of that art, in which the [work of] overcoming cultural barriers is part of the art-making process."[10] Although the group's practices build on the critical utopian experimentation born within the Euro-American artistic vanguard of earlier decades, it also draws strength and inspiration from cultural forms popular south of the border such as murals, *milagros,* altarpieces, pageants, and processions. The group's border-oriented events incorporate references to the heritage of peoples north and south of the border while applying the lessons of regional politics to broader global concerns, and vice versa. Their approach, that is, acknowledges the global and the local as two sides of the same coin.

One of the earliest site-specific manifestations, *End of the Line* (1986), was staged where the Tijuana–San Diego border fence formerly terminated at the Pacific Ocean.[11] Capitalizing on the dramatic potential of the site, BAW/TAF performers communicated with one another using both the words and gestures of neighbors exchanging greetings, as if to call attention to the porous character of the barrier separating them from one another. For the duration of the performance, the U.S.-Mexico border fence marked what literary theorist Mary Louise Pratt has called a "contact zone"—a space of creativity, discovery, and peaceful interaction—rather than a defensive barricade.[12] BAW/TAF subsequently displayed photo and video documentation of this event in several U.S. venues, contrasting their images of peaceful bicultural interaction to mass-media projections of the U.S.-Mexican borderland as a war zone.

Border Pilgrimage (1987) again engaged experimental performers from both sides of the border, but this time in a more aggressive scenario. Anglo, Chicano, and Mexican artists assembled at the tomb of Juan Soldado (patron saint of the undocumented) in the Tijuana municipal cemetery with the objective of crossing the border illegally under fictitious identities and documenting the crossing. The performance so successfully dissolved the distinction between theater and life that it failed, by virtue of its own realism, to be recognized by anyone other than the participants as a gesture of political protest (or art).

Refusing to be hamstrung by these limitations inherent in border art, BAW/TAF began to explore the interconnectedness of regional border politics and global concerns in less literal ways. In San Francisco, for instance, a number of BAW/TAF artists contributed to the creation of what a press release described as "an alternative news/information/analysis/criticism/distribution center to promote communication among different communities in Mexico and the United States."[13] This Border Axes initiative, sponsored by the Capp Street Project (a prestigious San Francisco–based artists' residency program and exhibition center), harnessed the latest available technology—at the time, fax and 800 numbers—to link the Capp Street site to institutions as disparate as an association of Latin-American artists in Mexico City known as Postarte and the Center for the Study of Women and Society at the City University of New York. These channels of communication enabled participants to conduct multinational dialogs—anticipating the way that blogs, online chatrooms, and wikis now function—around common concerns such as the drug wars, the AIDS epidemic, immigration, and labor legislation.

The art critic Robert Atkins cites a remark by BAW/TAF member Hicks that might have served as a manifesto for border art and social practice in the arts more generally: "We can't just talk about restructuring the art world; we have to talk about reconstructing society."[14] Not everyone agreed with this principle, however: Kenneth Baker of the *San Francisco Chronicle*, for one, dismissed the project as an attempt to "consolidate dissent under the cover of art,"[15] as if political activism and art could never comprise an alloy. In a dialog with Hicks performed at San Francisco's Galeria de la Raza that summer, Gómez-Peña quipped, in response to critics like Baker, that "in Latin America the artist has multiple roles. He/She is not just an image maker or a marginal genius, but a social thinker/educator/counter-journalist/ civilian-diplomat and human rights observer. His/Her activities take place in the center of society and not in specialized corners."[16]

The Capp Street Project enabled BAW/TAF to function as a sort of communications hub for radical artistic, academic, and political initiatives across the Americas. This breakthrough effectively edged the group from their starting point at the U.S.-Mexican border closer to centers of North American culture. The same gesture considerably raised the public profile of border art, investing the phenomenon with a new legitimacy. For a giddy moment, it seemed as though BAW/TAF had achieved its agenda; it had brought the border into the spotlit center to reveal that forces inflecting border politics (such as xenophobia, racism, and classism) are central to all operations of the American way of life. It had demonstrated, as the art historian Jo-Anne Berelowitz has eloquently observed, "that in a deep ontological sense the border lies within us all as the limiting barrier to the attainment of an unbounded humanity."[17]

Meanwhile, back in the Southwest, border artists, including some members of the original BAW/TAF group, began to profit from what the poet-activist José Antonio Burciaga describes as the "amigoization" of the American culture industry, a market-driven boom in Latino visual culture that brought media attention, grants, "the French filmmakers, the German journalists, and following them a myriad of dilettantes and cultural tourists who wanted to experience the border extravaganza."[18] As it turned out, "the success of border art turned out to be BAW/TAF's undoing, banalizing the border metaphor,"[19] and bringing about "the resignation of all but one of the original members, the only white male of the group."[20] Gómez-Peña complained that, around 1989,

> dozens of mediocre artists who were painting outdated surreal or abstract art before the boom became born-again border artists overnight. Major institutions, whose previous histories and interests were almost exclusively Eurocentric, suddenly organized conferences, festivals, and blockbuster exhibits about border this and border that, without consulting or including the creators of the movement.[21]

Major museum shows such as "La Frontera/The Border: Art about the Mexico/United States Border Experience," organized by the Museum of Contemporary Art of San Diego, initially seemed to represent a critical mainstreaming of art that engaged with issues of cultural identity such as border art. Yet these mainstream events also deadened the work's political thrust by promoting style over content and framing social activism as a fashionable artistic trend.

Who benefited from this short-lived border-art boom? The only Latino border artists to benefit, Gómez-Peña reckons, were, in addition to himself, four other artists from the BAW/TAF group (Isaac Artenstein, Robert Sanchez, David Avalos, and Richard Lou), "sadly all male."[22]

> But who else? Certainly not the migrant workers or the Tijuana artists or the Chicano cultural organizations. If the answer is a group of Anglo artists and major organizations, something went fundamentally wrong. A movement that began as an attempt to dismantle Anglo-Saxon patriarchal authority ends up being appropriated, controlled, promoted, and presented by Anglo-Saxon patriarchs.[23]

Although some of these newly successful border artists may have hoped to see mainstream cultural spaces (museums, galleries, universities) radicalized by their borderline thinking, these former outsiders often found their powers of political persuasion quickly neutralized once they crossed the institutional threshold.

While Gómez-Peña points the finger at the novelty-hungry capitalist art establishment, opportunistic Anglo artists, and politically naïve neophytes, Berelowitz rightly shifts some of the responsibility for the failure of BAW/TAF's vision back onto the shoulders of its original members. One of the most problematic issues to beset the group was that of gender inequity. Of the seven founding members, only two (Jude Eberhardt and Sara-Jo Berman) were women, and they were married to key male members (Artenstein and Gómez-Peña respectively). Women continued to enter the ranks primarily via their relationships with male group members.

In 1988, a number of BAW/TAF women organized to transform their individual grievances concerning the group's failure to address gender and sexuality "as borders requiring renegotiation" into a collective agenda.[24] They took a new name, Las Comadres, a term with multiple meanings (godmother, gossip, midwife, friend). Their numbers swelled from an original core of eighteen to a loose affiliation of about thirty women, all involved with the arts or art education in one way or another. This ethnically diverse consciousness-raising/support group methodically explored the intersections of feminism and multiculturalism. Together, they studied texts by multicultural feminist intellectuals such as Anzaldúa, bell hooks, and Trinh Minh-ha. After reading Trinh's "Grandma's Story," an essay on women and storytelling, they began to explore the ways that personal narrative, community-building, and larger historical circumstances interconnect. "Unlike written history," Berelowitz observes, "storytelling is an art of the body, transmitted from mouth to ear and from heart to heart, establishing a chain and continuum between the generations who pass it on, thereby providing a link between past, present, and future."[25]

Trinh's essay suggests that the storyteller's power is the power of bringing people together.[26] In contrast to the Western notion of the *author*, an individual who generates literary texts, the *storyteller* is a repository and narrator of collective experience. Her power, then, is not the power of ownership, but of communion. Storytelling, in that it operates outside established systems of critical evaluation, without the cachet of the author's signature or the benefit of copyright, has the effect of "deterritorializing language," as the postmodern philosophers Gilles Deleuze and Félix Guattari have argued.[27] The deterritorialization of language is a kind of unmooring, or freeing, of culture from official sites of articulation. Cultures, according to Deleuze and Guattari, are better understood as portable or mobile in an age of globalized media and performance. They describe culture in nomadic terms, as a constant process of encounter with and adaptation to "outside" influences that is global in its scope and that challenges received ideas about the rootedness or "organic" character of cultural identity. Thus, the term *deterritorialization* has exciting implications with respect to both globalization and border art.

If we were to imagine culture as evolving within an endless process of fluid exchange among peoples of different origins, would geopolitical boundaries still figure prominently in our narratives of cultural heritage? Or our art-making? Emily Hicks, a founder of Las Comadres, former BAW/TAF member, and tenured professor of Chicana/Chicano studies and comparative literature at San Diego State University, has rethought the operations of deterritorialization from feminist and multicultural perspectives in both her border art and "border writing."[28] She adopts holography (the creation of a multifaceted photographic image registering multiple perspectives) as an organizing metaphor for her creative work. Border zones, she argues, set in motion cultural interactions that reveal how two-dimensional our ideas about cultural heritage and ethnic identity can be. Hicks's shape-shifting "holographic reality" opens new vistas beyond the impasses of colonial history and embattled border politics. In an interview with the educator Peter McLaren, Hicks affirmed that "the habit of code-switching, necessary to survival in a border region, may strengthen one in terms of ability and agility with regard to perceiving and comprehending common notions" without diminishing one's sensitivity to the significance of cultural, historical, and economic differences.[29]

Hicks offers a kind of ethical blueprint for artistic intervention into the arena of border politics. Take, for instance, the actions she organized, together with other members of Las Comadres and BAW/TAF, in response to the right-wing "Light Up the Border" anti-immigration campaign of the early 1990s. Light Up the Border was a vigilante initiative spearheaded by Roger Hedgecock, former mayor of San Diego, who enlisted citizens to line their cars up on the border at dusk on the third Thursday of each month and to train their headlights on the no-man's land between the United States and Mexico. Hedgecock's vigilantes intended to spotlight both literally and figuratively the issue of illegal border crossing, and thus to highlight the efficacy of heightened surveillance. At the movement's apex, as many as a thousand automobiles aligned themselves on the border to shine their brights toward Tijuana.[30]

In response, Las Comadres hired a plane to barnstorm the parked cars trailing a banner that read: "1000 Points of Fear—Another Berlin Wall?" The banner's slogan makes reference to both President George H. W. Bush's contemporaneous "thousand points of light" State of the Union message (January 29, 1991) and the wall that had divided Berlin from 1961 to 1989 (and, symbolically, divided East from West). The slogan—with its disparate points of reference—thus draws an analogy between the Tijuana border fence and Communist Bloc strategies of social control that were vilified throughout the "free" West. At the same time, the formulation ironically compares the chain of headlights strung out across the Southern California landscape to the first President Bush's inspirational figure of speech, uttered as United Nations troops invaded the Persian Gulf.[31] By connecting apparently unrelated events to form a compound "holographic" meaning, the banner linked social justice concerns across time and space while questioning Euro-America's claims of enlightenment.

On the ground, BAW/TAF members also organized a multicultural coalition of counterprotestors who paraded the borderline equipped with mirrors to deflect, and reflect back, the Light Up the Night headlamp beams. These actions turned the tactics and idioms of Light Up the Night back on itself while refuting the "us and them" logic of pronouncements insisting upon the sanctity of national borders. At a time when the signing of the North American Free Trade Agreement (NAFTA) captured media attention, Las Comadres refocused the debate on the cruel contradiction inherent in opening the border to the free flow of capital while simultaneously closing it to the flow of labor. Their actions highlighted the extent to which immigration laws, vigilante border policing, and other xenophobic campaigns express anxieties about *internal* social dynamics as well as external pressures. These anxieties, once codified in antimiscegenation legislation, concern the mixing ("contamination") of populations and bodies whose "purity" upholds race-based social hierarchies. These are the stakes of maintaining, or failing to maintain, racial as well as national boundaries.

Stereotypes play an important role in maintaining both the internal and external cultural barriers that border artists aspire to dismantle. Stereotypes of the Other replace the complexities of cultural difference with something more understandable, something two-dimensional. In the mid-1990s, Gómez-Peña, still working the border as a site of creative political engagement, called attention to the ways stereotypes operate to dehumanize and thus rationalize xenophobic foreign policy. In a piece titled *Seditious Members of La Pocha Nostra*, for instance, he and his collaborators enacted a comic dramatization of "barbarian hordes" from Mexico invading the United States.

Seditious Members plays on several imagined threats to civilization north of the border, from peasant uprisings to national liberation movements to modern-day bandits. Running ahead of a monstrous premodern armored vehicle with a pirate's death's head mounted on its hood, Gómez-Peña's motley army of invaders, resembling stock characters from *Zorro* and other vintage Hollywood B-movies, managed, as the historian of visual culture Irit Rogoff notes, "to address all possible threats attributed to potential Mexican immigration; they negate modernity and its technologies and invoke mechanical backwardness; they perform a violent and aggressive invasiveness and they defy the codes of politeness set out by corporate culture."[32] This kind of stereotyping, she concludes, "works to put into quite ridiculous perspective" the degree to which such cultural clichés mask the complexities of actual cultural interaction among Latin America, the Caribbean, Mexico, and Chicano populations in the United States, not to mention indigenous American cultures. The border, like the stereotype, labors to reduce the complexities of this constellation of cultural influences by reducing them to a geographically localized Mexican-U.S. border "problem" (associated, in the imagination of many U.S. citizens, with serious economic and cultural threats).[33] *Seditious Members* thus aims to parody the stereotypes embodying America's obsession with the menace of Mexican immigration in order to attract attention to the human stakes of corporate-driven American foreign and domestic policies.

The lampooning of stereotypes, a Gómez-Peña hallmark, also plays an important role in one of his most widely publicized collaborations, enacted together with the performance artist Coco Fusco. *The Guatinaui World Tour* featured the pair as a couple of Amerindian specimens recently "discovered" on the tiny (fictitious) island of Guatinau in the Gulf of Mexico. The two performers, caged like circus animals and costumed like sideshow "savages" (with all the proper accoutrements: his feather headdress, strings of teeth slung around her neck, her grass skirt, his Aztec breastplate), appeared throughout 1993 in various public venues to be photographed and gaped at by passersby.

Informed by historical research, the team performed a hypertheatrical simulation of the humiliating conditions that "exotic" human displays such as the so-called Hottentot Venus had known as colonial spectacles throughout the nineteenth century. It was the artists' intention to heighten public awareness about the racism implicit in ethnographic displays such as those found in many natural history, ethnographic, and anthropological museums to this very day.[34] The American Museum of Natural History, for instance, until very recently displayed dioramas containing representations of Plains Indians along with other forms of "prairie life." The museum's magnificent collection of Inuit artifacts, moreover, would be more appropriately housed in a museum emphasizing "culture" rather than "nature." Gómez-Peña and Fusco attempted to turn the tables on display practices that "naturalize" racism.

"The performance was interactive, focusing less on what we did than on how people interacted with us and interpreted our actions," Fusco explains.[35] The performers, in fact, compiled data about the demographics and patterns of response they encountered as they toured the project. Gómez-Peña describes this practice as "reverse anthropology," in that the spotlight is directed at the spectator's characteristics (age, race, class, gender) and actions (gaping or refusing to gape), instead of the character-istics and actions of the "specimen."[36]

The Guatinaui World Tour dramatizes the extent to which racial and eth-nic stereotyping infiltrates not only Hollywood's dubious confections but also high cultural institutions like museums—and, perhaps more importantly, the political and natural sciences that shape our understanding of, and inter-actions with, the world. With their sideshow parody, Fusco and Gómez-Peña created a theatrical space that disarmed the defenses of their spectators, ena-bling them, as Gómez-Peña puts it, "to reflect on their own racist attitudes towards other cultures."[37] The success of the piece hinges on both the view-ers' and the performers' willingness to cross the border separating "us" from "them," to look beyond the bars of the cage, to view one another eye-to-eye, and to refuse the anonymous safety offered by stereotypes of Otherness. Fusco and Gómez-Peña's sardonic reenactment of a shameful form of popu-lar entertainment demonstrates that the cultural "Other," the people on the other side of the bars (or the borderline), can perform different roles than those assigned them by Euro-Americans. Rather than reaffirming the domi-nance of white races, as per received colonialist scripts, cultural difference (if not systematically reduced to cultural inferiority) may have the power to reflect, to refuse, to rewrite historical narratives, and to actually provoke posi-tive social change.

The artistic strategies and social agendas that distinguish the work of Gómez-Peña and Fusco have inspired a new generation of artists now coming to maturity. To cite just one example, the Proyecto Internacional de Tierra-Boya (PITB)—an initiative launched by Linus Lancaster, a high school art teacher in Healdsburg, California, in collaboration with several of his honors students (Cruz Calderon, Jose Montes, Abraham Rica, Jeovani Garcia, Steven Mota, Paul Nichols, Sared Gutierrez, and Adrian Silva)—employs a similar blend of brashness, humor, ingenuity, and politi-cal conviction. It addresses issues of borders and international relations through the creation of portable territorial markers (land buoys) that serve as props for political street theater, political lobbying, and the constitution of narratives of resistance to ultranationalism and corporate globalization through performance documentation. The group's enterprises are grounded in rigorous historical research and studiously informed by politi-cal theory. Organizer Lancaster explains that the project draws inspiration from Michael Hardt and Antonio Negri's notion of "imperial reversal."[38] This is something other than a 180-degree turn, or "reversal" as tradition-ally defined. *Imperial reversal* describes, rather, a form of inertia within the consumer sector brought on by capitalism's own excesses and the ensuing depletion vital material resources. Capitalism, by these lights, would exceed *itself* politically and be forced into a radical shift, an operational change that Lancaster describes as "productive aporia."[39] An *aporia* is a seemingly insoluble impasse in a line of investigation, often arising from contradictions at the point of origin.

These ideas of "aporia" and "reversal" materialize in the objects and actions generated by the PITB. One example, *El Gobernador*, illustrates the usefulness of these concepts particularly well. This "portable sculpture" is a

Weber barbeque fitted with outsized knobby all-terrain tires. A Cohiba cigar dangles from the "lips" formed by the lid and the charcoal basin (the cigar, Lancaster explains, "is significant in that the original Cohibas were promoted after the Cuban Revolution by Che Guevara").[40] The contours of the Weber give the world map painted in red on its black enamel surface a globelike effect. The tiny American flags that dot the surface of this map plot the global reaches of U.S. commercial and military imperialism.

In a letter to California governor Arnold Schwarzenegger explaining the appearance of the object on Capitol lawn, Lancaster notes that *El Gobernador* borrows its name from a massive steam locomotive built by the Southern Pacific Railroad and named after railway tycoon Leland Stanford (who had also once served as California state governor). The engine, designed to pull freight cars up the steep Tehachapi grade along the railway connecting Sacramento and Los Angeles, was mounted on an extrawide "Mastodon" wheelbase, to which the Weber's knobby wheels pay tribute. Stanford imported over ten thousand workers from China to build his railway. Once the line was completed, they were laid off. Stranded in California, they sought employment in the Sierra gold, silver, and copper mines, where the competition for jobs provoked violent responses from Euro-Americans competing for the same work. As a result of the ensuing social tensions, California's Chinese Exclusion Act passed into law in 1882, the very year the *Gobernador* was constructed. Ironically, the *Gobernador* did not turn out to be as powerful as its engineers had predicted (and here we return, rather literally, to the notions of aporia and reversal). On the way up the Tehachapi grade, the excessively large engine had to stop every few hundred yards to consume massive reserves of cord-wood fuel. When it finally reached the summit, the train, too unwieldy to turn around, had to back all the way down the mountainside. After only a few years, the costly and impractical showpiece was scrapped.[41]

Thus, *El Gobernador*, the PITB's contraption, functions as a mobile, tongue-in-cheek "monument" to failed acts of territorial/economic conquest. This and the group's half a dozen or so other land buoys, by claiming space and commanding attention in venues associated with the production of official culture and policy, signal the existence of channels of resistance to campaigns of cultural supremacy and expose the fragility of seemingly all-powerful regimes. *El Gobernador*, like all the highly tendentious art objects that the group produces, claims any space it occupies as a forum for conversation about political resistance. Whether dispatched by mail or escorted personally to a site, the PITB's objects serve as emissaries of the anti-imperialist revolution and participate in an exchange of cultural energy, a readjustment of political agency, or an oceanic intervention into imperialist cartography that aims to level out, if only in the popular imagination, an historically uneven sociopolitical field.

Soil samples also play an important role in the PITB's consciousness-raising campaigns. In response to the escalation of "border wars" between Mexico and the United States since 1993—a year marked by the passage of California's Proposition 187 (a ballot initiative designed to deny undocumented immigrants social services, health care, and public education) and the ratification of NAFTA—the project has mobilized Mexican soil to reclaim sites of symbolic significance, such as the California State Capitol in Sacramento.

On one occasion, group members mixed Mexican soil with water and painted the steps of the Capitol building with the resulting slip. They then composed an open letter to the California state assembly, tracing the intricacies of the relationship between election fraud in the United States, U.S. intervention in Mexico's electoral process, and the economic imperatives of NAFTA. The letter concludes with the following admonition:

> If you believe that this is not our problem and that your office is not the appropriate battle ground, we beg to differ. To that end we have taken the liberty of converting your office to sovereign Mexican soil through a transubstantiation process that our group has initiated. If you came to work last week, the soil of Mexico is on the bottom of your shoes and was tracked into your office.[42]

A copy of the letter was mailed, along with a soil sample, to California senator Dianne Feinstein in Washington, D.C. The Mexican soil samples found their way to other symbolically significant locations. A District of Columbia collaborator sprinkled Mexican soil on the White House lawn, for instance. Another correspondent integrated Mexican soil received by post into the environment of New Haven, Connecticut, a self-declared "sanctuary city" where Hispanic communities have been subjected to forceful campaigns of federal retribution. In return, the PITB solicits and receives soil samples from centers of resistance to the politics of U.S. domination and corporate globalization worldwide. In this small way, and with seemingly limited resources, the Proyecto Internacional de Tierra-Boya fulfills a large ambition: to reconfigure the geopolitical world by provoking a shift (however slight) in global political consciousness.

The group shares this ambition and a strong spiritual connection with the Ejército Zapatista de Liberación Nacional (Zapatista Army of National Liberation). Indeed, the group photograph posted on the PITB website foregrounds an EZLN banner. The EZLN views itself as part of the wider social movement and cultivates alliances with like-minded individuals and groups north of the border and around the world. The Zapatistas defend the rights of indigenous peoples and oppose neoliberal policies (NAFTA, for instance). The Intercontinental Encounter for Humanity and against Neoliberalism, held in the Mexican state of Chiapas in 1996, laid the groundwork for ongoing alliances with antiglobalization activists under various banners (the "alterglobalization" and "glocalization" movements, for instance) in Argentina, Venezuela, Bolivia, Cuba, Ecuador, Spain, Italy, Austria, Germany, Switzerland, Great Britain, France, and the United States.

Hardt and Negri, in their influential book *Empire*, argue that the Zapatistas, while still engaging in older forms of armed revolt, represent a new breed of revolutionary, born in the era of globalization and adept at the staging spectacular image-intensive campaigns via the World Wide Web.[43]

Gómez-Peña concurs, observing that "from the onset, the EZLN was fully aware of the symbolic power of the military actions." They strategically began their rebellion the day that NAFTA went into effect, and from day one of the conflict, have "placed as much importance on staging press conferences and theatrical photos as on their military strategy."[44] Their armed rebellion was conducted, one might even argue, as if it were a performance for world audiences, with each skirmish quickly translated into digital images for circulation on the Internet.

The Internet—with its First World, white-collar, technocratic associations—may seem an unlikely tool for revolutionaries concerned with the both class politics and the negative impact of corporate globalization on local populations. While proponents of the World Wide Web have extolled its democratic potential, critics have vigorously refuted this claim, citing class-based inequalities in access to phone lines, computers, Internet service providers, and other technical resources as significant barriers to universal participation. The EZLN fully understands, however, that material put into circulation online is readily available for dissemination via a range of other media. EZLN website postings are broadcast by word of mouth, reproduced in community news bulletins, and picked up by local and sometimes international news agencies, for instance, revealing the Web as only one aspect of a much wider communications network.

Although the Northern California–based PITB relies somewhat paradoxically on low-tech devices and traditional modes of communication (such as the U.S. Postal Service) more than twenty-first-century technologies, its awareness of the EZLN and its political goals and methods can be attributed to directly to the Internet. The PITB's penchant for low-tech media and the EZLN's embrace of high technology can be differentially explained. In a cultural field reconfigured by the advent of the cellphone/camera/videorecorder/computer/TV and virtual social relations, the PITB's quasi-obsolete (and ecologically low-impact) methods stand out. They imbue the PITB's projects with a form of sincerity, or genuineness, that virtual modes of communication do not typically foster. "We look to the Zapatistas as inspiration," Lancaster acknowledges, "rather than as a model for conscious resistance to global capitalism ... because the conditions in Chiapas are quite different from those in most of the United States."[45] The ambition to form communities of affinity, to create coalitions across all sorts of borders, to operate in solidarity with global struggles for human rights and dignity, without reducing human diversity to a set of convenient stereotypes, aligns the PITB with border-art forerunners such as Las Comadres and BAW/TAF, whose sympathies with socialist and populist revolutions south of the U.S. border are a matter of public record.

Throughout this chapter, I have stressed the commitment that border artists have demonstrated to the public domain in general, and especially to the creation of new forms and forums of what might be described as both public art and public education. (Not one of the artists I have discussed thus far creates work with the prospect of gallery sales in mind.)

The last example I will introduce, Chris Gilbert's exhibition "Now-Time Venezuela: Media along the Path of the Bolivarian Process," extends this pattern of social responsibility into the arena of the university art museum.

The first installation of this two-part exhibition—a multiscreen projection examining Venezuela's worker-controlled aluminum, textile, cocoa, tomato, and paper-product factories—was commissioned by Gilbert and produced by Dario Azzelini, a writer and political analyst who lives between Mexico City and Berlin, and the Austrian artist Oliver Ressler. The team conducted interviews with workers in five factories participating in Venezuelan president Hugo Chávez's campaigns to combat poverty and social injustice via the implementation of democratic socialist economic models and to bring to fruition the wars of independence waged by Venezuela's first president, Simón Bolívar, early in the last century (this accounts for the reference to the "Bolivarian Process" in the exhibition's title). In one of the video interviews, a worker describes his sense of empowerment within the worker-controlled Venezuelan workplace by saying, "We are the protagonists.... We don't think as Comandante Chávez does, Comandante Chávez thinks like us and that is why he is there and we will keep him there."[46]

Gilbert (who prefers the title *organizer*, with its political connotations, to *curator*) brought this work to the University of California's Berkeley Art Museum in 2006 as part of a yearlong cycle that he imagined would "not merely document but also contribute to" the social revolutions under way south of the U.S. border, specifically in Venezuela.

Part two of the exhibition revolved around a selection of programming made by Catia TVe, a Caracas television station operated by community activists. "This is a departure from a tradition of political art and exhibitions," Gilbert affirms in the manifesto he created for the exhibition, "in that it acknowledges that works of art can be part of the new world that revolutionary art brings into being rather than simply reflecting upon them."[47] Here, Gilbert adds his voice to the chorus of artists, scholars, and activists, including some of those discussed in this chapter, who believe that, by raising political consciousness, art can significantly shift public opinion and thus policy. Gilbert makes no apology for his overtly political agenda, offering his didacticism as a countermodel to the "ideology of neutrality" that he perceives as having a particularly "virulent" effect in American university settings.[48]

In April 2006, Gilbert resigned from his curatorial position at the Berkeley Art Museum when the museum's administration demanded that he delete a passage of his exhibition wall text proclaiming "solidarity" with the socialist revolution. Explaining the reason for his resignation, Gilbert wrote:

> The museum administrators—meaning the deputy directors and senior curator collaborating, of course, with the public relations and audience development staff—have for some time been insisting that I take the ideas of solidarity, revolutionary solidarity, out of the cycle. For some months, they have said they wanted "neutrality" and "balance" whereas I have always said

that instead my approach is about commitment, support, and alignment—in brief, taking sides with and promoting revolution.[49]

Predictably, Gilbert's act of refusal, and the circulation of his letter of resignation on the Internet, generated all the more interest in the show.

Part two of the cycle opened only days after the news of Gilbert's resignation broke, while the organizer's letter of resignation circulated on sites such as Indybay.org, Metamute.org, and Rhizome.org. The letter was picked up by other sites, excerpted by bloggers, and commented upon by journalists both online and in the print media, where debates over artistic freedom, curatorial responsibility, and government censorship ensued. The *New York Times* critic Holland Cotter acknowledged that "it is hard to deny the commitment and excitement of [Gilbert's] vision of the museum as an ethically charged experience, a psychologically fraught encounter, a stage for disruptive, possibly dangerous, ideas." He added, "It isn't just a place where you go to look at old things, but a place where you see in fresh ways."[50] Many others voiced support for Gilbert, applauding his initiative to "radically transform the role of arts administrator into that of engaged, political participant."[51] Skeptics, however, accused him of stealing the show, and making himself . . . the story.

In a letter to *ArtForum*, Gilbert ultimately renounced art and its institutions as a significant staging ground for revolutionary struggle. He concluded that "cultural institutions (such as museums and *ArtForum*) are part of a deeply corrupt bourgeois representational context, but to target them as the primary site of struggle is not radical in that it does not go to the root of the problem."[52] Even as Gilbert slipped away to Venezuela, controversy around the debacle continued to ramify, with censorship in the arts as a central theme. Most commentators (whatever their opinion of Gilbert or the Berkeley Art Museum) agreed that, in the current U.S. political climate, powerful censorship initiatives from both the private and the public sector pose equally disturbing threats to the freedom of artistic and political expression.

Gómez-Peña numbers among those who have expressed deep concern about both institutional censorship and self-censorship at a time when the arts are policed not only by museum directors but even by the Joint Terrorism Task Force.[53] In his essay "Cyber-Placazo: Gómez-Peña on Censorship in the United States," the performance artist discusses his strategies for preempting incidents of censorship, for example, posting an ironic proviso on the door of the exhibition or performance venue.

I always try to create a funny disclaimer that heightens the specific fears of the curator or the institution—something like: "Think twice before you cross this border." Or, "Patriots should think twice before entering into an internationalized space." Or, "The artists are not responsible for identity crises audience members might endure during the performance.'"[54]

Yet, of course, art activists like Gómez-Peña (to name only one representative practitioner within the rapidly expanding public art arena of border art) *are* responsible for subjecting the public to the discomforts of border crossing, and for the identity crises and crises of conscience these crossings provoke. That is indeed the purposeful effect of border art as it moves to, and speaks to, the heart of America.

In today's post-9/11 political climate, the xenophobic rhetoric of "the alien" has reached a fevered pitch. Those from outside our borders, and their kin within, are too often perceived (and processed by customs and immigration authorities) as enemies. Their fingerprints are indexed, irises scanned, and documents and baggage scrutinized at every port of entry. They are detained or turned away at the slightest pretext. Their visas are subjected to strict restrictions and dubious national quotas. Their purchases, communications, and movements are tracked. In a society where information technology-based surveillance, the fortification of national frontiers, and the growing prison-industrial complex extend and rework procedures of surveillance and control associated historically with totalitarianism, critical thinking about representations of alien identity should be recognized by all of us as an urgent imperative. Border artists like the members of BAW/TAF, Las Comadres, and the PITB have taken up this challenge. Like Chris Gilbert, they are rewriting the narratives of evolutionary and cultural development that have long served to justify territorial conquest and racial domination. They are redefining the borderlines that have served to separate and alienate. They are aligning themselves with social revolutions and revolutions of consciousness across the globe and here at home. They are teaching the global arena local lessons and waging local struggles for global stakes.

NOTES

1. The cultural anthropologist Arjun Appadurai describes the formation, under these conditions, of new "communities of sentiment." This is a useful way to think about global cultural interactions. See Arjun Appadurai, "Disjuncture and Difference in the Global Cultural Economy," *Theory, Culture, and Society* 7, nos. 2–3, 1990: 295–310.

2. Although the artist's social role is rarely featured in Euro-American accounts of the creative personality, the artist-as-public-intellectual is a venerated figure in Latin American cultures.

3. New Mexico State University, Center for Latin American and Border Studies home page, http://www.nmsu.edu/~clas/.

4. Mikhail M. Bakhtin, "The Problem of Content, Material, and Form in Verbal Artistic Creation," in *Art and Answerability: Early Philosophical Essays by M. M. Bakhtin*, translated by Vadim Liapunov and Kenneth Brostrom and edited by Michael Holquist (Austin: University of Texas Press, 1990), 274.

5. See Gloria Anzaldúa, *Borderlands/La Frontera: The New Mestiza* (San Francisco: Aunt Lute Books, 1987).

6. The founding members of BAW/TAF were Isaac Artenstein, David Avalos, Sara-Jo Berman, Jude Eberhardt, Guillermo Gómez-Peña, Victor Ochoa, and Michael Schnorr.

7. BAW/TAF, "General Statement," http://borderartworkshop.com/statement/statement.html.

8. Madeline Grynsztejn, "La Frontera/The Border," in *La Frontera/The Border: Art about the Mexico/United States Experience*, edited by Kathryn Kanjo (San Diego: Centro Cultural la Raza and Museum of Contemporary Art of San Diego, 1993), 25.

9. California College of the Arts recently launched a social practice program in its Fine Arts graduate division. This is one of several instances of institutional acknowledgment of an emerging field of practice. This field has been discussed by Nicholas Bourriaud, director of Paris's contemporary art space at the Palais de Tokyo, as "relational aesthetics" because of the displacement of emphasis away from the production of traditional genres and toward social transactions. More than twenty years ago, artist Suzanne Lacy identified this shift as a "new genre" of public art.

10. Emily Hicks, "What Is Border Semiotics?" cited in Andrew D. Hershberger, "Bordering on Cultural Vision(s): Jay Dusard's Collaboration with the Border Art Workshop/Taller de Arte Fronterizo," *Art Journal* 65, no. 1 (Spring 2006): 93n40.

11. The fence now extends well beyond the low-tide line out into the ocean depths. This extension of an armored fence beyond the shoreline into the ocean's unbounded expanse visually underscores the artificiality of national borderlines generally.

12. Mary Louise Pratt, "Arts of Contact," in *Ways of Reading*, 5th ed., edited by David Bartholomae and Anthony Petroksky, 33–40 (New York: Bedford/St. Martin's, 1999).

13. Press release cited in Robert Atkins, "Border Lines: The Border Arts Workshop Goes High Tech," *Village Voice*, September 26, 1989, available at http://www.robertatkins.net/beta/witness/artists/formats/border.html.

14. Quoted in Atkins, "Border Lines."

15. Quoted in Atkins, "Border Lines."

16. Quoted in Atkins, "Border Lines."

17. Jo-Anne Berelowitz, "Las Comadres: A Feminist Collective Negotiates a New Paradigm for Women at the U.S./Mexico Border," *Genders* 28 (1998), available at http://home.znet.com/marquesa/art/artreview/las/lascomadres.html.

18. Guillermo Gómez-Peña, "Death on the Border: A Eulogy to Border Art," *High Performance* 14 (Spring 1991): 9.

19. Hershberger, "Bordering on Cultural Vision(s)," 93.

20. Gómez-Peña, "Death on the Border," 9.

21. Ibid.

22. Ibid.

23. Ibid.

24. Berelowitz, "Las Comadres."

25. Ibid.

26. See Trinh T. Minh-ha, "Grandma's Story," in *Blasted Allegories: An Anthology of Writings by Contemporary Artists*, edited by Brian Wallis (New York: New Museum of Contemporary Art/MIT Press, 1987).

27. Gilles Deleuze and Félix Guattari, "What Is a Minor Literature?" in *Out There: Marginalization and Contemporary Cultures*, edited by Russell Fergusson, Martha Gever, Trinh T. Minh-ha, and Cornel West (New York: MIT Press, 1990), 60.

28. D. Emily Hicks, *Border Writing: The Multidimensional Text* (Minneapolis: University of Minnesota Press, 1991).

29. Emily Hicks and Peter McLaren, "Interview with Emily Hicks," *International Journal of Educational Reform* (2000): 83.

30. Extending this logic, in June 2006, Texas governor Rick Perry announced a plan to create a virtual border watch program enlisting the voluntary participation of private landowners in the placement of surveillance cameras (endowed with night vision equipment) at strategic points of entry along the Texas-Mexico border. The ultimate objective was to post the raw video feed on the Internet so that self-appointed virtual border patrollers throughout the United States could observe border activity in real time and report it to authorities via a toll-free number.

31. "We have within our reach the promise of renewed America. We can find meaning and reward by serving some purpose higher than ourselves—a shining purpose, the illumination of a thousand points of light." George H. W. Bush, State of the Union Address, January 29, 1991, available at http://www.infoplease.com/ipa/A0900156.html.

32. Irit Rogoff, *Terra Infirma: Geography's Visual Culture* (London: Routledge, 2000), 117–19.

33. Rogoff, *Terra Infirma*, 119.

34. Saartjie "Sarah" Baartman (1789–1815) was the most famous of at least two South African women who were exhibited as sideshow and World's Fair attractions in nineteenth-century Britain and France under the moniker "the Hottentot Venus" ("Hottentot" was what Dutch and English colonizers called the Khoi people, and "Venus" referred to the goddess of love depicted in so many European works of art). Baartman, the slave of Dutch farmers, was shipped to England and put on display in 1810. Her corporal proportions, skin, hair, and facial features were advertised to European audiences as typical of her people. She had large buttocks, which exhibition visitors were allowed to touch for an additional fee. After abolitionists made trouble for her handlers in London, Baartman was shipped to Paris and passed on to an animal trainer, who exhibited her at fairs. She aroused the curiosity of naturalists, anatomists, and ethnologists and was the subject of numerous scientific illustrations and scholarly publications. When she died of smallpox in 1815, her cadaver was dissected and her skeleton, genitals, and brain were preserved for display in Paris's Musée de l'Homme. Her fate came to public attention anew when American biologist Stephen Jay Gould published an account of her life, "The Hottentot Venus," in the 1980s. In 1994, Nelson Mandela, newly elected president of South Africa, demanded that the French government return her remains, which it finally did, after years of debate and negotiation, in 2002.

35. Coco Fusco, *English Is Broken Here* (New York: New Press, 1995), 50.

36. Gómez-Peña has often used this formulation in his writings and lectures. The title of his March 21, 2003, lecture at the BP Lecture Theatre at the British Museum, for instance, was "Performance as Reverse Anthropology."

37. Guillermo Gómez-Peña, *Dangerous Border Crossers: The Artist Talks Back* (London: Routledge, 2000), 39.

38. See Michael Hardt and Antonio Negri, *Empire* (Cambridge, MA: Harvard University Press, 2000).

39. Linus Lancaster, "Colocacion, Conquistar, y Quebrantamiento (Location, Conquest, and Disruption): Opening Movements of Proyecto Internacional de Tierra-Boya (The International LandBuoy Project)," M.A. thesis, Sonoma State University, 2007.

40. Letter signed by Linus Lancaster, Cruz Calderon, Abraham Rico, Jose Mones, Steven Mota, and Geovani Garcia, addressed to California governor Arnold Schwarzenegger, dated November 11, 2006.

41. I paraphrase an account rendered in the project's letter to Governor Schwarzenegger dated November 11, 2006.

42. Open letter to the California State Legislature and Federal Legislature, reproduced in Lancaster, "Colocacion, Conquistar, y Quebrantamiento," 33–35.

43. See Hardt and Negri, *Empire*.

44. Guillermo Gómez-Peña, "The Subcomandante of Performance," in *First World, Ha Ha Ha! The Zapatista Challenge*, edited by Elaine Katzenberger (San Francisco: City Lights, 1995), 90.

45. Lancaster, "Colocacion, Conquistar, y Quebrantamiento," 29.

46. Worker featured in "Now-Time Venezuela," quoted in Peter Selz, "Berkeley Art Museum Gets Radical with 'Now-Time Venezuela,'" *Berkeley Daily Planet*, April 21, 2006, available at http://www.berkeleydailyplanet.com/article.cfm?issue=04-21-06&storyID=23957.

47. Quoted in Selz, "Berkeley Art Museum."

48. Quoted in Wendy Edelstein, "Who Said the Revolution Won't Be Televised?" *Berkeleyan*, April 13, 2006, available at http://www.berkeley.edu/news/berkeleyan/2006/04/13_video.shtml.

49. Chris Gilbert, statement on his resignation from the UC Berkeley Art Museum, May 21, 2006, available at http://www.meamute.org/en/node/7834/.

50. Holland Cotter, "Leaving Room for Troublemakers," *New York Times*, March 28, 2007, available at http://nytimes.com/2007/03/28/arts/artsspecial/28ESSAY.html.

51. Gregory Sholette, http://transform.eipcp.net/correspondence/1150120940.

52. Chris Gilbert, http://g-rad.org/lamb/archives/2007/01/the-chavista-cu.html.

53. The raid on artist Steve Kurtz offers a dramatic case in point. Kurtz, a member of the performance art group Critical Art Ensemble, is primarily known for his work in Bio-Art, which occasioned his arrest by the FBI and Joint Terrorism Task Force in May 2004. Kurtz, also an associate professor of art at the University of Buffalo, was not indicted on any terrorism charges, but faces twenty years in jail if convicted on charges of fraudulently obtaining biological microbes. Because the Critical Art Ensemble often deals with social criticism, many see the artist's treatment by authorities as a form of intimidation, tantamount to censorship by the federal government.

54. Guillermo Gómez-Peña, "Cyber-Placazo: Gómez-Peña on Censorship in the U.S.," December 2, 2005, http://www.pochanostra.com/dialogues/category/gomez-pena-solo/.

CHAPTER 9

"True Things That Bind Us": Globalization, U.S. Language Pluralism, and Gay Men's English

William Leap

The most visible consequences of globalization, in Arjun Appadurai's phrasing, are the massive flows of "ideas and ideologies, peoples and goods, images and messages, technology and techniques" across local, regional, and national boundaries.[1] The worldwide circulation of these elements is not accidental; however, Appadurai adds:

> Globalization is closely linked to the current workings of capital on a global basis. Its most striking feature is the runaway quality of global finance which appears remarkably independent of traditional constraints of information transfer, national regulation, industrial productivity or "real" wealth in any particular society, country or region.[2]

While it is important to think of "global capital" as a global phenomenon, this perspective yields only a partial understanding of the "runaway quality of global finance"[3] in the current moment.

While I agree that global capital circulates independently of traditional constraints and boundaries, global capital is still invested locally. Each place global capital touches down—for example, in factory farming and industrial parks in rural India or Brazil; in city-center renewal projects in Washington, DC, or Singapore; in entertainment facilities in Tokyo, Saigon, or Bahrain—the projects assume the availability of local terrain for the production of capital and its intended global circulation. Securing such a terrain requires the removal of residents, either voluntarily or through forceful means. Ironically, once investment projects are under way, employment opportunities and related concerns bring new residents into the area—construction workers, other laborers, and those who provide services to them. So there are several reasons why *people* as well as *ideas, goods, images,* and the like, need to be included in the list of "objects" that globalization has set "in motion."[4] Once people are set in motion, *languages* also become caught up in the dynamics of globalization, and here begin the issues that I want to address in this chapter.

The people displaced by globalization are speakers of local languages or local varieties of national languages. Whether these speakers end up in neighboring communities, urban centers within or beyond the immediate region, or locations outside of their national boundary, globalization moves them into places where unfamiliar linguistic practices are the norm and where their own language skills disrupt the conditions of linguistic fluency and meanings of language diversity in their "new homeland." Those already resident in the homeland do not always take kindly to such disruptions. Thus, as Appadurai observes, while the "most striking feature" of globalization may be "the runaway quality of global finance,"[5] other "striking features" of globalization include *new/unexpected forms of language pluralism* and *more intense forms of linguistic backlash.*

Such has certainly been the case in recent years in the United States. Language pluralism has been a part of U.S. cultural history since the earliest days of the colonial period. But the number of languages other than mainstream English (hereafter LOTEs) has increased dramatically since the 1950s due to heightened immigration from South and Southeast Asia, Central and South America, and the Middle East. Fluency in English did not spread evenly within these immigrant communities, and even when English fluency did emerge, knowledge of English did not necessarily displace fluencies in LOTEs once immigrants and family members had settled into new communities, gained employment, and secured citizenship.

The widespread presence of LOTEs in the context of an otherwise English-speaking America is a good example of the "disjuncture between vectors"[6] that Appadurai associates with the workings of globalization. Some Americans have responded to that disjuncture with proposals designed to establish English as the country's national language. These proposals are not only about language, of course; they assert the need for a homogeneous "U.S. culture" and invoke rhetorics of patriotism and loyalty, as well as articulating a common voice as the appropriate means of obtaining it. Other Americans respond to the disjunction by reshaping the texture of their linguistic practices to ensure that their evidence of a LOTE and references to its presence are carefully managed during English conversations.

This chapter examines one category of language use in the United States in which the disjuncture between language diversity and linguistic nationalism is unfolding in especially intriguing ways: the linguistic, cultural, and social practices that I have elsewhere referred to as "Gay Men's English."[7]

Granted, certain ways of speaking English have long been associated with the presence of homosexual men in various U.S. public settings. Many of these speech practices have been recast into stereotype and ridicule: the lispy voice, exaggerated gestures, female pronouns and feminine nicknames to mark gay male personal reference ("Oh, Mary, would you look at her!"), and so forth. But the Gay Men's English (GME) I focus on here is a more subtly and strategically constructed linguistic resource, affording protection from public disclosure as much as it allows displays of gay identity in the public terrain.

These heavily sexualized linguistic codes have been reconfigured, now that LOTEs, and particularly same-sex-identified speakers of LOTEs, have become a part of everyday U.S. speech settings. These reconfigurations, along with the emergence of ways of talking about sexual sameness that are not dependent on GME, are some of the consequences of "globalization here at home"[8] that are of interest in this chapter.

GLOBALIZATION, LANGUAGE PLURALISM, AND OUTRAGE

Let me begin by discussing some of the characteristics of language diversity that have unfolded in U.S. settings in recent years in response to the influence of globalization. In 1940, the U.S. Census Bureau determined that the mother tongue of 18.6 percent of the national "white" population was a language other than English. For 60 percent of these persons, the language in question was German. Spanish was the fourth most frequently spoken LOTE reported in the enumeration.

The 1970 census showed that 16.3 percent of the entire national population (that is, of all persons, regardless of race/ethnic background) had a mother tongue that was a LOTE, and Spanish was now the most frequently reported language in this category. German had dropped to the second most frequently spoken LOTE. In 1975, the Census Bureau calculated that 17.9 percent of members of the national population age 14 and over spoke a LOTE as their mother tongue.[9]

During the 1980s, U.S. census figures showed a 38 percent increase in the number of persons in the U.S. population who spoke a LOTE at home, while the overall population increased by less than 10 percent during that period. The number of foreign-born Americans increased by 41 percent during the 1980s, which suggests that the source of U.S. language pluralism lies in immigration and other forms of outside renewal, such as work sojourners.

Yet whether speakers were foreign born or native born, the 1990 Census data indicated that 94 percent of minority-language speakers in the United States also spoke English at some level. As these data suggest, fluency in a LOTE was and is not a barrier to fluency in English; indeed, LOTE speakers can acquire English fluency without renouncing loyalty or proficiency in their first language.[10]

And according to data collected during the Census Bureau's 2000 household survey, LOTE speakers are doing precisely that. This survey identified 28 million persons who are speakers of Spanish at home, more than 26 million of whom also speak English at some level and over 20 million of whom speak English "very well" or "well." The census reports similar statistics regarding levels of English proficiency for persons who speak Chinese, French, German, Tagalog, Vietnamese, or Arabic at home.[11]

Thus, increasing numbers of LOTEs and LOTE speakers in the United States do *not* mean that English fluency is now on the decline. A careful reading of U.S. Census data suggest a very different profile: LOTE speakers are willing to acquire English proficiency, but find ways to do so without renouncing proficiency in their home/community language tradition. Doing so allows LOTE speakers to engage with a range of personal and political concerns within and outside of the LOTE community settings; in the process, their linguistic practices and priorities take on a texture that is very different from those commonly endorsed by speakers of English in the U.S. mainstream.

HOW LANGUAGE PLURALISM CREATES OUTRAGE

The linguistic differences are particularly upsetting to many native-born, first-language speakers of American English. English has never been officially declared the national language of the United States, yet there are many who assume that English occupies or should occupy such a position. There are many reasons people would uncritically accept this assertion, such as:

- English is the language of the national anthem.
- The Declaration of Independence, the Constitution, and other documents of national charter are printed in English.
- English is closely linked to the nation's Protestant religious heritage, the Pilgrims at Plymouth Rock, and related versions of the national origin myth.
- English provides the linguistic framework for the "oath of allegiance," by means of which immigrants are transformed into citizens.
- As the English-only repertoire of the nation's country-and-western Billboard charts will readily attest, English is the medium for everyday expressions of patriotism, loyalty, and civic pride.[12]

Thus we can understand why so many English-speaking U.S. citizens react so negatively when they learn that "21.3 million Americans are currently classified as *limited English proficient*—a 52 percent increase from 1990, and more than double the 1980 total" or that "one in twenty-five U.S. households [is] *linguistically isolated*, which means that no one in the household—older than age fourteen—speaks English."[13] Such statistics show how some speakers of a LOTE have resolved the tensions between English and LOTE proficiencies: they have simply chosen not to learn English. Read as a statement of personal choice, this linguistic solution need not be problematic to other members of the U.S. mainstream. However, these solutions can never be entirely personal and *always* spill over into the public terrain. For example:

- Massachusetts offers driver's license examinations in twenty-five different languages, Kentucky in twenty-three, New York in twenty-two, and

California in twenty-one. In all, forty-three states and the District of Columbia offer the examination to candidates in LOTEs.

- Hospitals and other medical facilities supported by federal funding are required to provide no-charge translation services to those clients who are seeking medical care and are not proficient speakers of English. Similar services must be provided to limited-English-proficient speakers of LOTEs in courtroom settings. And in districts where a viable percentage of registered voters come from LOTE backgrounds, federal law requires the availability of bilingual ballots or services of a qualified translator.
- A 2006 U.S. Army recruitment campaign uses the slogan "Yo soy el army" and similar linguistic phrasings to make military service more attractive to Spanish-speaking young people.
- To broaden its appeal to a Spanish-speaking clientele, McDonald's and other fast food restaurant chains now offer menus in Spanish as well as English. Counter personnel also often provide services to customers in both languages. English is no longer the sole language of commercial practice at such sites, and "fast food" is now a bilingual experience, whatever the customer's first language, under these circumstances.

For some Americans, the bilingual experience at the fast food restaurant has simply gone too far. A recent example is found at the McDonald's in Bogota, New Jersey. This franchise began advertising the availability of iced coffee on a billboard in Spanish, and Steve Lonegan, mayor of the community, demanded that the billboard sign be taken down. Otherwise, he promised to call for a general boycott of the local firm. "The advertisement is offensive and divisive,"[14] Mayor Lonegan explained. He continued, "The true things that bind us together as neighbors and community is [sic] our belief in the American flag and our common language.... When McDonald's sends a different message, that we're going to be different now, that causes resentment."[15] In effect, advocates for a "common language" are doing more than making a case for an English-based linguistic and cultural purity within the public domain. They recognize that voluntary initiatives are insufficient catalysts for change to that end and are demanding that there be government intervention to resolve what they see as a national linguistic problem.

The U.S. Department of Education and other federal agencies maintain conflicting policies in this regard. These agencies support language pluralism through education equity and equal employment initiatives, but favor English-centered linguistic practices through programs like the "No Child Left Behind" policies and inconsistent enforcement of affirmative action policies. Until quite recently, the U.S. Congress has been reluctant to take action to clarify the status of English in this regard. However, one section of the immigration reform bill S. 26110, which the Senate passed on May 25, 2006, proposed to promote the patriotic integration of prospective U.S. citizens by making English the national language of the United States. The House-Senate compromise version of S. 26110 was defeated on June 28, 2007, largely because of ensuing disagreements centered on the bill's provisions to grant amnesty for "illegal aliens" and create a "guest worker" system. Importantly, there was no floor debate—or dissent—over the national-language functions outlined in the compromise legislation.

States and localities have moved much more aggressively on the national-language question. As of November 7, 2006, twenty-eight state governments had passed legislation establishing English as the official language. For example, the Arizona act requires the Arizona state government "to conduct its business in English and limits governmental multilingualism to commonsense activities such as health care, public safety, judicial proceedings and tourism," according to Mauro Mujica, chairman of the board of the advocacy group U.S. English.[16] He continued:

> Rep. Russell Pearce and his colleagues in the legislature deserve a round of applause for their efforts to unite Arizonans under one common language.... Now that this measure has passed, I hope that those in opposition will join in returning our government's focus on English proficiency for all Arizonans. I think we all agree that we do not want to live in an "English-only" society, but we are equally opposed to the existence of an "English-optional" society.[17]

An "English-optional society" is a society where speakers make use of alternatives to English linguistic practice and find reasons to favor a LOTE in settings where English would otherwise be the expected language of public communication. Such conditions reflect the consequences of displacement, resettlement, and other components of globalization, but this time globalization is having its effects "here at home" rather than in some distant and exotic locale.

Mayor Lonegan's impassioned equation between patriotism and linguistic uniformity has already suggested that the close-at-hand effects of globalization raise fears about impending social divisions, threaten the integrity of neighborhoods and communities, and renew pleas for political, social, and linguistic unity. As the discussion in the following section will show, Lonegan is not the only U.S. citizen to voice such sentiments, or to act on them, under these circumstances.

GAY MEN'S ENGLISH, GLOBALIZATION, AND LANGUAGE PLURALISM "AT HOME"

The term *Gay Men's English* refers to the set of linguistic and cultural practices that appear in conversations, storytelling, and other forms of communicative work associated with a particular category of English speakers: same-sex-identified men. As is so often the case for gay-identified cultural practices in the United States, GME has been most closely identified with same-sex-identified men who are urban residents, relatively affluent, and predominately of Euro-American backgrounds. In that sense, GME has been and remains a language of whiteness.[18] At the same time, GME is not restricted, in occurrence or in appeal, to white terrain. While there are linguistic practices associated with experiences of sexual sameness within African American, Hispanic, Asian American, and Pacific Islander American speech traditions, there are African American, Hispanic, Asian American, and Pacific Islander American speakers of GME. How GME intersects with these non-English-based sexual languages is a matter of some interest in this chapter, and so is how GME intersects with the English usage of the U.S. mainstream.

One of the distinctive characteristics of GME is its expressive vocabulary, such as the words and phrases describing the political, social, geographic, emotional, and aesthetic, as well as the erotic, dimensions of a gay lifestyle. Given the close connections between expressive vocabulary and daily experience, changes in vocabulary become a helpful indicator of the changes unfolding in other areas of social and cultural life. I make use of this point when comparing materials in GME dictionaries and other texts below.

It is important to note that GME is more than a matter of vocabulary. Fluency in GME extends far beyond the boundaries of a gay-specific vocabulary and includes visual imagery and iconography, gesture and other forms of nonverbal communication, and other notions of style and taste. To some extent, the linguistic and cultural features found in GME resemble those found in other varieties of American English—particularly such varieties of English used by other socially stigmatized groups. Hence, the "gay" dimensions of these texts may not be apparent initially.

Some GME communication is unavoidably ambiguous in this regard, some of it deliberately so. These ambiguities ensure that the listener will be as actively involved as the speaker (or writer or artist or performer) in the work of GME communication. This yields a style of communication that differs from the speaker-centered, highly competitive exchanges that are widely attested in mainstream English conversations, particularly in conversations between heterosexual-identified men.[19]

Speakers of GME may also be fluent in varieties of English in which heterosexuality, rather than gay experience, is the orienting theme in linguistic practice. Similarly, "being" gay-identified or "doing" gay-related things are not prerequisites for fluency in GME. Some heterosexual persons are fully proficient speakers, and some gay-identified men never become familiar with GME—nor do they wish to. People often draw much sharper connections between language and sexual identity when they hear someone speaking GME, or what they believe to be GME, and they structure their responses to the speaker accordingly. Such is the nature of homophobia.

Viewed historically, GME is a decidedly North American/British construction. Its origins predate the struggles to move "out of the closet and into the streets" associated with gay liberation politics in the United States during the 1960s and 1970s. Its frame of reference has been shaped by subsequent conflicts between assimilationist and separatist gay politics, by the emergence of queerness as an alternative to gay identity, by mobilizations in response to the AIDS pandemic, by debates over "same-sex marriage," and (as I suggested above) by increasingly inescapable evidence that the "gay culture" with which GME is affiliated is a terrain of white-ness and privilege.

Currently, GME enjoys a worldwide circulation, both as a token of affiliation with North Atlantic gay experience and as a source of reference for naming and discussing sexual experiences when local languages and in-digenous sexual cultures offer no framework for such discussions.[20] This worldwide circulation of GME is closely tied to the circulation of global capital, and those ties strengthen GME's authority in local settings world-wide. Very different from existing frames of reference, which have older, indigenous, and therefore more "traditional" associations, GME becomes identified as the "modern way" to talk about same-sex experiences and desires in public and private conversations. The links between the circula-tion of global capital and GME often lets GME become identified as the best way to frame such discussions.

Inside the United States, GME has had a rather different articulation with global circulation. Here, GME is the "local language" and is already aligned with a very visible, vocal, indigenous homosexual culture. And here, rather than exporting GME, globalization has introduced LOTEs—and speakers of LOTEs—into the GME speakers' home terrain. As is true elsewhere in the globalizing world, English usage coincides with "mod-ernity" and "prestige" in public and private gay-related conversations, while LOTE usage receives a different positioning in these settings. In addition, there have been moves toward a white-centered, all-English-based gay lexical purism in recent years, as well as the emergence of racial/ethnically coded alternatives to a white-centered GME—and, with that, new forms of gay bilingual fluency and gay bilingual identity. All of these outcomes reflect a general uneasiness about "gay visibility" that resonate through-out much of U.S. society and a growing concern about the decline of standard English fluency. I examine each of them, in turn, in the follow-ing sections.

GME VOCABULARY: FROM DIVERSE RESOURCES TO LINGUISTIC PURITY

The gay liberation struggles of the 1960s and early 1970s produced major changes in the visibility of the gay experience in the United States.[21] Prior to that time, a dominant theme in middle-class gay experience was a carefully managed, discrete lifestyle vividly captured by the term "the closet." GME was a language of the closet, providing speakers with ways of disguising references to sexualized topics, concealing sexual identities, and otherwise mediating the risks associated with being homosexual in a largely unsympathetic "straight" terrain.

Yet even with this function, GME was in no sense a dull and unimagi-native linguistic code. Its vocabulary contained materials drawn from a va-riety of linguistic traditions, and the same was true for word construction, sentence structure, intonation, narrative style, and other features of GME linguistic practice. Particular traditions contributing linguistic practice in that regard included the languages of hobos, tramps, and sex workers; prison argot; African American urban and rural English; American Indian, Alaska Native, and Native Hawaiian languages; Yiddish and Yiddish English; Polari;[22] and other European, Asian, and African languages introduced to the United States during earlier periods of globalization.

Features related to the speaker's background also shaped GME linguistic practice. Particularly important were a speaker's ethnic/racial identity, class position, urban or rural residence, and expectations of secrecy and/or tolerance for visibility which each of these features associated with gay life during this time. Prestige dialects of GME were linked to domains of white gay affluence in certain East and West Coast urban settings. And there was also a remarkable amount of regional variation in GME vocabulary, suggesting that the secrecy and discretion dominating the years before gay liberation did not preclude the emergence of gay presence in the U.S. heartland.[23]

Bruce Rogers's introduction to *The Queens' Vernacular*,[24] one of several inventories of GME vocabulary from the pre-gay-liberation period,[25] speaks directly to the inclusive, broad-based focus of GME linguistic practice of this time. Rogers describes his object of study as "the street poetry of queens," a product of the gay ghetto, and a set of linguistic practices that are also "secretive, a form of protest and an expression of social recognition."[26] It is a way of talking that was "invented, coined, dished, and shrieked by the gay stereotypes ... by all those who find it difficult to be accepted for what they feel they are even within the pariah gay subculture."[27] As already suggested, the vocabulary that allowed this political work to unfold consists of words and phrases drawn from a range of sources and used with different levels of frequency. The entries in Rogers's dictionary usually display multiple synonyms for the reference in question, each with its own history and cultural associations, and each adding its own special framing to the given discussion.

For example, Rogers's entry for *a-hole* includes terms from German, Spanish, Louisiana (French) Creole, Swahili, and other non-English sources, as well as terms drawn from several varieties of English associated with the social margin. Some of the terms are highly descriptive and transparent in their meaning; others draw on metaphoric references or invoke specific types of cultural or social imagery. Rogers's comments note that some of these terms were widely recognized by speakers of GME in the 1970s, regardless of place of residence, while others were used only in certain areas of the United States or only by certain speakers in those areas.[28] In effect, as this entry suggests, there was no single "word" for *a-hole* in the GME of the 1960s and 1970s. There were many options, drawn from many different linguistic traditions, most of which were noticeably different from standard English phrasing. Taken together, those features helped GME maintain the "secretive ... protest and ... social recognition" functions that made it such an important resource for American gay men during this time.

Similar impressions about GME can be drawn from a review of the language use of same-sex-identified characters in gay fiction, drama, and biography from the 1960s and early 1970s. By way of example, I consider the use of English by several gay characters in one of these works, Mart Crowley's *The Boys in the Band*.[29] *Boys* is an especially rich archive of 1960s U.S. East Coast urban GME, as the following segment from the opening conversation in the first act of this play will suggest.

There are two participants in this conversation: Donald and Michael. Michael is a thirty-year-old, white, unemployed but seemingly affluent gay man; Donald is a gay man who is twenty-eight years old, white, and a part-time house cleaner. The play takes place in Michael's apartment, during an evening when he is hosting a birthday party for his friend (and ex-lover) Harold. Donald is the first guest to arrive. The two friends are chatting in Michael's bedroom as he is getting dressed for the party. Michael is waiting his turn to take a shower and change clothes:

Donald: You don't think Harold'll mind my being here, do you? Technically, I'm your friend, not his.

Michael: [Crossing to the bed table for a comb] If she doesn't like it, she can twirl on it. Listen, I will be out of the way in a second. I've only got one more thing to do. [He goes to the mirror.]

Donald: Surgery so early in the evening?

Michael: [Turns to Donald] Sunt! That's French, with a cedilla.[30]

Note the combination of linguistic resources that Crowley has Michael employ in this exchange: female pronouns to refer to a male-bodied subject ("If she doesn't like it, she ..."), an allusion to figure skating and particular forms of anal sex ("she can twirl on it"), and the invocation of a fictional, French-sounding term *sunt* complete with a continental-like spelling convention "with a cedilla." This is not usage ordinarily found in standard English contexts, but the features have particular significance in the context of *this* conversation. By framing his responses to Donald's remarks in these terms, Michael demonstrates his affiliation with an urban gay culture that is witty and creative, familiar with performing arts, and cosmopolitan in outlook, as well as catty, condescending, and, at times, misogynist. Thus, he confirms a proficiency in the linguistic practices—the GME—that membership in that culture requires. Notice that the array of linguistic resources Michael uses to establish affiliation and confirm proficiency is similar in scope to those suggested by the entries of Rogers's *Queen's Vernacular*.

Curiously, a very different array of linguistic resources is suggested in the dictionaries of GME and in the gay-related literary and nonfictional sources that begun to appear in the 1980s and afterward.[31] Items connected to gay-centered cultural and historical imagery are key elements in GME reference, according to these sources. However, items from LOTE sources no longer figure prominently in inventories of GME vocabulary or in GME conversations and narratives, compared to the case in the 1960s and early 1970s, and neither do words and phrases drawn from nonstandard varieties of English. Instead, as the dictionaries and literary materials indicate, the primary source for GME vocabulary is now mainstream English.

Consider, for example, the entries in *Gay-2-Zee: A Dictionary of Sex, Subtext, and the Sublime.*[32] Unlike the case in the GME dictionaries from the 1970s, the entries in *Gay-2-Zee* are very brief. They do not contain strings of multiple synonyms. The indicated words and phrases are drawn from a familiar, mainstream English vocabulary. There are very few terms from LOTE sources or terms from varieties of English based on the social margin. Even in instances where terms from nonstandard English sources are referenced, *Gay-2-Zee* says nothing about their origin or etymology. Apparently, unlike the case assumed by *The Queen's Vernacular*, the meanings of GME words and phrases can now be understood without any reference to their history.

Then again, the words and phrases in *Gay-2-Zee* do not require much historical discussion. The GME presented here is not exotic and deeply coded, in the sense of the GME in *The Queen's Vernacular*, but is largely a familiar idiom. The words and phrases could also be found in a conventional English dictionary and everyday, mainstream English conversations. These conditions lead *Gay-2-Zee*'s compiler Donald Reuter to question whether the seemingly distinctive English associated with gay experience in previous years is still part of gay life: "If I had been putting together *Gay-2-Zee* a few years earlier, things would have been much 'queerer' (if not clearer, fact wise)," he observes.[33] But within what Reuter refers to as an increasingly "post-gay era," gay language "is not just about ... words with a definite gay meaning. It is also about the implied, the alleged and the just may-be." It is, he explains, "as much about how we gay men say words," that is, intonation and innuendo, "as it is about the words themselves."[34]

Gay-2-Zee is not alone in suggesting that GME in recent years has begun to lose its distinctiveness and become more and more oriented around communication inside the mainstream setting rather than at distance from it or in opposition to it. GME conversations and narratives found in gay-oriented fiction, drama, and biography published since the 1980s provide the same impression. Some traces of the fast-paced, clever, and at times acidic repartee found throughout *The Boys in the Band* and other literary works from the 1960s and early 1970s can still be found in these sources, and so can references to the performing arts and other areas of popular culture. But not widely attested in these more recent sources are words and phrases from LOTEs or from varieties of English at distance from the mainstream.

Consistent with the image of GME presented in Reuter's dictionary, the vocabulary of these literary works consists of words and phrases that are based almost entirely within the U.S. mainstream English usage. Terms from other sources appear in these works only to provide additional expression of ideas already established in the discussion through mainstream usage. LOTEs and nonstandard English (like Michael's use of pseudo-French, above) are never used as a means of verbal combat or for some other argumentative purpose.

Terrence McNally's *Love! Valor! Compassion!* is filled with examples of such mainstream-centered GME usage.[35] This three-act drama tells the story of a group of gay men, three couples and two single men, who spend three holiday weekends one summer (Memorial Day, the Fourth of July, and Labor Day) at a country home in upstate New York. Gregory, who owns the home and is host for the weekends, is a choreographer and is trying to develop a new piece for New York production. Bobby, Gregory's boyfriend of several months, is in his early twenties; Gregory is in his early forties and takes great comfort in having a boyfriend who is half his age. Gregory talks with a stutter, and Bobby is blind. These are some of the ways that the play acknowledges the diverse biographies that have been included under the category "gay man" in recent years. So are the repeated references to the HIV-positive, symptomatic status of Buzz (in his mid-thirties) and James (late forties), the two unattached house-guests, who become a couple as events of the July 4 weekend unfold.

Act 1 takes place during the Memorial Day weekend. Arthur and Perry have been partners for several years and will be celebrating their anniversary on the Fourth of July weekend. Bobby is riding to the summer house with them. They are the last of the weekend guests to arrive. Already there is John, an older (late forties) and somewhat unpleasant individual, who is also James's identical twin brother; John's boyfriend-of-the-moment, Ramon, who is in his early twenties, Puerto Rican, a dancer, and someone who knows Gregory's work and is in awe of being in his presence for the weekend; and Buzz (James does not arrive until act 2).

In the following scene from act 1, Bobby, Arthur, and Perry are being welcomed by Gregory and Buzz while John and Ramon look on. Ramon moves forward to introduce himself to Bobby (Ramon's attraction to Bobby becomes a key element in act 1 and in the remainder of the play).

Ramon
(to Bobby):   Hi, I'm Ramon. [Ramon puts his hand out to Bobby.]
Gregory: I'm sorry. Bobby doesn't, um, see.
Ramon: I'm sorry. I didn't—
Bobby: Don't be sorry. Just come here! [He hugs Ramon.] Welcome—Ramon, is it?
Ramon: Right.
Bobby: Latino?
Ramon: Yes.
Bobby: *Mi casa es su casa.* I bet you were wishing I wasn't going to say that.
Buzz: We all were, Bobby.
Perry, Arthur,
Buzz: We all were!
Ramon: Listen, that's about as much Spanish as I speak.
Bobby: You're kidding.
Ramon: Sorry to disappoint you. The Commonwealth of Puerto Rico is a territory of USA. Imperialism ...
John: No speeches, please, Ramon. No one is interested.

Ramon: We speak American. We think American. We dress American.
              The only thing we don't do is move or make love Ameri-
              can.[36]

As in *The Boys in the Band*, *Love! Valor! Compassion!* depicts gay-identified men using English in a gay-centered social setting. However, the frequent references to gay popular culture and the rapid movement between
points of reference, of the sort found throughout Michael and Donald's
exchange, are not attested here. There are moments of noticeable topic
shift: Bobby's use of "Mi casa es su casa," a Spanish-language expression
which now has idiomatic status in the U.S. English mainstream, and
Ramon's brief reflection on the contradictions of Puerto Rican political
status. But, unlike in *Boys*, topic shift does not bring new gay meaning
into the discussion. Bobby's and Ramon's remarks could also appear in a
mainstream speech without difficulty.

The sharp and pointed verbal exchanges that give shape to Crowley's
script also help structure several points of the dialogue between McNally's
characters. However, these verbal duels are not dominated by the messages
of self-hatred that appear so frequently in *Boys* and which Michael con-
demns in the final moments of act 3.[37] In fact, John is the only person visiting Gregory's summer house who consistently voices acidic sentiments;
he is also the person whom Gregory's guests uniformly find to be the
most disagreeable.

Interestingly, and echoing the sentiments in Michael's comments twenty-
five years earlier, Ramon speaks out against these expressions of gay self-
hatred and their consequences. Midway through act 1, he observes, "I think
the problem begins right here, the way we relate to one another as gay
men."[38] Very differently from Michael, Ramon speaks as someone who is
new to the group he is addressing, someone who is racially/ethnically different from them, and (we later learn) someone has yet to become closely
aligned with key features of mainstream gay culture.[39]

Having the person who sees the damaging effects of gay self-hatred be
someone of minority background and someone who seems the least
assimilated into gay cultural mainstream is a useful dramatic device, and it
proves to be a focal point for events in the final act.[40] Yet this device also
makes a broader point about the connections between language fluencies
and the politics of gay culture in a 1990s U.S. context. Thus, *Love! Valor!
Compassion!* describes a world where LOTE speakers are not ordinarily
connected with mainstream gay experience, but also a world where the basis for those connections is familiarity with the conventional English displayed in *Gay-2-Zee*, not familiarity with the international cosmopolitan
code found in *The Queen's Vernacular* and used throughout *The Boys in
the Band*.

Certainly, words and phrases from LOTEs and from varieties of English
outside the mainstream are included in conversations and storytelling in
Love! Valor! Compassion! However, the frequency of these items and the
range of sources from which they are drawn are greatly reduced

(particularly so, the use of items from nonstandard English). As a result, the LOTE expressions in the script are limited to words and phrases that enjoy wide circulation in mainstream English conversations and are already included within American English dictionaries—for example, adverbial phrases from French (*C'est la vie*) and Italian (*Basta!*), idiomatic statements in Spanish (*Mi casa es su casa*), specialized vocabulary related to titles of works of classical music, technical dimensions of theatrical performance, or the preparation and enjoyment of gourmet food. Rarely does such usage carry the expressive or emotional weighting that it conveys in *The Boys in the Band*, another indication that the primary idiom of gay communication has become mainstream English centered.[41]

EXPLAINING THE CHANGES IN GME: MOVES AND COUNTERMOVES TOWARD GAY ASSIMILATION

What are we to learn from the prominent place given to words and phrases from LOTEs and nonstandard English sources in GME linguistic practice during the 1960s and early 1970s and the declining presence of such materials in those contexts in more recent times? Let me begin by drawing some parallels with the arguments made earlier in this chapter and suggesting some of the implications of those parallels.

Foregrounding mainstream English vocabulary and downplaying linguistic material from LOTEs and similar sources are, at base, attempts to "purify" GME. That is, these efforts are in some sense aligned with the broader campaign efforts to promote English as the national language and confirm its place as one of the "true things that bind us together as nation and community."[42] If GME is included within the national agenda for linguistic purity, speakers of GME must now be active proponents of that nationalist agenda, joining their heterosexual counterparts in voicing outrage in response to globalization's refiguring of U.S. linguistic and cultural diversity and actively reforming their own linguistic practices to guard against the threat of linguistic disruption within the gay English terrain.

In fact, the shift in linguistic positioning that moves GME from *The Queen's Vernacular* to *Gay-2-Zee* does reflect the broader changes unfolding in U.S. gay culture since the gay liberation struggles of the 1960s and early 1970s. As several writers have explained,[43] these changes have shifted gay culture away from the oppositional stance suggested in Rogers's depiction above and toward the "place at the table" politics advocated by gay neoconservatives such as Bruce Bawer and Andrew Sullivan.[44] These authors argue that activities that emphasize the differences between straight and gay cultures will do little to secure economic and social opportunities for sexual minorities. Rather than heightening the contrasts, gay men should disguise the specifics of homosexual desire, favoring instead a gay lifestyle that appears to be "virtually normal," in Sullivan's phrasing. Under such conditions, gay men's sexuality no longer hinders the pursuit of social and economic reward or unduly restricts the likelihood that those rewards will be obtained; in other words, "virtual normalcy" that is supposedly adopted freely and fully becomes a way for gay men to confirm their status as good citizens in an always suspicious U.S. society.

But to live in a world where those on the sexual margin are to become virtually normal, gay men would need to speak a language that supports the appearance of virtual normalcy. This language would still be associated with gay experience, but would not function (borrowing Rogers's phrasing) as a "secretive code, a form of protest and an expression of social recognition."[45] Instead, this language would be able to assist speakers in the work of assimilation by furthering their efforts to move without barrier within mainstream domains. Recalling how often mainstream experience, success, and privilege are defined in terms of race and class distinctions, this language would also invoke unmistakable associations with whiteness and downplay associations with other racial and social traditions. A language filled with vocabulary that is distinctive and different, whatever its source, would work against such goals—particularly a vocabulary drawn from LOTEs or from varieties of English at a distance from the mainstream.

Reuter spoke to this point when he observed that *Gay-2-Zee*'s treatment of an explicit homosexuality "would have been much 'queerer' (if not clearer, fact wise)" had he assembled the dictionary at an earlier time. In contrast, he continued, "our rapid assimilation into the mainstream and the broadening in scope of ranks has made it more difficult for our individual language to stand out and the sounds are growing harder to hear by the minute."[46] How extensive has this gay assimilation become?

There are some expectations of affluence embedded in the "place at the table" politics espoused by gay neoconservative politics. These expectations are not met by all gay men, according to recent studies of gay men's income data and practices of consumption.[47] Moreover, such factors as race/ethnicity, age level, urban or rural residence, employment, and career aspirations, as well as particular expressions of sexuality, further mediate the extent of gay participation in mainstream activities—and shape different gay men's interests in doing so. Understandably, as Richard Goldstein observed, "Inclusion isn't an issue for some of us, but it really is for others."[48]

For those for whom "inclusion isn't an issue," fluency in GME has now lost the allure that it commanded in earlier years. And because GME's association with the mainstream makes it an object of scorn, there is a search for alternative sources through which same-sex desire and experiences can be framed. I will review some of those alternatives in the next section.

When GME "really is an issue" for some, GME's connection to the mainstream makes it an especially valued cultural resource, particularly when other avenues leading to mainstream locations turn out to be sharply curtailed. GME was valued in the 1960s and 1970s for very different reasons, of course, and these differences point to broader changes in gay men's experiences taking place in U.S. contexts since the Stonewall period. Such fluency in GME may also present a problem.

As we have seen, the key marker of mainstream-identified GME usage is linguistic "purity." In earlier times, GME offered explicit references to gay experience and allowed speakers to underscore sexual identities in GME-centered conversation, but those resources are no longer viable. So what communicative resources do gay men now employ when they want to encode the fact that they are speaking as gay men in mainstream settings if GME is now more closely aligned with the "look and feel" of the English mainstream?

Some explicitly gay-centered linguistic practices still exist, of course, including the flamboyant speech of the drag queen or the exaggerated verbal posing of the leather clone. Nevertheless, social practices, rather than linguistic markers as such, provide a more workable solution to the public affirmation of gay identity in such instances. Particularly important options that have emerged in recent years include: participation in charity events, political fundraisers, sports activities, and other moments of public gay visibility; home ownership and property maintenance; securing a partner from racial/ethnical background different from one's own (the queer equivalent of the "trophy wife"); participation in marriage; and the adoption of children. All of these activities create affirmation of gay presence in terms that a mainstream audience will readily understand, and because these affirmations are framed in terms of mainstream notions of good citizenship and respectable civic practice, they provide unmistakable evidence that the "gay lifestyle" is safe, respectable, and entirely nonthreatening.

RESPONSES: SAME-SEX-RELATED VARIETIES OF LOTES

There have always been same-sex-identified women and men within the national LOTE population, and same-sex-identified persons have been part of the "new wave" of immigrants coming to the United States in recent years in the context of new forms of displacement, migration, and diaspora worldwide. Until 1993, U.S. immigration law allowed the exclusion of would-be immigrants on the basis of sexual orientation or the presumption that the immigrant might become homosexual. Even afterward, as Eithne Lubhéid says:

> Lesbian/gay migrants still face substantial barriers.... For example, the two most common ways to become a legal permanent resident (LPR) are through direct family ties or sponsorship by an employer. However, lesbian/ gay relationships—unlike heterosexual ones—are not recognized as a legitimate basis for acquiring LPR status.[49]

Similar to Sullivan's imaginings of virtual equality, much about the immigration process demands the appearance of sexual conformity and works against explicit affirmations of sexual sameness.

If sexual sameness is a part of the experiences of immigration and resettlement within the U.S. setting, then the linguistic dimensions of those experiences are of interest to this discussion, particularly as they pertain to issues of conformity. Do same-sex-identified men of a LOTE background learn GME when they come to the United States? Does learning GME facilitate their process of assimilation? Are there alternatives to GME fluency, and if so, what are their implications in the context of resettlement?

As explained in the preceding section, GME is now associated with mainstream gay experiences and is required for successful movement within that cultural terrain.[50] Becoming fluent in GME will be easier if the intended speaker is already familiar with other varieties of English, especially those connected to other areas of the mainstream. If the intended speaker comes from an area of the world where GME has already taken root because of the worldwide spread of a U.S.-based sexual culture,[51] familiarity with GME may also be part of the experience of border-crossing and resettlement. Developing GME fluency is an easier task if the intended speaker accepts the place-at-the-table politics and other assumptions shaping mainstream gay culture in the present moment. But not all same-sex-identified immigrants come from a background of English fluency or are willing to express their sexuality in a linguistic medium so closely linked to assimilation, mainstream-centered mobility, and whiteness—or to do so solely in terms of a white-centered frame of reference.

Not surprisingly, as the number of LOTE speakers continues to increase in the United States, LOTE-related alternatives to GME fluency have also begun to emerge in U.S. settings. These ways of talking about experiences of sexual sameness are grounded in linguistic practices found in the speakers' community of origin and adjacent settings, as well as those emerging in the contexts of U.S. resettlement. While they may show certain similarities with GME sentence structure or vocabulary, these LOTE-based varieties are self-consciously nested at a distance from the linguistic practices of the American (gay) mainstream. They assume the stance of oppositional codes, that is, ways of speaking that explicitly articulate (if not celebrate) the speakers' distance from GME and from the mainstream location that GME commands. Some speakers use these codes to create a momentary separation from the mainstream, as in E. Patrick Johnson's example below.[52]

Some of these varieties are recent formations, but others have considerable time-depth, as Rogers's depiction of linguistic diversity in *The Queen's Vernacular* has already suggested. Arguably, the oppositional code with the longest history is the "black gay language without gay English"[53] used among African American same-gender-loving men in United States. It may seem peculiar (and, admittedly, some say it is misleading)[54] to argue that speakers of Black Gay Language (hereafter BGL) are connected to a LOTE background. However, while BGL and the other forms of oral communication used in African American community settings are English related, they also have deep historical connections with West African and Caribbean language traditions, and features from those traditions have been maintained in African American oral communication in the U.S. setting both as an affirmation of (black-centered) racial/ethnic pride and as a consequence of (white-centered) racial/class oppression.[55]

The following exchange between two black gay men at a dinner party in Atlanta, from E. Patrick Johnson's "Mother Knows Best," provides an example of BGL and show how it differs from the GME of the (white) mainstream:

M1:   [Rising to leave.] Well, girls, I need to head out. I have company coming tomorrow, so I need to get home and clean my dirty house.

M2:   [The host] Can't you stay a little longer? You know your house ain't *that* dirty. I worked all week and still had time to cook and clean my house before y'all came over tonight.

M1:   Oh Miss Ann, puhlease. You know Consuela came over here and beat this place into shape—don't even go there. But I ain't mad at 'cha. If I was makin' your coins, Consuela would be up in my house, too.[56]

As this exchange begins, M1, one of the guests, explains that he has to go home and get things ready for tomorrow's visitors. M1's use of "girls" to refer to the other guests at the dinner party, and his use of "Miss Ann" to refer to the host (M2) calls to mind familiar practices from some arenas of GME conversation at earlier times. "I have such a problem with pronouns," Emory quips in *The Boys in the Band*; this phrasing is a deliberate attempt to provoke a negative response from one heterosexual guest at the birthday party.[57] But noting this similarity underscores the differences between BGL and the GME displayed in *Love! Valor! Compassion!* in which, consistent with the requirements of mainstream's virtual normalcy, no character has difficulties with pronoun gender-reference.

At base, the format of language use in this exchange resembles "playin' the dozens," a style of verbal dueling that is widely attested in African American English usage in informal settings. M2 begins the duel, when he suggests that *he* had worked all week and had been able to get *his* house ready for tonight's company, so M1 should be able to do the same without compromising *his* evening's fun. M1's reply deflates M2's attempt at self-conscious praise by undermining the claims in each of M2's arguments. First, M1 discloses that M2 has a housekeeper, thereby undermining M2's assertion of effective time management. Then, M1 pokes fun at M2's apparent achievement of middle-class status, a level of success not yet enjoyed by his friend ("If I was makin' your coins"). Note that the point in M1's remarks was not to reclaim the authority of his initial argument, "So see, I *do* need to go home now!" Nor is M1 attempting to silence M2's voice altogether and bring this part of conversation to a close: there are no words here in "French, with a cedilla." Instead, M1's remarks, while certainly pointed in focus, give M2 ample material through which he can continue the exchange and continue to demonstrate his linguistic competence in BGL.

There is nothing explicitly relating to GME about such usage, but there is something very African American about it. As Johnson explains, "Race distinguishes black gay men's usage of English from that of others because they draw from gay knowledge of language that circulates in black gay culture and from their identity as black men."[58] The messages about sexual sameness that this exchange conveys are framed according to that racialized linguistic tradition, and only secondarily according to the details of GME associated with the (white) gay mainstream.[59] Johnson concludes:

> As "outsiders within," black gay men incorporate their experiences as blacks in a racist society and gays in a homophobic society in order to create a "dark purple" ("blurble" in black vernacular) lexicon, as opposed to a "lavender" one, that speaks specifically to their subject positions.[60]

A more recently created set of LOTE-based varieties that also "speaks specifically to [the] subject position" of the same-sex-identified persons of LOTE background is now in use in Miami, Los Angeles, the Bronx, and other U.S. sites of Hispanic and Latino/a resettlement. These language varieties express aspects of same-sex-identified immigrant sexuality in ways that are simply not possible as forms of public discourse in the speakers' homeland.[61]

Susana Peña discusses one such set of linguistic practices used widely among persons of Cuban background who have settled in the Miami area since 1960. Its speakers call the variety *perra* and describe it as a "Cuban gay slang" whose use "marks a speaker not only as Spanish speaking but also particularly Cuban or Caribbean and gay."[62] In much the same way that (by Rogers's reckoning) the queens' vernacular facilitated "secretive[ness], ... protest and ... social recognition" for U.S. gay men during the 1960s and early 1970s, *perra* provides its speakers with the linguistic resources they need, as gay-identified Cuban men, to facilitate their struggles for "resistance, liberation, and freedom."[63]

Far from being a static code, *perra* is already in a state of change, as younger generations of Cuban Americans adapt the code's resources to fit their experiences as same-sex-identified Cuban American men. These adaptations involve, in part, incorporation of additional words and phrases from GME and other English sources into *perra* usage, where English joins expression from various Spanish sources and other linguistic traditions. Accordingly, and paralleling the significance of M1's use of "Miss Ann" in Johnson's example above, Peña notes:

> Men of Cuban descent invest the use of "gay" (and other cultural symbols of the U.S. gay movement such as freedom rings and pink triangles) with a range of meanings. We cannot assume that when a Cuban-American man says he is gay he means quite the same thing as an Anglo man in the United States would.[64]

This emergence of such "fractured" meanings of *gay* are additional reminders that globalization has effected a range of language-expressing messages about sexual sameness in U.S. society as well as GME.

RESPONSES: EMERGING FORMS OF SAME-SEX-CENTERED LANGUAGE PLURALISM

Besides making possible new forms of same-sex-related communication within contexts of immigration and resettlement, these LOTE-based alternatives to GME have prompted new forms of same-sex-related linguistic and cultural practices within the broader social terrain. LOTE-related varieties such as BGL and *perra* are used in public locations as well as private settings, and gay men who are not from LOTE backgrounds will be part of the listening audience and, at times, may even become participants in the linguistic exchange. The linguist recognizes these situations as moments for language contact and linguistic assimilation; however, as I have argued throughout this chapter, the particulars of contact need to be historicized.

At an earlier time, as the diverse sources for entries in *The Queen's Vernacular* suggest, speakers of GME simply incorporated LOTE words and phrases overheard in such settings into their GME vocabulary. Today, with GME oriented toward mainstream concerns rather than references from the margin, and with speakers of GME using nonlinguistic means (home ownership, marriage, adoption, and so on) to mark gay presence in public settings, the language learning in these settings is likely to have a rather different outcome: compound bilingualism. That is, the speaker of GME develops some level of second-language familiarity in the same-sex-oriented varieties of LOTEs.[65]

Contexts in which same-sex-related second-language learning might unfold include: personal relationships (momentary or long-term) between a speaker of GME and a speaker from a LOTE background; informal conversations between customers in bars or restaurants frequented by same-sex-identified men of specific racial or ethnic backgrounds and by men who are attracted to them; conversations between gay customers and LOTE-background service personnel (e.g., busboys, janitors, cashier's assistants) who may or may not be same-sex identified; and interactions between caseworkers and clients at social services agencies working with immigrant or displaced populations. Additionally, programs offering formal instruction in same-sexual-oriented LOTEs—and in how to adapt LOTE traditions to same-sex interests—are now available in some U.S. locations.

During the early 1990s, one of the lesbian/gay community centers in San Francisco offered weekly instruction in Swardspeak, the language closely associated with same-sex-identified Filipino men in the homeland and the diaspora.[66] Men of Filipino background as well as interested non-Filipino men regularly participated in these classes. Similarly, a lesbian/gay synagogue in New York City has sponsored classes in Yiddish for lesbians and gay men seeking a linguistic medium through which they can reconcile their sexual sameness with their loyalty to Hebraic tradition. Indeed, there is evidence that Gay Yiddish has become a medium for communication across national and ethnic boundaries on topics related to sexuality and religion.[67] Finally, there are the conventionally oriented summer language programs in cities like Guadalajara and Monterrey, Mexico, urban venues also well known for having an active gay scene and for welcoming to Anglo student-visitors, regardless of their sexual orientation.

Actual numbers of mainstream speakers of GME in the United States who have also become speakers of one or more same-sex-oriented varieties of LOTEs is difficult to estimate. And what level of fluency in the LOTE (or nonstandard English) the GME speakers have acquired in these settings is also difficult to specify. Conditions vary greatly, site by site and speaker by speaker. But as part of the work for this project, I have been observing conversations in Washington, DC, area gay restaurants between Hispanic/Latino service personnel and gay customers of Anglo/white backgrounds. Usually, the Spanish-as-second-language usage that GME speakers acquire through these exchanges is limited to topics and vocabulary connected to the service setting. On the other hand, regardless of the amount of the linguistic content that is transmitted between parties, the process of language learning becomes valuable in its own right, providing a starting point for discussion, which then allows additional linguistic (and other) issues to be explored.

I observed the following exchange between A, a gay man in his late fifties, and B, a busboy, at a gay-affiliated restaurant in the Dupont Circle area of Washington where A was having dinner on a July 2007 weekend, which illustrates some of the linguistic and social practices invoking GME-LOTE compound bilingual fluency in such instances:

A: What is your word in Spanish for this? [pointing to the yellow substance in the butter dish]
B: *Mantequilla*.
A: [Repeats the Spanish word, saying each syllable slowly] *Man-ti-key-yah*. In English, we say "butter."
B: [Grins, then repeats the English word, saying each syllable slowly] *Buh-tur*. [He smiles shyly.]
A: You say, "*quiero mantequilla*"?
B: [Smiles] *Si, si, si*. You want *y* I bring. [He leaves the table and crosses to the kitchen to fetch more butter.]
A: [Follows B's movement, nodding approvingly, as B moves into and back from the kitchen.]
B: [Returns to table.] *Buh-ter*. [Places dish on table.] And I bring more *pan*, uh, bread.[68]

When this conversation took place, A was seated by himself at a table in the front of the restaurant. My dinner guests and I were seated at a table to his right, close enough to observe the exchange with the busboy without difficulty. My note-taking was helped by the loud tone of A's comments, making me wonder whether he wanted his conversation with B to be overheard.

A had ordered his meal, was enjoying his cocktail, and was busy people watching. B was one of the people he was watching. B has been working at the restaurant for six months. This was his first full-time job since arriving in the United States from his home country in Central America. B is a fluent speaker of Spanish and also speaks one of the American Indian languages ancestral to his home community. I had heard him speaking in the ancestral language to another restaurant staff person some weeks before, and my questions about his language skills became the entry point for collecting details of the personal biography mentioned here.

Both A and B are engaged in language-learning in this example. In A's case, the language-learning is part of his attempt to make new friends and, where possible, find someone with whom he can spend what he termed "quality time." He visits this restaurant frequently and enjoys sitting in the front section because single men often sit there, dining alone, particularly in the late afternoon and early evening. "And," he told me when we started to chat table-to-table, "there's always the busboys." And did he speak Spanish? He has learned a few words and phrases, he told me, enough to get by in a restaurant or other commercial venues; and he uses his Spanish primarily when talking to the service personnel in those settings. Where did he learn his Spanish? Talking to people like B, in settings like the one I just described.

For his part, B is not "gay identified," but he has had sex with men, both in his home country and now here in the United States. He enjoys being the object of attention from some of the restaurant patrons, particularly the older men. Being a first-language speaker of Spanish, his command of sentence structure and vocabulary is much more complex than his very halting use of Spanish in the exchange with A might imply. Still, B used just enough Spanish to keep the conversation flowing and to maintain A's interest. And it gave him an opportunity to strengthen his English skills with someone who is a native speaker of that language, even if, as the sample conversation suggests, the range of English-based usage in the exchange was also limited.

But no matter: that the linguistic materials are limited does not alter the significance of the linguistic encounter nor does it weaken the significance of the location(s) where the encounter unfolds. As one of the consequences of globalization here at home, gay-identified men who are speakers of GME and have close ties with mainstream gay culture use gay-related commercial venues such as this Dupont Circle gay restaurant for same-sex-related second-language learning. So do men from LOTE backgrounds whose connections to U.S. gay culture are still in formation. The irony is that speakers of GME are learning to speak a same-sex-oriented LOTE at the same time that they resist incorporating LOTE words and phrases into GME usage. Interestingly, there is a linguistic "othering" that goes hand-in-hand with the bilingual fluency—and the GME purism—that emerges in these speech settings, even as (for the speakers from LOTE backgrounds) linguistic and social opportunities are also being created and extended.

These are not the outcomes I expected to find when I started to explore globalization's effects on GME fluencies in the United States. But the end product is consistent with the broader attitudes toward English—and toward language in general in the United States—as they have been (re)shaped by the consequences of globalization here at home in recent years. The alliances between GME linguistic purity and the broader expressions of cultural and political nationalism that are expressed within phrases such as the "true things that bind us" are similarly embedded within English-only arguments. Under the increasing pressures of globalization at home and within gay communities, these alliances cannot be ignored.

NOTES

My thanks to Michelle Marzullo, Harjant Gill, Ellen Lewin, and Denis Provencher for advice and comment during the preparation of this chapter, and to Michelle for her assistance in editing the final copy of the text.

1. Arjun Appadurai, "Grassroots Globalization and the Research Imagination," in *Globalization*, edited by Arjun Appadurai (Durham, NC: Duke University Press, 2001), 5.

2. Ibid., 4.

3. Ibid.

4. Ibid., 5.

5. Ibid.

6. Ibid., 6.

7. William Leap, *Word's Out: Gay Men's English* (Minneapolis: University of Minnesota Press, 1996); William Leap, "Studying Lesbian and Gay Languages: Vocabulary, Text-Making and Beyond," in *Out in Theory: The Emergence of Lesbian and Gay Anthropology*, edited by Ellen Lewin and William L. Leap, 128–54 (Urbana: University of Illinois Press, 2002); William Leap, "Language and Gendered Modernity," in *Handbook of Language and Gender*, edited by Janet Holmes and Miriam Meyerhoff, 401–22 (London: Blackwell, 2003); Liz Morrish and William L. Leap, "Sex Talk: Language, Desire, Identity and Beyond," in *Language, Sexualities and Desires: Cross-Cultural Perspectives*, edited by Helen Sauntson and Sakis Kyratzis, 17–40 (London: Palgrave, 2007). Critical reviews of these claims can be found in Deborah Cameron and Don Kulick, "Sexuality as Identity: Gay and Lesbian Language," in *Language and Sexuality*, edited by Deborah Cameron and Don Kulick, 74–105 (New York: Cambridge University Press, 2003); and Andrew Wong, "New Directions in the Study of Language and Sexuality," *Journal of Sociolinguistics* 9 (2005): 254–66.

8. Appadurai, "Grassroots Globalization," 5.

9. Dorothy Waggoner, "Statistics on Language Use," in *Language in the USA*, edited by Charles Ferguson and Shirley Brice Heath (New York: Cambridge University Press, 1981), 490–91.

10. James Crawford, "Demographic Change and Language," 1997, http://ourworld.compuserve.com/homepages/jwcrawford/can-pop.htm.

11. Hyes Shun, with Rosalind Bruno, *Language Use and English Speaking Ability, 2000* (Washington, DC: U.S. Department of Commerce, 2003), 4, available at http://www.census.gov/prod/2003pubs/c2kbr-29.pdf.

12. Even in instances when the country-and-western singers come from LOTE backgrounds, or nonstandard English contexts, the language of performance on the country-and-western stage is an English that the mainstream American public can understand. In some ways, that variety of English is itself nonstandard, but it rarely departs from the American English linguistic norms as dramatically as is the case for gangsta rap, bounce, or reggaeton.

13. Mauro E. Mujica, "English: Not America's Language?" *Globalist*, June 19, 2003, http://www.theglobalist.com/DBWeb/printStoryId.aspx?StoryId=3229.

14. Nico, "Right-Wing Mayor Calls for McDonald's Boycott over Spanish-Language Ads," July 10, 2006, http://thinkprogress.org/2006/07/10/spanish-boycott.

15. Ibid.

16. U.S. English, "Voters Make English the Official Language of Arizona: Passage of Prop. 103 Makes Arizona the 28th State with Official English," press release, November 8, 2006, available at http://www.us-english.org/inc/news/preleases/viewRelease.asp?ID=228.

17. Ibid.

18. Alan Berube, "How *Gay* Says White and What Kind of White It Says," in *The Making and Unmaking of Whiteness*, edited by Brander Rasmussen, Eric Klinenberg, Irene J. Mexica, and Matt Wray, 234–65 (Durham, NC: Duke University Press, 2001); Rosemary Hennessy, "Queer Visibility in Commodity Culture," in *Profit and Pleasure: Sexual Identities in Late Capitalism*, 111–42 (New York: Routledge, 2000); Charles Nero, "Why Are Gay Ghettoes White?" in *Black Queer Studies: A Critical Anthology*, edited by E. Patrick Johnson and Mae G. Henderson, 228–48 (Durham, NC: Duke University Press, 2005).

19. Jennifer Coates, *Men Talk* (London: Blackwell, 2003); Scott Kiesling, "Stances of Whiteness and Hegemony in Fraternity Men's Discourse," *Journal of Linguistic Anthropology* 11 (2001): 101–15; "Playing the Straight Man: Displaying and Maintaining Male Heterosexuality in Discourse," in *Language and Sexuality: Contesting Meaning in Theory and Practice*, edited by Kathryn Campbell-Kibbler, Robert J. Podesva, Sarah J. Roberts, and Andrew Wong, 249–66 (Stanford, CA: Center for the Study of Language and Information, 2002).

20. Tom Boellstorff, *The Gay Archipelago: Sexuality and Nation in Indonesia* (Princeton, NJ: Princeton University Press, 2005); Tom Boellstorff, *A Coincidence of Desires: Anthropology, Queer Studies, Indonesia* (Durham, NC: Duke University Press, 2007); William L. Leap and Tom Boellstorff, eds., *Speaking in Queer Tongues: Globalization and Gay Language* (Urbana: University of Illinois Press, 2004); Martin Manalansan, *Global Divas: Filipino Gay Men in the Diaspora* (Durham, NC: Duke University Press, 2003); Denis Provencher, *Queer French: Globalization, Language and Sexual Citizenship in France* (London: Ashgate, 2007).

21. John D'Emilio, *Sexual Politics, Sexual Communities: The Making of a Homosexual Minority in the United States, 1940–1970* (Chicago: University of Chicago Press, 1983); Martin Duberman, *Stonewall* (New York: Penguin Books, 1994); Stephen O. Murray, *American Gay* (Chicago: University of Chicago Press, 1996).

22. Paul Baker writes that Polari is "a secret language mainly used by gay men and lesbians in London and other UK cities with an established gay subculture in the first 70 years of the twentieth century"; Paul Baker, *Polari: The Lost Language of Gay Men* (New York: Routledge, 2002), 1.

23. Brett Beemyn, introduction to *Creating a Place for Ourselves: Lesbian, Gay and Bisexual Community Histories* (New York: Routledge, 1997), 1–7; John Howard, introduction to *Men Like That: A Southern Queer History* (Chicago: University of Chicago Press, 1999), xi–xxiii.

24. Bruce Rogers, introduction to *The Queens' Vernacular* (San Francisco: Straight Arrow Books, 1972), iii–iv.

25. Ronald A. Farrell, "The Argot of the Homosexual Subculture," *Anthropological Linguistics* 14 (1972): 97–109; G. Legman, "The Language of Homosexuality: An American Glossary," in *Sex Variants II*, edited by George W. Henry (New York: Paul B. Hoeber, 1941), 1149–79.

26. Rogers, *Queens' Vernacular*, iii–iv.

27. Ibid., iii.

28. Examined in 2007, which is thirty-five years after initial publication, some words and phrases included in the dictionary are familiar to today's speaker of GME, but many of them are no longer attested in GME conversations.

29. Mart Crowley, *The Boys in the Band* (New York: Samuel French, 1968).

30. Ibid., 8.

31. Wayne Dynes, *Homolexus: A Historical and Cultural Lexicon of Homosexuality* (New York: Gay Academic Union, 1985); Joseph P. Goodwin, *More Man Than You'll Ever Be: Gay Folklore and Acculturation in Middle America* (Bloomington: Indiana University Press, 1989); H. Max, *Gay(s)language* (Austin, TX: Banned Books, 1998); A. D. Peterkin, *Outbursts: A Queer Erotic Thesaurus* (Vancouver: Arsenal Pulp Press, 2003); Donald F. Reuter, *Gay-2-Zee: A Dictionary of Sex, Subtext, and the Sublime* (New York: St. Martins' Griffin, 2005).

32. Reuter, *Gay-2-Zee*.

33. Ibid., xii.

34. Ibid., xiv, xiii.

35. Terrence McNally, *Love! Valor! Compassion!* in *"Love! Valor! Compassion!" and "A Perfect Ganesh": Two Plays by Terrence McNally*, 9–142 (New York: Plume Books, 1995).

36. Ibid., 37–38.

37. Michael speaks directly to these attributes of this urban gay culture and to their consequences during the closing moments of *The Boys in the Band*. The party game he has orchestrated has backfired. Several of his guests are in emotional disarray, and everyone except Donald has gone home. Michael dissolves into a frenzy of anger, frustration, and tears. Then, recovering his composure, he turns to Donald and reflects: "If we ... if we could just ... learn not to hate ourselves so much. That's it, you know. If we could just not hate ourselves just quite so very very much." A few moments later, he adds: "Who was it that used to always say, 'You show me a happy homosexual, and I'll show you a gay corpse'?" (Crowley, *Boys in the Band*, 102).

38. McNalley, *Love*, 54.

39. Ramon is not merely referencing a state of psychological discomfort, however. He addresses here the problems that members of any minority group will face in the neoliberal context of self-managed economic uplift.

40. There is an African American character, Bernard, in Crowley's *The Boys in the Band*, but he manages his status within the group quietly, not with confrontation. For example, see his remarks about discrimination and endurance on p. 82.

41. For example, Ramon swears several times in Spanish and makes seductive remarks in Spanish to Arthur while they are alone on the raft in the middle of the lake, and Buzz uses a Yiddish word to disrupt the German title of a piece of classical dance.

42. Nico, "Right-Wing Mayor."

43. See, for example, Richard Goldstein, *The Attack Queers: Liberal Society and the Gay Right* (London: Verso, 2002); Daniel Harris, *The Rise and Fall of Gay Culture* (New York: Hyperion, 1997); and Michael Warner, *The Trouble with Normal: Sex, Politics and the Ethics of Queer Life* (Cambridge, MA: Harvard University Press, 1999).

44. Bruce Bawer, *A Place at the Table: The Gay Individual in American Society* (New York: Simon & Schuster, 1993); Andrew Sullivan, *Virtually Normal: An Argument about Homosexuality* (New York: Random House/Vintage Books, 1995); Andrew Sullivan, "The End of Gay Culture," *New Republic*, October 24, 2005, available at http://www.tnr.com/docprint.mhtml?i=20051024&s=sullivan102405.

45. Rogers, *Queens' Vernacular*, iii.

46. Reuter, *Gay-2-Zee*, xii.

47. Lee Badgett, *Money, Myths and Change: The Economic Life of Lesbians and Gay Men* (Chicago: University of Chicago Press, 2001).

48. Quoted in Kevin Riordan, "Attacking Queer Acceptability," *Washington Blade*, August 2, 2002.

49. Eithne Lubhéid, introduction to *Queer Migrations: Sexuality, U.S. Citizenship and Border Crossings*, edited by Eithne Lubhéid and Lionel Cantu Jr. (Minneapolis: University of Minnesota Press, 2005), xiii.

50. Conversely, the absence of gay English fluency has become a way of marking distance from the gay mainstream. This theme underlies Buzz's comments in act 1 of *Love! Valor! Compassion!* when he acknowledges Perry's and Arthur's familiarity with the lyrics from the Broadway musical *Annie Get Your Gun* and then observes: "Ethel Merman was gay, you know. So was Irving Berlin. I don't think English is Ramon's first language" (p. 37).

51. Boellstorff, *Gay Archipelago*; Boellstorff, *Coincidence of Desires*; William L. Leap, "Language, Belonging, and (Homo)sexual Citizenship in Cape Town, South Africa," in Leap and Boellstorff, *Speaking in Queer Tongues*, 134–62; William L. Leap, "Finding the Center: Claiming Gay Space in Cape Town," in *Performing Queer: Shaping Sexualities, 1994–2004*, edited by Mikki van Zyl and Melissa Steyn, 235–66 (Cape Town: Kwela Press, 2005); Manalansan, *Global Divas*.

52. For other speakers, as suggested in Susana Peña's discussion of *perra* below, these oppositional codes allow a more enduring distance from GME and the possibility of a "gay world without English."

53. E. Patrick Johnson, "Mother Knows Best: Black Gay Vernacular and Transgressive Domestic Space," in Leap and Boellstorff, *Speaking in Queer Tongues*, 252.

54. John McWorter, "An African Language in Philadelphia? Black English and the Mother Continent." In *Word on the Street: Debunking the Myth of a "Pure" Standard English*. Cambridge: Perseus, 1998: 153–199.

55. Phillip Brian Harper, "Eloquence and Epitaph: Black Nationalism and the Homophobic Impulse in Response to the Death of Max Robinson," in *Fear of a Queer Planet: Queer Politics and Social Theory*, edited by Michael Warner, 239–63 (Minneapolis: University of Minnesota Press, 1993; Geneva Smitherman, *Black Talk: Words and Phrases from the Hood to the Amen Corner* (New York: Houghton Mifflin, 1994).

56. Johnson, "Mother Knows Best," 252.

57. Crowley, *Boys in the Band*, 45.

58. Johnson, "Mother Knows Best," 252.

59. We need to rethink M1's use of Miss Ann in light of these remarks. As Johnson explains, *Miss Ann* is an African American English term that applies to any white woman or to any Black woman who is considered "uppity" or "acts white." If so, M1's usage is a same-sex appropriation of African American English message, and not merely a feature shared with GME usage.

60. Johnson, "Mother Knows Best," 253.

61. Certainly, there are varieties of Spanish in the homeland that are responsive to same-sex experiences. However, given the broader attitudes toward homosexuality in Central and South American settings, those varieties of Spanish serve as languages of private communication more often than they support public discussions and debates about sexual sameness. In much the same way, these varieties are associated with the experiences of the social margin more so than with that of the Central and South American mainstream.

62. Susana Peña, "*Pajaration* and Transculturation: Language and Meaning in Miami's Cuban American Gay Worlds," in Leap and Boellstorff, *Speaking in Queer Tongues*, 246.

63. Ibid., 247.

64. Ibid., 246.

65. Speakers of same-sex-oriented LOTEs may broaden their familiarity with GME in this setting, although, as explained, doing so also requires them to address a host of political and emotional issues.

66. Manalansan, *Global Divas*, 45–61.

67. For example, MyLanguageExchange.com offers opportunities to learn Yiddish by email. One of its clients wrote on the program's website: "I'm a 23 year old gay boy living in Israel and Germany and I would like to talk to and meet other gay boys" (http://www.mylanguageexchange.com/Learn/Yiddish.asp).

68. William Leap, unpublished field notes, 2007.

CHAPTER 10

The Globalization of U.S. Sports: From the Pros to the Playgrounds

Tim Wendel

> Back on the bleachers, Arthur and William watched Pingatore on the court, but they were lost in their dreams—of Isaiah, and of greatness. They thought about their friends and classmates, brothers and sisters, filing into their old rundown schools, so decrepit and dark, back home in the inner city. They felt enormously grateful. They were the lucky ones with the ticket in their hands, their dreams within reach.
>
> —*Hoop Dreams*

The 1994 documentary and book *Hoop Dreams* followed Chicago teenagers Arthur Agee and William Gates through four years of success and, ultimately, heartbreak playing high school basketball. From an early age, Agee and Gates dreamed of playing in the National Basketball Association (NBA), the top professional basketball league in the world. Perhaps this was the only dream either of them had for much of their adolescence. In the end, neither of them came close to playing in the NBA—the land of Isaiah Thomas, Michael Jordan, and LeBron James.

From the Bronx to Watts, the promise of a professional basketball career has long held many neighborhoods together. Even though the dream becomes reality for only a tiny percentage of those who play as kids, it provides a structure and discipline that other parts of our society often covet. Maybe that is why the dream of playing sports, winning an athletic scholarship, even making it as a pro, exists beyond the inner city.

Yet this widespread acceptance of *Hoop Dreams,* and the accompanying dreams of glory in a wide variety of sports, occurs when so much of the world, due to globalization, is up for grabs. According to The Institute for

Diversity and Ethics in Sport (TIDES) at the University of Central Florida, the percentage of players from outside the United States continues to grow in American professional basketball, soccer, baseball, and football. What we are witnessing is the opening chapters of the global sports age. This trend will create a harsh new reality for U.S.-born players—especially for the African American athletes who dominate some of these sports.

A 2005 *Sports Illustrated* article documented that the percentage of African Americans players in Major League Baseball (MLB) has fallen from 19 percent to 10 percent in the last decade.[1] Sports-talk radio and newspapers reported the drop as an isolated event. About the only connection made with the global marketplace was that Latino players have seen their numbers increase significantly at the professional level. But what is happening in basketball, baseball, and other major U.S. sports is often similar to what we have seen happen globally in the economy and elsewhere. The world is becoming flatter in sports, too.

International prospects usually cost professional teams less and often are considered to be more fundamentally sound than their U.S. counterparts, says Dr. Harry Edwards, a University of California sociology professor and a consultant for the San Francisco 49ers. He maintains that basketball is going the way of baseball, as foreign-born players increasingly take roster spots that in the past have been filled with U.S. players. "In ten or fifteen years, the question won't be, 'What happened to the [American born] black athlete?'" Edwards says. "The question will be, 'Who *needs* the black athlete?'"[2] Sports activist Richard Lapchick disagrees with Edwards's prediction, but he acknowledges that U.S. coaches and players need to "change their style of play, be less individualist, to compete against this new wave of talent."[3]

In 1994, the year *Hoop Dreams* came out, the first ten picks in the NBA draft were from the United States, and all had attended college. In 2002, however, Yao Ming from the Shanghai (China) Sharks was the top pick, an Italian forward was drafted at number five, and a Brazilian center was number seven. More recently, a high school kid, LeBron James, went number one, a center from Serbia-Montenegro was next, and a French forward was eleventh.

For decades, basketball has been a blessing to the black community. Although playing in the NBA always has been a long shot, the percentage of African Americans at the professional level has held steady at more than 75 percent, according to TIDES.[4] In comparison, black participation continues to fall to record lows in baseball and recently dropped slightly in the National Football League, too. In basketball, what we are seeing is more foreign-born players being taken higher in the two rounds of the draft. U.S. players, many of them college stars, go undrafted and have to fight their way onto a pro roster by playing in the NBA's summer league.

John Saunders, host of ESPN's *The Sports Reporters*, claims that foreign-born players are now the best in the game. At center, there is Yao from China. Saunders goes on to name Germany's Dirk Nowitzki as the top strong forward and Canada's Steve Nash as the best point guard. Nash also is the NBA's two-time most valuable player.

Charles Barkley, a former NBA star and now a television analyst, wishes "kids, especially black kids, didn't dream so much about playing in the NBA." But he agrees that the game kept the stars of *Hoop Dreams*, Agee and Gates, in school and close to their families, friends, and community. As adults, Agee went on to start a foundation to help children and Gates became a pastor. Gates remembers his fifteen minutes of fame, accentuated by the award-winning film and book, as "a blessing," even though he never came close to his improbable dream of playing in the NBA.

Still, in this age of increasing globalization, we need to be much more realistic about how difficult it is to play professional ball. Parents need to realize how long the odds are for a budding superstar to even get a whiff of a college sports scholarship in this growing age of globalization. According to the National Collegiate Athletic Association (NCAA), fewer than 5 percent of the kids playing youth and high school sports will receive any kind of collegiate sports scholarship, whether full and partial. As I recently told a friend who has a thirteen-year-old tennis star son: Don't chase the athletic scholarship, focus on academics. I know that sounds "old school," but the chances of a scholarship are much better for a kid with good grades in high school than for the star of the basketball or football team.

Edwards says too much emphasis has been placed on sports in the black community, but he notes that sports may be "our last hook and handle" to today's youth. Midnight basketball, Saturday football, and the local recreational facility "put them back in contact with the clergy, mentors, health workers, counselors, government workers, with people from the economic and corporate sector," he told *ColorLines* magazine. "Without that, we have no way of getting them at all, except through police and judicial action."[5]

Steve Boyd, vice president for the Hoop Dreams Scholarship Fund in Washington, DC, says that the globalization of sports makes "groups like ours even more important." His fund, which began as a charity basketball event, now mentors about a hundred inner-city students a year. "All that kids are bombarded with these days is that sports and entertainment are the only avenues of success," he says. "We're trying to show them that there are a lot of different ways to be a hero."[6]

Maybe young black men will eventually view sports as just recreation and a chance to learn something about life. That will not happen overnight, however, and more mentors and role models with a global outlook are needed.

Take James Smith. For twelve seasons, he has been the head basketball coach at Coatesville High School near Philadelphia. Among his former players is Richard Hamilton, now with the NBA's Detroit Pistons. Smith says basketball is changing faster and more profoundly than its fans and those who dream about playing the game for a living truly realize. "Anybody who questions where this is going just has to look at the recent [NBA] drafts," he says. "Basketball is not always going to be the U.S. game."

Smith did not return his coaching job last winter. Instead, he returned to school to pursue a master's degree in education. "It's something I've put off for a long time," he says. "But I need to show the kids that I can do something else. Be something more."

A generation or so ago, the top stars in high school played three sports. They moved with the seasons—football in the fall, basketball or hockey in the winter, and baseball, lacrosse, or track in the spring. Now kids are more likely to play a single sport year-round, usually in a top-flight league. They do this because the best leagues, the travel teams, and elite squads, make sports specialization more convenient than a generation ago. In addition, the pint-sized superstars follow this path because their parents and guardians often believe that this path is the best way to secure a college sports scholarship, perhaps even make a living in the professional game. The globalization of sports has directly influenced U.S. youth sports in this way.

In 1990, Little League Baseball began "Second Season," with 350 leagues participating in nontraditional fall and winter play. A decade later, there were nearly 2,500 such leagues. Participation in off-season basketball programs run by the Amateur Athletic Union (AAU) has tripled nationally. (Former Georgetown University basketball coach John Thompson says that the AAU coach, not the high school coach, is now the more important figure in many young players' lives.)[7] The American Youth Soccer Organization saw its ranks double in recent years, and "the great majority are playing year-round," a spokesperson says.[8] In youth swimming, kids participating year-round rose by 10 percent while seasonal memberships declined.

"It's very unfortunate," says John McGinnis, former president of the National High School Athletic Coaches Federation. "I try to stress to kids in ninth and tenth grades that they should still play a number of sports, but I wonder if I'm getting through. Too many parents think their kids are going to get a college scholarship. When a coach tells them their kid has potential in a particular sport, too often they lock them in. That's it."[9]

With the sports world increasingly altered by globalization, many parents believe this is the best option for their children. But some of the best athletes who ever played took a far different path to the top. Growing up, Hall of Fame quarterback Joe Montana pitched perfect games in Little League baseball and was so adept at high school basketball that North Carolina State offered him a scholarship. Baseball slugger Mark McGwire quit baseball temporarily his sophomore year in high school to play golf. If he had not become caught up in the ongoing steroids controversy, he would probably be playing in more pro-ams and perhaps be a fixture on the Senior PGA Tour. He was almost as good with a golf club in his hands as he was with a baseball bat. Deion Sanders was such a well-rounded athlete that he became the only athlete to ever play in both a World Series and a Super Bowl. "Parents need to make the major decisions that affect their kids' lives," Sanders says. "But when it comes to play, they shouldn't discourage a broad approach. When a child wants to color, do you tell him to use just one black crayon?"[10]

That is precisely what we're doing with our budding sports stars. We continue to push them down this path even when the chances of winning a college scholarship, and certainly of playing professional ball, are becoming more remote, thanks to globalization. Because of the influence of travel teams and the tantalizing hope of a college sports scholarship, the days when kids marked the seasons by the sport—football in the fall, basketball in the winter, and baseball in the spring, for instance—are over. One wonders what would have happened to Montana, McGwire, or Sanders if they were young sports stars in this day and age.

"We have reached the point of saturation—a vicious revolving door of never-ending seasons," says Fred Engh, founder of the National Alliance for Youth Sports and author of *Why Johnny Hates Sports*. "Children can't even take a couple of months' hiatus from a sport for fear of falling behind their peers and being excluded from teams the following seasons. Those elite teams, all those trophies—that's what the parents want."[11]

Summer hockey, fall baseball, indoor winter soccer, elite year-round teams that travel far from their neighborhoods—these are all part of a new kid-centric culture in which specialization supposedly breeds success. Says sports psychologist Rick Wolff, author of *Coaching Kids for Dummies*: "Excelling in sports has become as much a part of the American dream for parents as getting their kids into the best school and living in the best neighborhoods."[12]

But here's the dirty little secret: few make the jump from high school to the collegiate level. Only 3.1 percent of players make it in women's basketball, 5.8 percent in football, and 5.6 percent in baseball, according to the NCAA. Even worse, for most sports, the odds of a college athlete playing professionally are less than two in a hundred.[13]

"Parents are using their kids as a lottery ticket," Sanders says. "Before all this money came along, moms and dads didn't go crazy at games. They didn't curse their kids and get on them to play better. It was just fun. Now, there's a Yellow Brick Road, and parents think it's their ticket." In making youth sports so specialized, so adult, we're killing our children's joy for the games. More than 70 percent of those who begin playing organized sports in elementary school will have quit by high school, according to the Institute for the Study of Youth Sports at Michigan State University.[14]

"Starting out, most kids just want to play. It's the parents who keep score," says Christopher Andersonn, author of *Will You Still Love Me If I Don't Win*. "They can kill the love a kid has for a sport. Once that's gone, it's very hard to recapture it."[15]

The American Academy of Pediatrics (AAP) cautions about overuse injuries (tendonitis, stress fractures) in children specializing or training year-round in sports. "More injuries, more signs of psychological stress and more cases of early burnout are the results of specializing too young," says Stephen Anderson, sports medicine expert and chair of the academy's committee on sports specialization in children. According to the AAP, signs of sports overload include chronic injuries and illness, weight loss, sleep disturbances, and falling grades in school. When any of these problems present themselves, Anderson says, "the sport, the intensity, the source of motivation and the fun level need to be closely examined."[16]

In addition, this era of increasing specialization comes as globalization affects not only the professional and college ranks, but high school as well. Stu Vetter, who became a coaching institution in the Washington, DC area, has long embraced foreign-born players to gain a competitive edge. He has gone as far as to set up a team house near the high school where he now coaches in suburban Maryland. In recent seasons, that home has included players from Nigeria, Japan, Korea, Argentina, and Russia. Vetter and teams like his travel the country to play in the most prestigious tournaments. He insists he isn't the only one recruiting internationally. "Everything has changed in the last few years," Vetter told the *Washington Post*. "It's a level playing field. We might have been ahead of the curve once, but those perceptions have changed. If we were on the cutting edge before, now we're right in the middle."[17]

As my two kids have grown up, I've coached them in soccer, basketball, baseball, lacrosse, and ice hockey. I've told the stories about Montana, McGwire, and Sanders to the parents who have children on my teams. Afterward they smile, as if I'm teasing them, and then the puzzlement creeps across their face as they realize I'm dead serious. Most of the best athletes of our time played just about every sport growing up—usually in the backyard, in the street.

That's not to say my family hasn't been affected by our society's single-sport obsession. In almost every sport my kids have played, high-powered coaches and commissioners have tried to steer us away from local leagues to more elite teams, even travel teams. They have often urged my children to play their particular sport year-round and attend intensive sports camps. Sometimes, we've said no. But other times we've been caught up in the sports hype, occasionally with disastrous results. My son, who is a pretty good swimmer, recently announced he had had enough. Competitive swimming just wasn't fun anymore.

At such times, I vow to do a better job as a parent, and I remember something Montana said years ago, when he was an All-Pro quarterback for the San Francisco 49ers. It was after another game in which Montana had rallied his team for a last-minute victory. When reporters asked Montana about one of the pivotal plays, in which he evaded a blitzing defender coming from his blindside, he smiled that Cheshire cat grin of his and said, "Didn't you guys recognize that move?"

Puzzled looks all around. Nobody knew what he was talking about.

"It's an old basketball move," Montana explained. "Spin away from your man, remember? You guys forget I was a pretty good basketball player. They offered me a college scholarship in that, too."[18]

If anybody wants to see the future of sport in the era of globalization, they need only look as far as professional baseball. The way the game is played and how the talent is mined in this day and age is indicative of the path most other sports will eventually have to follow.

Junior Noboa stands in the shade of the first-base dugout and surveys his baseball kingdom. The former second baseman for the Montreal Expos operates one of the thirty or so baseball academies now in the Dominican

Republic. Establishments such as Noboa's are modeled, in large part, after Days Inns or Holiday Inns. The effect can be jarring to a visitor to the island. Dirt roads in the jungle dead-end at vast complexes with emerald-green fields and residence hotels that would be at home off any U.S. interstate. "We try to make it as close as we can to what they'd find in America," Noboa says. "If we don't, the odds of them making it aren't too high."[19]

In the back-and-forth debate over immigration reform, one footnote likely to be overlooked is the fact that Major League Baseball has its own type of guest-worker program. Despite decades of frustration and failure, the longtime national pastime learned that an effective policy for immigrant labor not only made business sense but was good citizenship, too. The approach has allowed the sport to foster young stars and a new fan base.[20]

Often, baseball seems antiquated compared with the rest of popular culture. American kids won't play the game because it isn't as high-paced as video games or as cool as the *sport du jour*, basketball. But when it comes to demographics, MLB is surprisingly cutting-edge. For the 2006 season, more than a quarter of the players on U.S. major-league teams are foreign born. At the minor-league level, overseas players make up 45 percent of the roster openings, with the majority coming from the Dominican Republic, which is the top exporter of baseball talent.

Fans who might object to day laborers have little problem cheering on immigrant stars. After all, MLB's attendance reached an all-time high last season.[21] "Without the influx of Latin players, we certainly wouldn't have thirty major-league teams," Chicago White Sox executive Roland Hemond told the *Kansas City Star*. "So they've been a great boon for our game, its growth in franchises as well as in quality of play."[22]

Sixty years ago, Jackie Robinson broke the color barrier in U.S. sports. While MLB did not volunteer for the role, it did show the rest of the country that black and white could not just get along but also work hand-in-hand on the same team. A similar evolution continues today between white, black, and brown. But assimilation in baseball hasn't been easy. Soon after Robinson, Orestes "Minnie" Minoso arrived from Cuba to play for the Chicago White Sox. Early on, he faced many of the same biases and insults that plagued Robinson. "When I played, I sometimes had to play the clown," he says. "I had to listen and laugh, even if I was crying inside. But never did I let them see that it bothered me."[23]

In the early 1960s, San Francisco Giants manager Alvin Dark declared that only English would be spoken in the clubhouse and dugout. His edict might very well have kept a team filled with Latino stars—Orlando Cepeda, Juan Marichal, the Alou brothers—from ever winning a World Series. In the hypercompetitive world of professional sports, such division in a locker room is poison for team chemistry.

Though that was four decades ago, today's immigration debate echoes similar themes. Throughout this country's history, immigrants—legal or not—have faced resentment for economic and cultural reasons: "They take our jobs." "They don't speak the language." "They're changing our communities." In fact, the Senate last year debated immigration legislation that declared English to be the national language of the United States. Another measure deemed it the "common unifying language." It can be, but only if used as a tool to bring people together rather than a wedge to drive people apart. Unifying? Just ask the Giants team of the early 1960s.

But baseball's own model of assimilation can provide good lessons for the nation as a whole, even if they cannot be duplicated on such a massive scale. Major leaguers are afforded the same work permits reserved for internationally recognized artists and entertainers. Today, many teams have bilingual coaches, trainers, and front office personnel from rookie ball on up to the majors. The Cleveland Indians and New York Mets not only teach their top prospects English but have also begun to send them to school in the Dominican Republic so the prospects can receive a high school education while they're playing for their organizations.[24] "Even if they fail as ballplayers, they are given tools that enable them to go on with life," says Alan Klein, author of *Growing the Game: The Globalization of Major League Baseball.* "This isn't the case in other [U.S.] industries making use of temporary workers."[25]

So in today's game, these players fold into American society—whether they become U.S. citizens or not. David "Big Papi" Ortiz, from the Dominican Republic, has become a folk hero in Boston. Another Dominican star, Vladimir Guerrero, is a crowd favorite in Southern California. In New York, Omar Minaya, the first Latino general manager at the major league level, has created "Los Mets," including Johan Santana, Pedro Martinez, Carlos Beltran, and Carlos Delgado.

Major League Baseball makes America accessible to these players, thus making these players accessible to American fans. If other industries dependent on immigrant labor—the agriculture and construction trades, for instance—would make even slight efforts to help their workers assimilate, the benefits would flow through American society. And then perhaps instead of two sides screaming at each other across a divide, we could have a civilized debate about immigration reform—regardless of what language we're speaking.

A few years ago, I asked Roger Jongewaard, longtime scout for the Seattle Mariners, where he had been in search of new baseball talent. During his nearly three decades in the game, Jongewaard had signed such prospects-turned-superstars as Darryl Strawberry, Ken Griffey Jr., and Alex Rodriguez. Jongewaard told me that he had been to the team's academy in the Dominican Republic. But after that, he said he "got a little carried away." He ended up traveling around the world, signing what he felt were top prospects from China, Russia, Italy, Holland, and Croatia.[26]

"Many Anglo players who never learned Spanish in school now know some of the language, and they've learned something about Latin American geography and customs," George Gmelch writes in *Baseball without Borders.*

International players, whether from Latin America or Asia, inevitably also introduce American baseball fans to their countries and culture, whether it is the customs mentioned by TV color commentators or cultural geography introduced through ESPN specials like those that followed Sammy Sosa or Pedro Martinez around their hometowns in the Dominican Republic.[27]

The impact of Latinos in baseball will be as important to the sport specifically, and our society in general, as the rise of the African American athletes was in the 1960s and 1970s. Anyone who has seen baseball as it is played in the Dominican Republic or Cuba knows how exciting the game can be. Outside the borders of the United States, runners relish taking the extra base at every opportunity. Pitchers aren't reluctant to challenge hitters. This quicker, more passionate, even more confrontational style of play is what's being brought to the United States. In essence, globalization is turning back the clock to a more exciting time for the sport.

Years ago, I watched rough edits from the PBS television series *Baseball* with its director Ken Burns. At one point, as we viewed snippets of a game between the old Brooklyn Dodgers and New York Giants, Burns complained that you didn't see that style of play anymore—so aggressive on the base paths. Instead, too many major league managers simply plan and pray for the three-run home run. I told Burns that the old style of baseball still exists in places like Havana and Santo Domingo. And thanks to globalization of the game, such a style and passion for the game is being brought back to our shores.

"Of all the sports, we Latins believe that baseball requires the greatest amount of skill," Hall of Fame player Orlando Cepeda says. "That's why we take such pride in playing it well."[28]

Often, baseball offers us the comfort of continuity, a link from one generation to another. What we're only beginning to realize is that the game also can connect Americans to worlds with which we thought we had little in common.

But baseball, of course, isn't the true national pastime anymore. In the mid-1980s, football surpassed baseball in terms of general popularity. A 2003 Harris Poll called professional football the favorite sport of 29 percent of Americans, followed by baseball at 13 percent, professional basketball at 10 percent, and auto racing at 9 percent.[29] Among U.S. sports, nothing has been a bigger success story than football. Some would contend that baseball had no choice other than to embrace a global marketplace. It needed to do so in terms of talent and fan base to survive. But football, at least at first glance, seems impervious to the pressures of the new global age, especially when one considers how fast and how far it has come. Four decades ago, the first Super Bowl took place at the Los Angeles Coliseum. The stadium had 30,000 empty seats. "Nobody cared," Green Bay Packers' receiver Max McGee later told HBO.[30]

As part of the merger agreement between the National Football League (NFL) and its upstart rival, the American Football League (AFL), commissioner Pete Rozelle had only a month to put the event together. The stitch marks showed as NFL and AFL owners glared at each other at the pregame cocktail party, with their wives on the verge of a catfight.

After the Kansas City Chiefs owner, the late Lamar Hunt, called the event the Super Bowl instead of its official name, the AFL-NFL World

Championship Game, the media made the nickname stick. When CBS, which carried the NFL games, and NBC, which had the AFL contests, each claimed first dibs on the new event, Rozelle let both of them broadcast it. That's how desperate he was for any kind of publicity. A sixty-second commercial for Super Bowl I cost $85,000 (for the 2006 game, it was $2.5 million for 30 seconds).[31]

Super Bowl I was competitive for about two quarters. After halftime, the Packers took control and trounced the Chiefs, 35–10. That evening, on the network news, sports commentator Haywood Hale Broun called the game "too predictable to be memorable." From such humble beginnings, Rozelle made his championship into the world's biggest sports event. "He consciously positioned it as a bigger, grander, more concentrated event than baseball's World Series," says Michael MacCambridge, author of *America's Game: The Epic Story of How Pro Football Captured a Nation.*[32]

But to do so, Rozelle knew he needed a few breaks along the way. The first watershed moment came in Super Bowl III. Vince Lombardi's Packers had handily defeated AFL teams in the first two championships. Days before Super Bowl III, Rozelle acknowledged that the NFL "might tinker with tournament brackets," MacCambridge says, "so that two teams from the old league [the NFL] could play each other in the final game." The rationale made sense to most fans. The old NFL was considered to be a much superior league at that point in time. Amid such negotiations, Joe Namath, the brash quarterback for AFL champion New York Jets, predicted his team would win. Then he backed up such brave talk by leading the Jets to a stunning 16–7 victory over the Baltimore Colts.

Through the years, football has steadily refined its annual showcase. The days before the game are used to hype the event, with the hopes that another player will be as outspoken as Namath. Instead of Al Hirt or Up with People as the entertainment, the NFL has turned to top pop stars in recent years (U2, Paul McCartney, the Rolling Stones). A younger and a more worldwide audience followed.

Apple's legendary "1984" Macintosh commercial helped establish Super Sunday as the most important day of the year on Madison Avenue. In 2005, Emerald Nuts and the men's deodorant Degree made successful Super Bowl debuts. In some viewing circles, the ads—not the game—have become the draw.

The contest between the Pittsburgh Steelers and Seattle Seahawks in 2006 was viewed by an estimated 90 million Americans and was beamed to thirty-two countries worldwide, including Australia, Brazil, and most of Europe. The Super Bowl had a global visionary in Rozelle, somebody who was willing to speak his mind in Namath, and a marketing staff that burned the midnight oil. The result? An event that has transformed the sports landscape around the world.[33]

No network footage of Super Bowl I exists today. Legend has it that the game was taped over for a soap opera. For this was the era before TiVo and VHS. Tape units were as big as refrigerators. One of the few who owned one back in 1967 was Playboy's Hugh Hefner. Even though

Hefner says he's been "hooked on football" since his college days at the University of Illinois, he didn't bother to tape Super Bowl I. "The first one wasn't worth the trouble," he says. "But we're having a big party at the mansion (in Los Angeles) this time. The Super Bowl? There's nothing bigger now."[34]

For the 2006–07 season, pro football was seemingly everywhere on U.S. television. *Monday Night Football* moved to ESPN, while its former announcers John Madden and Al Michaels jumped to NBC to do that network's new *Sunday Night Football* games. ESPN countered with more football, airing college contests those evenings. Forget about the leaves changing—a sure sign of autumn has become a classic slowdown like Oklahoma–Texas, Florida–Tennessee, or Ohio State–Michigan or, better yet, ESPN's Chris Berman ranting about this week's hero "rumbling, bumbling, stumbling" toward the end zone.

Perhaps we've embraced football so much because as a sports nation we're not much good at anything else anymore on the world stage. From Tour de France winner Floyd Landis testing positive to no U.S. singles player, male or female, making it into the quarterfinals at Wimbledon to our nation's quick exit from soccer's World Cup, it was a lousy 2006 on the international stage for U.S. teams. In the inaugural World Baseball Classic that spring, a highly favored Team USA didn't reach the finals. The American basketball squad hasn't won a world championship or Olympic title since 2000 (and that year, they barely got to the finals after Lithuania missed a buzzer beater). Legendary Duke University men's basketball coach Mike Krzyzewski was brought in to right the ship, but even Coach K struggled in his first foray into the global arena: Team USA only won the bronze medal at the 2004 Summer Games after being upset by Argentina. Certainly Tiger Woods has reaffirmed himself as the standard in pro golf, but U.S. fans seem to have had their fill of international play and "We Are the World" lineups.

Football prides itself on being the new all-American game, and a recent survey from TIDES bears this out. The report states that the NFL has made strides bringing in people of color into the front offices and broadcasting booths. But, unlike baseball and basketball, the NFL has the smallest percentage of international players of any professional sports league in the United States. In fact, the percentage of international players on the American gridiron fell from 4 percent in 2003 to 1 percent in 2005.[35]

If you listen to the NFL, they're as eager to be international as anybody else. Eighty foreign-born players were in NFL training camps this summer, according to ESPN. Last year the Arizona Cardinals and San Francisco 49ers played in Mexico City—the first regular-season game outside of the United States. There is talk about a preseason game in China, perhaps even an NFL franchise overseas at some point. But for the immediate future, football will focus on staying number one in the U.S. market.[36]

Richard Lapchick, director of TIDES, says football remains the U.S. sport least affected by international forces: "The NFL has been extremely successful marketing itself within this country," he says. "But it hasn't been as successful marketing itself overseas as our other sports."[37]

How long will the NFL's game plan of using all-American athletes while playing in more international places hold up? In Canada, winning at hockey was once considered a birthright. That lasted until 1972 when the Soviet Union outplayed Team Canada in an epic home-and-away series. Almost overnight, the world hockey title was up for grabs. Sweden, Canada, and the Czech Republic are the recent winners of the Olympic gold. How long will it be before more of the world falls in love with our version of football? More importantly, what happens when they want to play here—on the largest, most profitable stage in the world?

If the documentary *Hoop Dreams* were being filmed today, how much of the U.S. sports landscape would have changed due to increasing globalization in sports? I'd like to think we can take a page from how they play youth baseball in the Dominican Republic or youth basketball in Russia. It's time that we, as parents and youth coaches, embrace globalization as a chance to reinforce the real lessons of sports and hand them down to the next generation. Thanks to globalization, the odds of winning a college athletic scholarship and certainly a professional contract have certainly grown significantly longer. So, why not use that as an excuse to turn back the clock to sports' glory days, on and off the field?

Sports can still teach children much about how to react to rejection, determination, and perseverance. In my writing class, we talk about how the only thing you can do sometimes is wait for everybody and everything to catch up to what you have to offer. *War and Peace*, *The Fountainhead*, *Watership Down*, and *To Kill a Mockingbird* are just a few of the notable books that were initially rejected by publishers. James Joyce's *Dubliners* was not only turned down twenty-two times but, when it did come out, somebody bought up the first run and burned the copies. Somewhere along the line, everybody gets rejected, even humbled. The key is what happens next.

According to Joseph Campbell, the author of *The Hero with a Thousand Faces*, there are only three basic reactions to rejection. The first is easy to identify with. You say "to hell with them," Campbell writes, and then retreat to protect your ego and perhaps the gift that you've tried to offer to the world. The second response to rejection is to ask, "What do they want?" You believe you have a talent, a skill. You try to figure out the marketplace, to give them what they want in a commercial sense. But there is a real danger here: You have to be careful not to totally renounce your particular insight to the world in trying so hard to develop a public career. The third response is "to find some aspect of the domain into which you have come that can receive a little portion of what you have to give," Campbell says. Of course, that isn't easy to do.[38]

My first novel, *Castro's Curveball*, was rejected thirty-three times. To this day, I don't know if I should be proud or embarrassed about that. But the experience taught me that failure and rejection don't have to be the same thing. Failure has such finality to it. It's all over. Case closed. Rejection certainly stings, but *we* decide when the process is over. Going through so many rejections taught me that you don't need an army of supporters early on, only one or two people who believe as much in the project as you do. Find them, and you're on your way.

I also became convinced that any dreamer must occasionally speak with passion, even eloquence, about his project. *Castro's Curveball* was sold soon after I spoke to an editorial meeting at Ballantine Books. Somebody asked about Cuba, where the novel is set. I remember thinking to myself that when I leave this room, I need these editors and executives to love me or hate me. Playing it safe isn't going to cut it. So, I told them about Havana at dusk and how the Cuban people have this great gallows humor that allows them to still laugh when so much of life is stacked against them. Three days later, Ballantine bought my novel.

Everybody gets rejected. But many of my students really don't believe this. They think if they align themselves with the right agent or high-powered editor, they'll be impervious to such heartache, just as most college athletes are convinced they'll make the pros. So, I tell them one last story.

Years ago, I met the famous photojournalist Galen Rowell. We chatted between appearances at a local radio station. A bit star-struck, I asked how things were going.

Rowell replied that he was going through a rough patch. Several of his story pitches had been turned down. I couldn't believe it. After all, Rowell was a contributor to *National Geographic* and other magazines, as well as the author of several books. He was so matter-of-fact about this string of rejections that he could have been discussing the weather. Sure, it was raining today, but the sun would soon come out.

That evening, when I got home, I pulled down my favorite Rowell book, *In the Throne Room of the Mountain Gods*. Decades before the best-seller *Into Thin Air*, Rowell chronicled a star-crossed attempt to climb the second highest peak in the world, K2. On that expedition, of which Rowell was a part, everything that could have gone wrong did. The all-star team of climbers fought among themselves. The army of porters required to lug the gear went on strike several times for higher wages. The weather was abysmal. As a result, the expedition fell well short of the 28,741-foot summit.

Rowell returned home with haunting images and an epic, though cautionary, tale. For those looking for a quick result, too busy with the next text message, that would have been enough. Yet months later, Rowell was invited to join a new expedition to K2. "With a deeper understanding," Rowell writes, "of both the men and the mountain than I had possessed the first time I made such a decision, I answered, 'Yes. Count me in.'"[39]

After a game, players on my youth teams soon learned to gather around "the book." Especially in sports like basketball and baseball, the book shows how many points they scored or how many base hits they had. In fact, after some youth games, the crowd of players and parents around the scorer's table can delay the start of the next contest.

Early on in my kids coaching career, I had a group of seven-year-olds who believed only the official book. It didn't matter what I or their parents told them, their assessment of how well they had done was totally tied up in those rows of numbers. Most official scorebooks, especially at the youth level, merely keep track of points. Any of the coaches in the 2006 Final Four—UCLA's Ben Howland, Florida's Billy Donovan, LSU's John Brady, and George Mason's Jim Larranaga—will tell you a winning team has to be much more than that.

When the stakes get as high as they are in mid-March in college basketball, with a national championship at stake, a team of all-stars at every position usually doesn't win. The champions, like the best companies, church groups, or community organizations, often have the best role players, the people who are willing to give up their individuality for the good of the team.

"When teams are mismatched, the stronger teams can sometimes get by on talent and technical discipline," says Robert Quinn, author of *Change the World: How Ordinary People Can Achieve Extraordinary Results.* "When teams are playing at the highest level of competition, synergy really matters."[40] Barry Posner, professor of leadership at Santa Clara University, says that in pressurized decision-making situations, "cooperation beats competition hands down."[41]

Too often in sports, he adds, teams fail because the star players try to do it all. At a basic level, they are more concerned about their own performance than that of the team. They often can't help it. That's the way they've been raised. They've spent too much time looking at the official scorer's book.

"Professional hockey has it right when it rewards players not just for goals scored but for assists on goals scored by others, too," Posner says. "[Wayne] Gretzky did this for his teammates, no matter what team he was on."[42]

The 2006 Final Four teams in college basketball arrived at the pinnacle of their sport because at crucial moments they put team ahead of individual glory. Time after time, role players were crucial to their club's success. Glen "Big Baby" Davis may have been the biggest star at Louisiana State since Shaquille O'Neal. Yet he would have been watching the Final Four at home on television if his teammate Garrett Temple hadn't shut down Duke's J. J. Redick. UCLA missed fifteen of their first twenty-one free-throw attempts in the Oakland Regional. In fact, when the Bruins' Arron Afflalo hit back-to-back free throws, the crowd gave him a standing ovation. Afflalo went on to pace his team with fifteen points, including nine of ten from the charity stripe.

And then we had the improbable tale of George Mason. An afterthought in a part of the country that includes traditional powerhouses Georgetown and Maryland, the Patriots' roster was filled with players the other schools passed over. One could argue that Mason had no real stars, only role players. Against top seed Connecticut, a squad that boasted five NBA prospects, Mason stood at least four inches shorter at every position when the starting teams took the floor. But it didn't matter. Despite having the Huskies send the game into overtime, the Patriots prevailed and shocked the basketball world. "They don't measure heart by inches," Connecticut's Hall of Fame coach Jim Calhoun said afterward.

"On any kind of team that has performed above expectations, the participants say things like, 'We were all on the same page and pulling together, it was amazing,'" Quinn says. "The word amazing suggests that we normally are not all on the same page and pulling together."[43]

That's why I decided several years ago that our local basketball team would have its own book. Over the years, I've added categories besides points—rebounds, steals, assists, blocked shots, even key defensive stops. I've tried to get across to the players that to succeed we have to do all of these things well.

To my surprise, most players eventually buy in. I've even had parents ask how many rebounds or steals their kid had before even mentioning points. I'd like to think my teams, win or lose, share something in common with the game's best. Everybody on the roster knew they had a role to play. They knew that the book over at the official scorer's table told only a small part of the story.

Playing sports can be an important ingredient in any kid's upbringing, especially if the age of globalization continues to shift the focus off improbable college scholarships and professional contracts to such intangibles as life lessons. Watch any pro team and usually the last thing they go over in practice is how to score when the game is on the line. NFL teams practice their two-minute offense; NBA and college squads run that one particular play they believe will bring them a basket with time running out. Just imagine how much better our schools, government, and companies would be if the best people were running the best possible plays at "crunch time."

Sometimes I fear we adults, especially at the youth sports level, are so concerned with equal playing time and the allure of advancement through sport that we lose track of this basic principle. When I coached my kids' teams I had weekly conversations with my assistant and co-coaches about which players should be on the field at the end of the game. There was a pecking order for that moment. It could change from week to week, and I told the kids this was something to strive for. Only if the game was out of hand would the best players not finish the game. During the season, everybody would get a chance to start. But only the best players heading into that weekend would close things out.

We followed this game plan, regardless of gender and even experience level. One of the best teams I ever coached was a coed hockey squad. The kids ranged in age from six to nine. I had three girls on that team, and if we were ahead late, they were part of the unit that went out to hold the lead. The boys on my team, especially the scoring stars, couldn't believe it. So, after practice one night, I tried to explain it to them. "If we're ahead and time's running out, we don't need another goal," I said. "I want players that stay in position. Know where they need to be."

One of my favorite sports stories involves writer John McPhee and Bill Bradley, then a basketball star at Princeton. McPhee was profiling the country's leading scorer for the *New Yorker*. This was long before Bradley became a professional player for the New York Knicks and then a politician and presidential candidate.

One night, after practice, Bradley was coming off the practice floor, and McPhee fell in alongside to ask some more questions. Bradley still had a ball in his hands. As he neared the sidelines, without a backward glance,

Bradley flipped the ball over his shoulder and it improbably flew through the air and into the basket.

McPhee was incredulous. He wanted to know how Bradley did that. Bradley answered, "It's a sense of where you are." That became the theme of the article and the title of McPhee's later book about Bradley.[44]

Certainly there was an element of luck in Bradley's shot. But there was also a confidence and comfort level that athletes of any age can achieve. When players talk about being "in the zone," I believe they've found that sweet spot where fun can be found in the most pressurized of situations. They may not win, but they know enough about themselves and the game to do their best when everything is on the line. This is the lasting influence sports can have for anybody. If anything, this opportunity can become even greater as the sports world is further altered by the globalization of sports.

Just think how Arthur Agee and William Gates, the heroes of *Hoop Dreams*, would think of their sport today if they had been allowed to focus on the spirit of play, rather than training so long and so hard in a single-minded effort to win a scholarship and even one day play with the professionals. In this era of globalization, we often talk about opportunities lost. But in the realm of sports, such strong undercurrents may also force us to turn back the clock and perhaps think about sports in a more realistic way.

"Choices shape a child's life," Deion Sanders says. "These days, parents want to take away their kids' choices when it comes to the games they play. I don't think it's fair. Let a child be a child."[45]

That's something we can do in the era of globalization.

NOTES

1. "Declining Numbers in Baseball," *Sports Illustrated*, October 26, 2005.
2. Harry Edwards, interview on ABC News, August 6, 2003.
3. Richard Lapchick, interview by author, September 18, 2003.
4. Richard Lapchick, interview by author, September 19, 2003.
5. Harry Edwards, interview in *ColorLines*, September 2003.
6. Steve Boyd, interview by author, August 19, 2006.
7. John Thompson, interview on WTEM-AM radio, July 16, 2006.
8 Interview by author, February 18, 2002.
9. John McGinnis, interview by author, March 6, 2000.
10. Deion Sanders, interview by Dennis McCafferty, *USA Weekend*, August 27, 2000.
11. Fred Engh, interview by author, September 7, 2000.
12. Rick Wolff, interview by author, September 8, 2000.
13. National Collegiate Athletic Association, "Estimated Probability of Competing in Athletics beyond the High School Interscholastic Level," August 5, 2005, available at www.bankjr.com/teachers/tDoc.jsp?subject=FACS&doc=Pro-Sports.html.
14. Author interview with spokesman at Institute for the Study of Youth Sports, Michigan State University, August 27, 2000.

15. Christopher Andersonn, interview by author, March 6, 2001.

16. Author interview with Stephen Anderson, April 14, 2000.

17. "World Games," *Washington Post*, August 16, 2005.

18. Joe Montana, interview with author, October 19, 1986.

19. Junior Noboa, interview with author, January 20, 2003.

20. Tim Wendel, "A Tip of the Cap to Pro Baseball," *USA Today*, June 14, 2006.

21. Ibid.

22. Ibid.

23. Ibid.

24. Ibid.

25. Alan Klein, interview with author, June 7, 2006.

26. Roger Jongewaard, interview with author, July 28, 2003.

27. George Gmelch, *Baseball without Borders: An International Pastime* (Omaha: University of Nebraska Press, 2006), 311.

28. Orlando Cepeda, interview with author, May 15, 2002.

29. Wendel, "Tip of the Cap."

30. Tim Wendel, "How 'The Game' Became Super," *USA Today*, January 31, 2006.

31. Ibid.

32. Michael MacCambridge, interview with author, January 16, 2006.

33. Wendel, "How 'The Game' Became Super."

34. Ibid.

35. Tim Wendel, "In Life (and the NFL Draft) Stars Blaze Their Own Path," *USA Today*, April 26, 2006.

36. Ibid.

37. Richard Lapchick, interview with author, March 16, 2006.

38. Diane K. Osbon, ed., *A Joseph Campbell Companion: Reflections on the Art of Living* (New York: HarperCollins, 1991), 81.

39. Galen Rowell, *In the Throne Room of the Mountain Gods* (San Francisco: Sierra Club Books, 1986), 320.

40. Author interview with Robert Quinn, March 3, 2006.

41. Ibid.

42. Ibid.

43. Ibid.

44. Ibid.

45. Deion Sanders, interview by Dennis McCafferty, *USA Weekend*, August 27, 2000.

CHAPTER 11

Retaining Faith in the Land of the Free

Sara Heitler Bamberger

At the dawn of the twenty-first century, two transnational phenomena garner significant attention: globalization, in all its economic, political, and cultural complexity; and religious fundamentalism. These are not discrete phenomena, but rather two sides of the same coin: as globalization creates an increasingly interdependent, networked, homogenized world, it produces social, economic, and cultural dislocation.[1] This dislocation exposes millions of people to the existential vulnerability of clashing worldviews, thus bolstering religious identity and affiliation.[2] While allowing for differences based on geography, faith, and individual experience, this chapter seeks to create a typology for the relationship between globalization and religious adherence as it plays out in the American context.

In addition to affecting quantifiable changes in political, economic, and social relations, the process of globalization includes the dispersion of a subtle but distinct set of values. Among these are the value of material consumption, the belief that something new is inherently better, the value of popular culture, the mobility of labor, and the use of technology to enable rapid and constant communication. Although these values have found a captive market in the United States, they are not precisely or exclusively American values. Instead, they are globalization values, spread with Nokia phones, Toyota cars, and Coca-Cola. While the impact of these globalization values on non-Western countries and cultures has been widely documented, few scholars have explored whether and how Americans themselves resist the allure of their secular, materialistic utopia.[3]

Globalization values have permeated modern American life and are widely hailed as the benign by-products of a free, democratic, and prosperous world. For zealous adherents of specific faiths, however, these same values can be threatening, anathema, or even lethal, as they often conflict with a traditional, religion-based value system. How, then, in our famed melting pot, do Americans go about protecting, preserving, and transmitting distinct religious traditions?

Although the movements and institutions this chapter depicts are often branded as "fundamentalist," that nomenclature is misleading for at least three reasons. First, the term was coined to describe a specific Protestant movement in the early twentieth century and thus does not accurately capture the posture of faithful non-Christians. Second, its current usage in the media, as in "Muslim fundamentalist" or "Hindu fundamentalist," is laced with negativity and derision and has acquired an association with violence that almost never occurs in America. Third, by labeling all religious adherents as "fundamentalists," the term masks the very diversity that this chapter attempts to reveal.

To preclude misunderstanding, I instead employ the term *faith retainers,* which intentionally invokes two different associations. First, these religious adherents seek to retain their faith, and sometimes their distinct ethnic and religious culture, in its authentic form. They are not stripping culture from the fundamentals of their religion, but rather trying to retain their religion as it has been practiced up until the modern period. The second implication is that faith retainers attempt to protect their faith from penetration or dilution by global values and secularization. Here, the image of a retaining wall serves as a metaphor for the types of barriers these groups seek to create. Although some faith retainers do proselytize, that is not a characteristic of all faith-retaining groups, as many prioritize retention, preservation, and transmission to the next generation over the making of new converts.

In an effort to balance depth and breadth, I have restricted the case studies in this chapter to those of the Abrahamic faiths of Christianity, Judaism, and Islam. I hope to show the diversity of strategies within each tradition as well as the similarities and differences between them. I have focused my inquiry on trying to identify common themes and patterns around the following constellation of questions:

- How are faith retainers affected by the globalization of labor markets? Do changes in how the faithful earn their livings affect their religious observance and beliefs?
- How do faith retainers adapt their religious activities to an era in which communication is instantaneous and often ubiquitous?
- How do faith retainers view innovation, given their commitment to the preservation of age-old traditions?
- How do faith retainers respond to America's culture of materialism, which has only deepened with the availability of ever less expensive goods due to globalization?

In their strategies for addressing these challenges, faith retainers can be categorized into three broad groups, each corresponding to various degrees of acceptance of globalization values: *globalization restrictors, globalization negotiators*, and *globalization utilizers.*

GLOBALIZATION RESTRICTORS

The first response to globalization values is that of globalization restrictors. Members of these groups uphold traditions of their ancestors, including traditional language and dress, and eschew modern technologies to varying degrees in an attempt to establish what Samuel Heilman calls "enclavist" identities.[4]

Old Order Amish

Perhaps no American subculture is more romanticized and well known than the Old Order Amish, the most recognizable tradition within Christianity that can be identified as a globalization restrictor. Founded in England in 1693, the Old Order Amish established their first settlements in the New World between 1717 and 1736.[5] In the early twenty-first century, they number almost 200,000 and are growing at one of the fastest rates in the country. As Anabaptists, their theology is based on the premise that the worldly order and the Kingdom of God are irreconcilable, and thus the trappings of modernity only distract from experiencing God on Earth.

On the surface, the Amish appear to have fully renounced the consumption habits, rapid communication, and commitment to innovation of American culture. They use only horse-and-buggy transportation, dress in plain, uniform clothes, live in unpretentious homes without electricity, and enroll their children in one-room parochial schools and only until eighth grade.[6] For many years, the Amish prohibited telephone communication, based on the belief that true community bonding occurred only with frequent face-to-face encounters.[7] In recent years, however, phones have entered Amish life, although other, more recent innovations such as the Internet, have not.

Had they lived in a vacuum, the Amish would have preferred to be globalization deniers, because, more than any other group, they have organized their lives around a theology that depends on warding off modernity. But since the 1980s, changes in the local economy have forced this community to adopt new economic models. Malls and suburbs have increasingly infringed on their land and have led to the rapid dissolution of farming life. Despite their best efforts, the Amish have found modernity's encroachment impossible to fend off.

Though some argue that the microenterprise that has resulted in the burgeoning tourism industry of "Amish country" in Pennsylvania and elsewhere demeans and objectifies the faith and its faithful, the Amish have found the commercialization of their unique culture sometimes financially beneficial, given the paucity of other options that do not involve interaction with the globalized economy. With the burgeoning number of microenterprises that produce Amish furniture, food, and quilts, Amish culture has become a major commercial institution, which has in turn precipitated changes in the Amish's interactions with the outside world.[8]

Whereas previous interactions between the Amish and the "English," as the Amish call non-Amish Americans, were extremely limited, the tourism industry has forced them to come into contact with non-Amish on a more regular basis. Even more disruptive to Amish life than contact with the outside world, however, has been the change in family dynamics that results from the transition from an agrarian to a market economy. Whereas previously the Amish lived in a highly gendered world, now unmarried Amish men and women come into contact with each other regularly, blurring the gendered communication patterns and hierarchy.[9] As Amish microenterprises continue to thrive, time will tell to what extent participation in the tourist economy will erode their parochialism and self-sufficiency, or whether they will be able to maintain their traditional lifestyle, albeit with some accommodations to economic realities.

Haredim

The Jewish analog to the Amish is the Haredim (*Ha-rei-deem*), or "those who tremble before God." For these Orthodox Jews (often referred to as ultra-Orthodox), life revolves around pursuing sanctity and keeping out the *gashmiut*, or material preoccupation, of the secular world. Numbering roughly 200,000—the same population size as the Amish, and with the same soaring birthrates—they constitute about 30 percent of Orthodox American Jews.[10] The Haredim live in tightly knit communities with other Haredim, with the largest communities in the Northeast, in such towns of Crown Heights, New Square, and Kiryas Joel in New York and smaller communities near cities such as Boston, Philadelphia, and Baltimore.

The priority of the Haredi community is religious and spiritual development, not material success. A large house, fancy car, or degree from a prestigious university would be looked upon with disdain. Instead, the currency of value in this community is the sanctification of God. The creation and religious education of large families, adherence to Jewish law, and the study of traditional texts are the community's life-defining, norm-shaping activities.

When Haredim came to the United States in significant numbers in the 1950s, largely in the Holocaust's wake, they set forth on a very different course than most American Jews. Whereas the majority of Jews viewed integration into the mainstream as the goal of life in the New World, the Haredim staunchly rejected American values and culture.[11] They maintained and sometimes even resuscitated Yiddish as the *mama loshen*, the mother tongue of their American-born children. Like the Amish, they adopted styles of dress that prioritized simplicity and modesty. Perhaps most importantly, they built institutions: Haredi elementary schools and high schools in which girls and boys could be educated separately, synagogues, *gemaches* (charitable lending societies), and most importantly *yeshivot* (centers of Jewish learning), which men attend usually in lieu of a secular university. The yeshiva is the central institution of Haredi life, and men are expected to study Torah there as a form of service to God as long as they possibly can. Thus, as Heilman notes, "Extended time in a Torah learning institution, which might seem voluntary, is from the social point of view really mandatory. Torah study has become for Haredim a weapon in the war against the corrupting influences of life outside the Haredi cultural enclave."[12]

Despite the communal emphasis on learning—often full-time, for men, at the expense of being a breadwinner—somebody needs to make enough money to feed the children and pay the bills. To the surprise of outsiders, the women often shoulder responsibilities both for child care and income generation, believing that the best thing for the family is for the husband to "sit and *lern*." When men *do* work, it is often in a field that does not require a college degree. Industries that Haredim have historically worked in, such as the garment and diamond trades, have been largely outsourced abroad, where cheap labor and machinery have proven more cost-effective. The new industries that Haredim most frequently are drawn to are electronics and computing. The voluntary Haredi participation in the technology sector sets them apart from the Amish and underscores their belief that embracing "values associated with the eternal yesterday does not preclude an ability to master the instruments of today or tomorrow."[13] Thus, although Haredim often use the tools of globalization in their professional lives, they reject globalization values and try to keep exposure to the outside world to a minimum in their personal and religious lives.

Tablighi Jamaat

Globalization restrictors are to be found among American Muslims as well. Unlike Muslims in Europe, American Muslim immigrants are generally highly assimilated into U.S. society. They live in ethnically and religiously mixed communities and work in a variety of sectors that interact with the global economy.[14] However, small groups of Muslims within the United States shun such integration. Members of the Tablighi Jamaat, literally "Proselytizing Group," exhibit characteristics of globalization restrictors: for a period of time, they leave their normal lives and travel from community to community promoting simplicity, spiritual growth, and Islam.[15]

The Tablighi Jamaat was founded in 1925 near Delhi, India, to counter Hindu influences in Islamic practices in India. The movement explicitly rejected the advent of modernity, preached Islam's superiority, and advocated a stripped-down, simplified version of religion inspired by Sufi Islam and the more rigid aspects of Sunni law, eschewing abstract philosophical debates.[16] Tablighis proselytize only to other Sunni Muslims and believe that anyone can preach religion, even without a classical Islamic education. Furthermore, the Tablighi Jamaat is avowedly apolitical. The movement does not adopt political causes or stances, to the frustration of some of its members. The Tablighi Jamaat encourages respect for political authority, which has allowed it to spread inconspicuously over a broad geographic region.[17]

Generally, little is known about the internal structure of Tablighi Jamaat, but it is commonly described as a nebulous net of loosely affiliated, itinerant *jamaat*, or traveling proselytizers, who overlap with a component of the fixed, hierarchical network of *shura* (councils) at various local mosques. The jamaat travel in groups up to ten people and go on missions of varying lengths. Members visit mosques and college campuses in small missionary bands, preaching a return to purist Islamic values and recruiting others— typically young Muslim men—to join them on the road tour. During their missions, they stay at local mosques and rely on the hospitality of their hosts, although technically those who volunteer to go on preaching mission are required to spend their own money. The Tablighi Jamaat's simplicity, apolitical character, leadership hierarchy, and simple message enabled it to transform from a local South Asian movement to a transnational phenomenon. The movement spread to the United States in 1970s, along with the spread of Saudi Wahabism and South Asian Deobandism.

In the United States, the Tablighi Jamaat often operates out of Deobandi and Wahhabi mosques and Islamic centers. Many jamaat are centered in the Al-Falah Mosque in Queens, New York, but the predominantly South Asian missionaries visit Sunni mosques and Islamic centers across the country. In some reports, there are as many as 15,000 missionaries in the United States, although the actual number is difficult to determine because membership is unofficial and entirely fluid: those who identify with the Tablighi Jamaat can enter and leave at any time.

The jamaat shun globalization as a means of spreading their message. They do not use journals, printed publications, or the Internet to promote their objectives. All proselytization and communication between Tablighi Jamaat members occurs in person. Its members strongly advocate gender separation and veils for women, and they grow long beards and dress in the *gelbiyya* (a long, loose garment), following Muhammad's model. Like the Haredim and the Amish, their specific traditional, conservative dress serves as a marker of resistance to globalization. Tablighi members attempt to incorporate the Prophetic model of piety into their personal lives, and thus they eat meals on the floor and do not own televisions. In America, they shun voting, financial investments, and the banking system, and they minimize interactions with non-Muslims, as they believe these to be prohibited by Islam. At the same time, most members of Tablighi Jamaat in the United States are integrated into the global economy in their professional lives—many Tablighi members are university students, doctors, or engineers. Thus, once their period of participation in the Tablighi Jamaat comes to an end, they are virtually indistinguishable from other Americans, save for their personal religious practices.

What connections can be drawn between the Amish, Haredim, and Tablighi Jamaat? All three of these groups are enclavist: they adopt different forms of dress, renounce some or all technology, shun main-stream entertainment and pop culture, and emphasize person-to-person communication. They do not support or adhere to "globalization values" that emphasize material consumption, rapid communication, and innova-tion. Despite this, globalization restrictors have conceded to some realities of life in a global economy. In the case of the Amish and Haredim, global economic influences have caused significant innovations in their forms of livelihood. In the case of the Tablighi Jamaat, this problem is avoided by the temporary status of jamaat—Muslims leave their regular lives for a spir-itual pursuit, but with the understanding that such a status will be only for a certain period of time. Thus, while all three groups strive to deny or mute the impact of globalization, economic reality makes a fully imperme-able barrier impossible.

GLOBALIZATION NEGOTIATORS

Globalization negotiators, the second group of faith retainers, negotiate how to preserve and promote traditional religious observance and identity in American society. Whereas globalization restrictors perceive globaliza-tion's values as inherently negative, members of these groups believe that coming to terms with modernity is a core component of forging individual and collective religious identities. In order to do this, they have established communities that are both local and expansive, communities with high walls that separate the faith retainers from secular modernity, but open doors that keep relations with the rest of society fluid.

Latino Pentacostals

In the Christian context, Latino Pentecostals exemplify the globaliza-tion negotiator stance, albeit in very different ways from their Jewish and Muslim counterparts. Pentecostalism is by definition a globalized religion, as it was spread to the Global South by American missionaries. They gained converts at a rapid pace, and many of these moved to the United States in the 1980s and 1990s. Now, 25 percent of the United States' Lat-ino population, or about 6.2 million people, identify as Protestant, and 36 percent of those consider themselves Pentecostal—by far the largest denominational proportion.[18]

The relationship between transnationalism, globalization, and religion among Latino Pentecostals is multifaceted and layered.[19] For some adher-ents, the church becomes the hub of a binational identity. For example, La Iglesia de Apostoles y Prefetas church in Washington, DC, serves a pri-marily Salvadorian constituency. As such, ties with El Salvador run largely through the church: the church collects money to contribute to support Salvadorian mission work, as well as to help the friends and relatives of community members who remain across the border. Thus, the church becomes the physical embodiment of its members' new transnational identities as Salvadorian Americans.[20]

Another common model for Pentecostal churches is as a mini melting pot of Latin and South American immigrants. In the Gran Comisión Church in Paterson, New Jersey, for example, members forge a new sense of Hispanic identity with the Chileans, Dominicans, Cubans, Argentineans, and Peruvians with whom they worship. Thus, affiliation with the church "leads to the reaffirmation of Hispanic roots and the formation of a pan-Latino identity as a defensive maneuver ... against the discrimination they suffer" as low-paid immigrants to America.[21]

The turn to Pentecostalism can yield not only a new ethnic identity, but a moral one as well. As Pentecostals, these faith retainers vow not to drink, smoke, gamble, or be promiscuous. In this teetotaling process, the church often becomes the center of their American life, a moral anchor in a land of temptation. Here again, the church becomes the locus of globalization negotiation between the licentious behaviors that unbounded freedom can elicit and a life committed to more conservative, God-oriented value system.

Finally, Pentecostals' theology embodies the give and take of the globalization negotiator stance. Pentecostalism is unique as a faith retainer in that it places the presence of the Holy Spirit in human history—and not religious beliefs, rituals, obligations, or texts—as the defining element of religious ethos and organization. Thus, as Manuel Vasquez explains, "The Holy Spirit is at once the sign and vehicle of charismata (gifts like glossolalia, divine healing, prophesizing, and exorcisms, all marks of justification) and of the imminent second coming of Jesus Christ."[22] On the one hand, Pentacostalism is rooted in traditional Christianity and includes clear commitment to Jesus, the Bible, and Christian theological principles. On the other hand, it has pioneered a new vision of Christianity. In its privileging of intense, emotional religious experience, Pentecostalism is particularly well suited to the age of globalization. If instant communication is possible in the human realm, why not also with the Divine? By pairing traditional beliefs with a focus on personal experience of the Holy Spirit, Pentecostalism has been highly successful at negotiating globalization values into Christianity.

The phenomena cited above—the creation of binational identities, the creation of multinational Latino identities, the adoption of a stringent moral code, and the creation of contemporary Pentecostal theology that resonates in the era of globalization—are some of ways that Pentecostals negotiate globalization. While I have focused on a few examples, the scale of these experiences should be noted: millions of American immigrants from Africa, Latin America, South America, and the Caribbean negotiate their geographic, economic, cultural, and theological identities through the prism of a Pentecostal church that has strong ties to its members' country or regions of origin.[23]

Modern Orthodox Jews and Yeshivat Chovevei Torah

Within the Jewish context, Yeshivat Chovevei Torah (YCT) is an Orthodox seminary geared to the Progressive end of the 450,000 Americans who identify as Modern Orthodox Jews.[24] As an Orthodox seminary, its mission is to "professionally train open Modern Orthodox rabbis who will lead the Jewish community and shape its spiritual and intellectual character in consonance with modern and open Orthodox values and commitments."[25] To do this, its goals are "inspiring a passionate commitment to the study of Torah ... and the scrupulous observance of Halakha [Jewish law]; cultivating spirituality—God-consciousness, piety, and ethical sensitivity—and integrating it into all learning, religious practice and worldly pursuits."[26]

Despite its Orthodox affiliation—meaning that all of its students accept the binding nature of Jewish law—YCT prides itself on encouraging intellectual exploration, questioning, and critical thinking as essential components of one's full service to God. Founded in 1999 by Orthodox leaders who perceived Orthodoxy as becoming increasingly insular and right-wing, it increasingly serves as a counterweight to Yeshiva University, the primary center of Orthodox rabbinic ordination in America.

The word *openness* pervades YCT's promotional materials. In addition to offering courses in the biblical, rabbinical, medieval, kabbalistic, and Hassidic perspectives one might find at a Haredi yeshiva, YCT also teaches modern, postmodern, and non-Orthodox perspectives on traditional texts. Two required classes of note are "The Rise and Development of Jewish Denominations" and "The Challenges of Modern Orthodoxy"—classes that encourage a historical and theological self-reflection that globalization restrictors would shy away from.[27] YCT's curriculum is based around the premise that members of the Modern Orthodox community negotiate globalization on a daily level, so the rabbis that YCT trains should be equipped to deal with their congregants' questions.

Whereas Haredim have created institutions to isolate themselves from globalization values as much as possible, Modern Orthodox Jews have a much more complicated relationship with modernity. In some ways, they appear much like their non-faith-retaining counterparts: they believe in secular education and aspire to send their children to elite universities; they work in every aspect of the global economy, with a preference for fields that require advanced degrees; they often earn high salaries, live in affluent suburbs, and see no religious problem with using their disposable income to purchase large houses and amenities. They are as likely as their non-faith-retaining counterparts to own BlackBerries, cell phones, laptops, and other "time-saving" devices that often end up making adults connected to their work at all times. But despite "buying in" to globalization values, Modern Orthodox Jews consider themselves bound by Jewish law, and thus their lifestyle looks quite different from that of the average American.

To understand how Modern Orthodox Jews justify reaping the benefits of globalization values while maintaining their commitment to a traditional Judaism, one must examine their relationship to time. In the world of globalization values, there is nothing wrong with doing things that have minimal redeeming personal or social value, such as watching Hollywood movies, playing video games, or surfing the Internet. By contrast, the Modern Orthodox lifestyle is animated by a set of activities called *mitzvot*, ritual and ethical commandments, which obligate adherents and often end up consuming large amounts of time. These activities include studying Jewish texts, visiting the sick, giving charity, helping to prepare weddings and funerals, observing the Sabbath and holidays, helping the poor, and many other ethical and ritual obligations. Living a life defined by mitzvot mitigates the pervasiveness of globalization values: one can work, but not all the time; one can buy things, but one also has to give money away; one can be virtually connected most of the time, but sometimes one needs to just *be*.

Modern Orthodox Jews embrace what Mary Douglas calls "contrapuntal belonging."[28] In this worldview, negotiating a multiplicity of worlds—American and Jewish, individual and communal, local and global, profane and sacred—forms the essence of being a Jew in the Diaspora.

Zaytuna Institute

A primary example of globalization negotiators among American Muslims is the community that has formed around the Zaytuna Institute, located in Berkeley, California. This nonprofit, educational institute and school for Islamic studies is led by Hamza Yusuf and Zaid Shakir, both nationally respected teachers as well as converts who have studied extensively in the Middle East. The institute offers a traditionalist approach to Islam, as evidenced by its traditional methods of pedagogy and curriculum. Zaytuna teachers are classically trained, almost always in Islamic *madrassas* in the Middle East or North Africa.

As an institute of Islamic studies, Zaytuna's goal is to "cut through the illusion of contemporary nihilism and materialism and transform human beings."[29] It does not deny its need to encounter or respond to the globalized value system; in fact, it embraces this challenge. However, Zaytuna's leaders believe that the proper mode of response is for Muslims to deepen their understanding of their faith and incorporate it into their lives. The traditional scholarship it teaches is based on interpretations of respected scholars who lived in the early Islamic period.

Zaytuna has a large following among Bay Area Muslims and uses the Internet to reach a virtual community around the country and the globe. While it engages in some community outreach, its scholars do not proselytize, and their focus is on disseminating religious knowledge to interested Muslims. Zaytuna's highly polished, well-designed website explains that its mission "is to serve our Lord and honor our Prophet (upon him be peace) through providing the highest quality educational programs, materials, and training in the traditional sciences of Islam in the most beautiful way, using the most effective tools of our time."[30] The "most effective tools" include conventional means of informational distribution, including quarterly courses, newsletters, a semi-academic journal, and a fledgling full-time seminary dedicated to training indigenous American Muslim imams, as well as modern methods of communication: MP3s, video downloads and podcasts, and online courses. In short, while the Zaytuna Institute defines itself as being opposed to many globalization values, it embraces any techniques it can find to help its highly traditional teachings reach the broadest possible audience.

The local community and the broader virtual community that the scholars reach as they crisscross the country on fundraising drives are relatively affluent, educated Muslims who are interested in bringing spiritual and religious meaning into their lives. As one student commented, "We don't want to practice watered-down Islam.... Zaytuna presents Islam in its traditional clothing. They are not trying to modernize Islam, but teach us what is permitted considering we live in the modern world."[31]

The theme of trying to do what is permitted by faith while living the modern world is best reflected by globalization negotiators' dress. Zaytuna's male teachers and students dress in both Western and traditional garb, depending on the setting; Zaytuna's female students often cover their hair, but not always. Similarly, Modern Orthodox Jewish men will often wear a *yarmulke* (skullcap), but not always; women generally wear skirts and married women cover their heads, but not always. Pentecostals often wear the clothes of their home countries with pride at church, but Western clothes the rest of the week. This quasi-traditional, highly individualized dress code captures the globalization negotiators' commitment to contrapuntal belonging. Like globalization restrictors, they seek to live according to guidelines of their religious tradition. But unlike globalization restrictors, they aspire to accrue the material benefits of life in modern America, while maintaining a traditional outlook and practice of their faith.

GLOBALIZATION UTILIZERS

The third group of faith retainers comprises the globalization utilizers. Globalization utilizers are faith retainers who see as their *primary religious duty* to bring others—either strayed members of their own faith or in some cases new converts—into their flock. In this pursuit, they embrace the ubiquity of globalization values and try to reappropriate them to attract converts. Globalization utilizers attempt to simplify age-old traditions into bite-size nuggets, portray religion as a means to clear answers, and try to help would-be converts connect to others with similar viewpoints. These groups are concerned with packaging their faith in a way that it reaches the maximum number of people and are often explicit evangelizers. Although globalization utilizers see themselves as transmitters of ancient traditions, skeptics would questions whether truncating core beliefs into a single web page or offering prayer "experiences" that include multimedia presentations and loud rock music compromise religious authenticity.

Protestant Evangelicals

American Protestant evangelicals—largely affiliated with the Southern Baptist Convention—are globalization utilizers, as evidenced by their savvy use of the media to shape and transmit their message to the globalized world. The most prominent example of their embrace of globalization is the megachurch, the face of popular American evangelicalism. Mega-churches are outfitted with huge plasma televisions, conduct worship with grand musical productions (not limited to traditional hymns, but also including rock 'n' roll covers, original songs, and so forth), and recruit highly charismatic preachers. For example, Joel Osteen, the senior pastor of Lakewood Church in Houston, Texas, averages more than 47,000 attendees at weekly services.[32] Furthermore, the people in the hundreds of pews in Pastor Rick Warren's Saddleback Church represent only a small fraction of his flock; his book *A Purpose Driven Life* has sold 25 million copies and is the best-selling hardback book in American history, accord-ing to *Publisher's Weekly*.[33]

Modern technology plays an enormous role in "selling" evangelistic messages and saving souls. For example, evangelicals have embraced the concept of media access and have established their own conglomerates to steer this form of communication, particularly evident in the various popu-lar televangelist ministries. The Trinity Broadcasting Network was one of the original televangelism outlets to claim success in the United States. And building on the traditional Christian notion that dropping money on the collection plate brings material as well as spiritual rewards, pastors have found that a global audience also means a very large collection plate. For example, Pastor Paul Crouch, who is known for his "inspired salesmanship and advanced telecommunications technology," has managed to create an efficient financial machine through his ministry.[34] Similarly, Pastor War-ren's ministry and book sales generate more than $100 million each year, most of which he donates back to the church and its charitable activities.[35]

In addition to the medium of television, American evangelicals also use their own online bookstores. The Evangelical Christian Library hosts online books for Christian readers, and its purpose "is to bring glory to God by teaching the truth of His Word, the Bible, and thus pointing peo-ple to Christ and to a deeper love for the Lord. We pray that our Heav-enly Father will consecrate our online books for the spiritual growth of each reader."[36] Through the use of such technologies, religious messages are spread around the country and the globe.

By crafting Christian messages that are easily digestible, highly mar-keted, and delivered in a charismatic way, evangelicals utilize the tools of globalization to enable millions of people to supplement their globaliza-tion values with Christian values.

Chabad-Lubavitch

In the Jewish world, the best example of the globalization utilizer is Chabad-Lubavitch. Chabad-Lubavitch is a philosophy, a movement, and an organization. The word *Chabad* is a Hebrew acronym for the three in-tellectual faculties of *chochmah* (wisdom), *binah* (comprehension), and *da'at* (knowledge). The movement's system of Jewish religious philosophy emphasizes understanding and recognition of the Creator, the role and purpose of Creation, and the importance and unique mission of each human being. This philosophy guides a person to refine and govern his or her every act and feeling through wisdom, comprehension, and knowledge. Although Chabad-Lubavitch is in many ways religiously traditional, by stressing certain aspects of Judaism, including outreach and messianism, it offers an innovative response to the globalized age.[37]

The movement is guided by the teachings of its seven spiritual leaders (*Rebbes*), beginning with Rabbi Schneur Zalman of Liadi (1745–1812). The most recent Lubavitcher Rebbe, Rabbi Menachem Mendel Schneerson (1902–1994), known simply as "the Rebbe," guided post-Holocaust Jewry from the ovens of concentration camps to a multinational Jewish organization that embraces globalization even as it rejects some of its values.

Under Rabbi Schneerson's dynamic leadership, Chabad cultivated a brigade of Jewish emissaries to help these Jews around the world stay connected to their tradition. Thus, the core of Chabad's activities is carried out by four thousand *shlichim*, full-time emissary families who are dispersed to every corner of the globe. Sent from Chabad headquarters in New York to countries from Argentina to Vietnam, and to cities in all fifty states, the shlichim use their own initiative to figure out how to best serve the local Jewish community—as educators, ritual slaughterers, prayer leaders, counselors, Sabbath meal hospitality providers, or most importantly outreach organizers. Globalization has brought Jews everywhere, and Chabad has followed, helping them build more Jewish lives.

Chabad's zeal for Judaism is almost matched by its enthusiasm for virtual communication. Its website prides itself on being the virtual one-stop shop for any Jew seeking information or inspiration. Over one hundred graphic designers, computer programmers, editors, and writers work on it, making it an almost comically comprehensive site for all things Jewish.

Online, Chabad does not just educate about the importance of doing mitzvot, it tries to pitch them in the language of the assimilated viewer it targets. With an ironic, youthful voice, Chabad advocates putting up what it describes as "strange looking doorbells" (affixing a *mezuzah* to one's doorpost), "lighting up" (Sabbath candles, that is), soul food (keeping kosher dietary laws), and wearing "black leather" (the injunction on men to bind one's arm and head with leather boxes, known as *tefillin*, every morning).[38]

While such mitzvot are a core part of Jewish ritual observance, Chabad's promotion of these "quickies" seems particularly well suited to the globalized value system. Needing little preparation, and in the realm of action rather than reflection, they resonate with assimilated Jews who view even religious life through the lens of globalization values.

Perhaps the most intriguing aspect of Chabad's approach is its emissaries' ability to market themselves to a Jewish community that embraces globalization values, while still maintaining a Haredi-like dress code and way of life. On the one hand, Chabad aspires to "transcend all boundaries, serving the religious and the nonobservant, affiliated and nonaffiliated, young, old and all in between."[39] But despite the diversity of their constituents, Chabad emissaries are usually young, married couples, often with many children. The men wear traditional Hasidic garb of black pants and white shirts, and women wear skirts and hats or wigs to cover their hair, observing the Jewish commitment to modesty. Chabad emissaries see it as their mission to bring spirituality to the secular world, while holding onto their distinctive dress, their strong commitment to observing Jewish law, and their own Chabad traditions. As globalization utilizers, they use globalization in whatever ways they can to help bring people closer to their heritage and their faith.

AlMaghrib Institute

Similarly, a group of Muslim Americans adopts many of the same techniques as Christian evangelicals and Chabad to publicize their religious message. As a globalization utilizer, the AlMaghrib Institute is a largely virtual organization with traveling teachers, in many ways a modernized version of the Tablighi Jamaat. AlMaghrib's office is in Houston, but it does not have a single geographic hub for its activities; rather, it offers seminars that take place on location and rotate in mosques and colleges throughout fourteen cities in the United States and Canada. Founded in 2001, it is currently the largest Islamic educational institution in the United States, enrolling about seven thousand students. The AlMaghrib Institute offers Double-Weekend Degree Seminars that consists of a six-day, two-weekend format. Seminar topics include the biography and narrations of the Prophet, Qu'ranic sciences, Islamic law, fundamental beliefs, marriage and family, and others. AlMaghrib's instructors all speak English, ascribe to the classical Islamic tradition, and hold degrees from Islamic universities.

Like other globalization utilizers, AlMaghrib disseminates a very traditional body of Islamic knowledge and promotes the values of patience, wholeness, meaning, and spiritual growth. The content of its seminars and its instructors are deeply rooted in Sunni Islam, as are Zaytuna's courses. What, then, distinguishes AlMaghrib from Zaytuna; in other words, what makes it a globalization embracer rather than a globalization acceptor?

The answer lies in the way the AlMaghrib Institute uses not just the tools but the very values of globalization to disseminate religious knowledge. For example, students enroll online and the website is colorful, clearly laid out, and easily navigable. In its own literature, AlMaghrib uses slang terminology and portrays its approach as revolutionary, hip, cool, and fun. Seminar titles are often exaggerated sound bites and are accompanied with colorful, kitschy posters, dramatic descriptions in large fonts, and quotes from AlMaghrib students such as, "These seminars are really the sweetness of my life" and "AlMaghrib rocks!"[40]

AlMaghrib markets itself as taking an innovative approach to traditional studies. On its website, the institute includes a comparison of traditional versus modern learning. It first lists problematic characteristics of traditional classes, such as lecture format, limited use of technology, and lack of assessment, and concludes: "You'll be delighted to note that not only did we throw this list out, we shredded it with one of those cool shredders you can get at Wal-Mart."[41] This explicit nod to globalization is significant. However, the institute then suggests that the "modern" techniques it is using can in fact be found in the tradition of the Prophet and within Islamic heritage. "When someone applies these techniques, they are not, in reality, departing from 'traditional' learning. On the contrary, they are looking deeper into the techniques that the Prophet ... used."[42] Thus, there is a desire to preserve tradition, albeit in a new, flashy package.

Lastly, unlike Zaytuna Institute, AlMaghrib suggest that global values and Islamic values do not necessarily conflict. This is stated on their website:

> Unlike traditional Islamic institutions, AlMaghrib Institute does not intend to produce typical "Islamic students of knowledge." ... Rather, it wishes to help the average Western-raised Muslim to appreciate the complexities of the classical sciences of Islam in a practical and pragmatic way.[43]

In reading between the lines, it becomes clear that for the AlMaghrib Institute, the traditional Islamic sciences need not be presented as an alternative to globalization values, but as compatible with life in modern America.

CONCLUSION

In looking at globalization resistors, negotiators, and embracers, which approach is most effective? Not surprisingly, the three groups have very different priorities. For globalization restrictors, the main goal is preservation and transmission of a tradition. By creating enclavist communities— either in space or in time—they successfully ward off what they perceive to be the corrupting influences of globalized values, modernity, and America, despite having to make some concessions to economic realities.

The globalization negotiators, by contrast, are not interested in living in an enclave. Instead, their approach to religion attracts Americans who appreciate the economic and social benefits of globalization but perceive globalization values as insufficient when contemplating questions of faith, ethics, and spiritual growth. They advocate a return to traditional texts and traditions, while recognizing that we live in the twenty-first century and face challenges unique to the modern age. To walk this tightrope, they try to mitigate the impact of globalization's secular values by tethering themselves to a global religion, to a local religious community, and ultimately to the Divine.

Finally, the globalization utilizers' goal is to attract a generation of Americans steeped in globalization values back to traditional faiths. They utilize flashy multimedia creations for recruitment, worship, or both, and they package thousands of years of religious traditions into user-friendly, bite-size morsels of advice. They have been highly successful at bringing new souls into their respective folds. Whether the connection of these new recruits stays on a shallow plane or develops into a religious identity with nuance and depth is a question beyond the purview of this paper.

In surveying this group as a whole, how do the faith retainers profiled in this chapter compare with fundamentalists around the globe? I would argue that they share many ideological similarities. For example, they are concerned with the erosion of religion and its proper role in society; they selectively emphasize aspects of their traditions they believe to be most important; they generally subscribe to a Manichean worldview that separates the purity of the faithful from the contamination of the outside world; and they believe in the inerrancy of Scripture.[44]

But while their ideological characteristics are similar, the globalization negotiators and globalization utilizers differ from globalization restrictors and fundamentalist groups in the rest of the world in two significant ways. First, they lack many of the organizational qualities that typify fundamentalists, such as a clearly defined membership, sharp boundaries, authoritarian leadership, and strict behavioral requirements. In these ways, the "flattening" effect of globalization seems to have reached these religious communities as well.

Second, the perceived enemies of most fundamentalist groups, which include the religious establishment, the secular state, civil society, and religious competition, are much less oppositional in the United States than they are in many other countries. Whereas faith retainers often (although not always) define themselves in opposition to the pervasive secularism and materialism of American society, they rarely employ the militant, adversarial techniques that typify fundamentalists in other countries. Possible reasons for this include the United States' democratic political structure, the freedom of religious practice, the separation between church and state, the population's relative affluence, economic stability, and the enfranchisement of religious groups. Thus, as Emmanuel Sivan writes, in America "religion is likely to be shed lightheartedly, often unwittingly. Tradition succumbs to a pleasant infatuation and dies a sort of sweet death, a painless euthanasia, if you will."[45]

It is therefore not surprising that in America, a movement of faith retainers who see their religion as demanding a violent overthrow of America does not exist. In the Christian context, the far right groups like Christian Identity and other neo-Nazi ideologies claim to draw inspiration from Christianity, but their beliefs differ so significantly that to describe them as faith retainers would be inappropriate.

In the Muslim context, Salafi Jihadi Islam, the largely Saudi-funded brand of Islam that has taken root in many parts of the world, has not succeeded in mobilizing a broad swath of American Muslims.[46] In America, Salafi Jihadi ideology lacks charismatic leaders, large numbers of followers, or identifiable institutions.[47] Although an extremely small number of American Muslims do espouse radical views, most of them are immigrants who were reared under hate-filled regimes, and to describe their beliefs here would be to erroneously suggest that such ideologies are subscribed to in much larger numbers than they are.

In different ways, each of the groups described in this article challenges the hegemony of globalization values in America. Although their challenge is largely peaceful, sometimes political, and sometimes only implicit, they enliven the discussion of values in America. Ironically, the American values of tolerance, pluralism, and diversity that faith retainers have rallied against are also responsible for their flourishing. This phenomenon may be not only benign but positive. Faith retainers challenge the secular majority to wonder, if only occasionally, whether the values we so zealously export in the name of globalization are the best values, even for ourselves.

NOTES

1. See Robert Holten, "Globalization's Cultural Consequences," *Annals of the American Academy of Political and Social Science* 570 (July 2000): 140–52, for an excellent summary of the various theories of how cultural globalization spreads.

2. See, for example, Samuel P. Huntington, *Clash of Civilizations* (New York: Touchstone, 1996), for the most influential version of this thesis. Benjamin Barber, *Jihad vs. McWorld* (New York: Random House, 1996), explores the same clash on a religio-cultural plane.

3. See Frank Lechner, "Fundamentalism and Sociocultural Revitalization in America: Sociological Interpretation," *Sociological Analysis* 46, no. 3 (Autumn 1985): 243–59.

4. Samuel Heilman, *Sliding to the Right: The Contest for the Future of American Jewish Orthodoxy* (Berkeley: University of California Press, 2006).

5. See Donald B. Kraybill, *The Riddle of Amish Culture* (Baltimore: Johns Hopkins University Press, 1989).

6. Donald Kraybill and Steven M. Nolt, *Amish Enterprise: From Plows to Profits* (Baltimore: Johns Hopkins University Press, 1995).

7. For a detailed description of the role of the telephone in Amish society, see Diane Umble Zimmerman, *Holding the Line: The Telephone in Old Order Mennonite and Amish Life* (Baltimore: Johns Hopkins University Press, 1996).

8. Ibid., 36.

9. See Kraybill and Nolt, *Amish Enterprise*, 136.

10. Marvin Shick, *A Census of Jewish Day Schools in the United States, 2003–2004* (New York: Avi Chai Foundation, 2004), available at http://www.avi-chai.org/static/binaries/publications/second%20census%202003-04_0.pdf.

11. See Samuel Heilman, *Defenders of the Faith: Inside Ultra-Orthodox Jewry* (Berkeley: University of California Press, 1999).

12. Heilman, *Sliding to the Right*.

13. Ibid., 150.

14. See Pew Research Center, *Muslim Americans: Middle Class and Mostly Mainstream* (Washington, DC: Pew Research Center, 2007), available at http://pewresearch.org/assets/pdf/muslim-americans.pdf.

15. See Nicholas Howenstein, "Islamist Networks: The Case of Tablighi Jamaat," USIP Peace Briefing, United States Institute of Peace, October 2006. www.usip.org/pubs/usipeace_briefings/2006/1011_islamist_networks.

16. For example, see Said Amir Arjomand, "Unity and Diversity in Islamic Fundamentalism," in *Fundamentalism Comprehended* (Chicago: University of Chicago Press: 1995), 183.

17. Howenstein, "Islamist Networks."

18. See David Martin, *Tongues of Fire* (Oxford, UK: Blackwell, 1990).

19. Manuel A. Vasquez, "Pentecostalism, Collective Identity, and Transnationalism among Salvadorans and Peruvians in the U.S.," *Journal of the American Academy of Religion* 67, no. 3 (September 1999): 617–36.

20. Ibid., 620.

21. Ibid., 623.

22. Ibid., 621. Also see Donald Dayton, *Theological Roots of Pentacostalism* (Metuchen, NJ: Scarecrow Press, 1987).

23. See Edith Blumhofer, *Restoring the Faith: The Assemblies of God, Pentecostalism, and American Culture* (Chicago: University of Illinois Press, 1995).

24. Heilman, *Sliding to the Right*, 63.

25. "Mission and Values," YCT Rabbinical School, http://www.yctorah.org/content/view/1/49/.

26. Ibid.

27. "Academics," YCT Rabbinical School, http://www.yctorah.org/content/view/4/47/.

28. Mary Douglas, *In the Wilderness: The Doctrine of Defilement in the Book of Numbers* (Sheffield, UK: Sheffield Press, 1993).

29. "About Zaytuna Institute," Zaytuna Institute, http://www.zaytuna.org/about.asp.

30. Zaytuna Institute, http://www.zaytuna.org/zrelocation.asp.

31. Geneive Abdo, *Mecca and Main Street: Muslim Life in America after 9/11* (New York: Oxford University Press, 2006), 26.

32. Lillian Kwon. "Joel Osteen Resonates in Society Where Damnation Messages Don't." Christian Today, Oct. 20, 2007. christiantoday.com/article/joel.osteen.resonates.in.society.where.damnation.messages.don't/14090.htm.

33. "Rick Warren," PurposeDrivenLife.com, http://www.purposedrivenlife.com/en-us/aboutus/abouttheauthor/abouttheauthor.htm.

34. "TBN's Promise: Send Money and See Riches," *Los Angeles Times*, September 20, 2004.

35. Malcolm Gladwell, "The Cellular Church: How Rick Warren's Congregation Grew," *New Yorker*, September 12, 2005, available at http://www.newyorker.com/archive/2005/09/12/050912fa_fact_gladwell.

36. Evangelical Christian Library, http://www.ccel.us/.

37. The movement is not without its critics, particularly due to the adoration heaped on the previous Rebbe, whom many followers believe was actually the Messiah. For more on this, see David Berger, *The Rebbe, Messianism and the Scandal of Orthodox Indifference* (New York: Littman Library of Jewish Civilization, 2001).

38. "Ten Absurdly Simple Ways to Live Higher," Chabad.org, http://www.chabad.org/library/howto/wizard_cdo/aid/142434/jewish/introduction.htm.

39. Ibid.

40. See the AlMaghrib website at http://www.almaghrib.org/.

41. "What Is AlMaghrib?" AlMaghrib Institute, http://www.almaghrib.org/aboutus.php#page_3.

42. Ibid.

43. "AlMaghrib Curriculum," AlMaghrib Institute, http://www.almaghrib.org/curriculum.php.

44. For a much more nuanced explanation of these concepts, see Gabriel A. Almond, R. Scott Appleby, and Emmanuel Sivan, "Fundamentalism: Genus and Species," in *Fundamentalisms Comprehended*, edited by Martin E. Marty and R. Scott Appleby, 402–11 (Chicago: University of Chicago Press, 1995).

45. Emmanuel Sivan, "The Enclave Culture," in Marty and Appleby, *Fundamentalisms Comprehended*, 15.

46. Abdo, *Mecca and Main Street*. See also Khaled Abou El Fald, *The Great Theft: Wrestling Islam from the Extremists* (San Francisco: HarperCollins, 2005), and Kamar-Ul-Huda, "The Diversity of Muslims in the United States: Views as Americans," U.S. Institute for Peace, February 2006, available at http://www.usip.org/pubs/specialreports/sr159.html.

47. After conducting numerous case studies at the Combating Terrorism Center at West Point, research has demonstrated a pattern for radicalization among

Americans who embrace jihad, whether foreign or U.S. born. The cases of the Lackawanna Six, the Portland Seven, and the Virginia Jihad Group, as well as John Walker Lindh, Adam Gadahn, and others, demonstrate that Muslim extremists always travel overseas to receive training, because sufficiently radical institutions do not exist in America. For more information, see Chris Heffelfinger, "Behind the Indoctrination and Training of American Jihadis," *Terrorism Monitor* 5, no. 15 (August 2, 2007), available at http://www.jamestown.org/terrorism/news/article.php?articleid=2373588.

Index

About the Editor and Contributors

Sara Heitler Bamberger is coordinator of the Religion, Politics, and Globalization Program at the University of California, Berkeley.

Andrew L. Barlow is professor of sociology at Diablo Valley College and visiting associate professor of sociology at the University of California, Berkeley.

Michelle Bertho is program coordinator for the France-Berkeley Fund and French Studies Program at the University of California, Berkeley.

Paul A. Cantor is Clifton Waller Barrett Professor of English at the University of Virginia.

James Cohen teaches political science at the University of Paris VIII (Saint-Denis) and at the Institut des Hautes Études de l'Amérique Latine in Paris.

Diana Crane is professor emerita of sociology at the University of Pennsylvania.

Susanne Janssen is professor of sociology of media and culture at Erasmus University, Rotterdam.

Tirza True Latimer is associate professor and chair of visual and critical studies at California College of the Arts, San Francisco.

William Leap is professor of anthropology at American University.

Ronnie D. Lipschutz is professor of politics and codirector of the Center for Global, International, and Regional Studies at the University of California, Santa Cruz.

Tyler Stovall is professor of French history at the University of California, Berkeley.

Tim Wendel is a novelist, journalist, and member of the faculty in the Writing Program at Johns Hopkins University.

Howard Winant is professor of sociology at the University of California, Santa Barbara, where he is also affiliated with the Black Studies and Chican@ Studies departments.